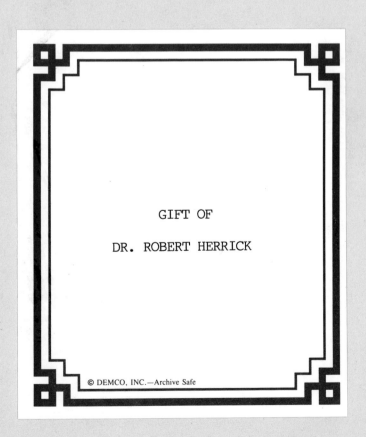

**WILL
HERBERG**
*FROM RIGHT
TO RIGHT*

Will Herberg

FROM RIGHT TO RIGHT

BY HARRY J. AUSMUS

WITH A FOREWORD BY

MARTIN E. MARTY

THE UNIVERSITY OF

NORTH CAROLINA PRESS

CHAPEL HILL & LONDON

Library of Congress Cataloging-in-Publication Data

Ausmus, Harry J., 1937–

  Will Herberg, from right to right.

  (Studies in religion)

  Bibliography: p.

  Includes index.

  1. Herberg, Will. 2. Religion historians—United
States—Biography. 3. Scholars, Jewish—United States—
Biography. 4. Jews—United States—Biography. I. Title.
II. Series: Studies in religion (Chapel Hill, N.C.)

BL43.H47A94 1987   296.3'092'4 [B]   86-19357

ISBN 0-8078-1724-4

Portions of this work are from

Harry J. Ausmus, *Will Herberg: A Bio-Bibliography*

(Westport, Conn.: Greenwood Press, Inc., 1986).

© Harry J. Ausmus.

Reprinted by permission of the publisher.

*To my friend
the late Dave McClellan
who advised:
"Make damn sure what you want in life—
you might just get it!"*

The productions of our youth
and of our maturer age
are equal in all essential points.

William Blake

CONTENTS

FOREWORD

One hundred fifty years after the United States disestablished its Protestant churches, an unofficial Protestant establishment endured. Catholics numbered in the tens of millions, Eastern Orthodox and Jews in the several millions, and other religious forces were making their presence felt. Yet by the middle of the twentieth century this pluralism was not fully recognized in the American ways of life. The liberal Protestant weekly with which I have been associated since 1956, *The Christian Century*, in 1951 bannered an editorial: "Pluralism: A National Menace."

Then, during the 1950s, the situation began to change. No longer could Protestants claim privilege except insofar as they could win it by weight of their numbers. American law, polity, power situations, and sense of fairness, to say nothing of the developing voice of non-Protestant groups, brought a need for new ways of conceiving national religious life. With that need came another one: there had to be people, plausible people, with voices, articulate and clear voices, to provide terms for conceiving the change.

Today, with pluralism seen as far more confusing than it seemed then, we look back on the names of a few major reconceivers. These included, for Protestants, figures like theologian Reinhold Niebuhr, who moved beyond circles of Christian ecumenism to determine ways for Protestants to relate to Catholics, Jews, and secularists. Father John Courtney Murray, S.J., joined by other prominent priests and lay leaders like the editors of *The Commonweal* did the same for Catholicism. They helped clear the way for the election in 1960 of the first Roman Catholic president.

For the first time, in the 1950s, Jewish thinkers began to have a strong and positive impact beyond Judaism. The suburbanization of the Jewish community meant the breaking down of almost literal and certainly spiritual ghetto walls. Who would speak for this new Judaism? In theology the most eloquent spokesman was Rabbi Abraham Joshua Heschel. At his side, as it were, was a layperson, a sociologist and part-time theologian, Will Herberg, the subject of this book. While Herberg explored a kind of Jewish existentialism, he also wrote a classic book, *Protestant-Catholic-Jew* (1955), a popular work of sociology. Herberg contended that a single American-Way-of-Life religion prevailed, but that Americans attached themselves to it or "prismed" it through at least three large basic faith communities. His synthesis may not long have held, but it was effected at precisely the right moment, in terms that were both challenging and reassuring. He became the Jew-in-pluralism par excellence in his time.

Who this Will Herberg was was somewhat difficult to say, and remains so, though this book goes a long way in identifying him. It was difficult not because he was not an energetic, accessible, and engaging (if contentious) partner in interfaith conversation. What made things difficult were Herberg's own changes, both before the 1950s and after. He invented some details about his past, obscured others, and in his later battles sent up confusing schedules about his earlier stances. It was known—there was no secret about it—that in the 1930s Herberg had been a Marxist and, in his own way at times, a Communist.

He converted, he would say, and Ausmus tells much of what can be known about the change. He often fought his past, as did so many of the Marxists of the 1930s who turned rightward in the 1950s. Max Scheler says of the rene-gade—and renegade is what Herberg seemed to be to his left-behind leftish comrades—that he had as his chief goal to "engage in a continuous chain of acts of revenge on his spiritual past." Yet Herberg did not become a crusader. Indeed, he became more of a crusader in the 1960s when he overtly lined up with conservative causes, as he did through identification, for instance, with William F. Buckley, Jr., and his *National Review*. Now Herberg did confuse people who had seen him as a moderate in the 1950s.

Ausmus has his work cut out for him sorting out these turns and changes. The purpose of a foreword is to signal something of what one should watch for, to locate significances, without giving the plot away. Let me set this on the table then on this early page: Ausmus's is and will be a controversial reading of Herberg. He will keep the reader awake and the critics busy. The title of the book, with its puns about orthodoxies and political slants, does its own signaling. Ausmus is going to raise the issue of just what got converted and what remained continuous and what it means for readers who are convinced one way or another.

This is not intended to be a psychologically rich biography; Ausmus will leave probing of the Herberg psyche to historians who lug their couches with them. Members of the psychobiographical school would certainly do more than relegate to a couple of lines and a footnote or two the issue of Her-berg's deception concerning his birthplace, birthdate, and academic degrees. Ausmus hurries on to certain questions of metaphysical attachment and politi-cal loyalty that he sees to be more informative. These foretastes of his argu-ment may seem somewhat obscure now, but they serve a purpose. Ausmus presents plenty of evidence for his case.

In the early pages one gets as a bonus a kind of "Who's Who" of the American intellectual left, seen through the career of a very busy and reflective participant in it. In the middle portion are chapters dealing with the Herberg most Herbergians knew best. Here Ausmus traces continuities—for example, in Herberg's constant fear of fascism as a point of reference. The last third deals with the other transformation in Herberg, the detailing of his turn to the second "Right" of the book's title. All along the way there are, free of extra charge, short courses on leftish editorial writing, labor organization, Jewish and Christian conversion, existentialism, biblical thinking, wrestling with the issue of "prophecy" in a republic, and the older new conservatism.

On these pages there are quotations that should infuriate all but the most uncritical Herberg groupies. It is hard to picture someone capable of recreating the circumstances in which he formulated his positions, yet such recreation would be necessary for true empathy. And on these pages there are many occasions that might evoke an "I get it!" or "Aha!" or "Now I see!" type of reaction, for Ausmus has a gift for making Herberg make sense when connections would not seem to be patent. It is in Chapter 12 that the full thesis finally gets expounded, and on those late pages Ausmus poses issues that force readers to come to terms with Herberg, with aspects of Americana, and perhaps with conflicting elements in their own philosophies and outlooks.

Herberg dealt with unfinished religious, secular, and national traditions alike. Many aspects of his pilgrimage duplicate aspects of others' journeys and should be of help as they—or, I should say—we look for ways on that unfinished, never-to-be-finished journey.

Martin E. Marty
The University of Chicago

PREFACE

Will Herberg is an example of those people who seek a reason for living even if life is meaningless. He first found meaning in Marxism, but when that god failed he turned to the biblical God, who, as tautologically defined, can ultimately never fail. As such, Herberg's life exemplifies *in concreto* a theory that was developed in my earlier work, entitled *The Polite Escape: On the Myth of Secularization*. His life demonstrates the interchangeability of political and ideological language with theological language, and provides further evidence of Nietzsche's contention that the discipline of history has become a disguised theology. Nietzsche, of course, was not the first to suggest this position. His philosophical opponent, Hegel, constructed his philosophy on the assumption that he was substituting philosophical language for religious language. Herberg's thought can only be rightly understood from this same perspective. For, as will be shown, he, if not deliberately then most assuredly unwittingly, chose biblical language over the language of Marxism knowing full well that the language of Marxism is derived from the biblical tradition.

In this great age of "democracies"—whether open or closed, whether pluralistic or monolithic, whether that of John Stuart Mill or Jean Jacques Rousseau, in the age of the "great levellers," to use Nietzsche's phrase—some people tend to forget that our language is still aristocratic in nature and hierarchical in structure. Hence, despite the tendency to view everything politically in an age in which politics is religion, the reader is requested to view the conclusion of this work metaphysically rather than politically. Metaphysics, as well as theology, precedes politics, given the hierarchical structure of our language. Only after having read the conclusion from a metaphysical perspective can one then proceed to read it from a political perspective. Having done so, the reader will observe that the Eastern bloc countries and the Western bloc countries are in essential agreement, and differ only over what Reformation theologians called *adiaphora*. The disagreement today between communistic and pluralistic societies is but the secularized continuation of the Reformation debate between *sola ecclesia* and *sola gratia*. In general, Communist countries today are those that historically have minimized the significance of the principle of religious toleration.

I mention this perspective in order to suggest that I have approached Herberg in a "Herbergian" fashion. The first eleven chapters attempt an objective and mostly uncritical presentation of the development of his thought. Some readers may be disappointed that I have not written a "life and times" of Herberg, which is not my intention. (In fact, some of the details of Herberg's life had to be deleted for reasons of economy.) Rather, the focus is on Herberg as he viewed his "times." Indeed, I have taken the unconventional approach of relating what Herberg thought in various periods of his life even to the point of repeating in later chapters some of the ideas already presented in earlier chapters. I have done this to inform the reader at every stage how Herberg's thought was remaining the same in some areas while changing in others. My own critical comments are reserved for the conclusion, and yet, in scholastic manner, they presuppose all that has gone before. They represent what I consider to be important problems that ought to be of significance, especially for students of theology and metaphysics who seek to "speak" to the modern world. In a word, the unresolved problem of the day is "nihilism." Those whose sensitivities might make them hesitate to traverse such thinking can find consolation in the thought of Herberg as presented in the earlier chapters.

A word is in order concerning the title of the work, *Will Herberg: From Right to Right*. Political terms such as "right," "left," "conservative," and "liberal" often are used disparagingly, and as a consequence frequently conceal important matters of substance. In the case of Herberg, he considered himself to be a "conservative" Marxist-Leninist in the 1930s and a "conservative" with respect to the American political scene by the 1960s. As will be shown, Herberg's thought reveals an underlying consistency, even after his formal rejection of Marxism. And, except for a brief period in which he questioned the ethics of Marxism, Herberg believed himself to be ethically "right."

The reader should know that I have taken a rather unconventional approach to documenting my quotations from sources. The traditional method, of course, is to document each quotation. However, had I used this traditional method in my attempt to provide an accurate portrayal of the development of Herberg's thought, the note numbers would have been in the "hundreds." Consequently, what I have done, in order to minimize the number of notes, is to cluster the sources in one endnote on a given topic. This approach may have unfortunate consequences for the researcher who seeks to find the source of a single quotation. To do so would require researching all the sources in a single endnote. I apologize for this method, but I am sure that most readers will sympathize with the economy it entails.

Herberg used the term "man" in his work to refer to both men and women. I have followed his pattern in my generic use of the word, deviating therefore from the publisher's policy of gender-neutral language in its publications. Similarly, the use of "Negro" rather than "black" throughout this book results from my effort to reproduce Herberg's thought in the language he himself used.

Numerous people have been of inestimable assistance to me in my research on Herberg. Donald G. Jones, of Drew University and the literary executor of Herberg's estate, invited me to write the book and was a constant source of information and assistance throughout the whole process of researching and writing the manuscript. Donald M. Vorp, formerly the theological librarian at Drew University and now of Speer Library, Princeton University, was an invaluable guide through the mountains of Herberg material that had been collated and filed expertly by students at Drew University Library under his supervision. Indeed, the preliminary work done by Vorp and his staff minimized tremendously the amount of time required to complete the research, and I can only feebly express my deep appreciation for what they accomplished. Alice Brent Nilva, now retired from the International Ladies Garment Workers Union (ILGWU) and a close friend of Herberg's, painstakingly led me through Herberg's years at the ILGWU and introduced me to Jay Lovestone, the late Charles S. Zimmerman, and the late Saby Nahama, all of whom graciously submitted to interviews about their relationships to Herberg. She also directed me to Robert Lazar, director of the ILGWU Archives, whose staff had compiled the Zimmerman Papers which also contained much information on Herberg, and, like the papers compiled by Vorp and his staff, reduced to a minimum the time required to research that period of Herberg's life.

Donald G. Jones and Douglas Webb were responsible for an almost complete bibliography of Herberg's writings, totaling over six hundred entries, part of which is published here. For a complete and partially annotated bibliography, the reader might wish to consult my work, *Will Herberg: A Bio-Bibliography*, published by Greenwood Press, Westport, Connecticut. William F. Buckley, Jr., in his inimitably genteel manner, happily granted access to his personal papers at Sterling Library, Yale University. Herberg's brother, Theodore, gracefully agreed to an interview about Herberg's early years, the recollection of which was certainly a painful experience for him.

Others have offered valuable assistance by way of correspondence, telephone, or personal conversation. Because they all were so charitable to me, I trust they will forgive the mere listing of their names for the useful information they offered: Robert J. Alexander, Alan Anderson, Bernard W. Anderson, June Bingham, Stanley Brown, J. Wade Caruthers, Charles Courteney, Mrs. T. S. Eliot, Lewis S. Feuer, Richard Fox, Nat Godiner, Robert Goff, Harry

Goldberg, Robert T. Handy, Sidney Hook, Ralph Luker, William May, Daniel P. Moynihan, Mrs. Reinhold Niebuhr, Thomas C. Oden, Gail A. Peterson, Richard D. Quigley, Francis P. Quilliam, Michael Ryan, Alvin L. Schorr, Hillel E. Silverman, Leo Steinberg, Bard Thompson, Richard A. Underwood, and Mrs. Bertram D. Wolfe. If I have omitted anyone whose name should be listed, I apologize for either my weak memory or my poor system of keeping records. And I also want to thank those who requested that their names not be listed.

There are individuals without whom any book of this nature would rarely be completed. I refer to those who struggled through the original manuscript, offering polite suggestions where even forceful demands would have been insufficient. Martin E. Marty, Arthur R. Kelsey, and Barry C. Fox willingly and graciously accepted that responsibility. Their recommendations were taken with the utmost seriousness and I am extremely grateful for their assistance. They of course cannot be responsible for the final product. In addition to reading the original manuscript, Marty also agreed to provide the interesting and informative foreword to the book. Ruth Landow accepted the onerous task of plowing through broken syntax, questionable semantics, split infinitives, dangling participles, and misplaced modifiers. Whatever lucidity, clarity, and communicativeness the book may contain is due in great part to her expert, but sympathetic, efforts. My wife and children had to endure the more practical inconveniences required of writing a book—the paper or books all over the floor of my study, the blank stares while I was thinking of something else, and the early morning "ideas" that had to be put on paper immediately. They are the brave souls. Finally, I wish to thank my computer which, on numerous occasions, when it would not do what I wanted it to do, had to bear the suffering of acrimonious disputes in a cloud of blue.

Harry J. Ausmus
Cheshire, Connecticut
23 April 1986

WILL
HERBERG
FROM RIGHT
TO RIGHT

I
THE
FORMATIVE
YEARS
1901–1929

The person who would later write about the impact of immigration on American religion was himself an immigrant. A Protestant by theological inclination, a Catholic by temperament, and a Russian Jew by birth, his most famous work was *Protestant-Catholic-Jew*. Claiming to be a synthesizer of thought and not a creator, he traversed the intellectual spectrum, moving from the catholicity of Marxism to the Protestantism of Reinhold Niebuhr and then to the Judaism of Franz Rosenzweig and Martin Buber. Frequently recalling that mankind will not stand still, he was an active Communist who became an avid anti-Communist with a lifelong respect for Karl Marx and V. I. Lenin, an enthusiastic supporter of American labor who was critical of the impersonality of the labor bureaucracy, and an eloquent defender of the American Constitution who argued on behalf of public aid to parochial schools. Throughout his life he was a traditionalist and a conservative; he opposed Joseph Stalin with the same vehemence with which he opposed Joseph McCarthy. In effect, he himself represented his own model of that American who lives in a society that can be envisioned as simultaneously pluralistic and religious.

William Herberg was born on 30 June 1901 in the small czarist-Russian village of Liachovitzi, located in the Poliese woods near the city of Minsk. His father, Hyman Louis (1874–1938), and his mother, Sarah Wolkov (1872–1942), were also born in this same *shtetl*. Although the conditions under which they lived cannot be exactly detailed, the Herbergs were presumably not among the destitute. Hyman Louis, for example, managed to graduate from the gymnasium and become successful enough as an electrical contractor to move his family to America, where, soon after their arrival, the fourth member of their family, Theodore, was born on 17 December 1904. In America, however, the family's condition deteriorated. Living in the midst of a largely poor Jewish neighborhood in Brooklyn, New York, Hyman Louis neglected his business. As the family's economic situation worsened, the relationship between husband and wife became increasingly strained. Although they managed to remain married for well over a decade, they eventually separated and finally divorced. Regarding the subsequent history of Hyman Louis two stories are told—one, that he lived a poor man's life in a wretched apartment room only to be buried, by his two sons, in a potter's field; and two, that he moved with another woman to South America where he died in 1938.

Sarah Herberg, apparently a strong-willed and determined person, rarely discussed her marital problems with relatives, some of whom had in fact emigrated with the financial assistance of Hyman Louis. Rather, she spent most of her time earning money by doing housework and by braiding and knitting belts. Will and Ted frequently assisted in the latter task, alternately knitting and reading aloud to each other. As far as religious instruction was concerned, the sons received little. Sarah and her husband were not atheists or materialists; they simply placed little emphasis on traditional Jewish values. At one time they would attend the synagogue on high holy days, but this practice was eventually dropped. Neither of the sons, by their own choosing, had a bar mitzvah. By far the greater concern was that their sons be educated. Sarah lived to see her younger son receive bachelor's and master's degrees from Columbia University but never to see her older son, Will, achieve a worldwide reputation as a scholar. She died in 1942 of cancer, and, contrary to Jewish tradition, was cremated in New York City.

After attending public school in Brooklyn, Will Herberg entered Boys' High School in February 1915. Here he began a period of intense intellectual activity, in which, unlike his father, he was neither dabbler nor dilettante. Rather, he pursued mathematics, physics, and the German, Hebrew, and French languages to exhaustion, showing, at the time, comparatively little interest in history. He also became interested in poetry to such an extent that, much later, he would write poems, on request, in the style of a poet selected. During this period Herberg developed what his brother referred to as his three major motivations: to fulfill himself, to capture every last bit of intellectual content, and to make something of himself in terms of a public image. With such aims he graduated from Boys' High School in June 1918 and entered the College of the City of New York (CCNY) in September.

At CCNY, he continued his exhaustive studies in mathematics, English literature, and the physical sciences while also growing increasingly interested in Freudian psychology. His brother, Ted, would go to the New York Public Library and copy Freud's works, chapter by chapter, in the German so that Will could translate them. His experience at CCNY, however, proved unsatisfactory. Although his grades in mathematics, the sciences, and the liberal arts were well above average, he received poor grades in hygiene and in military science and did not meet the college's physical education requirement of a hundred-foot swim. He remained at CCNY until the fall semester of 1920, when he was suspended because of absences in military science, having completed 94 of the 131½ credits required for graduation. His brother explained Will's suspension as a result of his physical clumsiness and a bone deformation in the knees, a condition that may have contributed to Will's disdain for physical exercise. Also, apparently Herberg had an altercation with a military science officer which ultimately led to his dismissal. In any event, his suspension from CCNY in November 1920 concluded his known formal education.[1]

According to Ted Herberg, Will's trouble with the military officer and his subsequent dismissal, plus the poor conditions under which he was raised, led him to communism. The exact circumstances of his induction into the Young Workers League cannot now be determined. What is known is that Herberg administered the Otis intelligence test to several students of the league, seeking to prove that students within the Communist movement had, in general, a higher intelligence quotient than most other students. Although the results of the test are not extant, his brother cited its use as an early example of Herberg's intellectual-elitist attitude, an attitude that he retained all of his life. Through such efforts, Herberg was able to rise through the ranks of the league rather quickly. In October 1925, he was elected as a delegate from district number 2 of New York City to the national convention. In the 17 October issue of the *Young Worker*, the news organ of the league, Herberg is mentioned as having been elected to the national executive committee of the league, specifically as part of the Politburo. His major task consisted of serving as director of "Agitprop" (agitation and propaganda) and as a member of the editorial committee of the *Young Worker* along with Nat Kaplan, Sam Darcy, and Max Shachtman. Shachtman is listed as the acting editor of the *Young Worker* in the 24 October and 31 October issues, whereas in the 7 November issue Herberg is listed as editor. Apparently, as a result of some unknown internal difficulties, he was listed as such only for a single issue. In any case, the 7 November issue of the *Young Worker* contains Herberg's first known article, entitled "Coal Miners: Here and in Russia."[2]

In this brief article, Herberg attempts to deal with the "fiction" that Russian workers are more oppressed than those in Western Europe and America. He describes this notion as "utter falsehood, hypocrisy, and poisonous malice" largely prompted by such reactionary labor leaders as John L. Lewis of the United Mine Workers Union. Indeed, he adds, American workers are, in many cases, more oppressed than the Russian workers. For example, the anthracite miners know well "that the [federal and local] government is the right hand of the coal operators" whereas the left hand is the "official bureaucracy of the Miners Union." Quite the contrary is true in the Soviet Union; conditions are less oppressive there since the Revolution of 1917. Russian miners, according to Herberg, have received a 25 percent pay increase, work only six hours per day, and take a month's vacation. Herberg concludes that, in Russia, "all toilers, young and old alike, are engaged, shoulder to shoulder, in the gigantic and inspiring task of laying the foundation of a new society where the insane brutalities of capitalism will be totally unknown and where the exploitation and oppression of man by man will have no place." Such was the fervor with which Herberg wrote, a literary fervor that lasted for the next fifty years, through over six hundred articles and several books.

In the same year that he wrote his first article, Herberg married Anna Thompson. Also born in Russia, her parents, David and Ida Becherman Thompson, emigrated to the Brownsville section of Brooklyn. Shy, demure, and timid, Anna apparently had few friends, only very close acquaintances who knew little of the details of her background. Research revealed few particulars of her life other than simply suggesting the image of a woman totally dedicated to her husband. Her commitment to his interests was such that they decided, according to Will's own testimony, not to have children because of the demands that would be made on them by the Communist party, which he described as a "movable seminar." She supported him with unfaltering dedication, whether he was a Marxist, a theologian, or a spokesman for American conservatism. Frequently, as Will and Ted had done, Anna and Will would alternately read aloud to each other over the dinner table. That Herberg was widely read and read widely was due in part to his wife's influence and her affection for him. She was, as numerous people suggested, the maternal foundation on which his scholarship rested.

She was not, however, merely a passive partner in this relationship, for she too was active in the party and on one occasion wrote an article for the *Young Worker* entitled "League Fighting Religious Dog: Begin Drive against New York Schools Sudden Zeal for Bible."[3] Referring to religion as "dope," Anna maintains there that bosses and their servants recently discovered that church and school were too far apart in New York City for the masses to be dominated effectively. Accordingly, they introduced religious training in the public schools. They "have come out strongly in favor of the proposed plans of mobilizing the public schools in the campaign to poison gas the workers' children with the religious dope." Consequently, the children who participate in religious training are dismissed early from school, whereas those who do not participate are persecuted by having to remain in school where they are lectured, scolded, and otherwise demeaned. Some teachers even "dispense" this "dope" in the classrooms. In response to this situation, the Young Workers League, according to Anna, planned to hold a series of protests, to distribute leaflets, and to organize parents against such repressive measures. The article concludes, in bold type: "Down With The Religious Poison In The Schools!!! Down With Religion, The Tool of Bosses!!!"

Although the marriage continued childless, Herberg's constant concern from the beginning of his literary career was the education of the young. Between 1926 and 1928, he wrote three articles dealing with the significance of young workers to the Communist movement. In a *Workers Monthly* article entitled "Lenin and the Youth," he raises the question, Why was Lenin not concerned to organize the youth?[4] The answer is quite simple, according to Herberg: the young are already, in effect, in the party! There is therefore no need, from Lenin's point of view, to have an independent youth organization because the young, and especially the students, are in the vanguard against czarism. Moreover, the young suffer as much, if not more, under capitalism, where they often are forced into labor and drafted into the army. Accordingly, Lenin believed that the young constituted the genuine hope of international socialism vis-à-vis social reformism and opportunism. Herberg thus concludes that "the youth movement owes its consciousness and understanding of its own role and destiny" to Lenin.

Part of that role concerns what Herberg referred to as the "coming war." In "The War Danger and the Youth" he maintains that the Soviet Union would be forced into a military confrontation with the "imperialist front" led by Great Britain and the United States.[5] This war would differ, however, from the war of 1914 in that the young and able-bodied workers would have to fight for the Soviet Union and for the revolutionary movement in China. In other words, Herberg explains, they would have to fight for the defeat of their own countries on behalf of revolutionary countries. Civil war in those countries opposed to the Soviet Union would result. "This will lead to world revolution," thus making the next war "a forerunner of proletarian revolution." Among those in the vanguard of such internal confusion in America would be the Young Communist League.

Military training for the young worker was therefore essential, according to Herberg. In an article on this subject in the *Daily Worker*, he notes that many in the party opposed such training for young comrades in the league's summer schools.[6] Herberg does not find such opposition surprising inasmuch as "America is the classic land of pacificism," a land of "petty bourgeois pacificism" where this sentiment has even affected the labor movement. Recalling his own experience, Herberg remarks that this question can be legitimately raised: "What kind of face will you have when, on the one hand, you fight military training in the City College of New York and other colleges, and, on the other hand, you institute military training in your own schools?" According to Herberg, the Communist movement does not oppose war and militarism per se, but only bourgeois war and militarism. Indeed, the movement favors *revolutionary* war and so opposes "pacificism," which opposes any war. By the 1950s Herberg would still oppose "pacificism," then called pacifism, but on the theological ground that it was utopian and bordered on idolatry.

What the young workers needed, according to Herberg, was a new orientation.[7] In recent times, the league has been overly concerned with internal affairs and with the complications of Marxist theory. It is now time to orient the league toward the masses in order to seek some unanimity of theory and practice. For Herberg, the path to this harmony could be achieved through education. To this end, he gave a lecture, apparently his first, at the Workers School in New York City, entitled "Militarism, Pacificism, and the Role of the Young Communist League," and also taught his first course in the Workers School, called "Problems in the Pioneer [Youth] Movement." Further attempts to educate the masses can be seen in two articles Herberg wrote in 1926. The first, entitled " 'Employee Education' in Economics," encourages the Communist movement to adopt the tactic that modern corporations have instituted, namely, to educate the employees in economics.[8] Of course, he writes, capitalist corporations offer their employees such seminars for spurious reasons: to exploit the employees and thus increase profits, and to prevent the spread of class consciousness that would otherwise revolutionize the workers. As Herberg notes, the very phrase "employee economics" means that the whole truth is not being taught and that employees are being seduced into class collaboration. Nevertheless, despite this kind of appeal to the employees, the "historical tendency" of capitalism is the destruction of capitalism and the employer. In Marxist language, "History promises us success if we play our proper role in its development." Meanwhile, the proper role of the proletarian vanguard must be to educate the workers about this trend. One way to do so is to adopt the propaganda techniques of the employers and managers, that is, to use noonday meetings, bulletin boards, educational pamphlets, and the like to inform the workers. To achieve this goal, Herberg asserts, the entire factory should not be the nucleus, but the shop itself.

The second article is entitled "The Steel Making Minerals and Imperialism."[9] In it, Herberg maintains that iron and steel form the basis of the modern world economy: "It is steel that forms the material basis of the latest stage of capitalism." Essential to the production of steel are the ferroalloys, such as manganese, nickel, tungsten, chrome, and vanadium. But these alloys are not found in large quantities in Europe and the United States; thus, they must be looked for elsewhere, and especially in the underdeveloped countries. For example, manganese is found largely in India, Brazil, and Africa; nickel is found in Australia, Ontario, and especially China; chrome is found in Rhodesia, India, and New Caledonia; and vanadium is found in Peru. Consequently, these countries are exploited by imperialist countries, a situation that can only be remedied by the development of a "unified world economy."

Herberg knew that, for a Communist, to unify the economy of the world required unity within the Communist International (Comintern). In 1929 such was not the case, for the increasing power of Joseph Stalin would eventually lead to an internal struggle with Nikolai Bukharin, the chairman of the Comintern's executive committee. Stalin, of course, won, and on 30 July 1929 Bukharin was relieved of his duties. Herberg, in agreement with Jay Lovestone, opposed Stalin, an action that led to Herberg's discharge from his position in the American Communist party. On 9 August, Max Bedacht wrote to Herberg:

> Dear Comrade:
> The Secretariat was advised of your activities in behalf of the opposition to the Comintern Address in the Party and in the League. The Secretariat considers it incompatible with work in the Central Committee of the Party to carry on activities other than those necessary to put the policies of the C.I. [Comintern] and the Party into effect. For these reasons the Secretariat decided to releave [sic] you of the duties you have heretofore performed in the Agitprop Department of the Party.[10]

The letter was signed, "Fraternally yours." Having sided with Bukharin, Herberg and the other Lovestonites were branded "right deviationists," a phrase first applied to Bukharin by Stalin.

2
THE
MOVABLE
SEMINAR,
PART I
1929–1933

In terms of the sheer quantity of articles written, Herberg's most productive years ran from the year of his expulsion from the mainline American Communist party (CPUSA) to the year of the dissolution of the Lovestonites in 1942. During 1929–33 alone, he delivered several special lectures and conducted numerous courses in the Marxist-Leninist School, later known as the New Workers School. However, Herberg was not alone in these efforts. Out of over five hundred expelled from the party,[1] Herberg's closest associates were Jay Lovestone, Benjamin Gitlow, Bertram Wolfe, and Charles S. Zimmerman, among others. These constituted the leadership of the CPUSA-Majority, as they called themselves, changing their name later to CPUSA-Opposition. On 10 October 1929, the CPUSA-Majority met and agreed to continue the revived *Revolutionary Age*, a weekly party newspaper that had first appeared in 1919 when it was staffed by John Reed, C. E. Ruthenberg, Gitlow, and Wolfe. Herberg was elected to the national bureau of the CPUSA-Majority and, within the year, became the managing editor of the *Revolutionary Age*, with Lovestone as editor, Wolfe as associate editor, and Harry Winitsky as business manager. The initial task of the revived newspaper was to inform other Communists of the presumed real situation behind all of the expulsions from the mainline CPUSA.

THE
LOVESTONITES
AND THE
COMINTERN

The first edition of the new *Revolutionary Age* was issued on 1 November 1929. In it Herberg's position on the expulsions, which was essentially the position of the Lovestonites, is described in the first of five articles on the Tenth Plenum of the Executive Committee of the Communist International

(ECCI), held in November 1928.[2] For Herberg, the crisis was precipitated, not so much by Bukharin's dismissal, but by a move to the left by Stalin. In other words, the Lovestonites were neither for Bukharin nor against Stalin, but for maintaining the Marxist-Leninist line. He viewed the whole difficulty as occurring on two levels: the struggle in the Communist International (Comintern) and its resultant relationship to the CPUSA.

Bukharin, in keeping with Lenin's doctrine, had held that there would be three periods of capitalist development after the world war: (1) a period of relative chaos, followed by (2) a period of stabilization, and (3) a period of reconstruction and economic recovery from the war. At the Sixth Congress in July 1928, Bukharin had spoken on behalf of this view. However, Stalin had covertly opposed this position, maintaining that the third period would be replaced by a period of ever-increasing revolutionary fervor. This latter interpretation was overtly stated at the Tenth Plenum, where the idea of a period of capitalist reconstruction was rejected outright. Accordingly, Herberg accused the Tenth Plenum of taking a "revisionist anti-Leninist line." Some, such as V. M. Molotov, even suggested that there would be no fourth period because the third period, as described by Stalin, would end in revolution. However, Herberg held that the Tenth Plenum was merely substituting "revolutionary-sounding phrases for an actual Leninist examination of the situation." What was needed, he insisted, was an economic analysis of the world situation, not merely "vague impressionistic phrases." Lenin had quite correctly maintained that, in a period of general decline in capitalism, there could nevertheless be momentary spurts of advance in capitalism, a position reiterated by Bukharin. To argue against Bukharin's position was therefore to argue against Lenin, who, at the Third Congress, had called opposition to his view an ultra-leftist view that would be disastrous for the whole revolutionary movement.

According to Herberg, the Tenth Plenum also rejected Lenin's view on the radicalization of the working masses, which process, for him, could only gradually move them toward a revolutionary position. In like manner, it rejected the idea of a "united front" with other Social Democrats in the trade unions, condemning the Social Democrats with such ambiguous terms as "fascists" and "social-fascists." The Tenth Plenum presumed that the trade unions had been turned into "agencies or appendages of the capitalist state." But one had to distinguish between the Social Democratic workers in the trade unions and the trade union bureaucratic leaders, those "obsequious leaders" who were constantly "cringing at the feet of imperialism." To deny this distinction between the leaders and the "sincere but mistaken masses" was to break with Leninism. To deny this distinction and to oppose the "united front" within the trade unions would be to adopt the position of syndicalism. Certainly, in Herberg's words, "the new trade union line of the ECCI as laid down in the X Plenum is not the line of Leninism."

The effect of those developments on the CPUSA was, in Herberg's opinion, devastating. The first hint of an attack on the American party was launched by A. L. Lozovsky at the Fourth Congress of the Red International of Labor Unions (RILU or Profitern) in March 1928. Lozovsky accused the central committee of the CPUSA "of 'dancing quadrilles around the American Federation of Labor,' that is, of being so stupid as to want to win for communism the reactionary leaders of the [Samuel] Gompers unions." With such assistance from Lozovsky, a revived American faction composed of William Z. Foster, Alexander Bittelman, and James P. Cannon attended the Sixth World Congress where they presented a minority report entitled "The Right Danger in the American Party," which was supported by such ultra-leftists, to use Herberg's term, as Besso Lominadze, Ernst Thalmann, Heinz Neumann, and other Stalinists. The Sixth Congress, however, dismissed that report as unfounded. Nevertheless, the Foster faction intensified its assault and increasingly the Comintern, with its changing leadership, tried to alter the political line of the CPUSA. Finally, in March 1929, the ECCI sent two representatives, Harry Pollitt and P. Dengel, to the CPUSA with an open letter that not only praised the CPUSA but also suggested some organizational changes within the party's structure. The majority of the party overwhelmingly rejected the suggested changes. As a reaction, the party elected a delegation, led by Lovestone, to travel to Russia to plead its case against these organizational changes directly before the ECCI. Instead of an open hearing, Lovestone and the delegation had to endure abuse and slander from the members of the ECCI. Three days after Lovestone returned from Russia, he "was expelled from the Party by the so-called Polburo [Politburo] without even a hearing." Thus began the "enlightenment campaign," the name the Foster faction gave to the new line of the party.

Herberg cited six considerations that were at issue through this whole development. The first could be called "exceptionalism," which for Herberg meant the Leninist view that each country, "because of the uneven development of capitalism," must proceed according to its own concrete conditions rather than mechanically follow a tactical line laid down by the Comintern. Second, with respect to the idea of the stabilization of capitalism, the Lovestonites rejected the notion that capitalism would collapse in the third period because of a new revolutionary wave among the workers. On the contrary, throughout the world of capitalistic countries, some were in decline while others were moving upward, and it was therefore pure self-deception to believe that all the workers in the world were becoming revolutionary. Third, the CPUSA-Majority rejected the idea that American imperialism was in decline. Fourth, the Lovestonites called for a united front, a position that for years had been held by Lenin and the Comintern. Fifth, with respect to trade union tactics, the CPUSA-Majority rejected the syndicalist view of the RILU and insisted on working within the trade unions, however reactionary, in order to win the workers to the revolutionary cause. In this regard, the charge of "social-fascism" against the Social Democrats and other workers in reactionary organizations was a dangerous theory that could only result in constructing a wall between them and the Communists. Finally, the CPUSA-Majority supported "inner party democracy" and "democratic centralization" as taught by Lenin and the earlier Comintern, and it opposed the present campaign of expulsion and terror. Herberg insisted that these six issues were not uniquely American but were international in scope: "The return of our Party to its Leninist course is directly bound up with the return of the ECCI to the line of Leninism."

From Herberg's perspective, there now existed three major groups: the Trotskyites, the Stalinists, and the opposition, of which he himself was a member. Stalin was deemed the most powerful, and the Trotskyites were seen as unwittingly following the "new turn." Only the opposition groups could bring stability, not by forming separate organizations, but by restoring the Comintern. Indeed, "the ECCI struggle against the ultra-left," such as the Trotskyites, "is only a sham battle because the ECCI itself is the source of the ultra-left sickness."[3] The logic of ultra-leftism was to develop an erroneous tactical line based on a false perspective of the world situation. The essential feature of this situation was the gap between the success of the proletarian revolution in Russia vis-à-vis the slower pace of the revolution in Western Europe and America. Not to recognize this gap would lead the ECCI to a false estimation of the objective situation in the capitalist world. However, in little more than six months after the expulsions, Herberg noted a change in the ECCI, a "strategic retreat" on the part of Stalin whereby he called for a concerted effort by the Communists in the trade unions. Such an action was not accidental, according to Herberg, proving indeed that the expulsions were not based on the objective situation but on a cynical factional advantage and internal politics. Herberg warned, nevertheless, that this "new turn" would fail because the ECCI was leftist in its orientation and would continue to be so. Only by a return to Leninism could the situation be corrected.[4]

THE
LEFTWARD
DIRECTION
OF THE
COMINTERN

Herberg's constant purpose was to display what he considered the shallowness of the ultra-left position of the Comintern.[5] The Comintern, in his opinion, was repeatedly arriving at "sacred ultra-left prejudices" concerning the present crisis and persistently failed to recognize the relationship between economic problems and the political problems that constitute revolutionary situations. He explained that, for Lenin, a general political crisis consisted of a critical breakdown in the policy of the ruling class as well as the consequent development of a situation in which the masses no longer wanted to retain the ancient regime. For a revolutionary situation to exist, what was needed was increasing activity by the masses, led by a vanguard that would carry out the wishes of those masses. But, according to Herberg, the current crisis was not of that nature. Some countries were presently in the situation described by Lenin, whereas others were not. In Germany, Spain, India, and Poland, the conditions for revolution existed whereas in France, America, and England, they did not: "To speak of a revolutionary situation in any of the [latter] countries is absurd." In America, the masses were not active but passive. And even in Germany, the revolutionary class was not strong enough to overthrow the regime, and the masses appeared to be moving to fascism. Nevertheless, the *Communist International*, the organ of the Comintern, continued to maintain that a revolutionary situation existed in all affected areas. The Eleventh Plenum of the Comintern, only two years after the Tenth, persisted in this unrealistic view of the current crisis.

Herberg believed that the Eleventh Plenum was in direct contradiction to the Tenth. Whereas the Tenth Plenum had announced that capitalism was "shattered" and being "liquidated," the Eleventh Plenum retreated to the position that capitalist stabilization was coming to an end. Whereas the Tenth Plenum had announced that the world was in a revolutionary situation, the Eleventh Plenum retreated to the position that there was a "growing increase" in revolutionary spirit. Thus, what was considered right wing at the Tenth Plenum was considered the party line at the Eleventh. Herberg added, rather sardonically, that "this is the 'new turn' strategy in action." There were, however, some remaining crucial differences. The Eleventh Plenum did not mention one word about the leftward trend among Social Democratic movements. It still rejected the policy of the united front. With regard to trade unions, the Eleventh Plenum called for organizing revolutionary workers only, thus creating a division among workers, which action Herberg called a "sectarian tactic." And there was no mention of the CPUSA or the need for the reunification of all Communist parties, a factor that Herberg referred to as "petty trickery, dishonest manovuers [sic], [and] criminal irresponsibility."

Herberg's opposition to the ECCI, however, cannot be construed as opposition to the Soviet Union itself. Consideration of the Soviet Union is essential to any effort to achieve Communist unity, and the "general line" of the Soviet Union was, according to Herberg, fundamentally correct. The general line represented the main strategical course in Socialist construction for the specific period under consideration. For example, at one time the concrete embodiment of the general line was "war communism," later the New Economic Policy, and still later the Five-Year Plan. This last, according to Herberg, would require some sacrifices, such as emphasizing heavy industry as opposed to light industry, which change would lead to a reduction in consumer commodities. Yet to oppose this emphasis and still want socialism was "the veriest petty bourgeois philistinism." Herberg even concurred with the mutual diplomatic recognition, in 1933, of the United States and the Soviet Union. Such arrangements were politically necessary but were not to be taken with any ultimate seriousness, especially in view of the fact that, on the same day of the agreement, the Comintern issued a manifesto calling for American workers to overthrow their capitalist government. To disparage such collaboration with capitalist governments constituted, for Herberg, "a sort of perverted political puritanism." Thus, despite the numerous expulsions from the mainline Communist organization, the Lovestonites approved of the Soviet Union and desired reunification with the Soviet-led party.

In fact, the Lovestonites made the first overture toward reunification with the CPUSA in February and May 1932, but to no avail. The reunification would never occur. One suggestion, by Herbert Zam, was even eliminated by Herberg.[6] Maintaining that after four and a half years the Communist opposition was now obsolete, Zam suggested the establishment of a new Communist party in America and a Fourth International. But, argued Herberg, the Soviet Union would never agree to such an arrangement, and the Fourth International would have to be an international without the presence of the Soviet Union. Such an organization "would either be no International at all or else it would be an anti-communist body, living only by virtue of an inevitable anti-Soviet orientation. This is the most obvious logic of class politics." Instead, the logic of the situation called for open discussion of differences. "Open discussion" for Herberg meant "freedom of thought," but freedom within the limitations of the fundamental aims and goals of Marxism.

MARXISM AND
FREEDOM OF
THOUGHT

Herberg's understanding of and attachment to Marxism was quite definite: "Marxism is the 'pure' class ideology of the proletariat—revisionism in whatever form reflects the pressure of bourgeois or petty bourgeois ideology." In contrast, he considered Christianity "the religion of spiritual enslavement," a mere cult of Judaism, which gave illusory solutions to a real situation— "After Spartacus comes Jesus."[7] In characteristic Marxist fashion, Herberg considered religion a means of class domination, and in such a society there could be no "freedom of thought."[8] In a class-dominated society, all "thought is class thought" even though its members might give lip service to freedom of speech. Only the Communist movement "holds out the promise of the realization of free thought as an actual reality." Membership in the Communist party was voluntary, Herberg claimed, and its major demand was that one agree with the fundamental aims and ideas of the movement. However, he added, agreement with these aims and ideas should not lead to mental stagnation. On the contrary, Marx, Engels, and Lenin did not represent the end of all thinking, nor did they eliminate the necessity for further investigation: "Such an idea is the very contrary of the spirit of Marxism." The genius of Marxism was that it freed thought from class domination and thus made it more socially effective. One therefore did not have to agree with every implication or proposition of Marxism; "this would convert the Communist Party from a political party into a religious sect." As Lenin pointed out, one could, if he chose, even believe in God, although Marxism was atheistic. The party member who believed in God was thereby educated about oppression. To insist dogmatically on uniformity of thought could only lead to inquisitions and heresy hunting. According to Herberg, Lenin's viewpoint on freedom of thought was "the viewpoint corresponding to the best traditions of the proletarian revolutionary movement, and, until recently, it was the viewpoint of the Communist International. It is a tragic manifestation of the present crisis that this viewpoint should have been deserted by the official leadership of the Communist International in favor of a semi-theological dogmatism that spells stagnation and ideological impotence."

In this regard, the approach of the Stalinists, Herberg concluded, was counterproductive.

In the 1 December 1930 issue of the *New York Times*, Walter Duranty reported on an interview with Stalin. In his review of Duranty's article, Herberg pointed out the contradiction in Stalin's current position on the political situation in the world.[9] According to Herberg, Stalin said that the depression begun in 1929 would not last and, contrary to his previous position, capitalism was strong and might recover from its current economic woes. That capitalism was strong, however, was the position of both Bukharin and Lovestone as early as the summer of 1929, before the "crash" in October. And, contrary to Lenin's expressed belief, Stalin maintained that a Communist society and a capitalist society could coexist. Consequently, Herberg attacked Stalin, giving full vent to his spleen: "That Stalin is a political ignoramus— this we knew long ago. But that he should harbor such absolutely incredible ideas for one who claims to be a follower of Marx and Lenin and should not hesitate to give public expression to them is certainly something that deserves the concern of the Communists and revolutionary workers of all countries." But Herberg's venomous attack against Stalin and against the ECCI for having expelled so many dedicated Communists gave him the opportunity to turn his attention to a Marxist-Leninist analysis of Trotskyism, of Rosa Luxemburg, of the relationship of intellectuals to the proletarian movement, of science, of the plight of the Negro in American society, and of American labor.

LEON TROTSKY AND
ROSA LUXEMBURG

From Herberg's perspective, Leon Trotsky was a major Marxist intellectual who was guilty of the shoddiest thinking and of the most perniciously faulty logic in the revolutionary movement.[10] Trotsky wanted only to "internationalize" a sectarian position and as such was only distantly concerned with class struggle. Trotsky, argued Herberg, sought only to universalize the notion of the Thermidor as found in the French Revolution of 1793: "Trotsky is himself politically and historically responsible for theories of Thermidor in *every* form." He believed that a Thermidorean reaction would occur in Russia, and he equated the Stalinist period with that of Alexander Kerensky in 1917, in which the dictatorship of the proletariat existed alongside the dictatorship of the bourgeoisie. Yet in the break between Stalin and Bukharin, Trotsky accused Stalin of being an ultra-leftist and wrote articles against the decisions of the ECCI. In effect, he borrowed from such "right-wingers" as the Lovestonites. Nevertheless, like Stalin, he too maintained "a mantle of infallibility." What occurred, however, was that the ECCI adopted Trotsky's own platform without giving him the credit. As a result, many Trotskyites, such as Karl Radek, happily returned to the party. Even Trotsky himself, during the Manchurian Crisis, delivered the slogan "Unconditional Defense of the Soviet Union!" On the other hand, some Trotskyites, seeking to be consistent, opposed Trotsky's maneuvers. Consequently, a split developed—especially in Germany, France, and Belgium—among the Trotskyites, a rift that could be witnessed in the Trotskyite organization in America.

Herberg indicated that Trotskyism had made little impact in the CPUSA until 1928. Some Communists, including Max Eastman, called themselves Trotskyites, but, according to Herberg, Eastman in particular was of "no significance whatever" because he had no contact with the American labor movement. James P. Cannon was largely responsible for organizing the Trotskyites in 1928. Together with the Foster group, a minority bloc was formed against the central committee of the CPUSA. However, Cannon did not make public his connection with Trotsky, and the Foster group attempted to suppress continuing rumors that the Cannon group was composed of Trotskyites. Finally, in October 1928, the Cannon group was positively identified with Trotsky, and Cannon, along with others, was expelled. Immediately the *Militant* was founded as the organ of the Trotskyites, although its mainstay was the articles written by Trotsky himself. Their effort among the labor movement was minimal; they spent most of their time distributing copies of the *Militant*. As Herberg wrote, "Peacefully—with the peacefulness of suspended animation—the Trotskyites pursue their interminable discussions about questions that have only the remotest connection with the American and international class struggle." So, according to Herberg, the major characteristic of American Trotskyism was "its ineradicable taint of charlatanism," its political frivolity, its unprincipledness, and its cynicism, a characteristic that could be observed in Trotsky's estimation of the situation in Germany.

Referring to Trotsky as the "Genius of Error," Herberg maintained that every prediction he had made was wrong. To hold, as Trotsky did, that Hitler was only a cover for the successful capitalist, Alfred Hugenberg, and that, by 1933, Hitler had already reached the zenith of his power, was, for Herberg, a fantastic "confusion of error." Trotsky was quite simply becoming a "Champion of Reformism" with respect to Germany, especially in his call for the restoration of bourgeois democracy, the restoration of the Weimar Republic. In

Herberg's opinion, this approach would only make the emancipation of the proletariat more difficult. He accused Trotsky of taking a non-Marxist position, mainly because he was becoming a centrist, seeking a rapprochement with "Left Socialism," a position that Lenin condemned. In so doing, Trotsky was running the complete circle of political positions, and any trace of Leninism in Trotsky's thought was all but discarded. According to Herberg, Trotsky asserted that the victory of nazism led to a strengthening of "democratic tendencies" in other countries. This view was utterly false. On the contrary, the Nazi victory had led to the "degradation of democratic dogma" and the strengthening of fascistic tendencies. Moreover, Trotsky's call to promote a "strong democratic government" in such capitalist countries as the United States and Belgium would only lead to the concentration of further power in capital.

Compared to Herberg's vehement disapproval of Trotsky, his adulation of Rosa Luxemburg seems a mild expression of feeling.[11] Citing Lenin, Herberg said that Luxemburg, in spite of all her errors, "was and remains an eagle." As one of the best-recognized leaders of the revolutionary movement, she belonged not to Germany but to the world, presenting a model to the international proletariat of the essence of proletarian striving. Her major weapon against oppression was her pen, which she wielded through the world war on behalf of Marxism. She was always in the forefront—"the fiery agitator, the gifted organizer, the profound theoretician!" Thus, she represented a working relationship between theory and practice and served as a model for communism in general and Marxist intellectuals in particular.

INTELLECTUALS
AND CLASS
CONSCIOUSNESS

Herberg was especially concerned with the relationship of the intellectual to the Communist movement, although his approach was quite orthodox.[12] For example, when Upton Sinclair was recommended for the Nobel Prize in Literature, Herberg believed that Sinclair deserved the prize because he was an "American Socialist novelist." When "bourgeois critics" opposed Sinclair's recommendation, Herberg accused them of "narrow-minded philistine provincialism." But Herberg did not disregard "bourgeois" intellectuals— he only believed them to be misguided. Frequently, he asserted, such intellectuals have revolted against the inequities and contradictions in the capitalist system, but usually they have turned to anarchism, skepticism, cynicism, or "some fantastic and crotchety scheme for the regeneration of mankind," or some other form of utopianism and "vain dreading." Clearly, for Herberg, such views were not rooted in the realities of the proletarian consciousness. Marx, in the *Communist Manifesto*, held that, in the final stages of capitalism, some of the bourgeois intellectuals would side with the proletariat. Consequently, the bourgeois intellectuals could find a place within the Communist movement, either by surrendering their bourgeois viewpoints or by serving as auxiliaries to the movement from without. But, according to Herberg, there were two things that the intellectual could not do: "He cannot hope to stand 'above the struggle' nor can he aspire to mold the movement in accordance with his own private social conceptions." These restrictions applied to any intellectual, whether he was a literary man or a scientist.

Literary techniques, like ethics and philosophy, were for Herberg part of the superstructure of society that reflected the substructure of social existence. As a consequence, he maintained that, in both content and form, class relations were present in literature. The novel or short story was not merely a form or a technique independent of any class, in which case the novel or the short story mirrored a bourgeois bias. However, the proletarian writer might still use these forms of writing as a point of departure from which a strictly proletarian form of writing might be developed. For example, Soviet Russia was still in a period of transition, and, as such, it still retained some bourgeois elements alongside the obvious Socialist ones. The Russian writer would consequently display those bourgeois elements as well as the Socialist trends in his writing style.

SCIENCE
AND CLASS
CONSCIOUSNESS

With regard to science, Herberg cited Bukharin to the effect that even science reflected a class consciousness. In capitalist societies, Herberg pointed out, a division existed between those who worked and those who thought, with the result that there was a bifurcation between practice and theory. Science devoid of its relation to practical necessities often lapsed into mere "academism," as it did in capitalist societies. Hence, science developed into "a pretentious divorce of thought from life," a "preposterous affectation of academism." This condition occurred particularly in the highest stage of capitalism, with the devastating effect that the inner life, the dynamism of science, was destroyed. Science became interested, not in humanity, according to Herberg, but only in the narrow concerns of the class, such as armaments, new modes of profit, and further means of exploiting the worker. Marxism, on the other hand, offered a radical departure from these conditions. A new orientation was initiated whereby science was related to life and in which "creative thought is socialized." Science no longer reflected the petty shopkeeper's desire for profit. Rather, Marxism sought to emancipate science from this kind of enslavement "by providing it with an objective worthy of the very highest efforts of mankind."

One person whom Herberg admired for both his literary and scientific abilities was V. F. Calverton, who was the editor of the *Modern Monthly*. Herberg especially appreciated Calverton's *Liberation of American Literature* in which he analyzed American culture from the perspective of historical materialism. In reviewing Calverton's book, Herberg remarked that social consciousness in the United States was characteristically manifested in a religious form and that American literature had developed "in sterile subservience to British standards and forms," limiting for a long time the development of a genuinely native literature. For example, the Puritans, in Herberg's opinion, were generally hostile to art, and the impact of the rise of commerce and of the wealthy bourgeoisie stunted literary growth in the eighteenth century. Consequently, Herberg accepted Calverton's idea that the American frontier had finally broken the American bondage to Europe. But before a genuine American literature could have fully developed, the Civil War had intervened, leaving pessimism in its aftermath, as exhibited by the "two sides" of Mark Twain. Finally, in the twentieth century, American literature was gradually being liberated by the proletariat. Thus, according to Herberg, Calverton's approach brought "a new significance and a new precision" to Vernon Parrington's *Main Currents in American Thought* because it introduced a Marxist analysis of American literature.

Although Herberg greatly appreciated Calverton's approach to literature, he was somewhat less appreciative of Calverton's approach to the relationship of science and Marxism. Specifically, Calverton's understanding of the history of science was inconclusive. In his "Modern Anthropology of the Theory of Cultural Compulsives," Calverton distinguished two stages of the history of science: the classical stage of free inquiry followed by the second stage of class conflict in which science was used as an apologetic for a particular class ideology. For Herberg, these two stages were correct, but he added a third stage, namely, the stage of science under the aegis of Marxism, in which "its social basis is the revolutionary proletariat." Herberg agreed with Calverton that science without a class bias was impossible in a class society. However, Herberg further asserted that "not every class-bias has a truth-distorting effect." Indeed, the conflict between bourgeois science and proletarian science was beneficial and even necessary for the attainment of truth. Yet, as a good Communist, Herberg agreed that proletarian class bias in science was more progressive.

Herberg's interest in proletarian as well as bourgeois science led him to discuss the relationship of Einsteinian physics to Marxism.[13] In the 9 November 1930 edition of the *New York Times*, Einstein's article "Science and Religion" and Sir James Jeans's book *The Mysterious Universe* were reviewed. In reaction, Herberg describes both Einstein and Jeans as "God-seekers," with Einstein specifically dubbed a "shamefaced materialist" and Jeans a "shameless idealist." Both represent the final stages of capitalism: "The ignoble capitulation of science to religion marks the twilight of contemporary bourgeois thought." In keeping with his general Marxist vision of science, Herberg maintains that Einsteinian physics, with Einstein's attendant popularity, reveals a cultural and class bias. In the eighteenth century, the philosophy that aided the ascendancy of the bourgeoisie was naive materialism and determinism. This view, however, was shattered by the world war, which drained the bourgeoisie of its optimism in the wake of the chaos and confusion brought by the war. As a consequence, science also underwent a radical change. Rationalism gave way to mysticism, naive materialism gave way to idealism and spiritualism, and determinism gave way to indeterminism. Herberg thus holds that "it is precisely the historical function of the new 'anti-materialist' tendency in modern science to supply moribund bourgeois civilization with the comforting assurance that the black future threatened thru the inevitable operation of natural and social forces need no longer be feared since the very foundation of science—materialism and determinism—are no more than empty illusions." For this reason, Einstein, with his new interpretation of physics, appears as the "shining champion" of the bourgeoisie in the field of science.

His theory of relativity, according to Herberg, can only make sense when understood in the light of this social context. In fact, his theory lends credence to dialectical materialism. Einstein's physics is based on the idea, in contrast to Isaac Newton's, that space and time are not absolutes and that matter and energy are related. This idea is grounded on Einstein's dictum that "whatever cannot essentially be observed cannot be said to exist." This epistemological position has, in Herberg's estimation, been erroneously construed as idealism.

The logic is quite simple: what is not observed does not exist; but because observation is subjective, existence too is purely subjective; hence, idealism is true. However, as Herberg emphasizes, this is not what Einstein meant. Rather, he meant that the condition for being able to know anything is that the thing must enter into human experience. Otherwise, the thing cannot be said to exist. Accordingly, Herberg notes the similarity between Einstein and Lenin, who said, "The definition of a thing must be given thru its relation to human practice." With regard to space and time, and matter and energy, Einstein denied that these were absolutes and spoke of a space-time continuum and the equivalence of matter and energy. From this, Herberg concludes: "Out of disparate categories—dialectic unity!"

In Herberg's view, Einstein was really a "conservative" scientist. He held to the old theory of causality and determinism, which was being attacked by Werner Heisenberg's principle of indeterminacy and Max Planck's quantum theory. But these were in actuality idealistic theories that denied objectivity to the physical attributes of matter. These scientists discarded causality in favor of a "statistical concept." Because the position or velocity of a particle was impossible to measure, they claimed, its future path could not be predicted—it could only be statistically approximated. This approach led Heisenberg to what Herberg called a "scientific mysticism." In other words, the principle of indeterminacy was based on human ignorance, which condition was in a transitional stage of scientific history and had been elevated by Heisenberg to an eternal and paramount principle. Herberg agreed with Einstein that the statistical concept in the indeterminacy principle would eventually disappear and would be replaced by a deterministic theory. Meanwhile, according to Herberg, the principle of indeterminacy was an example of the self-destructive character of bourgeois science: "Bourgeois science has been transformed into its opposite and has thereby ended its own cycle of development." Proletarian science would develop a new science and prepare the way "for the mastery of nature in thought and in action."

Like Heisenberg, Charles Darwin was also an expression, however profound, of his own age.[14] Prior to him, a static-mechanistic view of the world dominated. With the preparatory work of Immanuel Kant, Pierre Laplace, Sir Charles Lyell, and others, Darwin's *Origin of the Species* marked the rejection of this view and the acceptance of a dynamic view of nature. Herberg explains that Darwin's theory is not in opposition to revolutionary socialism, as some social Darwinists maintain. Nevertheless, there are some basic differences. Evolutionism is absolutistic because, according to Herberg, it is based on capitalistic roots, which are also absolutistic. It is undialectical, inasmuch as even the social Darwinists do not see society as developing by contradiction. It is unilateral because the same pattern of development is considered to be universal. Herberg argues that the main reason for these discrepancies is that Darwin was simply not a philosopher, a factor that does not detract from his significance in the realm of the biological sciences.

THE NEGRO
IN AMERICAN
SOCIETY

Herberg was far less concerned with Darwinism, however, than he was with the situation of the Negro in American society. He initially came to terms with racial prejudice against Negroes in four book reviews.[15] In them he agrees with Bishop William Montgomery Brown that the Christian church has traditionally played a reactionary role in history and that the pope presently opposes the Soviet Union in order to side with reactionary politics, despite the pope's brazen declaration of "freedom of thought." According to Herberg, Brown proved that religion has not been the greatest originator of culture but that culture grows in times of "deep scepticism." Preachers are therefore mere "intellectual prostitutes of the exploiters." Yet the Negro church is almost the only place that the Negro can call his own. Radicals should therefore not too readily condemn these churches with indignant phrases. The major question is not one of the impact of religion on the oppressed. Rather, it is the problem of the roots of race prejudice and "white chauvinism." A Marxist analysis reveals that race prejudice is quite simply a bourgeois means of keeping the workers divided and therefore oppressed, but further analysis suggests a new perspective on the Negro situation in America.[16]

In Herberg's estimation, a fundamental reorientation to the Negroes' problem in America was required. To assert that Negroes should be servile because intelligence tests have proven their inferiority, he declares, overlooks the fact that the tests themselves are used by the bourgeoisie to reinforce racial prejudice. Moreover, northern Negroes score higher than southern Negroes. "It is the social environment that is the determining factor in the development of intelligence." Nor is it sufficient, Herberg continues, to argue that Negroes constitute a mere colony of American imperialism or that they constitute a nation within a nation. They are not a colony inasmuch as the Negroes are an integral part of the national economy. To say that they compose a "nation" is to take the same view as the Comintern and Stalin who perceive the American

Negro just as they do the Croats in Yugoslavia or the Germans in Hungary. This approach leads directly to Garveyism or Jim Crowism, which permit, among other things, the establishing of "special schools" for Negroes. In addition, this view creates divisiveness and effectively eliminates the possibility of a Marxist analysis of the situation. Therefore, the Negro question is primarily the question of "an oppressed race." Such a question, taken in a Marxist perspective, must view the Negro either as part of labor or as part of capital.

The worst "scourge" of any worker is unemployment, Herberg continues, and the percentage of unemployment for Negro workers is higher than for white workers. The Negro is the last hired and the first fired and frequently can obtain a job only as a strikebreaker or "scab." The American Federation of Labor even established Jim Crow unions for the Negroes. Indeed, the Negro's situation in America is analogous to the plight of the Jew in czarist Russia. On the one hand, the Jew was excluded from both agriculture and important branches of industry in Russia whereas the American Negro works both in agriculture and in heavy industry. On the other hand, both Jews and Negroes have been forced to live in ghettos because the Jew was considered racially undesirable and the Negro is considered racially inferior. Both have experienced restricted educational opportunities. Just as there are religious differences between Judaism and Russian orthodoxy, so too, in the United States, is the racial difference between white and Negro emphasized. Negroes, as were the Jews, are generally excluded from political activity. And just as such organizations as the "black hundred" were established to harass the Jews in Russia, so do such organizations as the Ku Klux Klan harass the Negro in America. All of these comparisons, Herberg maintains, are remnants of a precapitalist society. The Jew's status in Russia resulted from a larger cultural and religious bias derived from the medieval aristocracy and the church; the American Negro's status is the legacy of the semifeudal society of the South, augmented by backward white workers who are really bourgeois in perspective. In Russia, according to Herberg, such prejudice was eliminated only by the extirpation of these capitalist and precapitalist social relations. In America, this same elimination of prejudice can be accomplished by abolishing discriminatory laws and customs, by penalizing those who engage in violent acts against the Negroes, and by overthrowing capitalism and thereby destroying precapitalist social stratifications. In making such suggestions, Herberg also reveals the differences between his position and that of W. E. B. DuBois.

Herberg refers to DuBois as a "petty bourgeois intellectual" who nevertheless has played a relatively important role in the emancipation of the American

Negro. And he notes that DuBois had a high regard for the Russian Revolution and predicted the collapse of capitalism. Yet, Herberg maintains, some important differences exist between communism and DuBois's position. Whereas DuBois considered the Negro bourgeoisie politically weak, Herberg warns that, although numerically small, the middle class is nevertheless dangerous because it perpetuates a bourgeois mentality among Negroes. Whereas DuBois maintained that, since Booker T. Washington, the dominant Negro leadership has not been capitalistic, Herberg cited evidence to the contrary. Leaders such as Bishop Carey, Kelly Miller, and Marcus Garvey felt that Negroes needed to gain prominence by occupying important positions in the economy. To pursue this policy, according to Herberg, is to pursue a capitalist policy. Even the National Association for the Advancement of Colored People (NAACP), which with qualification DuBois supported, demonstrates its capitalistic outlook by seeking to abolish discrimination through quiet legal manipulations. Whether people are Negro capitalists or white capitalists, they are equally bourgeois. Finally, whereas DuBois held that the dominant Negro leadership reflected the poorer Negro, Herberg warns of the danger inherent in assuming that the poor will achieve proletarian class consciousness. They could more easily become bourgeois. For example, Alexander Hamilton was born poor but became "the most class-conscious, the most far-seeing and the most capable representative the American capitalist class has ever had." Consequently, Herberg concludes that DuBois was wrong: "It must be said that Dr. Dubois really does not understand the roots of the matter." Only the members of the proletariat serve as effective allies of the Negroes, and "between Kelly Miller, Bishop Carey, and Marcus Garvey, on the one hand, and the masses of Negro people, on the other, we must insist that a deep distinction be drawn!"

Herberg thus fervently maintained that this distinction between the proletariat and the bourgeoisie was the heart of the Negro question. For example, in late 1932, Oscar DePriest, a U.S. Representative from Illinois, called for a nonpartisan conference of the various Negro organizations to convene in Washington, D.C., for the purpose of discussing what united action should be taken to decrease discrimination in American society. The meeting concluded with a call for support of the U.S. Constitution and the Declaration of Independence while urging Negroes to join either the Democratic or the Republican parties and to vote for "fair minded" whites. In addition, the conference condemned communism. For Herberg, this was nothing more or less than "Americanism," the "counsel of abject servility," to which communism was unalterably opposed. Instead, he urged the Negroes to merge with other underprivileged groups and form a new party—a party of labor to fight oppression of all kinds. But this recommendation was not Herberg's only suggestion for ending racial inequities.

For him, racial prejudice was the ideological reflection of race subjection. In this light Herberg explained that several reasons have been offered to justify the existence of racial prejudice. Some have suggested that a "natural anti- pathy" has always existed between Negroes and whites; but, according to Herberg, this view has been totally discredited by scientific investigation. Others have suggested that the conflict between Negro and white workers is based on economic competition, but however Marxist-sounding this position may be, he asserts, it still does not get to the root of the problem inasmuch as some petty bourgeoisie never come into contact with Negroes and are nonethe- less highly prejudiced. Likewise, the theory that racism is a holdover from the period of slavery does not explain increasing prejudice because prejudices based on tradition have declined and even died out in the past. Another theory, that the capitalists foster racial prejudice to keep the workers divided, is only partly true, for this view does not account for the depth of racial prejudice as an ideology unto itself. Finally, racial prejudice is considered an essential ele- ment of bourgeois ideology, which assumption is more nearly correct, but the material basis of this ideology must be examined.

Herberg suggests a socio-historical approach. Since the Civil War, the Negro has been placed in a "peculiar economic status," arrested between a semifeudal and a proletarian stage. In other words, the Civil War was a "bourgeois-democratic revolution" that remains incomplete. With Reconstruc- tion, two possibilities were faced: the Radicals, such as Thaddeus Stevens and Charles Sumner, sought to complete the revolution by establishing a "bour- geois military dictatorship in the South." But such moderates as Andrew Johnson proposed the second course—compromise and reconciliation—con- ceiving of the next stage as "a sort of modified chattel slavery." The moderates were triumphant, Herberg exclaims. The Radicals failed largely because the West was beginning to open up and the Northern bourgeoisie preferred to expand its capitalist economy there. So it compromised with the old ruling aristocracy in the South. Also, the Northern bourgeoisie both feared the rising proletarian masses in the North and worried that a radical reconstruction in the South might lure away the Northern proletariat. As a consequence, the moder- ates permitted racial prejudice to continue unabated, and their success during Reconstruction "is the historical basis for the persistence of the racial subjec- tion of the Negro and of race prejudice to this day." Capitalism, in its declining stage, Herberg explains, attempts to protect precapitalist social relations and thus uses the precapitalist status of the Negro as a source of steady profits.

Racism accordingly becomes a part of the official bourgeois ideology, and thus the white workers are propagandized with the same mentality.

Herberg claims that the evidence of the continuation of this ideology can be seen in the Southern agrarian economy that developed after the Civil War. That economy continued to be based on cotton, the main agricultural product. The Negro was considered "free" while social relations remained unchanged. In other words, Southern agriculture "was reconstituted as capitalist agriculture operating on the basis of pre-capitalist forms." For millions of workers, both Negro and white, serfdom continued in the decades that followed, but some workers became sharecroppers, still using the tools of the landlord. Other workers managed to become small landowners, but 85 percent of these were whites who were little more than cash tenants, paying their rent in cash borrowed at usurious interest rates. Approximately 25 percent of these were unable to pay their taxes. For the most part, therefore, "human labor-power and the mule still dominate the scene," with the workers functioning in conditions of semipeonage under a social system of semiserfdom. Thus, "Southern agriculture is carried on basically as capitalist exploitation thru pre-capitalist relations." According to Herberg, the only means of overcoming this condition is by Socialist transformation.

The abolitionist movement, the Civil War, and Reconstruction, in Herberg's estimation, formed "one organic epoch" in American history—and American historians have been remiss in presenting objective analyses of this epoch. Without championing the fight against slavery, Herberg complains, they have only apologized for both the North and South and heaped abuse upon the Radicals. James Ford Rhodes classified the Civil War and Reconstruction as "war time passions" and as a conflict of "political parties." Charles Dunning explained Reconstruction as the result of original sin. Charles Beard, along with other so-called Marxist historians, such as A. M. Simons, James Oneal, and Anthony Bimba, "exhibit an incredible shallowness and vulgarity of historical judgment." Even Robert Morss Lovett maintained that Andrew Johnson and William Henry Seward "wisely" carried out Lincoln's program for Reconstruction. What Herberg believes is needed, therefore, is a reevaluation of this epoch from the point of view of the Marxian dialectic, a reevaluation both viewing the Civil War as the second American revolution based on bourgeois-democratic principles and interpreting Reconstruction as a conflict between the radical Jacobins and the conservative Girondins who finally won. For Herberg, the abolitionists hold a special place in American history. On the one hand, they constituted a vanguard movement, developing in isolation from the class they represented and often in antagonism to it. They were, in effect, "typical bourgeois-democratic revolutionaries" with a "mystical-utopian cast" and bearers of a transcendentalism reminiscent of the "vaporings of Gandhi." On the other hand, they were "the noblest, most progressive, most revolutionary movement in recent times." Yet their work remains unfinished; the task can only be completed by the American proletariat, the "truer guardians" of the heritage of the Civil War. "The American communist is the proletarian Abolitionist of today!" After the proletariat triumphs, the abolitionists will be remembered in the right light and the American Negro will be totally emancipated.

According to Herberg, the Negroes ask if the Communist, once in power, will betray them as the abolitionist almost did. Given the backwardness of the American white worker, asking this question is justified. But, Herberg holds, this view overlooks the fact that, if the economic basis of the Negroes' state of semiservility is destroyed, the whole superstructure will collapse too: "The very root of the caste subjection of the American Negro will be eradicated and the possibility of real social and political freedom and equality established." The American worker's first step is to become class conscious—just as the Russian worker's was with regard to the Jew: "Today, the liberation of the Jews in the Soviet Union is absolutely complete." For similar liberation to occur in America, the whole economic and political structure must be transformed.

THE PROLETARIAT AND AMERICAN LABOR

The state of the American economy and the condition of the American political structure were both in—to use Herberg's lifelong word—"crisis."[17] Under the presidency of Herbert Hoover, wealth gradually became concentrated in the hands of the wealthy; and, in contradiction to the "old" argument that the members of the proletariat would themselves gradually become successful capitalists, the misery of the workers had increased. That argument "crashed in 1928." Even the report of the Hoover Committee on Social Trends displayed a capitalist bias, according to Herberg, and was significant only because it proved that capitalist civilization was "heading rapidly for the abyss." The report consisted of two volumes of analyses by academicians whose shallow empiricism made them "intellectually blind and socially fatuous." It maintained that throughout the 1920–29 period employment rose from 50 to 57 percent; but this increase, in Herberg's opinion, only reflected the increasing number of women in industry. Actually, there was an "absolute decrease" in the number of workers in the manufacturing industries. Furthermore, although output increased by 3.3 percent per year from 1925 to 1929, according to Herberg, wages increased only 1.4 percent per year. Consequently, the "rewards of labor" were in reality decreasing during the years of so-called prosperity.

Herberg pointed out that membership in labor unions declined, a fact that displayed the lessening effectiveness of labor movements. Strikes had declined by 80 percent since the world war, largely because of the collaboration of the union leadership and the capitalists. Some corporations suggested "cooperative self-help" arrangements to assist the unemployed, proposing to allow employed workers to use idle machinery in order to provide for their own necessities. But, for Herberg, this approach was fraudulent and would only help the owners of the machinery and the plants to resolve an emergency situation at the expense of the working class. The mainline Communist party had no solutions either, offering only to organize a sectarian hunger march that would not be representative of the masses. The American Federation of Labor (AFL), one of the larger unions in the country, merely sided with the government.

The AFL, in agreement with Hoover, called for "rugged individualism" and "voluntary charity" to aid the unemployed.[18] Neither suggested emergency relief. Herberg recommended that the proletariat campaign for such relief, along with unemployment insurance, the six-hour work day, and the abolition of child labor while simultaneously organizing itself and propagandizing about the causes of unemployment. He noted that the AFL actually turned leftward at its 1932 convention in Cincinnati, where it scrapped the notion of "rugged individualism" and called for unemployment insurance, the six-hour work day, and the five-day work week. However, the union leaders made this change and adopted some of the demands of the militants in order to retain their own positions of leadership. Consequently, the AFL leaders would be little affected by Franklin Roosevelt's National Recovery Act (NRA); indeed, they would erroneously support it.

The real effect of the NRA, as Herberg interpreted title I of the act, would be to make the president a "supervisory dictator" over the economic life of the country for two years.[19] In sum, the NRA established state capitalism. Its benefits would accrue largely to big business: "From first to last, the National Industrial Recovery Act is a measure conceived by and dedicated to the interests of trust capital, of Wall Street." For the worker, it posed an inherent danger; namely, it "legalized class collaboration." Moreover, the act posed a threat to unionism in that the president took over the power to regulate wages and work hours and offered the possibility, in establishing the National Labor Board, of eliminating the right to strike. Such actions, Herberg felt, would put the workers at the mercy of their employers; thus, no substantial recovery should result from the NRA. By 1933, Herberg announced that the NRA was a failure. The recommendation of Dudley Cates, NRA assistant administrator of industry, that "vertical unions" be established and directed by the government, and the suggestion by Gerard Swopes, president of the General Electric Company, that the NRA be taken over by the U.S. Chamber of Commerce, if followed, threatened genuine unionism and bordered on Fascist unionism.

Although he did not feel fascism to be truly imminent, Herberg nevertheless feared that the United States might possibly turn to it.[20] Fascism was to him an expression of monopolistic capitalism and a "definite, tho not inevitable, stage in the political development of post-war capitalism." Similar to what Marx called Bonapartism, fascism, Herberg explained, arose in a time of crisis when the bourgeoisie had lost control over society and when the proletariat was still powerless. The members of the bourgeoisie then appealed to nationalism and created a "Saviour-leader" while calling for a socialism ambiguously based on private property. Nonetheless, they still sided with the capitalists. In Herberg's opinion, the situation in America had not yet reached this point. The two-party system still existed, labor was weak, and the conflict between capitalists and anticapitalists had not intensified. Consequently, to refer to Roosevelt as a Fascist dictator was "totally false," Herberg felt; unlike Hitler and Mussolini, Roosevelt had no extralegal armed detachment like the "brown-shirts." Moreover, fascism sought to destroy labor organizations, which Roosevelt had not done. The NRA, however, came closest to fascism with the establishment of state capitalism, but this maneuver could merely have been capitalism in its last stage and not necessarily fascism. In America, fascism was best expressed by the Khaki-Shirt Army and the Ku Klux Klan; and should it arise, it would be in the form of a peculiar brand of populism based on a peculiar socialism, led by a leader such as Huey Long. These conditions, however, were not present at the time. To prevent such barbarism from occurring, Herberg appealed to the proletariat to unite.

Herberg's own direct efforts among the workers began in December 1933, when Charles Sasha Zimmerman, a fellow Lovestonite and head of the International Ladies Garment Workers Union (ILGWU), Local No. 22, invited him to become the union's local educational director, a position he was to hold until 1954.[21]

3
THE
MOVABLE
SEMINAR,
PART II
1934–1937

The slogan that Herberg adopted for the educational department of Local No. 22 was "Knowledge is power." His own belief in this motto was exhibited not only in his role in the International Ladies Garment Workers Union (ILGWU) but also in his private life. While working for Local No. 22, he was totally absorbed in his private hours in intellectual pursuits, often to the detriment of his social life. He rarely socialized with either the members of the union or the members of the American Communist Party-Opposition (CPO). At his office on West Fortieth Street in New York City, he ordered his lunch and studied while eating. He frequently remained in his office until late in the evening, engaging in his own research. As Charles S. Zimmerman said, "The one thing he wanted, he never got—a Ph.D."[1] But his private efforts in reading and writing indicate that he sought to achieve the same end through less formal means. Yet his private hopes and labors in no way lessened his effectiveness as educational director of Local No. 22. As Saby Nahama, a colleague of Herberg in both the union and the CPO, observed, "No one would believe that anyone could do a job like Will." This view of Herberg's abilities was confirmed by Zimmerman, who wished that he had had a hundred men like Herberg assisting in the organization of a union.[2]

Zimmerman's aim in hiring Herberg was to educate the members of the union to the purpose of unionism. In this regard, Local No. 22 was not a Communist union but simply a union with Communists in it. Herberg himself was not concerned with the question of whether the members were Communists or not. If educated properly, he believed, they would become Communists on their own. To educate the union members about the purpose of unionism, Herberg invited numerous guest speakers, organized the Union Central School, scheduled classes for Spanish-speaking union members that were held at a public school in Spanish Harlem, and arranged art shows, musical groups, and recreational activities for the children of union members. He scheduled theater parties, in which members of the union might attend a Broadway play, after which a member of the cast would give a lecture. On one occasion, Herberg himself directed a play entitled "Miners Are on Strike." He also founded the *Union Dressmaker*, the official publication of the local, which was published in English, Spanish, and Yiddish. On 20 November 1936 Herberg wrote to Zimmerman, "The Educational Department activities are in very good shape."[3]

Education, for Herberg, was "really a vital matter to any labor union."[4] It was particularly crucial in the 1930s, given the current economic depression. Labor unions were increasing in strength. Workers who formerly were suspicious of organized labor were joining unions for protection and security. In August 1933, Local No. 22 staged a successful strike that led in so many new members that its ranks swelled to approximately thirty thousand. These factors further reinforced Herberg's belief that the National Recovery Administration (NRA) was a failure as a recovery program. It was not a "good angel" offering gifts to grateful workers. Rather, the NRA had not measurably increased buying power or substantially reduced unemployment or seriously improved business: "Unions must, therefore, rely not on the NRA but only on their own militancy and organized might." Herberg first directed, in agreement with several resolutions passed at a recent ILGWU convention, that labor must first of all understand all regulative NRA agencies as "essentially employer bodies, treating with them strictly along class lines." Second, industrial unionism must be promoted and the leaders of the American Federation of Labor (AFL) enjoined to merge craft unions with industrial unions. Third, "company unionism" should be condemned as divisive. Such a union "actually enslaves the workers under the hypocritical forms of 'employee representation.'" Fourth, workers should support the organization of a labor party "in the form of a political federation of trade unions, labor political groups and workers' organizations generally." And fifth, labor should oppose any form of racial discrimination and mobilize against fascism. As a consequence of these requirements, labor had an urgent need of militancy: "Labor can gain something under the NRA only if it is strongly organized and ready to fight and fight hard for its aims." And militancy in support of these aims required education of the workers.

Although Herberg never formally joined the union, his position as education director exposed him to the workers' actual conditions, conditions often divorced from the airy realm of Marxist politics and metaphysics. Nonetheless, his enthusiasm for communism and the CPO continued unabated. Indeed, his work with the union served to solidify further his already firm Marxist position. For example, he and Anna, along with others, did organizational work for the CPO in Harlem. But by far the greater emphasis was on his lectures at the New Workers School, where he continued to offer courses on Marxist theory and its implications. During the winter term of 1935, his course, as advertised in the *Workers Age*, concerned "Marxism and Modern Thought." The advertisement explained that the course would deal with the development of modern science in physics, biology, psychology, anthropology, and sociology.[5] Another course he offered was "The History of the Revolutionary Movement in the U.S.," which emphasized the development of the labor movement from 1783 to the rise of the AFL and the Industrial Workers of the World (IWW). In addition to his administrative and instructional activities, Herberg continued to write articles, many of which dealt with the ILGWU in particular and American unionism in general.[6]

COMMUNISM AND
AMERICAN LABOR

On 22 March 1934, the ILGWU, Local No. 22, held an election for the top position in the local. Zimmerman won as manager, and Herberg called it a victory for the Lovestonites inasmuch as Zimmerman was himself a Lovestonite at the moment. The mainline American Communist party (CPUSA) had believed the election would be a test of its own strength, but in fact, Herberg stated, the "Left," including the CPUSA, tallied only 27 percent in the election as opposed to 45 percent the previous year. In Herberg's estimation, the election represented a defeat, at least in the dressmakers' union, of dual unionism, which the CPUSA had supported and the CPO had opposed. With such a victory Zimmerman became not only a leading Lovestonite in Local No. 22 but also a spokesman for what Herberg called the "progressive" element in the ILGWU.

The ILGWU convention in Chicago in July 1934 was a testing ground for these new tendencies in the dressmakers' union. At the convention two groups emerged. There was, on the one hand, the "entrenched bureaucratic right" and, on the other, the progressives, led by Zimmerman with Jay Lovestone in attendance. The official CPUSA, according to Herberg, played no significant role. Through the efforts of the Local No. 22 representatives, the convention approved a resolution against Jim Crowism by calling for a boycott against the hotel in which the convention had originally met because of its discriminatory practices toward Negro union members. Also, the convention adopted a resolution to establish a fund of $50,000 to be used in the fight against fascism. The importance of such resolutions was demonstrated in the election of Zimmerman as vice-president of the general board of the ILGWU. As a consequence the members of the official CPUSA were thereby forced, according to Herberg, to languish in their own errors. Unlike the CPUSA, the CPO had warned a year earlier that it was fatal to assume that the ILGWU would lose ground. On the contrary, Herberg maintained, the International at the convention could boast of four to five times the membership of the previous year. The CPUSA attributed this sudden growth to the effect of the NRA, but Herberg felt that this unprecedented rise in membership was the result of successful strikes in New York City, St. Louis, Philadelphia, Chicago, and other cities. Indeed, the CPUSA did not offer a program or a single important resolution at the convention; in contrast, Lovestone was the first avowed Communist to offer a major address in the history of the American labor movement. His address, in which he opposed the NRA, significantly displayed the growing influence of the CPO in labor: "It was, in a very real sense, the official proclamation of the CPO as a recognized nation-wide force in the American labor movement." The CPUSA, on the other hand, with its policy of dual unionism and of divisiveness in regard to the AFL, was losing ground as a major factor in American labor.

Six months later the CPUSA made what Herberg called another "turn." He referred to a recommendation in the 26 January 1935 issue of the *Daily Worker* that the CPUSA move from dual unionism toward cooperation with the AFL. The reason offered by the *Daily Worker* for this maneuver was the increasing influx of workers into the AFL as a result of the NRA. In Herberg's estimation, this "turn" was only temporary and would be relinquished should the NRA be abolished. Nevertheless, this new position showed the contradiction inherent in CPUSA policy. For years the *Daily Worker*, as Herberg recalled, had denounced the CPO as an obstacle to labor unity. In 1930 the CPO called for progressive groups within the AFL. The CPUSA opposed this approach and charged the CPO with frustrating unity while calling the AFL a "company union" and demanding its destruction. In April 1931, the CPO urged industrial unions to merge with the AFL. Once again the CPUSA called the CPO an obstacle to unity. In September 1931, the CPO sought a merger of isolated furrier unions and AFL furriers. The CPUSA opposed it. By the 1935 international conference in Toronto, the International Fur Workers Union was calling for unification; since 1934, the CPUSA had been hopelessly isolated in the ILGWU. Herberg therefore concluded that the major obstacle to unity was not the CPO but the CPUSA: "We [of the CPO] are proud of our record of exposing and defeating every trickery scheme of fake 'unity.' " However, Herberg was not opposed to every position of the mainline CPUSA. In 1936, at the national meeting of the CPO on Labor Day weekend, he proposed that all Communists support and vote for the CPUSA political candidates: "Despite all deviations, [the CPUSA] is still the historical representative of communism."[7] Moreover, the two organizations shared a common distrust of capitalism in general and of the American government in particular, and they shared a common goal, however their methods differed, of worker unification.

The major hindrances to unification were the lines dividing the workers themselves, best represented by the conflict between the AFL and the Committee for Industrial Organization (CIO).[8] For Herberg, this disunity was exemplified in the fifty-fifth AFL convention in Atlantic City in 1935. It concluded, as Herberg remarked, with "incredible results." As a consequence of profound social changes in the preceding three years, the executive council of the AFL was divided for the first time through the actions of a powerful group that challenged the leaders of the union from the floor of the convention. The "old reactionaries," such as William Green and Matthew Woll, sought to turn back the clock by introducing a "red-baiting" resolution that would oust all Communists from the AFL. The progressives opposed this view while supporting, by a narrow margin, a compromise resolution excluding Communists from central labor bodies and state federations. Nevertheless, the progressive elements displayed their increasing strength: "The force let loose at Atlantic City will not cease until the entire A.F. of L. has been renovated from top to bottom." The real force for American labor was not the AFL but the CIO.

In Herberg's opinion, with the founding of the CIO in 1935, American labor was beginning to move at an "American tempo." While based on the more solid foundation of industrial workers, the establishment of the CIO introduced a new era in the history of American labor: "In the truest sense of the word, we have entered upon a new era that can be judged only in its own terms." According to Herberg, that the CIO was more progressive and less traditional than the AFL would doubtless lead to rivalry. The question of unity, therefore, would necessarily arise.

Herberg noted three possible ways of unification. The first possibility was to unify around the AFL, but this approach would be reactionary because it would be based on craft unionism and would lead to "the worse disaster that could possibly befall the American labor movement." Second, both organizations could adopt the policy of "peace at any price," but this tack would lead to an avoidance of the real issues and differences. The third possibility was to unite around the CIO and consequently on the basis of industrial unionism. Herberg himself supported this last position: "This is the only kind of unity in harmony with the fundamental interests of the labor movement; it is unity making for life and progress." In Herberg's estimation, if the CIO became the new forceful labor movement of the country, then the progressive elements of the AFL would drift toward the CIO. But the most pressing need in achieving such working-class unity was for the Communists and Socialists to agree on the road to the unification of all American labor.

Herberg noted that although the last Congress of the Communist International (Comintern) had stressed the need for unity, in America precious little progress had been made.[9] The Militant Socialists were not prepared to seek unity, and the CPUSA and other Socialists constituted a relatively small group in the country. He felt that, for effectiveness, they should embrace, without exclusiveness, the great masses of the American workers: "In order to be really fruitful, Socialist-Communist cooperation must be cemented on such a basis and on such a program as will most effectively mobilize the organized labor movement for action." The first step, in Herberg's opinion, was to unite the CPUSA, the CPO, and the Militant Socialists. But there were numerous obstacles to achieving this unification, all of which could be reduced to an "irritating sectarianism, overlaid with new opportunist errors." For example, the CPUSA should relinquish its support of dual unionism and should abolish the American League against War and Fascism because both were sectarian in character. And the CPUSA should avoid "hair-brained 'unity' schemes," such as a plan for the CPUSA to unite with the reactionary elements of the clockmakers' and painters' unions. This maneuver would only alienate the more progressive members of the two unions. A later scheme fostered by the CPUSA was to call for a "broad unity convention" composed of the AFL, the CIO, and the railroad unions. This approach, in Herberg's estimation, not only was utopian in perspective but would be positively harmful to the CIO as well. The CPO, on the other hand, stood on the principle of "Unity in and thru the CIO," and, equally important, it supported the formation of an American Labor party.

Herberg maintained that some essential principles must be followed in order to establish an American Labor party.[10] One was that form follows function; that is, such a party should not be organized along the lines of traditional political parties that function largely to lure people to the polls at election time. Of course, a labor party would seek votes also, but its primary aim should be the education of the masses. Second, a Labor party should be democratic in structure, allowing the trade unions to form the basis of its constituency but also permitting Socialists and Communists to participate because, as Herberg believed, they had always been the most class conscious. Above all, the Labor party should not function as a so-called People's Front, which, in countries like France, Germany, Czechoslovakia, and Poland, contained not only a coalition of Socialist and Communist but bourgeois parties as well. Such an approach would virtually be "political class collaboration." Nevertheless, this approach was precisely what the official CPUSA and the Trotskyites favored in their Labor party proposal. Herberg predicted that this kind of thinking would lead them to support Roosevelt for another term: "After all, if you can support Herriot in France, Bruening in Germany, Beneš in Czechoslovakia, why strain at Roosevelt in the United States?" In reality, he knew, the CPUSA supported the idea of a Labor party only if it could control it. But this aim was only a repetition of the old policy of sectarianism, not a desire for unity. The fatal flaw of the CPUSA was allowing the executive committee of the Comintern to dictate its position; by doing so, according to Herberg, it could never become the vanguard of the American working class.

For Herberg the Socialist party was no more effective in its tactics than the CPUSA.[11] In 1931 he described the militant element of the Socialist party as immature and politically shortsighted, but he predicted that the militants in the party would either move toward communism and withdraw from the Socialist party or capitulate to the demands of the moderates and the more conservative element lead by Morris Hillquit, James Oneal, and Norman Thomas. By 1935 Herberg, in asking, "Where do the SP Militants Stand?" welcomed the Militants' latest publicized program "as indicating a deepening of theoretical consciousness." The title of their program, as issued in September 1935, was "Draft for a Program for the Socialist Party of the United States." Yet, in Herberg's estimation, they still held to a reformist or centrist, and not a revolutionary, position. For example, the new program offered little economic analysis of American social conditions; it offered no practical program for the labor movement; it did not distinguish between revolutionary and parliamentary (bourgeois) democracy; and it failed to mention the need for a dictatorship of the proletariat. Its most glaring defect, in Herberg's view, was its failure to understand that fascism was a dictatorship of capitalists based on the petty bourgeoisie. And most disappointing of all, the document offered no Marxist analysis on the nature of war during the present stage of capitalism. The Socialist party, according to Herberg, apparently did not recognize the necessity of converting imperialist wars into civil wars. Thus, the Socialist party was still caught in the "vicious circle of centrism" and must ultimately choose between the democratic socialism of the old guard and the revolutionary socialism of Marx and Lenin: "And the choice must be made sooner than later for, here as everywhere, stagnation means retrogression."

In dealing with the question of the unity of the Socialists and the Communists on behalf of the American labor movement, Herberg accused the Socialist party of being "confused." For example, with regard to the formation of an American Labor party, the Socialist party, and especially Norman Thomas, displayed a "peculiar type of opportunistic sectarianism" characteristic of the militants among the Socialists. Thomas offered five conditions for the establishment of a Labor party, all of which Herberg considered unrealistic. First, Thomas held that a Labor party should be more than a reform party; Herberg noted that he did not specify what was meant by "more." Second, Thomas maintained that the Labor party should have mass support; in Herberg's opinion, the Socialists did not really elicit such support. Third, Thomas recommended that the Socialists should be the vanguard of such a Labor party; according to Herberg, this view would lead the Socialist party to "suicidal sectarianism" inasmuch as some in a Labor party might seek to ban Communists and Socialists from the party. Fourth, Thomas held that the Labor party should be national in scope and intention; Herberg knew that many labor parties begin on the local level—should they therefore be rejected by a Labor party that is national in its program? And fifth, Thomas maintained that a Labor party should be democratic and not bureaucratic in structure; Herberg warned that in the event a Labor party did develop a bureaucracy, that party might then be rejected outright. From all this Herberg concluded that Thomas, in effect, was really opposed to a Labor party: "The price of sectarianism is necessarily political blindness!" In 1930–32, the CPO accused the official CPUSA of this kind of sectarianism. From 1935 on, Herberg accused the Socialist party of the same kind of confusion. But the confusion in the CPUSA and the Socialist party was nowhere near the chaos created by the common enemy, the capitalists, specifically the American capitalists under the Roosevelt administration.

Herberg detected a marked increase in the level of hostility in the public reaction to labor between 1935 and 1937, which change he believed correlated with a two-year upsurge of interest and involvement in the labor movement. This hostility reflected "the historical backwardness of the American working class," which could not accept the fact that unionism was here to stay. Mass support for government regulation of unions merely proved that American workers "are still petty bourgeois-minded."[12] Labor unions, Herberg recommended, should view this situation in appropriate perspective, namely, a Marxist perspective centered on class struggle. For example, Herberg stated that the Supreme Court voided the NRA in 1935 on the ground that its regulations interfered with intrastate commerce and delegated improper power to the executive branch of government. As a consequence of this court decision, some (of bourgeois persuasion) called for constitutional reform, seeking to "cleanse" the bourgeois state. The path of reform should not be, according to Herberg, toward a reemphasis of states' rights, now the mainstay of reaction, just as before the Civil War the issue was the mainstay of slavery; Marx had opposed decentralization and had preferred a centralizing bourgeois government. Rather, reform should follow four major avenues: (1) it should raise the class struggle to a higher level; (2) it should emphasize the need for workers' councils (soviets); (3) it should seek labor's independence from capitalist political parties by establishing a labor party; and (4) it should not view itself as a panacea but should always maintain the class struggle as paramount. In sum, constitutional reform must take a backseat to the greater task of organizing labor to be strong enough to call forth an effective strike. To do this, the New Deal government's exact position toward labor must be clearly recognized and understood.

The beginning of the breakdown in capitalist production, according to Herberg, was in 1929. Roosevelt's "new gospel," which shifted to cartelization, offered economic relief, public works for the laborer, social security, and the encouragement of collective bargaining under government control and through unionism. Roosevelt and big business thus had the same goal—to preserve the capitalist system. American liberalism supported Roosevelt in this effort: "The social and labor policy of the New Deal makes such a striking impression today primarily because traditional American liberalism has always been so incredibly shallow and anemic." By placing unions under government regulation and depriving them of their independence, liberalism and the New Deal were repeating the age-old employer's method of crippling the worker. The idea of government-regulated unionism "is something that can take on bodily form only as fascism." As labor attempts to become stronger, Herberg asserted, the government will impose stronger controls. In this manner, liberalism and Roosevelt will have come full turn: "New Deal liberalism completes the circle and meets old-line reaction on its own ground." For this reason, unions should insist on their independence, an insistence made all the more difficult by the passing of the new wages and hours bill introduced by congressmen Hugo Black and William P. Connery in May 1937.

The Black-Connery Fair Labor Standards Act "marks a deeply significant event in the American social and political development, laden with far-reaching consequences for the organized labor movement." It set up a board composed of five people appointed by the President and approved by the Senate. The board had the task of controlling interstate commerce to a degree; it would establish minimum wages at about forty cents per hour, with a thirty-five- to forty-hour workweek; it would define and appropriately prohibit child labor;

and it would outlaw strikebreaking. According to Herberg, some of these
regulations, if adopted, would be advantageous to unions. But the bill contained possible pitfalls for the future. For example, some articles in the bill
provided that both employer and employee could make appeals to the board
and, if unsatisfied by the board's actions, could make further appeals within
the judicial system. This recommendation suggested to Herberg that there
were obvious loopholes in the bill that could be used by unscrupulous employers. What the New Deal sought, Herberg felt, was ultimately to take over
the functions of unions, thus making unions themselves superfluous. Consequently, organized labor should be pleased with the gains made in the Black-
Connery bill but "should never lose sight of its inherent limitations and
dangers."

Similar dangers could be found in Roosevelt's own policies. With regard to
foreign policy, the American economy, and American labor, the president was
in Herberg's opinion a much more farsighted capitalist than those who were
anti–New Deal and who referred to him as a "Red."[13] In his radio address of 3
January 1936, Roosevelt stated his opposition to autocracy and aggression,
both abroad and at home, whether in the form of Fascists, of Communists,
or of the American Liberty League. On the one hand, he proposed a twofold principle of neutrality in order to avoid war: prohibition of the export
of armaments to belligerent countries and discouragement of the export of
American goods of indirect military value to belligerent countries. On the
other hand, he expressed a fear of an autocracy at home based on the domination of government by financial and industrial interests—or, in other words,
the American Liberty League. Herberg cited Alfred E. Smith's warning that
Roosevelt seemed to oppose the "twin spirits" of autocracy and aggression
without any concern for private property. Needless to say, some, like Smith,
accused Roosevelt of fostering class conflict and following Marx and Lenin.
Even Gabriel Peri, the editor of the Communist journal *Paris Humanite*, in the
6 January edition claimed that FDR was following the line of the Seventh
Congress of the Comintern. Herberg explained that what was happening was
not that Roosevelt was moving toward Marx and Lenin but that, in fact, the
official Communist party was moving "in the direction of bourgeois liberalism!" This trend would prove dangerous for communism in America because
the heart of the New Deal was really the support of big business.

To clarify this point, Herberg referred to the U.S. Chamber of Commerce
proposal and the Gerald Swope plan to aid economic recovery in 1931. Both
sought modifications in the antitrust laws, with the chamber also recommend-
ing unemployment insurance, old-age pensions, shorter work hours, and a

national economic council. Before he was elected, Roosevelt had promised to take action to achieve these aims. Thus, he "was elected not against big business but with the support of the most decisive sections of the dominant capitalist interests of this country!" Even the NRA, passed in June 1933, was, according to Herberg, the "embodiment of a program for big business." H. I. Harriman, the president of the U.S. Chamber of Commerce, congratulated the directors of the chamber for having achieved a victory when the NRA became law. And Roosevelt's gold policy was endorsed by the wealthy industrialist J. P. Morgan. Nevertheless, Herberg admitted that, by 1936, big business was opposed to Roosevelt. The reason for this change was that the emergency of 1931 had passed, at least for big business. Profits were rising, wages were minimal, and big business was little concerned about unemployment because technical progress in machinery had decreased the need for labor. In other words, for big business the New Deal was no longer necessary whereas Roosevelt felt that some kind of long-range stabilization was required in order to avoid another economic collapse. The anti–New Dealers were therefore capitalism's backward element, the "Bourbons who seem unable either to forget or [to] learn anything."

The impact of Roosevelt's New Deal on the workers and the farmers reflected a deeper process taking place in the labor movement. Herberg predicted that, in the 1936 presidential election, many workers would vote for Roosevelt, not as Americans or as Democrats, but as *workers*: "The Roosevelt question has become a labor question." At the root of the workers' support of Roosevelt was the Roosevelt myth that "he is a friend of labor," a myth created largely by the old-line reactionaries: "His prime attraction as a candidate is the enemies he has made." On the contrary, Roosevelt in Herberg's estimation was taking a conservative course in the same way that Otto von Bismarck and Lloyd George were conservatives. Even the Supreme Court inadvertently helped to foster the myth. Those measures offered by Roosevelt most promising to labor were "largely nullified by judicial interference." Thus, Roosevelt retained the glamour of his original promises but did not have to fulfill them because of the "kindly interposition of the courts." In this manner, Roosevelt's presumed liberalism was for Herberg the "truest conservatism." Labor accordingly had only one major recourse and that was to organize an independent Labor party on a national scale. Otherwise, the entire country was in danger of being lulled into succumbing to the dangerous appeals of fascism.

*COMMUNISM
AND THE
THREAT OF
FASCISM*

Herberg's concern about the rise of fascism in Europe deepened as the
thirties wore on, and, in contrast to his earlier view, by 1936 he believed
that fascism loomed on America's horizon.[14] Fascism, he explained, arose in
times of economic and social crisis in which the bourgeoisie could no longer
control the masses through the usual means and the proletariat lacked sufficient political means to seize control. The disillusioned members of the petty
bourgeoisie then mounted an independent social movement of a "pseudo-
radical nature." However, because their ideology was contradictory and was
based on "an intensely reactionary mystical nationalism," they sought salvation through a leader. Opposed to both capitalism and communism, these
Fascists established a decadent socialism based on private property. The capitalists, in order to protect their own property and to preserve the state, turned
to the Fascists for assistance. Thus, fascism became "the salvation of capitalism in a blind-alley." The bourgeoisie, in effect, controlled the Fascist movement. As Herberg's earlier articles on fascism pointed out, the members of the
petty bourgeoisie were ultimately incapable of leading themselves and had
therefore to be led by either the proletariat or the bourgeoisie. If led by the
latter, then fascism resulted. Unlike the official Communist party and the
Trotskyites, who, according to Herberg, sought a broad-based movement
composed of mixed elements to oppose fascism and the possibility of war, the
CPO recommended that a united labor coalition, led by Communist vanguards,
should conduct such a movement. Inasmuch as the "whole of the [American]
people" was bourgeois and conservative, it could be progressive only under
the direction of the working-class proletariat. Consequently, Herberg opposed
a broad-based movement and preferred a movement founded on trade unions.

In this country, to Herberg, "the most authentic expression of native American fascism" was Huey Long. Its most immediate manifestation was Father Coughlin's National Union for Social Justice and the Black Legion. Herberg called them both "panaceamongers." Writing before Father Coughlin
announced as a third-party candidate on 17 June 1936, Herberg showed that
Coughlin's fascistic tendencies could not be identified with the church. The
church and fascism, he said, were unalterably opposed to each other; fascism
sought to subordinate the church to the state. Nevertheless, Father Coughlin's
movement exemplified the continuing degeneration of capitalism into fas-

cism—as did the Black Legion. Essentially a lower-class movement in the midwestern industrial sections of the country, the Black Legion was composed mostly of poor whites from the South. Exalting the native white American and denigrating foreigners, Negroes, Jews, and Catholics, the Black Legion was in effect a resurgence of the Ku Klux Klan and basically "Talmadgism transplanted," functioning largely as "the hired bully of big business." The aims of the Black Legion were to uphold the Constitution, to root out "disloyal elements," and to take hold of the government in the name of "true" Americans. Unlike its European counterparts, the Black Legion gloried in that frontier pathology, using and displaying firearms. The real danger, in Herberg's view, was that all of these disparate organizations might merge to form one movement around a cult hero, a leader who might be "worshipped as a veritable wonder-worker saviour." However anxiety-provoking the threat of such a merger might have been in America, fascism in parts of Europe had already taken hold and was gaining momentum while the Comintern had done little to stop it.

Herberg found a recent shift in Comintern policy toward fascism shocking. First of all, it recommended that the Communists agitate, not against the Fascists or the bourgeoisie per se, but against millionaires and "armament profiteers." Second, it sought to reconcile all, including Fascists and anti-Fascists, against these wealthy people. For example, the Italian Communist party announced that it would adopt the Fascist program of 1919 as its own. Germany's Communist party asked Communists to consider the National Socialists as fine progressive people and to accept the words of the Nazi leaders as genuine. Even the CPUSA, according to Herberg, in the September 1936 edition of the *Communist* called for joining Father Coughlin's National Union. The purpose of such tactics was to convert Fascist organizations into vehicles of the proletarian struggle. "Such is the new dispensation" of the Comintern, wrote Herberg. To him this trend was clearly dangerous. It was "utterly monstrous" to assume that Fascists could be offered the hand of reconciliation in the hope that they would help bring about a proletarian revolution. On the contrary, such a maneuver would only strengthen the power and position of demagogues like Hitler and Mussolini. The overthrow of the Fascist regimes in Germany and Italy required the participation of some Fascists "but only to the degree that they cease to be fascists." The Comintern deluded itself by assuming that rank-and-file Fascists could remain Fascists and still legitimately carry on the class struggle. This approach was the logical culmination of the "People's Front" strategy. This ultraopportunism of the Comintern, expressed in a "national front," was the ultra-leftism of the "third period," expressed in "a united front from below." According to Herberg, this policy of having Marxists agree to a coalition with a liberal regime had aided in bringing Germany, and especially Austria, under the "Fascist Heel" and had led to catastrophic results in Spain.

Since the world war and the fall of the Hapsburg monarchy in 1918, Austria had played a unique role in European history.[15] As Herberg wrote, "Austria has been the cockpit of Europe," trapped by the policies of the Germans, French, and Italians. Germany "desired some form of an Anschluss in the interests of the new German imperialism," Italy wanted an ostensibly independent Austria, and France attempted to save Austria from both the Germans and the Italians. Fascism within Austria took two forms: the Nazis and the pre-Italian Heimwehr, with Chancellor Engelbert Dolfuss associated with the latter. In February 1934, the workers of Linz spontaneously engaged in an insurrection that was crushed by the government within five days. Although the revolution was inspired by Social Democratic principles, the Communists played no part. This event nevertheless confirmed, for Herberg, the principles of Marxism. The Social Democrats had previously attempted to collaborate with the Dolfuss regime, which increasingly became more uncompromising. The Linz revolt proved the illusiveness of collaboration and confirmed the Marxist theory, as explained by Herberg, that class conflict moved along in a disguised fashion until there was open revolt. It demonstrated, as in Germany, that reformist socialism, championing parliamentary democracy, would fall prey to catastrophic consequences if the principle of the necessity of a proletarian dictatorship was forgotten. Such Austrian Social Democrats as Otto Bauer and Julius Deutsch were guilty of this charge: "It was not their personal devotion to the cause of labor that was wanting; it was their Marxist clarity and firmness of revolutionary principle that were missing." In effect, by seeking to collaborate, they became themselves barriers to a genuine revolutionary spirit: "Only under the hegemony of the proletariat, only under proletarian slogans, can a people's movement against Fascism grow strong and triumph!"

The same principle applied to the situation in Spain. Herberg maintained that the civil conflict there would "inevitably pass over into a socialist revolution," a requirement for the elimination of the remnants of a decaying feudalism.[16] The bourgeois liberal regime, brought about with the aid of a People's Front coalition of liberals, Socialists, and Communists, continued to suppress the peasants while promising land reform. This reform, Herberg recommended, could only be accomplished by a Workers' Alliance working against the liberal government, thereby following the pattern of the Russian experience in moving from a bourgeois to a Socialist revolution. Like Russia, Spain was in an arrested stage of capitalist development, with the peasantry in a strategic political position and the proletariat playing a relatively minor role in a backward economy. The bourgeoisie aligned itself with the peasantry to seek agrarian reform and to break "the clutch of the Church over the life and soul of the people." Yet, given this situation, the involvement of the proletariat would also be required in order to bring to full realization the revolutionary potential: "In the very nature of things, the proletariat is the only class in modern society that can lead any great revolution of today in a determined and thorogoing fashion, even tho it may be bourgeois in its social content." The major difference between the Russian and the Spanish revolutions was that, in the former, the Bolsheviks refused to support a provisional, bourgeois government whereas in the Spanish revolution the People's Front supported the liberal government, acting somewhat like the Mensheviks and Social Revolutionaries of 1917. The Spanish proletariat should have maintained its political and organizational independence after the election of 16 February 1836. Herberg predicted that, as in Germany and Austria, the bourgeois element of the People's Front would become reactionary and might even oppose its former allies.

At the Magdeburg Congress of Social Democrats in 1910, August Bebel warned that coalition parties of proletariat and bourgeoisie would benefit the latter. According to Herberg, this situation existed in Spain in 1936. The program of the Spanish government was not a program of bourgeois democrats but one of bourgeois republicans. Unwittingly, the workers who were members of the People's Front supported suppression of the peasantry by the Manuel Azana government. He was their ally and the workers themselves were partly responsible for stultifying the force of the revolution. The logical reaction, said Herberg, would be a Fascist counterrevolution similar to the Kornilov Putsch in Russia in 1917, which led to the collapse of the Kerensky government. Herberg predicted that the Fascist forces would be defeated and that there would be either a return to the liberal regime or a proletarian Socialist regime. Should the liberal regime maintain its control, it would have to either progress toward a genuine revolution or go backward by establishing "a ruthless bourgeois dictatorship." In either case, the Marxists in Spain would hold its future in their hands.

By August 1936, Herberg claimed that Europe, and especially Spain, was divided into two camps, the Socialists and the Fascists: "Socialism against fascism—on the Spanish front—is now being fought a great and bloody battle in this mighty war upon which so much of the fate of mankind depends." England, "the proud mother of parliamentary democracy," supported the Fascists, wanting no "Red Menace" in Spain, the neighbor of Portugal, a virtual British colony. England, Herberg held, had greater need of the new Spanish fascistic dictator, Francisco Franco, than of Mussolini because of British lifelines in the Mediterranean area. France, according to Herberg, followed the most despicable policy: "The most miserable example of criminal, suicidal futility parading as foreign policy is exhibited by France, by that renowned People's Front government whose praises are sung so vociferously in the socialist and official communist press." The French government called for a nonintervention pact banning the sale of arms to either side of the Spanish dispute. Such a proposal, if enacted, would have aided merely the Fascists in Spain. Even the French radicals took the same position as England—do not offend the Italian and German Fascists over the Spanish question. Thus, all of Europe was aligned along ideological lines, such alignment serving to accentuate the danger of war because ideological interests usually reflect national and class interests.

In view of these world alignments, Herberg recommended that the Spanish Marxists, the Partido Obrero de Unificación Marxista (POUM), take a "Jacobin defense" in the Spanish civil war—that is, oppose both Franco and the bourgeois regime of Juan Negrin and Indalecio Prieto, the latter being supported by the Stalinists. In so doing, the POUM should attempt to change the policy of the government to a revolutionary policy. During the French Revolution, the Girondins called in 1792 first for political unity in order to win the war, after which attention could be turned to the revolution at home. But the Jacobins called first for the immediate completion of the revolution in order then to win the war. The Jacobins, as Herberg explained, "proved to be the saviors of France" by opposing the common enemy as well as the Girondins. During the American Civil War many, including Lincoln, maintained that the slavery issue could be solved only after a military victory. As a consequence of following this policy, oppression of the Negro continued. Instead, the Jacobin defense, like Lenin and the Bolsheviks vis-à-vis the Kornilov and Kerensky regimes in Russia, was "the only kind of defense in consonance with the immediate and long-range interests of the masses of the people!" To do otherwise was to follow the dubious logic of the People's Front as enunciated by the Stalinist-controlled Comintern.

In the Ethiopian crisis of 1935–36, the Comintern again confused the genuine tactics of the Communists with the reformist tactics of the Social Democrats.[17] Writing in August 1935, Herberg discussed the Italian plan to invade Ethiopia in order to create, as Herberg interpreted it, a colonial reserve for Italian capitalism. The League of Nations, in his estimation, was incapable of halting this aggression, mainly because of the vested interest of the major member states. Even the USSR had not raised its voice against the Italians; and the Soviet foreign minister, Maxim Litvinov, suggested that the Ethiopians capitulate to the Italians. From this Herberg concluded that the Soviet Union "has now manouvered [sic] itself into a situation where it appears as the errand-boy of the unscrupulous League politicians intriguing against the life of the last independent nation in Africa." A month later, however, the Soviet Union officially condemned Italy, and Herberg noted that it thus regained much of its prestige. However, in a report to the National Plenum of the CPO in February 1936, written after the Italians had invaded Ethiopia, Lovestone and Herberg again accused the Comintern of following a misguided course in the Ethiopian crisis. Although the Soviet Union attempted to force the League of Nations to invoke "collective sanctions in general and oil sanctions in particular against Italy," it nevertheless only engaged in diplomatic, parliamentary tactics in dealing with imperialist powers. This approach in itself was not inappropriate, but it did mask a real danger: "Instead of exposing the predatory interest of the imperialist powers, they [the sanctions] tend to nourish popular faith in the desire or interest of these powers in effecting peace or in protecting colonial peoples against aggression." In short, the sanctions should have been antiimperialist, not proimperialist, sanctions.

Herberg recommended that labor demonstrate a united front against Italian imperialism in every country, by mounting strikes, by preventing the transportation of war materials to Italy, and by refusing to grant any financial-aid credit to Mussolini. In other words, the working-class strategy outside the Soviet Union did not need to be identical to, or even modeled on, Soviet diplomacy. The Soviets might collaborate with imperialist powers in diplomacy, but that did not mean that the workers in each country must do so. Consequently, the CPO was "uncompromisingly" opposed to the Comintern policy requiring labor in every country to advocate sanctions against the Italians in order to support Soviet diplomacy. However correct Soviet diplomacy might be, according to Herberg, it would amount to collaboration to support bourgeois approval of sanctions in capitalist countries like America, England, and France.

For Herberg, proletarian-centered foreign policy had two major goals: (1) to aid the proletariat throughout the world, and (2) to protect the Soviet Union. He considered these two aims to be in complete harmony; any policy in conflict with one conflicted with the other. The rationale was quite simple: the Soviet Union would be the first country to achieve socialism in its purest form.[18] The seeming inconsistencies in both domestic and foreign Soviet policy merely reflected the contradictions of the ongoing dialectic. The Soviet Union, too, had emerged from the womb of capitalism and thus shared with others some of the defects of their origins. Nevertheless, this "grand dialectic scheme" was "organically integrating the various contradictory phases in a pattern culminating in the new socialist order." With the institution of the Second Five-Year Plan, the Soviet Union had established the conditions that would make a classless society not only a practical possibility but also an immediate possibility. Marx had given no full-fledged policy. The policy must arise out of the experience of the proletariat in the light of Marx's general theory. Or, as Herberg wrote in a spirit similar to his later theological position: "There are no sacred dogmas or unalterable principles standing above all criticism. Authority and tradition, the authority of a great thinker such as Marx, Engels, Lenin or Rosa Luxemburg, the tradition of the socialist-labor movement precipitated from the experience of decades of struggle, may be very valuable guides if properly employed. But they must be applied *concretely*, with careful regard to time, place and circumstances. To tear a sentence from its practical context and convert it into an absolute dogma, is a grave sin against the spirit of Marxism and it becomes all the graver if it is Marx or Lenin who is thus mistreated." With this perspective in mind, the labor movement in America should agree on these goals and seek to achieve them through independence of action, free of class collaboration.

Agreement was made all the more difficult, according to Herberg, because of differences between the CPUSA and the CPO. After all, the Communists should constitute the united vanguard of the American labor movement. But the differences between the two groups were considered to be too deep for reconciliation. Herberg dealt with several topics that divided them.[19] One, in 1936, concerned support of Roosevelt's reelection. According to Herberg, the CPUSA gave unofficial support to Roosevelt's campaign largely because it feared a Republican victory and because Earl Browder believed that Roosevelt, like Woodrow Wilson, would keep America out of war. However, this position in Herberg's opinion would still place the workers in the hands of the capitalists' two-party system; in effect, the CPUSA was agreeing with the old-guard Socialists.

The second topic concerned pending neutrality legislation currently before Congress, specifically the two bills introduced by congressmen Key Pittman and Sam D. McReynolds respectively. For Herberg, the two bills differed very little. Both called for an embargo on munitions in the event of war, with the latter bill specifically exempting "American Republics." But, in Herberg's estimation, this legislation, if passed, would be utterly futile because it could not keep the United States out of war: "It is a dangerous illusion that a country like the United States can be isolated from the rest of the world, can be 'protected' from the plague of war by a 'cordon sanitaire' of neutrality laws." Such legislation would merely lull people into a false sense of security. The official CPUSA, in the 22 February 1937 issue of the *Daily Worker*, called for invoking the Kellogg Peace Pact in the event either of war or of the danger of war in order to enforce an embargo against an "aggressor." But, Herberg held, the CPUSA overlooked the fact that the term "aggressor" was ambiguous, so much so that imperialist powers could define the term in such a manner that the Soviet Union might be called the aggressor in a war against Japan or Germany. In practice, this approach of invoking the Kellogg Peace Pact was meaningless; moreover, Herberg continued, the CPUSA wanted to outlaw and repudiate any armed party that sought to overthrow a democratic government. But, in Herberg's estimation, this view would inevitably lead to opposition directed against working-class insurrections.

The third and most hotly debated item was the notion of "dual unions," that is, the establishment of Communist unions alongside existing unions. For Herberg, dual unionism was definitely a departure from Lenin's expressed opposition to sectarian unions, described in his essay "The Infantile Sickness of Leftism." Nevertheless, in 1934 the CPUSA, following instructions from the Comintern, adopted the principle of dual unionism. But the CPUSA was inconsistent even with respect to its own position. In 1928, William Z. Foster had supported Lovestone's opposition to dual unions; in 1930, the CPUSA referred to the AFL as a "company union" and called for its destruction. A year later the CPUSA was involved in attempting to organize within the ILGWU, within the Amalgamated Food Workers Union, and within the millinery union. By 1935, the Seventh Congress of the Comintern had come around to condemning the sectarian course of dual unionism and so did the CPUSA. But according to Herberg this new line was only a sham policy inasmuch as some dual unions still existed, such as that, for example, in the anthracite region of Pennsylvania. The CPUSA, Herberg claimed, was merely trying to take advantage of the recent influx of workers into the union as a result of the NRA. What would the CPUSA do in the event that the NRA was abolished? Herberg felt it would return to the policy of dual unions.

TROTSKYISM
AND THE
COMINTERN

However critical of the presumably ambiguous policy of the CPUSA and the Comintern Herberg may have been, his ongoing attacks on the thought of Trotsky and the Trotskyites continued unrelentingly.[20] The thrust of his argument was that the Trotskyites were following a policy of centrism. For example, Trotsky at one time had lectured on the necessity of the independence of Marxist organizations, regardless of size, from other reform organizations like the Socialist parties. In 1932 he argued for Marxist independence from the German Fascist movement. By 1934, however, he was calling for Marxists to join Socialist parties in England and France and for negotiations with the American Workers party in the attempt to seek a merger. This new centrist line, according to Herberg, was a result of the collapse of the Trotskyite faction in Russia. In 1933 the Russian Trotskyites had hoped for a failure of the First Five-Year Plan and the disintegration of the Soviet economy at the same time as they were attempting to control the Communist party of the Soviet Union. Yet they "religiously abstained from any direct contact with the class struggle and prided themselves on their sterile existence as a small propaganda sect." But the Five-Year Plan succeeded, and Trotsky's speculations about it went unrealized. His only recourse was to maintain that the Soviet Communist party could not be reformed, that it was essentially dead, and that a new party had to be formed in order to challenge the existing Soviet Communist party. In Herberg's estimation, Trotsky was in effect attempting to return to 1919, a charge Trotsky himself had made against Stalin: "It would be well for the Trotsky of today to ponder his own words of five years ago." Trotsky and the Trotskyites were in Herberg's view quite simply no longer members of the Communist movement.

Even the false tactics of the Comintern were a result of Trotsky's efforts. It was falling headlong into "the morass of opportunism," a path first taken by that "genius of error." For example, the Comintern took the position that the way to fight fascism was through bourgeois democracy, a position taken by Trotsky in the *Militant* of 9 December 1933. His view became the view of the Comintern. Similarly, Trotsky, speaking of Germany, called for a revamping of the Weimar Constitution; and the Comintern subsequently called for a constituent assembly in Fascist Poland. According to Herberg, the French chauvinism of Maurice Thorez was the other side of the coin of Trotsky's anti-Soviet position. Thorez maintained that, as a result of the Franco-Soviet Pact of 1935, France demonstrated that it was not an entirely imperialistic country whereas Trotsky maintained that Soviet Russia was not entirely proletariat. Herberg criticized both for failing to understand that the pact was derived from special interests, not from an underlying similarity. And Herberg considered Trotsky a prisoner of his own ideological system, which prevented him from understanding the real significance of the Moscow trials of 1937: "The Moscow trials were thoroly reactionary in their political significance and content; they were the initial stage of a thoroly reactionary wave of terror reflecting the last stand of an outlived burocracy fighting with tooth and nail to preserve its power and status."

Herberg thus criticized Trotsky's centrism and his sectarianism. As Herberg noted, Lenin had opposed centrism on the ground that it was trapped ambiguously between bourgeois democracy and proletarian dictatorship, between reformist socialism and revolutionary internationalism. Centrism really embodied the wishful thinking of reformism and was thus not a halfway house to communism but a barrier. As Herberg wrote, "The road to Communism lies over the corpse of centrism." Earlier, Marx had criticized sectarianism as being "religious," an appellation that Herberg applied to Trotsky. What the Trotskyites and others had forgotten, according to Herberg, was how Lenin had laid the groundwork for the various Communist parties. He maintained that the way to revolution would proceed at differing paces in different countries, at a faster pace in Russia than in America. The unity of all the parties would be through the Comintern, which Lenin definitely did not view "as the tail-end of the Russian Communist Party." Rather, "a genuine International must be a federation of parties standing on the basis of real equality." Herberg further explained that Lenin emphasized party centralization and party democracy. The two were interrelated, with the former avoiding anarchy and the latter avoiding arbitrary bureaucracy. The Trotskyites, as well as the CPUSA, in America and internationally, had, Herberg claimed, forgotten these basic Leninist principles.

SIDNEY HOOK
AND ORTHODOX
MARXISM

Herberg also maintained that orthodox Marxist-Leninism had not merely been forgotten but had been misinterpreted by Sidney Hook, who at the time was a professor at New York University and was an eminent intellectual spokesman for Marxism.[21] Herberg referred to him as the "chief theoretician of the 'new revolutionary party' in the United States." Earlier, in 1931, Herberg wrote to Hook proffering a mild critique of the professor's understanding of Marxism. A year later Herberg wrote to Hook explaining that his motive for writing was the "not altogether benevolent purpose" of publishing a critique of Hook's understanding of Marxism from the point of view of orthodox Marxism, an explanation he repeated in 1933. By 1934, Herberg had already begun his critique in the *Workers Age*. In his opening salvo he called Hook a "thoroly false Marxist," mainly because of Hook's presumed break with Marx's theory of the state. At the heart of the criticism was the notion of "the dictatorship of the proletariat," which Hook rejected in favor of the phrase "worker's democracy." According to Hook, Marx referred to "the dictatorship of the proletariat" only rarely; therefore, there was no need to insist on its usage. Herberg did insist, however, that the dictatorship of the proletariat was the very essence of Marx, citing several passages in which Marx used the phrase and pointing out that both Marx and Engels signed the statutes of the World League of Revolutionary Communists in which the phrase appears. Moreover, according to Herberg, Lenin maintained that the dictatorship of the proletariat was the essence of Marx's theory of the state, a position that Lenin argued against Karl Kautsky, who, like Hook, minimized the importance of the phrase. As Herberg concluded, Hook "does not know that he is only echoing Kautsky somewhat belatedly."

Referring to Hook as "our learned historian," Herberg noted that Hook attempted to reduce the concept of the dictatorship of the proletariat to a mere "dictatorship of the Party," which Hook considered to be tyrannous. Consequently, Hook preferred a multiparty system within the Soviet regime. This view, according to Herberg, was "an outright repudiation of Marxism." Following Lenin, Herberg argued that one must distinguish between the party and the working class. The task of the party was to mold and to guide the proletariat, which did not always know what road was most beneficial for the class itself. For example, the working class supported an imperialist war in 1917 and backed Warren G. Harding in 1920 and Roosevelt in 1932. These actions were not in harmony with the program of the party: "In fact, the program of the revolutionary worker's party is in essence the expression of the real interests of the workers, even tho this party may be a tiny minority and the workers may scorn and persecute it. This is the most elementary Marxism." Herberg thus claimed that Hook was suffering from "democratic fetishism." He assumed, in effect, that the voice of the working class was the voice of God, "a result of his philistine worship of the abstract forms of democracy to the exclusion of any appreciation of its concrete social content!"

In other words, Herberg criticized Hook for confusing the dictatorship of the proletariat with bourgeois democracy. The bourgeoisie required several parties in order to accommodate its varying special interests whereas, as Herberg cited Marx, the members of the proletariat had more in common than those of the bourgeoisie and therefore required only one party. Herberg further explained that there were three fundamental political tendencies in the working class: (1) revolutionary socialism (or communism); (2) reformist socialism, which was contaminated by bourgeois liberalism; and (3) anarcho-syndicalism, which was contaminated by petty bourgeois radicalism. But as all agreed on the need for revolution, why have separate parties? Even after the revolution a two-party system would not be necessary inasmuch as one of the parties would inevitably be reactionary. Thus, Herberg maintained, Hook's desire for a multiparty system in the Soviet regime "suffers from its unreality, from its lack of tangible reference." The Soviet system broke with parliamentarianism and permitted the party to be the "trustee of power."

Hook responded in the *Modern Monthly* to Herberg's articles with an article of his own entitled "Literary Manners and Morals of Apache Radicalism." In it Hook refers to Herberg's position as the "Communist-Catholic theory of infallibility" in which the party somewhat mystically intuits what is good for the working class as a whole. Herberg denied the mystical process and replied that he found little value in Hook's article, especially as a contribution to a genuine discussion of Marxist theory: "I am really somewhat at a loss to account for the very unphilosophical peevishness exhibited by this eminent philosopher, to the point where it quite beclouds his reasoning powers!" He accused Hook of failing to deal with fundamental issues while engaging in personal attacks and concluded: "I feel a little bit sorry for him." Apparently, a degree of cognitive dissonance between Herberg and Hook continued for a long time after this debate. Several decades later, in the margin of one of Hook's articles, Herberg wrote, "Poor Hook! He is such a bore." In similar words, Hook, who was later puzzled by Herberg's conversion "to a kind of Jewish Christianity by Reinhold Niebuhr," would write: "Poor Herberg . . . one can't help feeling sorry for him. If he were truly reborn as a believing Jew or Christian why would he continue the deception [about having a Ph.D.]?"

MARXISM
AND RELIGION:
V. F. CALVERTON

*F*or that matter, Herberg's position on institutionalized religion remained unchanged during most of the decade. One of the few sources of information about his position during the mid-thirties is a review of Calverton's *The Passing Gods*.[22] There, Herberg agrees with both Calverton and the Young Hegelians that any modern critique of religion must seek "the annihilation of religion thru social consciousness." As Herberg points out, Calverton's book raised the question of why religion has persisted despite its "manifest irrationality." From the viewpoint of dialectical materialism, religion, he says, is a social phenomenon, not a private, individual reality. It is, as Calverton called it, a "cultural compulsive," which has persisted because it promises man control over his material environment. Through "self-conscious rational action" religion can be overcome only in a classless society. Herberg agreed, in short, with Calverton's assessment: "That religion can be understood only if it is conceived as a practical instrument of power in the social life-process of mankind, seems to me to be almost unchallengeable." In 1936, Herberg offered a course at the New Workers School on Marxism and modern political thought. The lecture outline gives another source of information about his position; there he maintains that Christianity provides only an illusory emancipation when concrete social emancipation is impossible: "After Spartacus comes Jesus!" As we shall see, Herberg experienced a similar transition in his own life during the period 1938–41—after Karl Marx came Reinhold Niebuhr.

4
THE
NEW
DEPARTURE
1938–1940

I n July 1938, the Lovestonites voted in a national convention to change the name of their group again, this time from the Communist Party-Opposition to the Independent Labor League of America (ILLA). The new name reflected a new mood. They had originally considered changing the name to the Independent Communist Labor League but decided against the use of the word "communist" because of its poor public image in America. The New Workers School also received a new title—the Independent Labor Institute. There Herberg and others offered lectures and courses that emphasized this "new departure," as Herberg called it. For example, Herberg gave a lecture entitled "Some Central Problems of Socialism" and offered a course called "Democracy-Fascism-Sovietism," which was described as a "critical examination of contemporary state forms from the point of view of their historical origins, structure, function and social significance." Herberg, Jay Lovestone, Bertram Wolfe, and Lewis Corey lectured on the topic "New Problems in Marxism" at the Progressive Labor Institute in Philadelphia. Even the *Workers Age* was altered. It not only attempted to appeal to the masses of workers as it had been doing, but now it also attempted to appeal to "hard-pressed middle-class people."

Regardless of these alterations in titles and procedures, the group was still avowedly Communist in aim. As Herberg explained: "In this country, we strive to operate realistically and effectively in a non-revolutionary situation as an organic part of a non-socialist labor movement that is just beginning to find itself. On the other hand, we are part of an international tendency working under circumstances where the labor movement must be revolutionary or nothing at all."[1] This position, he held, was "really new." Proclaiming radicalism of any sort to be bankrupt, Herberg maintained that for too long American radicals had looked to Europe for inspiration and guidance. In so doing, they had erroneously imposed European models and ideals on a country whose conditions greatly differed from European ones. Moreover, American radicalism had been dualistic in nature, seeking to establish a labor movement along independent Socialist lines and then hoping the American worker would join it. Thus, as Herberg wrote, "For us, the very crux of the new departure must be a break with these unwholesome traditions." The task, therefore, was not to attempt to impose the radicals' own image of what they thought labor should be upon the American labor movement but to become an integral, vital element within the movement. Acting in relation to the American labor movement as an advanced group, a kind of "pep group," the ILLA sought to bring "greater clarity and class consciousness" to the movement itself. This task would be accomplished by analyzing the situation in America on its own merits and by applying European models only where they were concretely applicable. In other words, the ILLA would not interpret the American labor movement and American events in terms of official communism or even in reaction to Stalinism. Rather "we are on our own," and the point of view of the ILLA would be a uniquely American point of view. This new party line found expression in Herberg's articles on topics ranging from the obvious, American labor, to the less obvious, the ethical problems of Marxism.

AMERICAN LABOR, MARXISM, AND STALINISM

The American Federation of Labor (AFL) still remained, for Herberg, a union characterized by "craft fetishism" whereas the Committee for Industrial Organization (CIO) represented a higher level of class consciousness.[2] The AFL, following a kind of "conservative syndicalism," opposed sit-down strikes and in general opposed government action on such social and labor issues as the wages and hours bill. The CIO, in contrast, moved in the direction of independent labor politics, supporting legislation without compromising this independence. According to Herberg, the future of American labor was thus in the hands of the CIO. Yet labor should not be divided, he warned. The path to unity, for Herberg, lay in the direction of a grand council of labor composed of the CIO, the AFL, and the railroad workers' unions with the major thrust toward such unity initiated by the CIO. But there were inherent dangers in this push for unification, particularly, "the utter inadequacy of the top leadership of the CIO." Centralized control of the unions was required in order to fight big business, but at the same time the unions must be democratic, with the leadership acting as a federated council. One danger was that the top leadership might take on the characteristics of an international board, undemocratic in spirit. By 1939, Herberg perceived the CIO as showing this tendency; the leadership seemed to be developing into a supercentralized controlling agency over affiliated unions. For example, the Steel Workers Organizing Committee was established in 1937, but after two years it still did not have the rights of full-fledged membership. Essentially the same situation existed for the Textile Workers Organizing Committee and the United Automobile Workers. The leadership, in Herberg's estimation, should avoid such Stalinistic tactics and should recognize that a union is composed of real men and women and that, like all institutions, a union "has many sides and bears the marks of the contradictory features of human nature and human society."

Overlooking this contradictory human situation, according to Herberg, was one of Stalinism's major faults.[3] Unlike Stalin, Lenin was flexible in strategy and tactics; with him "Marxism was, indeed, no dogma but a manual for action." Stalin's inflexibility, on the other hand, resulted in "a totalitarian police state" based on a twofold dictatorship of the proletariat and the bureaucracy, both resting firmly on the shoulders of the dictator himself, Stalin. The manifest expression of Stalin's dictatorship occurred early in 1938 with the executions of Bukharin, whom Lenin called the most valuable theoretician of the party, and seventeen others. As a result of such purges, from 1938 on, Herberg described Russia as subject to the rule of "Soviet totalitarianism," with Stalin the source of a "New Imperialism." As he wrote, "Between Stalinism and communism, there is a vast chasm filled to the brim with the blood of the victims of his purges." These kinds of actions should be rejected, according to Herberg, not only from a political point of view but from a moral point of view as well.

Herberg predicted that Stalin was preparing the way for a shift in Russian foreign policy, which would be dutifully followed by the Communist International (Comintern) and which spelled disaster for the international working class. In a "sudden declaration," as Herberg called it, Stalin announced in early 1938 that socialism was possible only on an international scale, that an attack against the Soviet Union by bourgeois states was inevitable, and that Russian socialism could only be maintained with the aid of the international proletariat. In essence, this declaration offered nothing new. What amazed Herberg was that Stalin announced this policy after the Seventh Congress of the Comintern had proclaimed that socialism in Russia was "final and irrevocable" and after Stalin had praised the policy of establishing People's Front movements. To Herberg, Stalin's enlistment of the international proletariat to assist Soviet Russia in a time of crisis was in fact a ploy to gain support primarily for Soviet foreign policy. Stalin's internationalism was therefore fraudulent: "Stalinism is not internationalism; it is the most grotesque travesty of it." For Stalin, international proletarian support for Russian foreign policy was even more important than support for Russian workers.

According to Herberg, Stalin was attempting to achieve what Trotsky had sought: "Trotskyism is in essence an inverted, frustrated Stalinism." For example, after the Russians invaded Finland in the fall of 1939, the Trotskyite press called for the workers of Finland to rise up and assist the Russians in taking over "bourgeois Finland." But, asked Herberg, did the Trotskyites call for the Spanish workers to support France, or, for that matter, for Ethiopian workers to support the Italians? Did the Trotskyites really believe that the Finnish government was the real aggressor? Some argued that the Russian army brought less evil to Finland than a Finnish government controlled by Wall Street and London. But how could one bring freedom to the Finns on the point of a bayonet? Others have argued, Herberg continued, that the Russian conquest of Finland would boost the Finnish economy. But to Herberg this viewpoint seemed precisely the kind of justification offered by imperialist powers in their wars. The Stalinist invasion of Finland was, quite simply, a cynical attempt to protect Russia by means of a sham revolutionary slogan. In reality, Stalinist Russia had adopted traditional arguments for imperialism: "It must therefore expect to be judged as any other imperialist power is judged!"

Behind this new imperialism lurked the Stalin-Hitler alliance and Russian domestic political struggles for power. Compared to these matters, economic considerations, asserted Herberg, were of relatively minor importance. Rather the Soviet Union, in invading Finland, sought outposts in the Baltic region. But, as Herberg again argued, thinking in terms of military considerations for national defense precisely reflected the logic of imperialism. Of equal importance to military considerations was the domestic situation. Russia was engaging in foreign adventures in order to take attention off the purges and repressions at home: "In a word, the resort to predatory foreign adventures on the part of the Stalin regime is the clearest proof that this regime had already exhausted the tremendous social resources left to it by the Russian Revolution." By engaging in imperialism, that is, the conquest of foreign lands by military force, conquest based not on the desire for expansion of monopolistic capitalism but on sheer "predatory aggression," Stalin's regime had negated almost all of the gains of the revolution. Having lost prestige before the masses of the world, Stalin was the "prize devil," not Hitler, against whom the capitalistic world would wage a second world war. Stalin had so altered conditions in Russia that what existed was no longer capitalism, socialism, proletarian dictatorship, or fascism; Stalinism was "an essentially new historical phenomenon describable only on its own terms." Herberg thus called upon the Finnish labor movement to fight for independence from both the London-controlled Finnish government and Stalinist Russia. In short, it should adopt a "Jacobin defense." And international socialism should keep its "deep faith" in the Russian Revolution while working toward a purge of Stalinism.

Herberg held that Stalinism had adversely affected the entire Communist movement: "The Stalinist party represents an entirely new type of social and political party."[4] The American Communist party (CPUSA), for example, had become simply an extended arm of the ruling clique in the Kremlin, a foreign agency of the Soviet government. The "social interest" that the CPUSA served was therefore not to be found in America but in Russia. As such, the concerns of the CPUSA were completely outside those of the American labor movement. It had even attempted to justify the Stalin-Hitler pact as a defensive peace maneuver. Such reasoning, according to Herberg, merely reflected the logic of the Popular Front strategy. When the war began in September 1939, Herberg noted that the CPUSA, following instructions from Moscow, switched from sloganeering in support of democracies against fascism to doing so to keep America out of the imperialist war. According to Herberg, this tactic was implemented as if the party had discovered overnight that the war was imperialistic. For him, the war was a resumption of World War I, and it would conclude with a "super-Versailles" treaty more rapacious and vindictive than the peace of 1918, to be followed by another war. Regardless of who would win the war begun in 1939, Herberg prophesied that "authoritarianism [would] be triumphant and democracy doomed" and the Stalinist danger would persist in the American labor movement because of the existence of the Stalinist CPUSA.

The CPUSA, in Herberg's opinion, was becoming "a frankly totalitarian outfit." While continuing to recommend that American Socialists should form a "Socialist Block," Herberg nevertheless accused the official party of promoting degenerate "communism." For example, Earl Browder recommended that the CPUSA adopt an amendment to its constitution to the effect that any group that might try to subvert or overthrow any or all institutions of the United States should be opposed. In short, as Herberg concluded, the party sought to support the American Constitution. But, he added, this amendment would be support for capitalism, upon which American institutions were erected. To defend the American Constitution "is surely nothing but a gross caricature of communism that Marx and Lenin stood for. Such a party is, or at least aspires to be, a bulwark of capitalism." Moreover, Browder, unlike Marx and Lenin, proposed to expel those members who advocated violence and terror. And he engaged in "chauvinism and idiocy" when he recommended that membership in the CPUSA be restricted to American citizens.

In similar fashion, the convention of the Communist-led American Youth Congress held in July 1939 considered two resolutions that reveal the rising political cynicism of the CPUSA: one condemned communism for its hostility to belief in God, human rights, and private ownership of property; and the second condemned all forms of dictatorship, whether Communist or Fascist. For Herberg, these resolutions were clearly confusing from the perspective of Marxist principles. But then the CPUSA, according to Herberg, was no longer concerned with principles but with power: "To the dyed-in-the-wool Stalinist, bred in the all-devouring cult of the great god Power, the very notion that there may be principles and ideals of supreme value in themselves, in the service of which alone power gains whatever moral legitimacy it has, is genuinely foreign and unintelligible. Power is the great all-in-all." The official CPUSA was therefore isolating itself from the American laborer and was creating a serious obstacle to the rise of socialism in America.

The Stalinists had even infiltrated the American Labor party (ALP) in spite of its constitution that included a prohibition directed against Communists as members.[5] Generally, Herberg had high regard for the ALP because of its forthright independence from both major political parties. It had made a limited arrangement with the Republican party in order to achieve the election of ALP candidates while backing acceptable and progressive Republicans. It had moved in the direction of dispelling the Democratic party's belief in itself as a labor party. However, Herberg warned that the ALP should both shun political careerists who merely wanted to use the ALP for their own political advancement and avoid using too many political analogies reminiscent of the British Labour party. Above all, it should make its position clear in relation to the Stalinists. To accomplish this, the ALP should appeal to the American masses, allow affiliated unions to participate actively in establishing policies, and place in assembly-district organizations active members who would have the task of keeping the Stalinists contained. Nonetheless, Herberg's warnings notwithstanding, the ALP succumbed to control by the official CPUSA by 1942.[6]

ROOSEVELT
AND THE
THREAT OF WAR

Although the ALP was an important political party to Herberg, its importance was minimized by the political situation in America under Roosevelt's administration.[7] What concerned him most was the threat of war and
how all Socialists should attempt to prevent it. With respect to the war threat,
Herberg maintained that Roosevelt was using foreign diplomacy as a screen to
hide domestic problems. For example, Roosevelt opposed almost all neutrality
legislation except the O'Connell Bill, which retained the spirit of neutrality
and which, however illusory, was wanted by the greater masses of the American people. But, Herberg pointed out, it would simply broaden the powers of
the executive branch of government to permit the president to decide who was
or was not an aggressor and what sanctions should be imposed against any
aggressor. According to Herberg, such arbitrary power could easily become an
instrument of imperialist diplomacy and would result in America's becoming
involved in a war. In short, the O'Connell Bill was not really a neutrality bill.

Should the United States get involved in a war, Herberg believed, it would
become a military dictatorship. It would become increasingly totalitarian. He
noted that the Roosevelt administration was shifting its foreign policy from
"collective security" to "continental defense" of North and South America.
The old New Deal sought economic and domestic recovery through social
welfare activities and by increasing consumer purchasing power. The new
New Deal directed funds toward military rearmament, which would result in
stronger government controls over industry and labor and a new alignment
between the government and big business. Herberg also chided Lewis Mumford for supporting this kind of war effort when he suggested that the United
States should convoy munitions to those "democracies" in need of assistance.
These "democracies," Herberg maintained, had paved the way for Hitler's
advances at the Munich Conference of 1938. Hitler's annexation of Czechoslovakia not only had galvanized these "democracies" but also had allowed
them to increase their own power bases at home. In March 1939, Herberg
predicted that the Soviet Union might seek a rapprochement with Germany,
especially if Hitler turned his attention to the West. Should this occur, Roosevelt, in Herberg's estimate, would only use the situation to consolidate his own
power and position.

Herberg believed, therefore, that the rush for armaments, the "war boom,"
was calculated as a way out of the Great Depression. But there were factors

other than merely economic ones to consider. Roosevelt sought to follow in the steps of Woodrow Wilson, to succeed where Wilson had failed. Because Americans "are the most missionary of people," they seek to save the world for democracy. This condition, Herberg held, suited Roosevelt's "Messiah complex." An isolationist when he entered office, Roosevelt had switched to salvationism as a means of connecting his foreign and domestic policies. The New Deal had failed to create a strong economy, so Roosevelt focused on foreign quarrels to take the minds of Americans off their domestic economic woes. Consequently, the New Deal, established for the purpose of economic and social reform, would become the "mechanism of military-authoritarian control in time of war." To avoid this situation, Herberg recommended Socialist unity.

As he wrote, "Only socialism can bring peace to the world."[8] The Socialists should therefore fight against increasing the president's powers, support the call for a war referendum, seek to isolate the United States from other imperialist countries, and try to have the arms embargo extended. Ultimately, a Socialist revolution would be required, but this could only be accomplished with the aid of the masses who were conscious of "all that is fine and enduring in our democratic tradition." Further, "it is this great tradition that must be absorbed and built upon by modern American socialism if socialism in this country is ever to be more than an exotic ideological growth, strange, unintelligible and somewhat terrifying to the masses of the people." The alternative, according to Herberg, was that America in time of war would bring a "semifascist dictatorship to this country as sure as fate." This development would of course be detrimental to the labor movement. Accordingly, at its national convention held in New York City during 2–4 September 1939, and in reaction to the Stalin-Hitler pact, the ILLA adopted a resolution asserting "Keep America Out of War."

THE FASCIST
MENACE

As in the previous two periods of Herberg's life, he feared the rise of fascism.[9] This concern was markedly heightened after the outbreak of the war, which led Herberg to publish seven articles on the subject "Does Fascism Menace America?" For him the possibility of fascism in America had been an ongoing one since the early 1930s. In 1938, he maintained that the Wagner Act establishing a fair wage above minimum wage had the potential to lead to "a governmental despotism bordering on fascist totalitarianism." With the outbreak of a war in 1939 in which there was a good chance that America would be involved, fascism in America became an imminent possibility. If fascism did take hold, it would not be the result of an invasion but would come from within, for the country in his estimation was undoubtedly "fascist-conscious." American fascism would be derived from the traditional and mystical nationalism that emphasized "100% Americanism." In this context, Herberg examined two paths to fascism, one based on the Italo-German model and the other on the latent French model. In other words, fascism could be arrived at from "below" as well as from "above."

Fascism from below would arise when the lower classes were unhappy with the prevailing social and economic conditions and the ruling class was unable to rule in its traditional manner. In fact, the petty-bourgeois masses would become disillusioned with parliamentary democracy. In this sense, fascism was really a plebeian movement, one that would fall under the influence of obscure groups composed of power seekers, disenchanted students, unemployed workers, nationalists, racists, criminals, and semicriminal elements. Organized around a so-called godlike leader, these often disparate entities would establish their own armies and oppose traditional political parties. They would gain power, not through revolution, but by connivance and convenient "arrangements" with the existing government. Eventually a one-party system would develop, and any opposition would be eliminated through "purges." In this manner, fascism "offers a middle-class substitute system for working-class socialism: national-race solidarity for class solidarity, national struggle (war) for class struggle, the authoritarian corporate state for the democratic-socialist state." On the other hand, fascism from above could achieve the same ends with different means. It, too, would occur in times of crisis. However, instead of groups organizing from outside the government, strategically placed groups from within the government would take the initiative and direct the government toward an authoritarian regime in order to control the existing situation. In either case, whether fascism came from below or above, the stated purpose for taking the reins of government would be to preserve a decaying capitalism.

For Herberg, "America [was] full of the raw materials of fascism." It had its share of "crack-pot reform movements," like the Ku Klux Klan, the Father Coughlin movement, and Huey Long's "share-the-wealth" movement, which, since the death of Long in 1935, continued through the Gerald L. K. Smith movement. Fascism in America, Herberg predicted, would develop along regional lines because the different sections of the country varied in their social and economic conditions. Following this development, the various organizations created would then unite around the American Constitution: "The heart of the political faith of American fascism is clearly Constitution-worship, the idolization of the Constitution as the sacred symbol, the ikon of 'national existence.' " Such fascism would be considered not only "constitutional" but "democratic" and "Christian" as well: "Fascism in order to save democracy—this would be the keynote of American fascism." However, Herberg offered two suggestions for avoiding fascism: (1) keep America out of the war, and (2) organize labor in such a fashion that a Socialist revolution, not a Fascist coup d'état, would occur. Should fascism succeed, the failure of labor to realize its mission would be partly responsible. Should fascism gain a foothold in the United States, the country would remain totalitarian after the war was over. American democracy would be dead.

Herberg viewed the war in Europe as a conflict between imperialist possessors and imperialist aggressors, between bourgeois-democratic states and totalitarian states. Although he opposed both, he nevertheless believed that, whichever side won, the future of socialism was threatened.[10] If the Nazis won, the dreams of socialism and democracy would be shattered for decades to come. If the Allies won, for a while socialism would have a limited scope within which to function, but totalitarianism would be the ultimate result of an Allied victory. Their victory would lead to a more ruthless Versailles Treaty and possibly the partition of Germany—or even the restoration of the German monarchy. Socialism was the only path by which these results could be averted. Consequently, Herberg recommended to American Socialists the "Jacobin defense" of remaining independent and attempting to keep America out of the war. For him, the future of socialism would be decided, not in Europe or in Asia, but in the United States. Accordingly, he proposed a "systematic opposition to the [Roosevelt] administration, its aims, policies, and programs." The major form of American national defense was a "planned 'attack' on unemployment, poverty, and low living standards," "a dynamic democracy, implemented with a program of social reform looking towards socialism." In terms of actual military defense, Herberg maintained that a broad national commission drawn from the ranks of workers and civilians should be established to determine actual military needs in the event that a threatened invasion actually materialized. This defense should be coordinated with other countries in the Western Hemisphere. But the United States should not engage in the illusions either that it could stay out of the war in Europe by assisting the British or that it could cooperate with Hitler should the Axis powers be victorious in Europe.

Herberg of course was not opposed to all aid to England because for him defeat of Nazi Germany was paramount. He nevertheless recognized the ambiguity inherent in the situation: America should stay out of the war and simultaneously give assistance to Great Britain. But the *kind* of aid offered was the crucial point. For example, certain kinds of assistance would eventually involve the United States in the war, such as carrying munitions to Britain on American ships, which would then be subject to attack by German submarines. Should this happen, the United States would again be brought into the war, just as it was in 1917, by means of the public reaction such an event would evoke. Therefore, the United States should sell munitions to England on a cash basis and require the British to use their own carrier vessels. In other words, Herberg opposed repeal of the "carry" provisions of the Neutrality Act, which, according to him, prohibited American ships from carrying war materials to foreign countries engaged in war. He equally opposed opening up American ports to British warships, which policy, in his opinion, would invite the war to American shores.

In considering what to do in the event the Nazis should win the war, Herberg definitely disagreed with Charles A. Lindbergh's recommendation that America should collaborate with the Germans in order to save Western civilization. This view, in Herberg's estimate, was nothing short of appeasement: "An alliance with Hitler to preserve 'western civilization' makes about as much sense as an alliance with Al Capone or Dutch Schultze to maintain the supremacy of the law." To assume that one can cooperate with Hitler would be "suicidal folly." Instead, Herberg suggested "returning to the traditional American policy initiated by Thomas Jefferson." The United States should maintain diplomatic relations with all foreign powers, regardless of their policies, but still keep all its natural resources for its own use. As he wrote, "A country [namely, the United States] that is really a continent in itself, with such vast resources of every kind and variety, inhabited by a people of unparalleled energy and technological ingenuity, ought not be scared out of its wits by the specter of unsalable surpluses." These resources and surpluses could be used to build a self-sustaining economy within its own boundaries while it remained relatively independent of other countries.

AN
ETHICAL
CRITIQUE OF
MARXISM

The Stalin-Hitler pact, the Russian invasion of Finland, the war, the continuing Stalinist line of the Comintern, and the Herberg-perceived decline of Marxist-Leninism in the official Communist party led him to a changed perspective on communism in general. From 1938 on, Herberg preferred the words "socialism" and "democratic socialism" over the word "communism." More importantly, he began to question the validity of Marxism from an ethical point of view.[11] As early as February 1939 he wrote, "Unless socialism is humanitarian, unless it makes the cause of suffering humanity its own, it is not likely to develop much beyond the level of ordinary power-politics, without real hope for the future." Moreover, "If socialism prevents us from acting and feeling as human beings should, there is surely something spurious about it."

With such a categorical imperative in view, Herberg began to interpret communism from an ethical perspective. He still admired Rosa Luxemburg but mainly because she had warned about authoritarian tendencies in the Soviet Union. In contrast, the CPUSA should be attacked, not as agents of American labor, but as agents of a foreign power. The Trotskyites were in his opinion engaging in trivial theological disputes, exemplifying a mere "political psychopathology." For them, important questions "are treated in a spirit quite as remote from present-day reality as the no doubt momentous conflicts over the nature of the Godhead that rocked the early Church councils, and some are almost as other-worldly in their substance." These disputes were "specimens of 'Marxist' political theology," replete with anathemas and bulls of excommunication, delivered by "the final authority of the priest of the Dialectic." The basic question for communism was, How did Lenin, who started with an ultra-democratic philosophy, construct a Bolshevik regime that took the road to totalitarian dictatorship? The answer, in Herberg's new perspective, could be found in the sinful nature of man, and, he added, "even Stalin can't improve on that."

The confirmation of this new position in Herberg's thought came from Reinhold Niebuhr's *Moral Man and Immoral Society*, which he finished reading on 17 May 1940. Herberg had probably read other works by Niebuhr, such as his article "A Lesson Well Learned," which was originally published in the Spring 1939 issue of *Radical Religion* and reprinted in the *Workers Age* on 12

April 1939. Nevertheless, the crucial work for Herberg, by his own admission, was *Moral Man and Immoral Society*. Having read it, he contacted Niebuhr at Union Theological Seminary where they met to discuss the book and its implications over coffee. Thus began a close acquaintanceship that would last until Niebuhr's death in 1971.[12] Although Herberg had already begun a critique of Marxism before reading Niebuhr's book, he proceeded to a more intensive critique after reading it. And like Niebuhr, Herberg based his evaluation of Marxist ideology on ethical considerations.

At the core of Herberg's analysis was the relationship of "means" and "ends."[13] According to Herberg, the fundamental goal of socialism was freedom, and the means of achieving the goal was collectivism. However, when the goal persisted in being rather vague and undefined, he perceived that the means tended to become more important than the goal. What occurred then was that the means became a fetish, and collectivism became identified with the goal itself. Hence a fetishism of collectivism developed, which, Herberg held, was in effect a "collectivist mysticism," what Jules Romains called "unanimism." This revealed an ambiguity inherent in collectivism—its capacity to develop in two different directions: toward totalitarian socialism and/or toward libertarian socialism. In recent history, Herberg noted, the trend had been toward totalitarian collectivism, a development that arose out of the very structure of collectivist organization. In any organization, two categories of people could be found: the leaders and the led. In other words, the very act of organization could set in motion a bureaucracy that had the potential to become authoritarian. Thus, far in advance of Milovan Djilas's *The New Class*, Herberg wrote, "Those who exercise indispensable and irreplaceable (non-interchangeable) functions necessarily acquire a position of privilege and power—and come to constitute a privileged group above the masses." From such bureaucrats, the "fetishism of organization" was established, and dictatorship became an imminent possibility.

Herberg believed that this thrust for power inhered in human nature. Theologians recognized the thrust as radically evil and knew it for original sin. Biologists called it an instinctive desire for survival. But the drive for power had essential moral ambiguities: considered positively, power, according to Herberg, was indispensable in achieving freedom; considered negatively, power inevitably produced coercion, self-aggrandizement, and repression. With the latter, power would become an end in itself, a fetish. In other words, socialism had to become a power machine if it was to achieve its goal, but the Socialist organization could become an end in itself. A dictatorship would result that would perpetuate itself and eventually attain a position so sufficiently entrenched that it would be perceived as "normal": "Both rulers and ruled become habituated to authoritarian institutions and procedures." For this reason, Herberg quoted Robert Michel to the effect that "Socialists may triumph—but socialism never."

Herberg admitted that he did not know how to resolve this dilemma. Because the means chosen to achieve socialism's ends often produced unintended results, he could only maintain that "here the Deed [of the Fall of Adam and Eve], which we learn was the beginning of all things, will have to have the last word as well." He did, however, offer a qualified approach, that is, to work for the establishment of a libertarian socialism. He referred to this brand of socialism as a kind of "socialist Jeffersonianism," which emphasized a government that governed least and which stressed the uniqueness of the human personality. Such a government would give the freest reign to the development of "spiritual individualism and independence" and would be "rooted in a humanistic conception of society." For Herberg, this view required a "new pluralism," a "neo-liberalism," in which political democracy went hand in hand with economic democracy. Libertarian socialism, if established, would create the conditions for this kind of society.

Some elements of Marxism should therefore be discarded whereas others could be retained. The most enduring element of Marxism, for Herberg, was its "instrumentalist pragmatism," its empiricism. His major objection to Marxism was its monism, its assumption that all things were interrelated. This view, quite simply, was theological, a belief inaccessible to scientific inquiry. The concept of history as a dialectical movement, with its dogma of progress, was a belief created by human imagination and was not an organic, objective process that inhered in the nature of history per se. From an ethical point of view, Marxism was based on universal values (such as courage, loyalty, and truth) not peculiar to any particular class of people. In this regard, Marxism condemned the exploitation of the proletariat, not in the name of values that were expressions of the interests of the proletariat—"that would be an absurd tautology." Rather, opposition to the exploitation of the proletariat, Herberg explained, was based on an ethical evaluation that transcended the special interests of any particular class and was considered binding on all mankind. As such, Marxism overlooked the point that an economic class might not be the only group to dominate a state. It could also be dominated by a militaristic bureaucracy or a party caste, as in the Soviet Union. Therefore, the essential failure of Marxism was its moral failure, its failure to analyze explicitly the values implied in its own ideology. It was consequently a religious faith in the dialectic operating as divine providence and assuring that all would be well in the end.

THE END
OF THE
LOVESTONITES

By December 1940, the end was near for the Lovestonite group. Besides opposing the Soviet-controlled Comintern in particular and various elements of Marxism in general, it was experiencing economic difficulties with the *Workers Age*; therefore, the ILLA had no substantial reason to continue to exist. Jay Lovestone summed up the mood of the group in that year: "For us, there were no sacred doctrines."[14] Consequently, at its national convention on 28–29 December in New York City, the ILLA voted to dissolve itself, thereby becoming the only radical organization of the day to take such an action voluntarily. In a declaration prepared by Lovestone and Herberg for the convention, which unanimously adopted it, the ILLA declared that communism in America had no ground on which to stand. The official American Communist party was condemned as a foreign agency of Stalin's dictatorship. What was needed was a new method for a new world. Every other approach had been shattered by the events of the last decade: "Old-line social democracy, traditional Marxian orthodoxy and Russian Bolshevism have all failed. We may learn a great deal from each, but we can never again look to any of them to show us the way to socialism." A "new start" was required.[15]

The last issue of the *Workers Age* was published on 25 January 1941. It announced the dissolution of the group and printed the formal "Declaration" adopted at its December convention. In an equally formal editorial "Farewell," Herberg recounted his years as editor of the *Workers Age*, maintaining that the paper had had a beneficial impact on the American labor movement and that it "will undoubtedly bear abundant fruit when conditions permit the rebirth of American socialism." And for Herberg himself, an equally "new start" was required.

5
THE
PERIOD OF
TRANSITION
1941–1950

For two years Herberg wrote no articles. Between 1941 and 1943, he read voluminously, desperately attempting to understand his disillusionment with the Communist movement. Some of his colleagues at Local No. 22 of the International Ladies Garment Workers Union (ILGWU) spoke of the states of despair Herberg suffered, especially after the death of his mother in December 1942.[1] Aside from performing his office duties, he spent much of his time absorbing knowledge. In 1941 alone, he read most of the works of Shakespeare, Chaucer, and Dostoevsky, along with Reinhold Niebuhr's book, *An Interpretation of Christian Ethics*. Also during these two years Herberg delivered only two lectures of note, both to the union school. One was "How to Defend Democracy," and the other, given in June 1942, was "The Basic Dilemma of Socialism: Another Aspect of the Problem of Ends and Means," which essentially repeated the articles by the same title in the *Workers Age* of 1940.

Herberg would be able to tell about his experience in moving over to a formally theological perspective only after several years had passed. In 1947 and 1948, he would explain how this new perspective had developed.[2] Marxism had been his religion: "Marxism was to me, and to others like me, a religion, an ethic, and a theology; a vast, all-embracing doctrine of man and the universe, a passionate faith endowing life with meaning, vindicating the aims of the movement, idealizing its activities, and guaranteeing its ultimate triumph." As a Marxist, he was committed to freedom, to justice, to brotherhood, to progress of "the unlimited redemptive power of history," and to the power of economics, "the invisible god of the Marxist faith." But whereas Marx, in his *Theses on Feuerbach*, stated that the criticism of religion led to politics and the criticism of politics led to political economy, Herberg traversed the reverse route from economics to politics to ethics to theology. From the fetishism, the idolatry, of economics, of the party, of Russia, and of the dialectic, Herberg turned to the question of the "true God." With a "stunning realization," he sensed, "vaguely and almost fearfully," that he was turning to formal religion. At this point, Herberg encountered the writings of Niebuhr.

The result was what he called his "first authentically religious experience" about which he could only say, "I cannot talk about it . . . but when it was over I had found my faith."

Herberg's positive theological affirmation led him, in his view, to become a better Socialist and "a better Marxist, taking Marxism in terms of its best insights and ultimate ideals." These insights and ideals centered on Marxist political action, social thought, and economic understanding, which Herberg now viewed from a theological perspective rather than from the perspective of a "shallow materialism." According to Herberg, the Judaic understanding of man emphasized not only the sinful nature of man but also the grandeur of man, steering clear of the extremes of "fatuous optimism," as with Jean-Jacques Rousseau, and "utter depravity," as with John Calvin. The dialectical struggle was found not only within history as a class struggle, but also more directly in man himself, as individual, as person. Man has therefore, he asserted, been cast into a "state of eternal struggle out of which is generated that tragic sense of life which is the mark of every high religion."

This Judaic view of the infinite worth of the individual person in Herberg's estimation had its social consequences, of which a democracy was perhaps the best expression: "Democracy is, in effect, a dynamic reconciliation on the social level of man's grandeur and misery, of his eminent dignity as a person and his perennial inclination to sinfulness as manifested in the egoistic self-assertion of power." As such, the biblical approach to social organization was incontrovertibly opposed to totalitarianism of any form because it was opposed to idolatry, to absolutizing the finite. Democracy, as opposed to totalitarianism, recognized the transcendent spiritual nature of man, his reason, his imagination, and his moral freedom. This biblical perspective on democratic society, which he later understood to have been the result of changes begun in 1940, provided the unifying theme of his thought from 1947 to the end of his life.

CHRISTIANITY
AND SOCIALISM

With the dissolution of the Lovestonites, then, Herberg found his political activity reduced to a minimum, joining the organizing committee of the Union for Democratic Action in March 1941. He also did little writing until 1943 when he published an article in the *Antioch Review* entitled "The Christian Mythology of Socialism," a project he had been working on since the spring of 1941.[3] By his own admission, this subject had been the focus of his thinking and reading since 1939. The fundamental thesis is that "the very nature of reality determines the dialectical-dramatic structure of both Christianity and Socialism, so that the two become at bottom variant mythological transcripts of a single essential reality, saying the same thing in different languages, on different levels of experience and meaning." Claiming a degree of originality in this thesis, Herberg here insists that he is not merely identifying Christianity with socialism, nor is he only asserting that socialism is religious, which Nicolas Berdyaev and Arnold J. Toynbee had already done. Anyway, according to Herberg, this fact had been obvious to him for years. Rather he has become convinced that there is a "virtual identity in structure of the belief-systems of Christianity and Socialism." In maintaining this view, he states that in no way does he intend to denigrate Marxism as a significant social movement. Indeed, as he wrote to Bertram Wolfe about this article in July 1943: "Marxism represents the only really valuable, realistic and effective approach in social knowledge." And he added, "If I have to call myself something I would call myself a Marxist—a very critical, revisionist Marxist but a Marxist anyway." He did, however, disagree with Marx's and especially Lenin's understanding of religion, which he considered to be "really a part of the incongruous baggage of 18th century rationalism that traditional Marxism carries with it."

In drawing out the structural identity of Christianity and socialism, Herberg suggests that it is possible "to compile a sort of lexicon of terms and expressions by which a proposition or doctrine in one belief-system can be 'translated' into its analogue in the other." For example, Christianity and socialism share three major stages of history: the primitive state of harmony, the intermediate stage of conflict, and the ultimate state of regained harmony, which would last eternally. The first stage, "Primal Innocency," is reflected in primitive communism and in the Garden of Eden myth: "Except that one is described in anthropological terms and the other in theological, Christianity's Eden and Socialism's Primitive Communism can hardly be told apart." The second stage, or the "Fallen State," results from Adam's sin according to the Christian view or from the lapse into private property and consequent class divisions according to the Socialist view. The third stage, "Regained Innocency," in which self-alienation, both spiritual and social, is overcome and harmony restored on a higher level, is reflected in the notion of the Kingdom of God or heaven on the one hand and social virtue derived from the establishment of communism on the other. In either case, the end of history has arrived: for Christianity this means the end of spiritual conflict, and for communism it means the end of social conflict. Both, Herberg argues, "are ultimate stages in which time is annihilated, [both are] stages of final perfection."

According to Herberg, these three stages can be viewed from the perspective of a triadic dialectic, and Marxian theory, he asserts, "swears by the Dialectic." The thesis equals Edenic paradise and primitive communism. The antithesis or negation is the sinful world of the fallen state and class society. And the synthesis or "negation of a negation" is the arrival of the Kingdom of Heaven and communism. This latter stage is heralded in Christian thought by a "great apocalyptic catastrophe" and the destruction of the Antichrist. In Socialist thought, the new order is ushered in by a proletarian revolution overcoming the reactionary forces of capitalism. Such was the "orthodox" Christian and Socialist understanding. On the other hand, both Christianity and socialism have "reformist" positions. In these, the new era arrives by a slower, more evolutionary process, a view based on the dogma of progress, of inevitable gradualism. However, the orthodox positions consider a "transitional period" prior to the final stage, which in Marxism is the period of the "dictatorship of the proletariat" and in Christian thought is the millennium. This transitional era is brought about by the Chosen People, by the Saving Remnant or the church, for Christianity, and by the proletariat or the party for Socialist theory. In both cases, these people are "elected" either through the suffering of a soul who receives saving grace or by enduring the suffering that is a consequence of economic and social woes that produce a class-conscious worker. In Christian thought, to achieve this status, a person must "die" to his own sinful nature, and in Socialist thought the proletariat must discard all remnants of bourgeois mentality. Throughout this entire historical process is seen the divine hand of Providence, or the dialectic.

From the similarity in the structure of Christianity and socialism, Herberg concludes that the Judeo-Christian tradition permeated the basic patterns of Western thought: "The significant philosophies and ideologies of modern Western civilization are in the last analysis derived from this source." This tradition is such a part of the collective unconsciousness that even those who try to oppose it cannot escape its hold: "It has, in very truth, become second nature to us." Even Socialists who oppose this tradition nevertheless share the same mythological way of thinking, "the imaginative filling out and transformation of experience into a dramatic struggle of personalized forces." Mythology thus forms the dynamic element of all higher religions and all great social movements because all great social movements are essentially religious.

The interrelationship of philosophical and theological language persisted in Herberg's thought from the 1940s on. One can find earlier intimations of this view as far back as December 1932, when he wrote: "Spinozism is materialism (atheism) in a theological cloak."[4] His appreciation for Marxism was not diminished by his discovery of its inherent mythological structure; as has already been mentioned, it made him a "better Marxist." Marxism became for him a secularized version of the biblical faith; but, as such, there existed a potential for demonic perversion of the faith inasmuch as Marx's own thought, to use Marxian language, is part of the social superstructure.[5] Although he never totally disavowed Marxism, he did dismiss its Russian version as an actual demonic perversion, as a worldwide conspiracy to subject all people to totalitarian slavery. Yet with regard to the idea of a utopian society, by 1950 he preferred Marx's theory as more realistic than Martin Buber's notion of *communitas communitatum*, of federations within a federation.[6] By 1969–70, in a seminar entitled "The Thought of Karl Marx," he maintained that Marx's thought had become so distorted and falsified that it had been reduced to a mere slogan. Nevertheless, he considered Marx "Mr. Europe of the 19th century." Socialism therefore remained an important element in his own thought, and his article in the *Antioch Review* provided the metaphysical justification for a socialism based on theological and ethical principles. For this reason, Herberg, in an outline for a 1947 lecture entitled "Capitalism and Socialism in the Light of the Judeo-Christian Ethic," could quote the British Socialist Victor Gollancz to the effect: "I am a more passionate socialist than ever I was."[7]

DEMOCRATIC SOCIALISM VERSUS TOTALITARIANISM

Herberg insisted that the choice was no longer between capitalism and Socialist collectivism.[8] Capitalism of the nineteenth-century brand was for him no longer viable in the modern world: "Collectivism in some form is here and is here to stay." Rather, the choice was between totalitarian collectivism and "democratic (libertarian) socialism," the latter being a socialism rooted in an ethic based on the uniqueness of each individual human personality. He referred to this approach as the "third way" vis-à-vis capitalism and totalitarianism. This personalist socialism would be, as Herberg rather vaguely called it, a "theologically grounded and religiously motivated socialism." Referring to himself as a Socialist of no particular party, Herberg based his position on the social thought of Berdyaev and Lewis Corey. According to

Herberg's interpretation, Berdyaev opposed the destructive elements of bolshevism while both promoting a philosophy that did not discredit the spiritual dimensions of man and consistently attacking any depersonalization of the human spirit. Unlike Marx, who was too dogmatically concerned with economics and the future utopia, Berdyaev grounded his social thought on the biblical view of the transcendent worth of every person. This personalist socialism sought a type of society that was pluralistic and decentralized and placed restrictions on state control.

Lewis Corey, a longtime Communist known, among other names, as Louis Fraina, in his 1942 essay "The Unfinished Task" also recommended pluralism, but his was specifically an economic pluralism with a "mixed economy" that fair-handedly avoided too much concentrated economic control either by the government or by private enterprise. In such an economy, collectivism would be necessary but not treated as an end in itself. As Herberg wrote: "Collectivism and planning are not ends in themselves, as much as traditional socialist thought has made them out to be; they are institutional devices to control the economic forces of the modern world *in the interests of freedom and justice* and are to be justified only to the degree that they serve this end." Consequently, following Corey, Herberg offered a five-point program for democratic socialism that included (1) enhancement of individual freedom; (2) employment of collectivism, but only when necessary to enhance freedom; (3) economic pluralism; (4) minimizing the economic power of the state; and (5) grounding the preceding four points on a personalistic ethic rooted firmly in "a dynamic religious affirmation in the spirit of the Judeo-Christian tradition." Such a social philosophy, Herberg believed, would avoid the excesses of both capitalism and totalitarian socialism and would be profoundly compatible with the "essential spirit of Judaism and Christianity."

The labor movement, one of Herberg's abiding concerns, would of course play an important role in this political view. The American Labor party (ALP) had unfortunately been "stillborn," according to Herberg. Even before the Communists captured the party in 1942, it was ignored, for the most part, by the Committee for Industrial Organization (CIO) and the American Federation of Labor (AFL). Its original goal had been to be an independent third party, but, from the first, political independence was "merely an empty ceremonial formula" and its program was hardly distinguishable from the New Deal itself: "The ALP was born an administration party." After the Communists captured control of the ALP, any hope of its developing into a powerful party became untenable. That a third party, "a broad-based labor-liberal party," might be formed in the immediate future, Herberg believed, was an impossibility even though the notion was supported by the Americans for Democratic Action and the Fellowship of Christian Socialists. The major obstacle to establishing a third party was, in his opinion, the questionable belief that a "labor vote" existed in America. Herberg doubted that a labor vote existed for two reasons. First, since 1938 labor itself had become part of both the New Deal and Roosevelt's political machine. Second, and this was a factor that Herberg considered fortunate, the American worker had never become self-consciously proletariat "to the exclusion of his broader interests as an American citizen." The American worker was more "wage-conscious" than "class-conscious." Consequently, labor, in Herberg's opinion, was almost unanimously opposed to the formation of a third party.

Since 1933, the United States had become, in Herberg's view, a front-runner in labor legislation. One result of this change was that the phrase "big labor" began to be used as a popular bogey alongside such phrases as "big business," "Wall Street," and "the Trusts." Anti-Roosevelt sentiment was transformed into antilabor sentiment. For this reason the Taft-Hartley Labor-Management Relations Act of June 1947 was passed, which act, in Herberg's estimation, strengthened the power of the employers and weakened, through prohibitions and restrictions, the power of the unions. The labor unions themselves were partly responsible for this situation, a responsibility that arose out of the paradoxical nature of a labor union itself. Unions originated to fight oppressive conditions for workers; yet frequently the rank-and-file member had less freedom in regard to his union than he did in regard to his employer. This situation was exacerbated by the dual nature of unions, which were forced to act as business organizations themselves while serving as expressions of "democratic self-determination." In other words, a conflict existed between the purpose of the union and its orientation.

To fulfill its purpose, the union had to develop a bureaucracy; yet it was oriented toward "idealistic, quasi-religious collectivity."[9] Gradually the bureaucracy became more important than that original orientation. Soon a chasm appeared between bureaucratic leaders and rank-and-file members. The leaders engaged in power politics and called on the membership to be more "realistic," more "practical." As a consequence, the union's ideals receded into the background. Herberg considered this development to be "very largely an impersonal objective process." When the bureaucracy became a "privileged caste," the possibility arose that "total" unions would develop—unions in which the civil rights of members would be restricted and the rank-and-file members would passively assent to the suggestions from the bureaucratic leaders. The task of bargaining would then be delegated solely to the leaders, with the members agreeing to the completed collective-bargaining contract. This kind of unionism, according to Herberg, bordered on totalitarianism and was contrary to the spirit of democratic society.

What was needed, in Herberg's view, was a "limited" union with a moral conscience. Although bureaucracies have always entrenched themselves, their evils could be minimized by guaranteeing civil rights to union members and by decentralizing the power and functions of union bureaucrats. As Herberg wrote: "What is most needed is a profound transformation in the moral atmosphere. What is needed is the creation of a labor conscience." He called this kind of morality "labor civic morality," which would be binding upon both the leaders and the led. The exact nature of this morality could only be understood, according to Herberg, not by some predetermined European model, but by American religious and democratic traditions seen from the perspective of a radical biblical realism.

Herberg sought to construct a theory of democracy that was in keeping with the historical traditions of American society.[10] Building on Anglo-American institutions, the Puritanism of the seventeenth century, and the liberalism of the eighteenth century, he maintained that at bottom these traditions shared a common view of human nature. Here again he repeated his understanding that human nature was both good and evil, rational and irrational. Agreeing with Kant and Bertrand Russell, Herberg affirmed his belief in the transcendent dignity of the individual person, a view derived from Judeo-Christian tradition.[11] Paradoxically, he felt, man has also been marred by sinfulness: "The lust for power is but the prideful self-assertion of the ego in its social dimension." Even the highest ideals of man have been complicated by the selfishness of those who promote them. Nevertheless, Herberg asserted, the ability of man to transcend himself has always made social order possible whereas man's sinful egotism has made democracy necessary: "Both aspects are indispensable to any tenable theory of democracy: one as a protection against the pessimistic cynicism that leads to tyranny; the other against the optimistic utopianism that leads to anarchy." Accordingly, Herberg opposed the naive optimism of Rousseau as well as the doctrine of total depravity described by Calvin: "If the notion of the essential goodness of man makes democracy unnecessary, the doctrine of utter depravity would seem to make it impossible." Both of these "oversimplifications" could have led and did lead to tyranny. Consequently, "there is no escape from the radical ambivalence of human nature."

Herberg maintained that the ambivalence of human nature has resulted in a corresponding ambivalence in the social order. By definition, a state has always endangered human freedom because a state has always needed a bureaucracy, the creation of which has entailed coercion. But the extremes of tyranny and anarchy could be avoided. They could be avoided, in Herberg's opinion, only by a democracy in which power was diffused through society, thereby creating a system of checks and balances. As he wrote: "That is what democracy is: an institutional system capable of sustaining and fostering social organization through the necessary use of power while guarding against its dangers and excesses at the hands of tyrannical rulers, oligarchical minorities, and despotic majorities alike." In other words, "democracy, in short, is the institutionalization of permanent resistance to human sinfulness in politics." This political democracy, for Herberg, also implied economic democracy, in which all consumers, as well as producers, would determine the course of their own economic lives. In attempting to correlate political democracy with economic democracy, Herberg was trying to unite economic radicalism with the political philosophy of the fathers of the American Republic. Although these views were frequently considered to be antithetical, Herberg said: "My point is that this antithesis is largely unreal." The founding fathers had a realistic understanding of human nature and of the human desire for power, whether political or economic.

Judaism, Christianity, anarchism, and "authentic Marxism" in Herberg's estimation shared the belief that the exercise of power over people was sinful and wrong. Nevertheless, the desire for power on everyone's part was a brute fact of human existence. The politician, for example, who sought to assist in people's welfare had to acquire the power to do so. The revolutionary who sought social justice was often only searching for an outlet for his own frustrations and discontents. The philanthropist who supported his favorite charity actually found self-satisfaction in feeling pity for underprivileged people. Consequently, all our ideals degenerated into permitting ends to justify means: "To the impurity of our weapons must therefore be added the ambiguity of our cause." Power was thus an inescapable element in all social and political situations. Neither perfectionism nor Machiavellianism would suffice. Perfectionism, the assumption that the moral law could be fulfilled, as in pacifism, was quite simply utopian and frequently deteriorated into cynicism, into "idealism gone sour." Machiavellianism was outright "unashamed worship of the devil" and denied all moral standards in politics. Communism was guilty of both of these fallacies. According to Herberg, the only reasonable path to take, given the nature of man, was democratic socialism.

Herberg held that the essential feature of democratic socialism was its emphasis on the uniqueness of each individual human personality. Totalitarianism equated the state with society and thereby denied individual autonomy. It penetrated every aspect, every interest, and every activity of a human's life. In this kind of collectivism, society and state could become "a pantheistic god." Such a view of socialism was erroneous, according to Herberg, and contrary to that of Marx who wrote in his *Economic-Philosophical Manuscripts*: "One must always avoid setting up a 'society' as an abstraction opposed to the individual. The individual is the social entity. His life is therefore an expression and verification of the life of society." For Herberg, capitalism, the other side of the coin, turned the individual into a mere cog in a giant economic machine. Democratic socialism called for creating the conditions that would allow a person to realize his full potential by combining political democracy with economic democracy and economic pluralism. Frequently calling this view "democratic collectivism," Herberg recommended "a balanced combination of state action on the one hand and cooperative individual action on the other, with *the presumption always in favor of the latter*." He continued, "The last phrase is important; it means that whenever individual or voluntary group effort can accomplish the purpose, the state is to keep out." Calling for an "economic constitution of the nation," Herberg maintained that the government should form the overall economic policy of the country but should not engage in the economic enterprise itself except to prevent unjust practices, such as unfair trade. In any action, whether by the state or by a private group, the uniqueness of the personality should be revered as the "touchstone of human endeavor." The foundation of this society would be the grand tradition of the biblical faith, of Judaism and Christianity.

According to Herberg, Marxism could only be preserved by grounding it in this Hebrew-Christian tradition.[12] To achieve this end, Herberg first defined his own religiousness in Christian terms. Indeed, he considered becoming a Roman Catholic. He maintained, however, that Niebuhr was responsible for convincing him to establish his religious perspective in Jewish terms. Catholicism had its Jacques Maritain and Neo-Thomism, and Protestantism had its Karl Barth and Emil Brunner and neoorthodoxy. What Judaism needed was "a great theological reconstruction in the spirit of neo-orthodoxy equally distant from sterile fundamentalism and secularized modernism."

Herberg based his theological approach on a Neo-Kantian opposition to positivism and humanistic naturalism.[13] In other words, he opposed the elevation of the empirical method and of devotion to humanity to the status of absolutes. Maintaining that his new position antedated Ignazio Silone's and Arthur Koestler's and that his own perspective changed in 1938–39, Herberg dismissed positivism outright as "demonstrably false": "The doctrine of positivism is not itself scientific knowledge and yet it claims to be true." Positivism was thus in the contradictory position of assuming the validity of the principle of empirical verification without being able to verify this principle empirically. Then Herberg criticized naturalism on two grounds. One, it unknowingly deified humanity, thereby raising it to the status of a religious belief and praising it to the point of idolatry. As such, it was inadequate and could not withstand critical examination. In other words, it elevated the relative and conditioned to the status of the absolute and unconditioned: "The religion of humanity is unworthy of the human spirit." Two, the very fact that man constructed a concept of nature showed that man's mind transcended nature. If everything were nothing more than nature and matter, both naturalism and materialism would be inconceivable and therefore meaningless: "In a word, *natural* science *presupposes* a vantage point *outside of nature*. Internally science is naturalistic, but no philosophical scheme that embraces all our knowledge-experience and assigns science its proper place in the structure can be naturalistic." Moreover, for all its emphasis on the ideals of humanity, naturalism could not rely on scientific facts to prove them because clearly values could not be derived from facts: "The values embodied in our ideals are, in the strictest sense, postulates of Kant's *Practical Reason* (or again faith)." Even orthodox Marxists, according to Herberg, were not naturalists.

Communism, not Marxism, was antithetical to the Jewish faith and stood in a position of irreconcilable conflict: "Communism is *reactionary* through and through . . . it is hostile to freedom, to human welfare, to personal self-realization, even to the ordinary security of social existence." In contrast, Judaism was "progressive" and "revolutionary" in its "affirmation of freedom and justice." The essence of Judaism was fivefold: (1) it was a "faith enacted in history," (2) it was "reenacted in the life of every individual," (3) it was a faith oriented toward Zion while recognizing the interdependence of the land and the Galuth in history, (4) it was grounded in the Covenant, and (5) it was a faith that generated a transcendent ethic for individual and social life. This understanding of Judaism was fortified by Herberg's study of the works of Rosenzweig: "Insofar as my life possesses any validity as Jewish existence, I can say that I owe it to Franz Rosenzweig."[14]

THE
THEOLOGY OF
FRANZ ROSENZWEIG

Herberg considered Rosenzweig among the first to observe that the faith of the ancient prophets was compatible with major elements of modern culture: "Rosenzweig blazed the trail of a new day in Jewish religious thinking—a 'third way' equally distinct from, and opposed to, the traditionalism of conventional Orthodoxy and the rationalistic modernism of 'liberal' religion." Herberg explained that, for Rosenzweig, religious thinking was existential thinking as opposed to scientific or so-called objective thinking. The teachings of religion were not subject to empirical verification but achieved the status of truth by becoming part of one's own existence through commitment, decision, and venture. Religious thinking was thus inseparable from religious experience, which expressed itself not in philosophy but in what Martin Buber called the "dialogic life." God has revealed himself through words and deeds and the "I" has reacted to the "Thou" in words and deeds also. Scripture was indeed for Rosenzweig a divine revelation of the personhood of God, according to Herberg; but having been written by generations of men, it was subject to all of the errors of human frailty. The Scripture "contains God's words nevertheless. It contains it, yet is not identical with it." Consequently, it has had to be interpreted over and over, creating a sensitive relationship between the written Torah and the oral Torah, between Scripture and tradition. Throughout, Herberg explained, Rosenzweig presupposed the divine appointment of Israel as special servant of God, affirming the Law (*halakah*), not by legalistic ritualism, but through personal appropriation. The Jews have therefore been uniquely chosen. But Christianity has also played its important role in history. As Herberg explained Rosenzweig's position: "Judaism and Christianity are to him essentially of one piece, one religious reality; Judaism facing *inward* to the Jews, Christianity *outward* to the Gentiles." Judaism has remained a constant reminder of the one God whereas Christianity has sought to spread this word to the unredeemed world. Together, they have constituted the fully revealed religion: "Only they are divinely ordained as God's appointed way for the realization of his kingdom among men." In such a manner Rosenzweig opposed both fundamentalism and modernism at the same time that he formed a "third way" on which Herberg himself continued to elaborate and expand.

For Herberg an important question was, What does it mean to be a Jew? He consistently asserted, in agreement with Rosenzweig and Buber, that Jewishness implied more than a race, a nationality, a culture group, or a religious denomination. Rather, Judaism was something unprecedented in history.[15] For him, Jewishness was expressed on three levels of unity and tension: (1) God and man, (2) God and history, and (3) God and Israel. On the first level, at the heart of the issue was the ambiguity of man, who has always stood at the juncture of "finity" and infinity, in search of a god, usually an idol and not the personal God of Judaism. Because of man's fallen nature, man did not find God—God found man, and man in response committed himself to the love and service of God. This view, according to Herberg, "is the true meaning of *shema*," a Jewish liturgical prayer. On the second level, Judaism was a historically oriented religion in which God directed the course of history toward the ultimate fulfillment of His purpose for history. And Herberg's third level concerned the election and vocation of Israel: "It is a supernatural community, called into being by God to serve his eternal purpose in history." As such, Judaism was not a system of propositions to which one gave intellectual assent, nor was it an esoteric knowledge mystically intuited. Rather it was a "faith enacted in history," consisting of the history of a particular people who constituted the history of God's people: "Jewish religion is thus, in essence, *Heilsgeschichte*, redemptive history," "a history which redeems." Herberg believed this history to be expressed in three great ritualistic festivals: *Pesah*, *Shabuot*, and *Sukkot*. According to him, "These three festivals are for us the living reenactment of the formative events in the redemptive history of Israel. Just as Israel became Israel through the events to which they refer, so the individual Jew becomes a Jew-in-faith by 'repeating' these events in his own life."

ZIONISM AND ANTI-SEMITISM

Herberg insisted that this view of Judaism should not be confused with nationalistic Zionism. In fact, Herberg believed that the 1947 bombing of the King David Hotel in Jerusalem by Jewish terrorists was a denial of the Jewish tradition. He believed that "by changing our course bit by bit in pursuit of the rising star of nationalism, we have reversed our destiny." Herberg pointed out that the early rabbis were neither nationalists nor internationalists, neither patriots nor antipatriots, neither militarists nor pacifists. Their central concern was the Torah and living according to it. This sacred tradition, and the freedom to live and teach according to it, was alone worth defending. Jeremiah, in Herberg's opinion, would today be considered a "collaborator." Israel was therefore not a nation or a folk, but a holy people under covenant with God: "Universalism and divine election thus stand in organic relation." Israel accordingly should not accept the normative values of other nations; indeed, Herberg claimed, Israel should act "abnormally" in opposition to the normal values of other nations. Otherwise, the desire to act as other nations would lead to a break with the Covenant. The pursuit of nationalism, which many Jews adopted, has the potential to reduce Israel to the dimensions of other nations. According to Herberg, such nationalism represented "the most radical perversion of the idea of Israel," and in effect constituted assimilation. On the contrary, the Jew could never live at ease in the world: "Palestine's destiny, rather, is to serve as the ideal pole of 'normality' in dialectic relation to the 'abnormality' of the Galut, each functioning as a norm and balance for the other." Consequently, even in Palestine, the Jew would always be alienated from the world. In this manner, Judaism would fulfill its destiny and not evade it. In this manner, *Eretz Yisrael* would retain its position of not merely being a political entity identified with a particular land, but it would be more—a "holy place," symbolizing "the Great Triad: God-Israel-Torah."

Recognizing that the Jew lived in the world but was not of the world, Herberg knew anti-Semitism would be a constant threat.[16] For him, anti-Semitism was not only a sociological and psychological prejudice—it was a theological position that pointed "straight to the heart of the spiritual malady of the contemporary world." Israel was a mystery that transcended the categories of nature and society, and it bore witness to the God of history vis-à-vis the spatial gods of paganism. Anti-Semitism was therefore a rebellion against God and the Law. Christians who engaged in anti-Semitism were thus guilty of lapsing into paganism and indeed were rebelling against the Jewishness of Jesus Christ: "Antisemitism, in short, is anti-Christianity," and, as Herberg further contended, "The pogrom is the reenactment of the crucifixion." To elevate a prejudice against Jews to the point that the prejudice led to pogroms was, for Herberg, to absolutize the relative, to engage in pagan idolatry. As he wrote, "Only God is absolute; everything else, literally everything else— society, institution, belief, or movement—is infected with relativity and stands under divine judgment." This list included anti-Semitism. Christians should realize that Christianity was the "Judaism of the Gentiles" and that an attack on Jews was an attack on Christianity.

Anti-Semitism, according to Herberg, existed in the Soviet Union to an appalling degree. Communism had not solved the "Jewish problem" in Russia, a point that put an end to the illusion that the abolition of capitalism would result in the abolition of racial and religious prejudice. Herberg saw that

Russian chauvinistic nationalism, which led to anti-Semitism, pervaded the entire structure of Russian history and institutions. Consequently, the mere passage of a law would not wipe out anti-Semitism in the Soviet Union. Herberg maintained that the Soviet attitude toward Jewry was formulated before the Russian Revolution by Karl Kautsky, whose position was adopted by Lenin and Stalin. The Jews and Zionism were considered reactionary, "nationalistic," and even imperialistic for seeking political hegemony over the Middle East. Herberg explained that Kautsky believed Zionism and anti-Semitism were both based on precapitalistic modes of production and would be eliminated by a Communist revolution. After the Revolution of 1917, Zionism was banned in Russia as utopian, as pernicious, as counterrevolutionary, and as "the last illusory gasp of Judaism." Thus, Herberg concluded, persecution persisted, and opposition to Zionism became a permanent part of Soviet foreign policy because it was viewed by the Russians as an instrument of Allied imperialism. Such was the policy of the Soviet Union from 1921 to the late forties, until the establishment of the state of Israel. At that time, the Soviet Union courted the new Israeli state but only for the purpose of bringing it into the Soviet sphere of influence. Inasmuch as he believed Israelis would resist such overtures, Herberg predicted a return of Russian hostility toward Zionism.

Despite anti-Semitism, indeed perhaps even as a result of both the extermination of millions of Jews in Germany during World War II and the establishment of the state of Israel, Judaism was entering into an era of resurgence, Herberg maintained. "There is a religious revival under way among American Jews today."[17] As evidence, he noted an increase in synagogue membership and attendance at services and a rise in building programs and religious schools. The reason for this upsurge, in Herberg's view, was the need on the part of Jews for Jewish identity in the wake of the events of the previous decades. This revival, however, would prove to be of greater benefit to the Conservative branch of Jewry, especially in America where the old distinctions of Orthodox, Conservative, and Reform were tending to disappear. One reason for this change was that during the war the rabbis in the armed services were concerned with meeting the needs of "Jewish" soldiers and not Orthodox or Conservative or Reformed Jewish soldiers. The blurring of these distinctions subsequently carried over into civilian life where, as Herberg predicted, a "new" Jew might arise in America and refashion the life of the synagogues. During this process, one important task would be to avoid a portentous trend among Jews to separate religious life from secular life: "Jewish faith knows no such separation between religion and the world; all of the affairs of life stand under divine law and divine judgment, and all are therefore the concern of religion." This task required an adequate theological position rooted in the biblical tradition.

Herberg reiterated his belief that the Jews were "the People of the Book," a book that was relevant despite the confusion of the age. Liberal theology, according to Herberg, was inappropriate for an age of crisis because it eliminated the tension between God and man, the "otherness" of God, and practically promoted a "secular cult of 'adjustment' " in the face of spiritual malaise. The more justified approach was that of Christian Neo-Reformation theology, which emphasized the tension between God and man and which was neither fundamentalist nor modernist, neither rationalist nor mysticist, but was existential, emphasizing that faith involved a decision made by man in confrontation with God. As a consequence, for Herberg it stressed the sinfulness of man and the self-transcendence of man while assimilating the best of Marx and Freud. It held to a "God-centered relativism," opposing both capitalism and totalitarianism, the deification of the state. This "third way," in Herberg's opinion, could be seen among Christians, both Catholic and Protestant, in the works of Maritain, Berdyaev, Barth, Brunner, Tillich, and William Temple. Jewish theology, he insisted, should pursue a similar path inasmuch as "the fate of the Jew has become essentially typical of the fate of contemporary man." He further contended, "In the Jew, the archetype of the outsider standing forever at the brink of nothingness, the alienation of contemporary man, his malaise and homelessness in the world, find their most intense expression." Herberg found this new approach to theological thinking among the Jews in the works of Buber, Rosenzweig, and some other Jewish theologians.

THE STATE
OF JEWISH
THEOLOGY

Martin Buber was of course the most famous at the time and Herberg held that he was among the greatest thinkers since Søren Kierkegaard. Buber's distinction between "I-Thou" and "I-It," between person-to-person and person-to-thing encounters, was a fundamental distinction in human relations. The I-Thou encounter was the basis of spiritual life, which consisted primarily of communion, not mystical union, with God. Here, Herberg held, on the one hand the uniqueness of personality was paramount. On the other hand, to construe a "Thou" as an "It," the objectification and thus depersonalization of the human personality, was one of the major sources of evil. For Buber, as Herberg explained, a genuine community, in contrast to a collectivity, always involved a "third person," namely God. For both Buber and Rosenzweig, the road to salvation was found in the people of Israel, although Buber was somewhat utopian and unrealistic in his view of the state of Israel, treating it as though it were the messianic kingdom. Nevertheless, Herberg held that, aside from Buber, Rosenzweig, and a few others, such as Gershom Scholem, Leo Baeck, Solomon Schechter, Louis Finkelstein, Max Kadushin, and Samuel S. Cohon, Jewish theology was nearly in a state of "unrelieved mediocrity." The reasons for this state of affairs were historical.

Herberg maintained that the Jews had entered the modern world belatedly. For example, in Eastern Europe, where the Renaissance had had little effect, the Jews moved directly from the assumptions of the Middle Ages to the thought of modern secularism. As a consequence, many began to disregard the two major polarities of Jewish spirituality, namely, the prophetic function and the priestly function. The biblical prophet, Herberg observed, acted in a time of crisis, calling on Israel to question itself. In contrast, the priest did not act in times of crisis; his was the task of accommodating the prophet's exhortations to everyday existence—the task, in other words, of smoothing out the prophet's thought. Herberg noted a constant tendency to reduce this polarity to a one-sided priestly function that maximized what was thought to be "normal" and that consequently resulted in the "draining of Jewish spirituality of its original [prophetic] force." He summarized the results of this developing situation thus: "For many generations now, priestly 'normalcy' has been taken as the true spirit of Jewish religion and every suggestion of prophetic urgency impatiently brushed aside."

In the midst of this questionable condition, Herberg felt, some Jews had mistakenly taken Jewish nationalism, Jewish culture, Jewish social services, and even antidefamation as the essence of the Jewish religion. In effect, Herberg held, they elevated a part of the Jewish religion to an absolute. For example, Zionism had frequently been raised to the level of "an idolatrous Ersatz-Judaism."[18] In reaction, Herberg called for a theology that would delineate the dialectical meaning of the Jewish faith.[19] A vitally relevant theology, he asserted, "tells us what we really believe in the affirmation of faith. It serves as a check upon arbitrariness of will and sentimentality of feeling in the religious experience. Above all, it helps us to expose, and thus to protect us against, the corrupting influence of ideologies that stem from commitments at variance with our supreme and overriding allegiance to the Living God."

A THEOLOGICAL
RECONSTRUCTION

When one works to develop a theology of this nature, Herberg felt one must deal with a number of problems. First, there was the difficulty of the relationship between reason and revelation. Herberg insisted that human reason would never attain to a knowledge of God and that "only divine self-revelation [could] bring to man the saving truth." This revelation was manifested in Israel, in the Scriptures, and in the scholarly tradition of form criticism of Scriptures. Inasmuch as theology attempted to go beyond nature and experience while using terms derived from nature and experience, a paradox necessarily arose, or, as Herberg put it: "Anyone who thinks he can formulate a valid Biblical theology without paradox is simply deceiving himself." Second, this theology should emphasize the absoluteness of God while elaborating the means of communication between God and man, much as Buber did with his notion of the "dialogic life." Third, the biblical view of man's sinful nature and man's ambivalence would have to be demonstrated. Such a demonstration would deal with man's propensity toward self-absolutization and also his self-transcendence, without omitting the tension between the misery and grandeur of man. Fourth, a theology of this kind would need to deal with the relationship history has with society, showing that because history was not a solution but was the very crux of the human condition, human institutions could only be viewed relativistically and not idolatrously. For Herberg, a theory of society based on biblical faith would avoid the pitfalls of "power-mad-cynicism, secular utopianism, and otherworldly quietism" alike. Finally, this theology should deal with the concepts of salvation, faith, and grace, carefully delineating between the need for grace sola gratia and the need for *teshubah*, the turning away from self-sufficiency.

In addition to these five general theological problems, Herberg suggested six additional issues specifically Jewish in content that a Jewish theology must address: (1) a theology of *halakah*, (2) a theological account of the Jewish liturgical year, (3) a theological interpretation of the inner relationship between Judaism and Christianity in the manner of Rosenzweig, (4) a theological analysis of the anti-Semitism utilizing depth psychology, (5) a theological evaluation of the present crisis in Israel and in the world, and (6) a realistic theory of society. This theology, according to Herberg, should use recent developments in Christian theology as a tool to elaborate Jewish religious thought, utilizing the insights of such theologians as Barth, Brunner, Tillich, Maritain, and others.

This whole theological reconstruction of Herberg would become the subject of subsequent works, the writing of which constituted a task that was to occupy him for several years. Throughout, Herberg constantly warred against what he considered to be idolatrous forms of thought. Of these, he most persistently attacked the philosophy of secularism which, since the eighteenth century, had become "the official voice of our culture" and which represented "the cultural climate of our time."[20] He described secularism as reflecting "the perennial effort of sinful man to establish himself in his self-sufficiency against God." Often witnessed in American thought, secularism found specific expression in some people's devotion to science. For Herberg, following the scientific "party line" in America was comparable to following the political "party line" in the Soviet Union, with this exception—in Russia if a person did not follow the party line, he could wind up in prison. Secularism had also infected the church and the synagogue, both of which frequently sought to confirm self-sufficiency on secular grounds. In many cases, churches and synagogues adopted the techniques of business and established adult or social educational centers and exclusive clubs where emotionalism took the place of worship and where lectures and classes were characterized as "inspiring" and "educational." Superficial dabbling in psychology became a substitute for pastoral care. In Herberg's view, if religion meant confrontation with and obedience to God, then "the contemporary church and synagogue [were not] to be regarded as authentically religious institutions." For example, if a Jew could be regarded as both "ethnic" and religious, then he could overlook the religious and emphasize the ethnic by supporting philanthropic organizations, Zionism, Yiddish culture, antidefamation, and the like. In other words, he could support "a whole host of ersatz-Jewish faiths" but not the biblical-rabbinic faith. In Herberg's opinion, such secularist tendencies usually ended up in "practical polytheism," "with each area of life subject to its own god."

Herberg pointed out that the secularist attitude frequently involved some particular perception of the state, usually an erroneous view. For example, the moral perfectionism of some pacifists, Herberg observed, did not allow them to recognize that it was not the state per se but society that demanded some form of coercion be required to direct man's self-centeredness. The result of such an error was that pacifists were characterized by an "imperturbable self-righteousness." In other contexts, some have even questioned religious institutions while relying on a dubious notion of the state. For instance, Paul Blanshard in his book *American Freedom and Catholic Power* displayed, in Herberg's opinion, an anti-Catholic bias grounded in a "secularist-statist philosophy that . . . is far more dangerous than anything in American Catholicism to which the book calls attention." Blanshard, Herberg maintained, had misunderstood not only Catholicism but the nature of the "pluralistic foundations of American society" as well.

Herberg therefore sought to draw the attention of the church and the synagogue to the secularist tendencies in their own organizations as well as in society generally. Indeed, he predicted a decline in secularism: "I think we can say that there is already beginning to emerge a mind that is *post*-modern," and many of the Jews who had adopted Jewish ersatz religions have almost unwittingly been led back to authentic Judaism. Herberg pointed out that many secularists themselves had come to recognize that science could be elevated to the level of an idolatrous commitment to that which was only relative and that the scientific way of thinking was not existential thinking. As for the church, specifically, the Roman Catholic church, Herberg recommended that its true model should be not civil society but the family. As such, he suggested five areas that the church should stress in its confrontation with the modern world: (1) the church must become a bastion of humaneness, (2) it should preach only the gospel because it is relevant to the concerns of the day, (3) it should abjure depersonalization of man in mass society, (4) it should never be identified with any social cause or movement (that is, it should assume the stance Herberg earlier called the "Jacobin defense"), and (5) it should be faithful to its appointed mission. In this manner, both the church and the synagogue could do their respective parts in bringing to an end this era of "human self-deification."

Herberg recognized that such efforts constituted a difficult task, as exemplified in the life of the French Christian Leon Bloy. Referring to him as a "Man of the Absolute," Herberg lauded Bloy for having led many, such as Jacques Maritain, from the aridities of positivism to the "Waters of the Absolute." Like Kierkegaard's writings, Bloy's novels displayed a contempt for the idolators of the day, which included both the church and the wealthy whom he frequently denounced with "prophetic wrath." Bloy was, according to Herberg, a man who attempted to stand outside all human viewpoints in order to judge the world. He had an "implacable hatred of mediocrity." His one weakness, however, was his French chauvinism, his assumption that France was God's preferred country. As Herberg quoted Bloy: "Mankind is explainable and plausible only by means of France." This idolatry, despite his great influence, was his nemesis.

In Herberg's view of the modern world, idolatry of the state, whether it was France, America, or otherwise, was difficult to overcome. He found one possible solution to this difficulty in Buber's *Paths to Utopia*, in which, at least according to Herberg, Buber sought to free socialism from its corruptions. Herberg agreed with Buber that the major enemies of society were centralism and authoritarian regimentation. But he only partially agreed with Buber's suggestion of a socialist pluralism as *communitas communitatum*, a federation of federations, a community of communities. As Herberg summarized Buber's position: "Socialism is the 'structural renewal' of society through the development of a network of communities, united in a free federation." Yet believing that the abolition of property was an eschatological task, believing in a "mixed economy," and opposing the excesses of both capitalism and communism, Herberg doubted that Buber's approach provided an operable mode of action in the United States with its "vast economic structure at various stages of monopoly and social control." Moreover, Herberg felt that Buber failed to recognize that some form of coercion would be necessary in society and too easily assumed that free cooperation could be developed and made readily available. Herberg also noted that although Buber's criticism of Marx was fairly accurate in general he overlooked the true significance of Marx, whom Herberg, quoting Hermann Cohen, maintained was the "ambassador of the Lord of history." Nevertheless, Herberg appreciated what Buber had attempted.

History for Herberg was the intersection of time and eternity, a "dialectic fusion" of the two.[21] Man himself was "fixed at the juncture of time and eternity." If the dialectic of time and eternity were ignored and time alone stressed, then one was left with mere change, or flux, or process, and, above all, meaninglessness. However, as Herberg noted, philosophers from Plato to Bertrand Russell had sought to escape from such meaninglessness by turning to the eternal and ignoring time. But Scripture has always held that time was "really real" and that the world and time were created by God and therefore ought not to be ignored. Both Christianity and Judaism were historical faiths that were "enacted in history." Easter and Passover were thus for Herberg not merely memorial days: "They are crucial moments in which eternity enters time, in which the temporal takes on the dimensions of the eternal." Just as "God was in Christ" for the Christians, so "in Israel the *Shekinah* (divine presence) is made manifest." The biblical understanding of the nature of God for Herberg was therefore not based on Greek ontology, but on what God has done—how God has functioned and acted in history. Man, who has always lived in time and in history, has communicated with God through prayer, an "I-Thou" dialogue with God. The deeds of God were acknowledged by faith and not subject to the inductive proofs of science.

Indeed, science itself, for Herberg, was ultimately religious. It presupposed the validity of the idea of the "uniformity of nature" from which was also derived the method of induction. The uniformity of nature, however, could not be proved, it could only be assumed and postulated. As Herberg maintained, the notion of the uniformity of nature was "a methodological postulate that is neither *proved nor provable* by science since science cannot start 'proving' anything unless and until it is assumed." It cannot be validated by experience because any attempt to use experience to validate anything must make use of this very rule. To use a principle to prove itself is obviously improper. Also, the inductive method, as David Hume suggested, rested on dubious grounds.[22] It assumed a constant relationship between events of certain kinds, and yet this relationship could simply have been a matter of habit. Moreover, the inductive method must fall back on the assumption of uniformity in nature for its validity. Thus, the core of the scientific method required a leap of faith. Herberg accordingly maintained that both science and religion were grounded in an unproved assumption or belief accepted as an act of faith, using the word faith in the Thomistic sense as "an intellectual assent motivated by the will." Science, like religion, Herberg believed, had an existential grounding. As for the biblical tradition, existence was religious and religion encompassed the entire realm of human existence—a view Herberg systematized in his first major work, *Judaism and Modern Man.*

6
GOD, MAN, AND ISRAEL

In February 1947, Harold Rosenberg took exception to Herberg's assertion that Herberg held to the same values as a religious person that he had as a Communist.[1] In the margins of his own copy of Rosenberg's essay, Herberg maintained that Rosenberg had missed his point entirely: "I assert: (1) that my values came to me from the Judeo-Christian tradition via socialism, which took them over in secularized form; (2) that socialism attempted to build its own theological foundation for these values in its materialist metaphysics; (3) that this Socialist theology has shown itself incompatible with and destructive of these values (i.e., its own values as derived from the Judeo-Christian tradition); (4) that only an authentically Judaic (or Judeo-Christian) theology can serve as an adequate metaphysical foundation of these values." In short, the values Herberg learned from socialism needed to be grounded firmly in their own historical source, namely, the Judeo-Christian tradition. Herberg then delineated these values in his book *Judaism and Modern Man*.

His original title for the work was "God, Man, and Israel: An Interpretation of Jewish Religion." He also thought highly of Milton Konvitz's recommended title "Between God and Man: An Interpretation of Jewish Religion."[2] Apparently, the editors chose the final title, a choice Herberg did not greatly appreciate; he wrote to Solomon Grayzel, the editor of the Jewish Publication Society of America, and explained, "The title is not unrepresentative but it seems rather pedestrian, doesn't it?" Nevertheless, the editors' title remained, and Herberg began writing in September 1947, completing the book in July 1950.[3] A few months before the manuscript was finished, he wrote to Rabbi Herschel Matt: "I am increasingly dissatisfied with what I have written" and "the book will be much too long." One of the readers of the manuscript, Milton Steinberg, felt differently. On the last page of the manuscript, a few days before his death, Steinberg had penciled: "This is the book of the generation on the Jewish religion. At last Judaism has found an expositor capable of articulating its timeless and essential insights in the idiom of our generation and as a response to its deepest questions." Herberg was deeply moved by Steinberg's comment: "If what I am doing in this book will even remotely deserve this judgment, it will be beyond my best expectations." Steinberg's comment would later appear on the back of the book jacket when the book was finally published in September 1951.

Herberg considered *Judaism and Modern Man* a restatement of Jewish tradition seen in the light of existential philosophy and from the perspectives of Martin Buber and Franz Rosenzweig.[4] He admitted that the work constituted both his own confession of faith and "a declaration of total commitment" to his existence as a man and as a Jew, as an individual dedicated to the biblical-rabbinical tradition. The first five chapters consider the plight of modern man, seeking the absolute in the midst of despair. Chapters six through sixteen examine the nature of God and man against the background of Jewish tradition. Chapters seventeen through nineteen delve into the mystery of the unique election of Israel. In other words, the book attempts to deal with the concerns of all great religions: the horrible condition of man and the means of salvation therefrom. For Herberg, the passage from the condition of man to the means of salvation was achieved by a "leap of faith." Throughout his analysis, Herberg was keenly aware of his scholarly dependence on Reinhold Niebuhr, Buber, Rosenzweig, and Solomon Schechter.

The book begins with the world in a state of "crisis" demanding resolution.[5] Since 1912 the Western world has been drastically altered from a world of optimism and belief in the ability of man to direct the course of his own history to a world of bewilderment, confusion, and despair. The past generation, Herberg points out, has witnessed two devastating world wars, the decline of capitalism, a threat to parliamentary democracy, and the explosion of nuclear weapons. In effect, Western civilization has been reduced to a primitive level of existence in which millions of people have been wantonly murdered, millions displaced from their homelands, and millions enslaved. In contrast to much of the world in 1912, freedom of thought, freedom of the press, and freedom of passage from one country to another have been replaced by state censors, propagandists, passports, and totalitarian governments. As Herberg explains: "Only yesterday man proclaimed himself 'master of things'; today he considers himself lucky merely to survive" (p. 6). The source of all this confusion, as Herberg describes it, is not merely economics, not merely existing institutions, not merely oppressive rulers, all of which reflect the character of a majority of people. Rather, the problem is man himself, every-man: "The horrors we glimpse are not merely the horrors of hell without; they are also—and primarily—the horrors of the hell within, the chaos and evil in the heart of man" (p. 6). In other words, man has made a god of himself and his own presumed self-sufficiency. This personally assumed divinity has become demonic and has brought man to the "brink of the abyss" in which he has very nearly lost his own soul.

Herberg holds, however, that the crisis is only temporary: "Nothing in history is eternal." Nevertheless, reflection on this current situation has revealed to him the "permanent crisis of life, the existential crisis which no time or history can cure" (p. 9). Man is confronted with the yawning abyss of meaninglessness, insecurity, and what Herberg calls "metaphysical dread." Our domestic, political, and social lives merely echo this continuing note of existential despondency and despair. Herberg describes how modern faith in science and reason has only served to confront us with the puzzling problems that all people of all times have faced. And the final verdict on one's personal existence is the fact of one's own death: "For death not only brings all of our enterprises to an abrupt end; it reduces them all to nonsense" (p. 14). Seeking the solution to this existential need within ourselves only results in the continuing and agonizing desire to achieve self-sufficiency, or, better, self-delusion. The only valid solution must, according to Herberg, be transcendental: "From this chaos there is no escape except by breaking through the natural conditions of life and seeking completion in something beyond" (p. 16). This "something beyond" requires a system of values, however relativistic they may be, that will vindicate human existence amid apparent human insignificance and meaninglessness.

Herberg considers modern philosophies to be inadequate for the task because, in their desire to achieve "objectivity," modern philosophies have in effect devalued human life. This result is the consequence of attempting to equate the findings of science with reality, whereby human "subjectivity" is relegated to a secondary role in the scheme of a corrosive relativism. As Herberg indicates: "If science is the 'real reality' of things, reality is void of value" (p. 19). What values there may be are considered to be relative to one's environment, social class, perspective, or position in history. The fault rests, not with science or relativism per se, but with those who naively equate the scientific method and relativistic philosophy with reality itself. With such a view some fixed point of reference is required: "If, indeed, values cannot claim some lodgment in reality, and right and wrong, true and false, good and evil, are no more than merely a matter of ideology or conditioning, then clearly nothing is ultimately better than anything else and everything is permitted" (p. 23). If so, then human life would be deprived of meaning.

Herberg describes the ersatz faiths that have been erected to fill the spiritual vacuum in the life of modern man. These substitute religions end in "delusive security" and often find expression in the absolutizing of a nation, a race, or a class. Three of the most common and most influential religions are science, Marxism, and psychoanalysis. Science has been viewed as a "wonder-working technology," capable of ushering in a veritable utopia, of producing "a life of carefree ease amidst material plenty," brought about by that miraculous wizard of the laboratory, the scientist. In Herberg's view, science can be a valuable servant; but, when absolutized, it can become a monster that leads to depersonalization, atomization, mass standardization, and "further stultification of man's aspirations toward a worthy and significant existence" (p. 27). Even more than science, Marxism (as opposed to the thought of Karl Marx) has become one of the most potent religions of the day. Herberg maintains that it is sheer folly to assume that Marxism can bring salvation. On the contrary, Marxism, with its notion of the dialectic of history, has unwittingly proved that "history cannot solve our problems; history is itself the problem" (p. 28). Marxism, which has in effect exalted the values of "bourgeois" liberalism within industrial society, thereby promising a better society in the future, in the final analysis is as bourgeois as the class it presumes to oppose so vehemently. It criticizes in the present that which it seeks to establish in the future. One consequence is to extol a power struggle that has led to shameless acts in the present, such as the antihumanistic deeds of the Soviet Union. Whereas science and Marxism have an external orientation, psychoanalysis seeks to analyze man's problems internally. As a result, the psychoanalyst has become "the priest and father-confessor of our time," offering "peace of mind." According to Herberg, this "quackery" has become one of the most delusive and dangerous religions of the era. Its main result has been to dull the conscience, to blunt moral sensitivity, and to encourage shamelessly "an almost lascivious preoccupation with self" (p. 29). In so doing, it overlooks that existential anxiety in need of metaphysical relief. Thus, psychoanalysis, like Marxism and scientism, along with nationalism and racism, are ineffectual in meeting the genuine needs of an ambiguous human condition. What is needed is a "leap of faith."

Herberg insists that the solution to the metaphysical problem of human life can only be found beyond life itself: "Life, if only to save itself, must find fulfillment in something beyond, in something more than life" (p. 33). Ideals, ideas, and institutions will not suffice. The only means of giving life to life is to ground it in a transcendent God who is "the Lord of life and history." This grounding cannot be achieved by science or by metaphysically constructing "proofs" for God's existence or by a mysticism that ultimately results in self-deification. Rather, it can only be achieved by a "leap of faith" that is "beyond experience, beyond science, beyond objective logic" (p. 36). This leap requires an existential logic that insists on decision and commitment and is concerned with the concrete, inward life of the individual. Here, one must decide between the idolization of that which is finite, such as the self, and that which is genuinely absolute and transcendent, namely, God. Such a decision for God "comes only after a desperate inner struggle in which the victory is never final" (p. 37). As he further explains, "The existential achievement of faith is never secure" (p. 39). It is "a battle in which the victory can never be final" (p. 40). Security, assurance, is therefore never complete, but, according to Herberg, faith nevertheless transfigures one's life: "Life acquires unity, direction, significance" (p. 40). It views reality from a different perspective, from the perspective of a transcendent goal beyond the relativities and frailties of human existence. For Herberg, this perspective is a historical one, seen through the eyes of the Judaic structure of faith.

Herberg distinguishes between Greco-Oriental religions, such as Buddhism, and Hebraic religions, which include Judaism, Christianity, and Islam. Both systems agree that there is an Absolute Reality, although Herberg insists that there is a fundamental difference between the two views of reality. Greco-Oriental thought emphasizes "goodness" rather than God, stressing an impersonal primal ground of all, such as Nirvana, Nature, or Pure Spirit, and is usually conceptualized in pantheistic terms. Hebraic religion, in contrast, views God as a living, personal Being, who is the transcendent creator of the universe. For Greco-Oriental thought, the empirical world is illusory and therefore reduces the significance of life and history to meaninglessness. Hebraic thought, contrarily, views life, history, and the empirical world as real, as a creation by God and as a construct under the direction of the will of God. As such, Herberg says, the Hebraic world view rejects the soul-body dichotomy of Greco-Oriental religion in which the body is the lesser part. It proclaims man to be a "dynamic unity" of both body and soul; the body too is part of God's creation. Given this position, disagreement also exists with respect to the nature of evil and the means of salvation. Greco-Oriental thought treats evil as the result of error and ignorance whereas Hebraic thought regards evil as the result of man's egocentricity and self-absolutization, as a result of sin. Salvation is therefore achieved through repentance and reconciliation, not through a denial of personality but through an affirmation of the personality in communion with God. Thus, whereas Greco-Oriental religion seeks the soul's escape from life, Hebraic religion asserts that life itself is precious and looks forward to the fulfillment of the whole man through the resurrected body that participates in the Kingdom of God under the direction of God himself.

Herberg clarifies that, for Hebraic religion, God is not merely an "idea." Rather, He is a living being. Herberg agreed with Pascal that God is not the god of philosophers but the God of Abraham, Isaac, and Jacob. As such, God is not a philosophical notion, nor is He an ethically emotive feeling or a cosmic process. In Hebraic religion, God is "a dynamic Power in life and history—and a dynamic power that is personal" (p. 59) yet incomprehensible to the mind of man. One can therefore only speak symbolically about God, and ambiguity and paradox will necessarily arise. We cannot know God as a thing or as an idea, but only as we confront Him, and He confronts us, as a Person, as, in Buber's language, a "Thou." To the uninitiated, this view of God is the grossest of anthropomorphisms, for God is characterized as having all the emotions common to man, like jealousy, compassion, anger, and so forth. As Herberg states, "This paradox of God who is beyond everything in nature and history, and yet is ever actively involved in both, goes to the heart of Hebraic religion." God is the absolute creator of the world, and all created things are thus subordinate to him: "Whatever is not God—and that means everything in the world, every society, every institution, belief or movement—is infected with relativity and can at best claim only a passing and partial validity" (p. 65). This view is also applicable to man's relationship with God.

According to Herberg, man is "an anomalous element" within creation. He is a creature and a part of nature, simultaneously having the ability to transcend nature and his own creatureliness: "Self-transcendence is the mark of man. Every aspect of his finite life opens up with infinite possibilities" (p. 69). This biblical understanding of the nature of man avoids the errors of naturalism and a body-soul dualism. In other words, it avoids the pitfalls of a materialistic view of man, as in naturalism, which views man as simply another animal controlled by deterministic forces. It also avoids the Greek and Oriental dualism that insists that man's immaterial soul is more important than his body. As Herberg asserts, Judaism, in contrast, "refuses to exalt nature as self-sufficient or to disparage it as inferior and unreal" (p. 70). Judaism holds that matter is a vehicle of spirit, of the personality, grounded in a relationship with others and with God. The point of contact between ourselves and others, between ourselves and God, is "the word," which man can understand because he is created in the "image of God." But there is a dark side to human nature, namely, man's sinfulness. As a consequence, man should never confuse his status with that of the Creator, unlike whom man suffers from *yetzer ha-ra*, an "impulse to evil." Freedom, which man retains and which is man's most glorious characteristic, is also the source of man's evil, which occurs through wrong use of freedom. That which makes man preeminent in nature is also the source of misery. This capacity for freedom leads man either to defy or to obey God. Freedom can be used either for self-aggrandizement or for obedience to God. Self-aggrandizement occurs when man elevates his own finitude to the status of infinitude; he makes a god of himself. Pride is therefore "the sin of sins." The only way out of this morass is by "turning back" to God, who then confronts man as both a "Judge" and a "Father," offering both justice and mercy. Every moment of our lives, everything we do, comes under judgment. At this point a decision for or against God must be made: "It is a situation in which man would be utterly lost were it not for the resources of divine love" (p. 79). God, acting as Father, helps us to make the proper decision, which affects the concrete existential circumstances of our lives. In this process, ethics are invariably involved.

From Herberg's perspective, ethics have unwarrantedly been distorted by the cultists of science, who seek to make ethics "scientific," and by philosophers who seek to make ethics "rational." Both of these views are essentially Greek in origin, holding that human values are revealed in nature and reflected in the human mind. In this scheme, religion is relegated to a minor place in the discipline of ethics. Herberg, on the other hand, feels that values cannot be derived from a "fact" of nature: "The distinction between that which is and that which *ought to be* is the starting point of all ethics; no one, however, can possibly infer the latter from the former" (p. 89). The study of the evolution of nature may inform us of where nature has been and where it might go, but it does not tell us that this path is good. A study of history may reveal the inherent tendencies of human society toward socialism, but it does not inform us that this tendency is what ought to be. Moral evaluation therefore transcends the natural and historical processes themselves. The capacity for ethical judgment is thus derived from religion, which position, in Herberg's view, is a decidedly Hebraic one. This view "starts not with self-sufficient nature or reason from which everything relating to human life is to be deduced, but with the will of God" (p. 91). And, Herberg insists, all of our Western values are derived from Scripture and must remain grounded in that tradition or risk becoming meaningless and invalid. The fundamental source of Hebraic ethics is man's God-given freedom, which permits man, despite the determinative factors of society or nature, to transcend causality and be self-determining. Given this freedom, one must choose between God and idolatry: "The ultimate imperative of Jewish ethics is . . . the affirmation of the Living God and the repudiation of idolatry" (p. 96). This affirmation results in the imitation, not the impersonation, of the ways of God and manifests itself in faith and humility. Accordingly, the love of God extends to the love of one's fellowman who is likewise, in the eyes of God, considered a "Thou." Jewish ethics is an ethic based on love. But it is also an ethic based on law.

For Herberg, the Hebraic emphasis on an ethic based on both law and love avoids the excesses of legalism and antinomianism: "A legalism that absolutizes law as ultimate must . . . be rejected. But so also must the antinomianism that rejects law as unnecessary in human life on the ground that relations among men should be 'regulated' in the spontaneous freedom of love" (p. 107). Perfect love is unattainable by sinful man, and, as a consequence, law is required but that law should be tempered with as much love as is humanly possible. The divine law, as described in Scripture, also cannot be perfectly achieved by man. Yet it functions as a regulative principle, serving as a guide for action and as a principle by which to criticize and to judge existing conditions while suggesting alternatives for action within given conditions. Most often, a person making a choice faces two evils between which his choice is the lesser evil as defined by the standards of law. The constant peril, therefore, is that one will view one's choice of a lesser evil as a positive good. Such an approach, in Herberg's estimation, erases altogether the distinction between good and evil. To avoid this error, the absolute but unattainable standards of the law must be preserved. Herberg thus holds that the moral law stands "over us as an eternal judgment reminding us that the best we can do is none too good and warning us against converting the inescapable necessities of practical life into standards of right and good" (p. 112). In effect, the law serves as a reminder of man's ultimate dependence on God. It reminds man of his weakness and emphasizes his need for salvation.

This need for salvation, as Herberg describes it, is a need for security against the fears, the anxieties, the perplexities, and the frustrations of the human situation. The final judgment of life itself is death. To escape this condition of metaphysical angst, man engages in all kinds of delusive enterprises, not the least of which is the hankering after self-sufficiency. But, according to Herberg, one can only achieve salvation in obedience to a Loving God, in which obedience the self is related to a "supernatural reality." Literally, nothing else will help. What is required to achieve this needed relationship with God is *teshubah*, a "turning." Repentance, a contrite heart, an emptying of all delusions of self-sufficiency all describe the nature of this turning. The result of this turn is faith, and, as Herberg claims, "Faith is at bottom right relation to God and that is salvation" (p. 123). Man responds to

God's grace with a decision of faith and thereby becomes a "new self." However victorious this event may be for man, the battle is not yet won: "Salvation, like faith, out of which it is born, can never become a secure possession of ours" (p. 125). The constant struggle for this security constitutes the "perennial struggle of life" even after the turning—it is "the battle of faith." Nonetheless, a shift in perspective is created whereby the repentant man now sees that ultimately, through God, freedom and justice will be achieved in the greater society erected by God, namely, the Kingdom of God.

One's turning invariably will have its social effects, and Herberg insists on the relevance of religion to social life. From the Hebraic point of view, as he describes it, life itself is religious and every area of life is affected by religion, whether the area of life be public or private, economic or political. As Herberg holds, "Hebraic religion is social in its relevance and bearing, or it is nothing" (p. 134). It affirms society at the same time that it calls society into question. Recognizing that society is part of God's creation, Hebraic thought nevertheless does not affirm any particular social order as unequivocally containing the truth. Any society that makes a claim to absoluteness receives a resounding no from Hebraic religion. Society itself cannot be affirmed as an idol: "Ultimately, man stands related to God and fellow-man in a bond which no society can comprehend or social institution embody" (p. 139). God's divine judgment falls on any society that claims to be greater than this bond, whether it be a totalitarian one or one that utilizes the economic institutions of capitalism. Religion consequently must discern both the divine as well as the evil within society; it must take the position, as Herberg puts it, of a "dialectical yes-no" to every society: "No absolute, no infallible rules, no simple confrontations of good and evil, right and wrong, are available" (p. 143). All choices in society are envisioned as judgments relative to the absolute Living God. Society and the individuals in it are therefore of genuine concern to Hebraic religion, but society per se cannot be sanctified. This weakness can be best witnessed in the ambiguous attempts that have been made to apply codes of justice within society.

Rejecting the idea of natural law as too rationalistic and too inflexible to account for wide divergencies of justice in varying societies, Herberg takes the position of Hebraic religion that seeking justice is a divine commandment: "To act justly is a universal obligation laid upon man by God" (p. 147). Justice is not merely a strict code of laws, nor is it a determinate standard to which all assent. Rather, the application of justice varies from culture to culture, grounded, for Herberg, in the Living God. The criterion by which the quality of justice rendered is judged is, again, the law of love: "Justice is the institutionalization of love in society" (p. 148). Because perfect love among men is unachievable, a system of justice becomes necessary. It too suffers from all the weaknesses of frail humanity and frequently lapses into bureaucratism and coercion, becoming a vehicle of self-interest. Herberg therefore insists that no system of justice can claim perfection—justice can never be fully satisfied. Nevertheless, Hebraic religion maintains that justice rendered should at all times be tempered with the transcendental element of love: "Only love can provide the leaven to keep justice fresh and ever changing and hence free from the corruption of idolatrous absolutization" (p. 151).

This problem of achieving justice is, as Herberg notes, particularly noticeable in the realm of economics which, he claims in agreement with Marx, is "basic to social existence." Herberg points out that Hebraic religion offers no specific program for an economic system. No economic system is divinely sanctioned. The ancient prophets merely affirmed that the fruits of nature were to be utilized for the enhancement of all human welfare, and all economic activity must be judged according to how well this end is fulfilled. The biblical standard for economic justice, therefore, is how well an economic system avoids using persons as means to an end. A person is an end in himself. The just economic system, as Herberg explains, avoids what Marx called *Verding-lichung*, "converting a person into a thing," into a cog in a giant machine. On this basis, every economic system, whether Communist or capitalist, fails. Herberg believes that a new system, composed of the best elements of both socialism and capitalism, is possible. It would be buttressed by the recognition that economics is a branch of ethics, which in turn is a branch of theology. In this view, no doctrinaire system can be universally applicable. All that can be done is to adopt an economic system, with attendant institutions, that tends to enhance human freedom and to minimize the evil that can be done to the people of a society. Its goal would be to achieve a higher level of justice. Genuine justice cannot be realized in the present because it is an "eschatological reality," which can only be achieved in the future Kingdom of God. For the present, the Kingdom of God functions as an ideal of how people ought to live.

Although the Kingdom of God is in the future, it is nonetheless present as a judicatory factor in current relationships among the state, the society, and the individual. The idea of the essential equality of all people, according to Herberg, must be affirmed because we are all children of one God. From an empirical point of view, equality cannot be justified. It can only be justified by recognizing every individual's unique relationship with God. As Herberg notes, the Mishnah holds that the world was created for the sake of one individual person. Therefore, every other person ought to be treated not only as God's creature but also as a neighbor, no one elevated higher than any other. Only through sinful egocentricity does one deny this equality for another. For this reason, some coercive authority must be established in society to minimize this sinful egocentricity, to reduce the quantity of sinful acts that could otherwise occur. Government itself is necessary to maintain peace and justice, even though government itself reflects the radical ambiguity of human nature. Consequently, that state is best that protects its citizens and simultaneously guards against its own excesses of power. This view, in Herberg's opinion, is the essence of democracy: "So thoroughly aware is democracy at its best of the inevitable moral dubiousness of all government that it embodies the principle of resistance to government in the very structure of government itself" (p. 181).

Hebraic religion, as Herberg understands it, condemns the notion, so prevalent, that state and society are identical. On the contrary, Hebraic thought affirms that society is more than the state and that the individual person is more than both state and society. To affirm otherwise is to run the risk of totalitarianism, which equates society and state and denigrates the uniqueness of the person. Neither does Hebraic religion favor an atomistic individualism. Rather, it insists that man's uniqueness is found in his relationship with God and with the community of believers, a community that also transcends state and society. As such, it opposes the idolatries of every society and every state. It opposes all pretensions to absoluteness, the result of which can only be slavery. Thus, as Herberg concludes: "The political thought that derives from Hebraic religion is built on a series of antitheses. Man free under God is confronted by the coercive state, the individual person by the claims of society, the community of believers by the authority of the secular world; at every point, there is a tension and polarity that cannot be resolved through any dialectic. Each side has its right and its necessity, even though the two can never be fully reconciled in this world" (p. 188). The resolutions to the contradictoriness of life, whether social or individual, can only be achieved in the Kingdom of God. Truth cannot be achieved within history.

Yet, according to Herberg, history is not without meaning. The sense of history as reality, in contrast to the ahistorical view that human doings are part of the veil of maya, derives from the Hebrew prophets: "The prophets were the first authentic 'philosophers of history'" (p. 194). For them, God is the God of history. As such, history is not something from which people seek to escape— it is in the hands of the ultimate creator of all reality, the Living God, who has a purpose toward which history is moving. The future is consequently the means by which past and present are interpreted. History, for the Hebrews, is eschatological, not cyclical, as was the Greco-Oriental perspective. It is viewed, not in terms of a "this-worldly naturalism" or in terms of an "other-worldly idealism," but in terms of a "trans-worldly messianism" in which the events of history are affirmed as real and significant, moving toward the resolution of all ambiguity and contradictoriness in an "end," beyond history. The only modern views that closely approximate this Hebraic view are found in the philosophies of Marx and Nietzsche, although Herberg views their eschatologies as "corrupted." As a corrective for these corruptions, Herberg offers "the authentic concept of Hebraic eschatology" (p. 208).

Herberg explains that Hebraic thought emphasizes that history is the second stage of a three-phase process. The first is a Creation and the third is the Kingdom of God, both of which transcend history and yet give it its meaning. In the Garden of Eden story, all of the elements of the order of Creation were suggested, such as personhood, marriage, and community. At the same time, man's potential for *yetzer ha-ra*, for "sinfulness," was present. When this potential was actualized and self-interest became the prime human motivation, history began. And history is the outworking of that which occurred in the Fall of Man. As Herberg asserts: "History is thus the implementation of the order of creation through social activities and institutions, but in such an ambiguous way that the order of creation is thereby both effectuated and thwarted, both realized and perverted" (p. 214). The reason for this ambiguous condition and the motivating force of history is self-interest. One's own special interest or idea becomes a collective fixation. In this sense, according to Herberg, Marx was correct in asserting that history is the history of "class struggle." Marx erred only in limiting his approach to economics; in fact, every area of history and all human doings are tainted by self-interest and sin. The dialectic, which is not therefore an immanent principle within history itself, is the interaction and conflict of divine intention and human self-interest. Ultimately, however, divine intention will be enforced in the Kingdom of God, a vision of which can be comprehended in the present only through faith. History can only be redeemed by God.

Herberg maintains that Scripture and revelation, not reason, validate this Hebraic vision of history. Ideas such as God and freedom cannot be empirically verified; they can only be believed: "The affirmations of religion all hinge upon a crucial presupposition and commitment that emerges on a level far deeper than the rational processes of philosophy or science" (p. 243). Reason and science are useful in interpreting Scripture and tradition, but they do not constitute the normative standard of judgment. Rather, the normative standard is revelation and the affirmation that Scripture is a revelation of God.

Rejecting the fundamentalist conception that Scripture is the verbatim revelation of God and rejecting equally the modernist view that Scripture resulted from mere "inspiration" on the part of its writers, Herberg insists that Scripture is not equivalent to a revelation of God but is a human record of man's encounters with God. It is a human account of *Heilsgeschichte*, of "redemptive history," which can only be acknowledged by and interpreted through the eyes of faith. As such, Scripture promotes one unified theme, despite the seemingly bewildering patchwork of sources from which it derived—the theme of God's acts of judgment and redemption in relation to man. Scripture thus tells us what God does, not what he is, in a strictly metaphysical sense. It is "a record of God's 'mighty deeds' and therefore a revelation of his 'ways'" (p. 250). But it has nevertheless been written by the fallible hand of man. As Herberg explains, "The Bible is the word of God, but it is also the work of man: neither side of this double affirmation may be suppressed or ignored" (p. 250).

Because biblical revelation, according to Herberg, is "ineradicably particularistic," it is viewed as a "scandal" by the modern mind. It not only emphasizes that God has chosen a particular people but it also reveals that certain particular historical events are of greater significance than others. God elected the Jews the standard-bearers of redemption by means of a particular event that occurred on Mount Sinai. This event is as significant for the Jews as the Christ-event is for Christians. All other revelations of God, before and after that event, have meaning only in terms of that event. Herberg acknowledges that a "general" revelation of God does exist, if for no better reason than because man is defined *Homo religiosus*, from which definition one could conclude that all men search for God. Usually, however, the interpretation of this type of revelation leads to idolatry. To avoid error, one must turn to Scripture and understand, through faith, the "special" revelation first given to the people of Israel.

For Israel, the substance of religion is history. Herberg believed that the essence of Hebraic religion could not therefore be found in mystical illumination or by intellectual assent to a set of theological propositions. Rather, it was "faith enacted in history, not to be experienced, understood or communicated apart from that history" (p. 261). It is *Heilsgeschichte*—a redemptive history that is an integral part of corporate history and yet is transcendent, in its source, to history. Moreover, the world can be redeemed only through this history of Israel. This view describes the "scandal of particularity," that God would choose to reveal himself concretely to a particular people under particular circumstances. Just as people interact on a special basis under particular circumstances involving particular personalities, so does the Living God reveal Himself. In Jewish faith, God's personality was given concrete expression in the Exodus-Sinai events, which signified God's love, showing His redemptive activity, and created the people of Israel, by means of divine Covenant, a community of the elect. However, this particular Covenant with Israel has its universalistic overtones. It was a revelation not only *with* and *for* Israel but also *through* Israel to the world. As Herberg explains: "When the vocation of Israel is finally and completely fulfilled in the Kingdom of God at the 'end,' Israel will lose its reason for existence and all mankind will again be one" (pp. 268–69).

Israel consequently is a unique sociological phenomenon: it is an anomaly. A Jew is not a person who belongs to a particular race, nation, culture, religious denomination, or people, even though a Jew is in some sense all of these. Crucial to a definition of Jewishness is an awareness of Israel's "calling" as a "supernatural community" to serve God's purposes: "Apart from [the] covenant, Israel is a nothing and Jewish existence a mere delusion. The covenant is at the very heart of the Jewish self-understanding of its own reality" (p. 271). For this reason, Herberg maintains that anti-Semitism is the other side of the coin of Israel's calling: "Antisemitism is, at the bottom, the revolt of the pagan against the God of Israel and his absolute demand" (p. 273). Consequently, the Jews must contend with anti-Semitism until the "end," inasmuch as there is a constant revolt against the Living God. As perennial witness of this Living God, Israel can never live "normally" in the world; it cannot live as other nations. "Israel," Herberg holds, "lives in both time and eternity" (p. 275). In its relation to Zion it is bound to no land, whether that land is America, France, or even the state of Israel. Yet, Zion is the Promised Land in the fulfillment of the messianic prophecy. Meanwhile, prior to such fulfillment, Jewish existence centers on "both Zion and the Galut," living in dialectical tension between the two. As Herberg maintains, "The tension between the two can never be resolved in history" (p. 276). He thus considers erroneous the idea that the complete Jewish life can be lived only in the state of Israel. The faithful Jew, no matter where he or she lives, will always exist in tension with the social environment because the Jew lives on the supernatural level as well as on the natural level of human social existence. The Jew always lives in a state of ambiguity; and the state of Israel, "however highly we may regard it, is, after all, but another community of this world" (p. 278). The state of Israel is not identical to the Covenant-community. As members of the Covenant-community, the Jew feels solidarity with other Jews, regardless of the country in which they reside. They are bound together by the Covenant. Nevertheless, Zion is at the heart of the Hebraic eschatological vision of a "new age" in which Jerusalem will be proclaimed the center of the Kingdom of God. Thus, through the Covenant, the particular people of Israel will be the vehicle, "the operative instrumentality," by which the whole world will be redeemed. Through the *Torah*, Israel will be the focal point all should follow on this historical path toward salvation.

Herberg explains that *Torah*, in Hebraic religion, means not only "law" but also "teaching and way": "It is a book, an idea, a quality of life. It is the Pentateuch; the Bible in all its parts; the Bible and the rabbinical writings; all writings dealing with revelation; all reflection and tradition dealing with God, man and the world" (p. 286). *Torah* is *Heilsgeschichte*. The Jew becomes genuinely Jewish through "the process of *existential identification*"—by making the Jewish tradition part of himself, by personally appropriating redemptive history, "by *re-enacting in his own life* the redemptive career of Israel" (p. 288). Liturgically, this process is demonstrated in *Pesah*, *Shabuot*, and *Sukkot*, which represent the Exodus-Sinai events of Israel's redemptive history. Expanding on his original view of this subject, Herberg insists that these festivals are not merely rites of commemoration, but decisive moments in which eternity enters time. The significance of these events in the liturgy become part of the Jew's own being, "not figuratively, but actually, through existential 'repetition'" (p. 289). Ritual is thus the existential *acting-out* of one's religious convictions, and in this manner religion is not only a way of thinking but also a way of doing. In its liturgical tradition, Israel combines the divine and the human, the *Torah* as Teaching and Law. Accordingly, as Herberg holds, "Law and Teaching constitute two aspects of the same reality, and that reality in unity and synthesis, is Torah as Way" (p. 301). To this Way, the individual Jew must choose, and affirm his choice, to live under the Covenant and make it an active part of his or her life. A decision is required and is crucial to the Jew's entire being as one of God's Chosen People.

In Herberg's conclusion to *Judaism and Modern Man*, entitled "Faith for Living," he asserts that "the problem of religion is the problem of existence" (p. 307). It is, in the final analysis, a question of one's devotion and loyalty. As such, it is a problem of the relationship of man to God inasmuch as one is always in search of a "god." Hebraic religion insists that the true God is the God of Israel. All others are idols that entice their followers down false ways of redemption and salvation. To extricate oneself from this hopeless condition of idolatry, only a "return" to God will suffice. Active faith is an essential requirement for this "return"—it involves personal commitment and decision. It is "personal" because the God of Israel is no abstract principle but the living God of Abraham, Isaac, and Jacob. For the Jew, the entire story that makes up the Jewish tradition is "quite literally the substance of his personal biography" in which *Heilsgeschichte* is appropriated into his own life (p. 309). This attempt at appropriation is constant and requires a persistent battle against all idolatries and constant declarations of affirmation to the Living God.

Herberg thus believed that Hebraic religion was the only "philosophy of life" adequate for the current crisis of the modern world. Those who reviewed *Judaism and Modern Man* generally agreed with his position. Most of the major reviews were positive that the book would serve to secure an important position for Herberg among American theologians, both Jewish and Christian.[6] Milton Konvitz believed that Herberg was too gloomy in his theological perspective and that he had omitted the possibility that God could also be found through joy and laughter.[7] Nevertheless, Konvitz agreed that the book had placed Herberg in the company of such distinguished theologians as Buber, Schechter, and Leo Baeck. Similarly, a reviewer in the *San Francisco Chronicle*, identified only as "J. B.," held that Herberg's book was more scholarly and more profound than similar works by Milton Steinberg and Philip Bernstein. W. E. Garrison in the *Christian Century* proclaimed that Herberg, despite his background in the labor movement, was "no mere amateur theologian." Most agreed that *Judaism and Modern Man* was lucidly and persuasively written. One exception was Michael Fraenkel, who apparently found Herberg's neoorthodoxy somewhat distasteful: "Long on God, neoorthodoxy is very short indeed on man."

By far the most penetrating review was the one Reinhold Niebuhr wrote. Referring to Herberg as a "lay theologian," Niebuhr contended that the book might well become "a milestone in the religious thought of America." He called it "a book of great value" for those interested in either the Jewish or the Christian faith, and he argued that the book should not be neglected by Christians because the word "Judaism" appeared in the title. Although Niebuhr agreed with Herberg's equation of the Christian doctrine of Original Sin with the Jewish idea of the "evil imagination," he nonetheless would have appreciated some explicit consideration of the popular notion that the Jewish faith was more optimistic than the Christian. Moreover, Niebuhr felt that Herberg had not dealt adequately with the relationship of Christian and Jewish legalism to the prophetic principle. In this regard, Niebuhr wrote: "Mr. Herberg's method is not to challenge interpretations with which he disagrees explicitly, but to state his own with great force and cogency. It is a very good pedagogical method which may have the limitation of obscuring the point at issue to the uninitiated." Nevertheless, Niebuhr was quite certain that the book would stimulate not only believers but doubters as well. Thus, through *Judaism and Modern Man* and by means of such reviews, Herberg became one of America's significant Jewish theologians.

7
THEOLOGY
AND
SOCIETY
1951–1955

Although *Judaism and Modern Man* served to make Herberg known as a theologian, it did not immediately serve to obtain an academic post for him. He had offered courses on a part-time basis at the New School of Social Research in 1948 and 1949 on the topics "The Philosophy of History from Augustine to Toynbee" and "Twentieth Century Philosophers." Meanwhile, his duties with the International Ladies Garment Workers Union (ILGWU) diminished to the point where, by 1954, his salary from the union amounted to only $320 and his occupation was listed on his income tax return as "writer and lecturer." Lecturing on college campuses and before religious organizations occupied much of his time, taking him to such diverse colleges and universities as Berkeley, Stanford, Iowa, Occidental, and Brandeis. His lecture tour of March 1952 was not entirely atypical—he participated in "40 lectures and discussions at 12 institutions in just over three weeks."[1] For a little over a year, he was editor of *Judaism: A Quarterly Journal of Jewish Life and Thought*. But by far his greatest effort was expended in writing articles concerned with theological issues and with the relationship of religion and society, presenting biblical doctrines without compromise and without dilution.[2]

THEOLOGIANS AND PROPHETIC RELIGION

Never far from the central theme of his first book, Herberg continued to emphasize the importance of a faith based on the biblical tradition as the only means by which one could meet the crises of the age.[3] Because he focused his attention on biblical faith, Herberg rejected the argument of cultural relativism that all theologies were of equal validity. His opposition to this position had a twofold basis: not all religious experiences were the same and, even if they were, not all theologies were equally valid. Rudolph Otto had already shown that religious experiences possessed certain definable characteristics, but this assertion did not mean that all religious experiences were the same. Just as there were different kinds of aesthetic experiences, so there were different kinds of religious experiences. Moreover, different people described similar experiences in different ways, and, as a consequence, different theories arose. In this sense, some theories were better than others. Likewise, in religion, according to Herberg, different theologies had to be clarified, not by culture, but by the categories of theology themselves: "The autonomy of the religious cannot be denied." And if there were different types of religious experience, it followed that some theologies were "relatively more true" than others. Herberg insisted that this belief did not mean that some theologies were absolute and infallible but simply that some were more adequate. The crucial error of cultural relativism for Herberg lay in its holding that, because no theology was infallible, all theologies were of equal adequacy.

To explain what he meant by a more adequate theology, Herberg compared Islam to the biblical tradition. For him, the crucial difference between the two perspectives came down to the fact that Islam had no sense of *Heilsgeschichte*. It knew God as sovereign Lord but not as Redeemer. In Herberg's perspective, Islam, even in it most mystical tradition, as in Sufism, forfeited the genuine faith of the biblical tradition. As such, Islam was a Jewish-Christian heresy, differing little from Oriental pantheistic mysticism, and was essentially like all other "paganized salvation cults." In this regard, Islam was, Herberg maintained, "an unbalanced, one-sided development of an authentic aspect of Biblical faith."

Herberg discerned that there were two ways of faith (both of which he had discussed in *Judaism and Modern Man*), which he now discussed in the Tillichian categories of autonomy, heteronomy, and theonomy. The two ways of faith consisted of the biblical approach, which was existential, and the Greco-Oriental approach, which he now described as "mystical self-deification." The former was based on transcendence, whereas the latter was based essentially on immanence. The first represented a theonomous faith that opposed philosophical totalism as idolatrous. It used reason but recognized the limits of reason: "Reason is needed to bring man to an understanding of his situation and thus to the point of decision; to define and illumine the terms of the decision of faith; and to elicit the implications and consequences of such decision. It cannot, however, either determine the decision of faith, which is a genuine 'leap,' or prove its assurances." Referring to the theonomous approach as "objective relativism," Herberg held that it was opposed equally to the pitfalls of absolutism and cultural relativism while preserving the positive elements of each in dialectical tension. Likewise, he viewed ethical humanism as self-defeating, leading either to self-righteousness or to complete despair. As a consequence, he stated, "ethics, too, raises the 'question of God.'" Biblical or theonomous faith was avowedly "a God-centered (objective) relativism." Religion, in this view, was not identifiable with any particular culture, nor was it in total opposition to it. Rather, genuine religion was in a state of dialectical tension with its culture, both for and against it, depending on the issue at hand. In this manner religion operated as the central integrating principle of a culture and as such pointed also to God. In our age, in Herberg's estimation, we have witnessed the collapse of a culture based on human autonomy and have observed the horrors of heteronomous cultures such as Nazi Germany and Stalinist Russia. The only hope for overcoming the anxieties and insecurity of the age would be to accept decisively the implications of theonomous culture. Existential anxiety could not be cured by technology or psychotherapy but by a "transcendental ground of integration in life beyond all the forces of disintegration that threaten us in our actual existence."

One of the most significant characteristics of theonomous or biblical faith, Herberg asserted, was its prophetic principle, its opposition to everything that was not God, whether a person, an idea, an institution, or a social and political movement. According to Herberg, the prophetic faith recognized that God was the only absolute—all else was to be perceived and experienced relative to God. Citing William James, Herberg agreed that God was the "Great Relativizer." In this perspective, communism, scientism, liberal humanism, fascism, and rationalism had all become the ersatz, idolatrous religions of the age. Even belief in democracy could become an idolatrous ideology. At the heart of all these "false faiths" was secularism, "man's belief that he is ultimate, the supreme power in the universe, entirely sufficient unto himself." Against these erroneous paths, Herberg offered prophetic religion, a God-centered relativism that proclaimed that "there is no salvation in history, but also no escape from it." As such, it was a religion of commitment and decision, one that affirmed both the love of God and the love of fellowman and protected against both cynicism and utopianism.

The key word for understanding prophetic religion for Herberg was still *Heilsgeschichte*, "redemptive history." Rejecting what he called the "heathen" view that reality was nature and the Greco-Oriental view that reality was the timelessly eternal, Herberg described the biblical view of the psychophysical unity of man. Man was truly part of nature yet transcendent to it in his capacity for freedom. Herberg maintained that, with this biblical view of the nature of man, man could for the first time be described as a genuinely personal and historical being: "History is the very stuff out of which human being is made:

human existence is potential or implicit history; history is potential or actualized existence." In sum, in Herberg's view we define ourselves by our history. Some only defined themselves in terms of partial histories, such as the history of America, and the result was the idolatry of Americanism. In this sense, one could make the history of America one's *Heilsgeschichte*, replete with holidays, symbols, and liturgy. Of course, this would be idolatry. Biblical faith, in contrast, was concerned with the history of God's involvement with his people. This history was represented in the rites of worship and the holidays of God's people and the hope that God has given them: "Remembrance and expectation are the two foci of existence in faith." This faith was appropriated in decision making and in action based on that decision made. In this manner, "sacred history" could become one's own history.

History also functioned for Herberg as the most essential element of hermeneutics. He defined hermeneutics as "the disciplined procedure for understanding man through his works. In other words, hermeneutics is an inquiry into the meaning of an artifact." In theology it has been directed toward interpreting the Bible, having raised the question about the meaning of a text, what the text really said, and what the text wanted to say. Early Christian hermeneutical methods were of two types. The allegorical approach, as utilized by Philo of Alexandria and Origen, sought to delineate the timeless metaphysical principles of a biblical story. The typological approach, as utilized by Chrysostom and the school of Antioch, insisted on a literal meaning of a biblical story while emphasizing the historical mode of understanding, presuming that an event foreshadowed the coming of a subsequent event. According to Herberg, the allegorical method prevailed through the Middle Ages, but with the Reformation the typological method grew more preponderant.

Herberg considered the nineteenth-century philosopher Wilhelm Dilthey the first to develop systematically the principles of hermeneutics. Following Vico and Hegel, Dilthey distinguished between historical doings and occurrences of nature, the latter having no meaning for man. Man could only *verstehen*, "understand," human doings, in the sense that, like an actor, he has *erleben*, "lived through," similar human doings—or could at least imagine living through them. Conversely, a person would not even imagine what it was like to be an object of nature, such as a stone. According to Dilthey, man's understanding was therefore restricted to historical understanding. Herberg explained that for Dilthey there were three manifestations of *Geist*, "the human spirit": human actions, human concepts, and the synthesis of these, *Lebensausserungen*, "life expressions." Hermeneutics was largely concerned with the latter, Herberg asserted, which was expressed largely in poetry, art, music, and the like. With this category, man was viewed neither as an object nor as a subject but rather transjectively, that is, through interpersonal relationships, in which one person could understand another person through intuition or insight or divination. In such a manner would an actor attempt to understand a character in a play. In the same manner, through sympathetic understanding a person could understand another person, whether from the past or in the present. With respect to a biblical text, Herberg pointed out that, for Dilthey, we could only get answers to a text if we asked certain questions beforehand that would permit us to be aware of our own preunderstanding of the text. Hermeneutical understanding was thus always historical understanding that contained three kinds of personal knowledge, namely, autobiography, biography, and historiography. Indeed, as Herberg reiterated, we have come to know God historically.

Taking Dilthey's perspective, Herberg considered the hermeneutical approach of the New Testament scholar, Rudolph Bultmann, to be inadequate. First of all, Herberg believed that Bultmann had overestimated the importance of the three-storied view of the universe for the writers of the New Testament. According to Herberg, Paul knew that the earth was round, as did the Greeks. But Herberg's stronger disagreement with Bultmann centered on his deviation from Dilthey. Both Dilthey and Bultmann agreed that a person came to a text with his own set of presuppositions, of which that reader should be aware. Yet Bultmann contended that a person should attempt to understand the New Testament only if he was seeking answers to the ultimate questions of human existence, with a concomitant desire to achieve "authentic existence." As Herberg explained Bultmann, "Only those who are existentially committed can understand." This approach, according to Herberg, was unnecessary. Rather one could say with Dilthey, "I am a human being and, because of affinity with other human beings, can understand expressions of their life." Herberg thus believed that there were "shared meanings" among people of seemingly different philosophical and theological perspectives and that we therefore could understand their positions without being committed to them ourselves. In the case of comprehending the New Testament, it was a matter not of commitment but of first-rate interpretation.

Although he disagreed with Bultmann about an appropriate hermeneutical method, Herberg had comparatively little quarrel with the theology of Reinhold Niebuhr.[4] He read Niebuhr's works, underlined them heavily, but added little in the margins by way of critical comment. His comments about Niebuhr were for the most part written in superlatives: "Niebuhr [is] the most creative and powerful theologian in America today—and already a national and world influence." His theology was "directly relevant to man's actual historical existence and problems." Herberg believed that Niebuhr's book *Faith and History* was his most important work next to *The Nature and Destiny of Man*; it was "the completion of a grand design." Herberg approached his own understanding of Marxism from a Niebuhrian point of view: "Marxism is of the 'children of light'—but Soviet Communism is a force of the 'children of darkness' which 'perverts' Marxism." Given the differences between the theologies of Niebuhr and Karl Barth, Herberg defended Niebuhr thus: "Barth has pushed the transcendental pole of his dialectic so far as to destroy the dialectic and make his theology irrelevant to discriminate judgments between the better and the worse in the actual world. Hence his 'abstentionism' and 'neutralism.'" Niebuhr's influence on Herberg can also be observed in Herberg's understanding of the nature of love and the self.

For Herberg, the nature of love was closely related to the self.[5] He defined love by means of the Greek terms *eros*, *philia*, and *agape*, or striving, mutuality, and "heedless, uncalculating self-giving," respectively. *Eros* and *philia* could be found among humankind, whereas *agape*, according to Herberg, was characteristic only of a redemptive God. As he wrote, "In the Bible, [*agape*] means the power of God in redemptive love: it is strictly God-descending, 'supernatural.'" Therefore, *agape* was the action of God's grace, given gratuitously to man. Where *agape* could be found in man, it was solely because of God's grace, it was "God's power in man." Because even the man of faith was riddled with sin, the *agape* of grace in man was still mixed with *eros* and *philia*, "no matter how high the level of love achieved." Nevertheless, if it were not for *agape*, *eros* and *philia* would destroy themselves. Niebuhr, in Herberg's estimation, expressed this viewpoint "with consummate insight and skill." *Agape* was the grounding of human character and the basis for any social cohesion. The danger in overemphasizing *eros* lay in the possibility that it could lead to autonomous social atomism. The danger of overstressing *philia* derived from the fact that it could lead to destructive collectivism, to what David Riesman called "other-directedness." In either case, a lack of transcendence existed that could only be provided by a redemptive God whose love was described as *agape*. The absence of this notion of transcendence had led many contemporary thinkers to erroneous perspectives in regard to love, man, and society.

Herberg's understanding of the relationship of love and society to the transcendent led him to criticize some of the philosophers and literati of the century.[6] He considered Jean-Paul Sartre to be a "muddle-head" whose writings were "at best, literature—at worst, journalism—rarely, philosophy." More to the point, Herberg described Sartre's philosophy as an attempt to equate the transcendent with nothingness, whereby man himself achieved that status of the transcendent and became identified with God. Ludwig Wittgenstein and his followers not only were guilty of not having any technical philosophical vocabulary with which to understand linguistic analysis but also actually had no use "for any vocabulary in the last analysis." And the major error of philosophers of science and those who made an absolute out of the scientific method was that they were seemingly unaware of their own presuppositions. According to Herberg, modern science was based on three major metaphysical assumptions: (1) the reality of the external world, (2) the knowability of the external world, and (3) the uniformity in nature, that is, that there is a natural or preordained harmony in nature. In comparison, the major difficulty with art was that it presented the world as if Paradise still existed. In other words, art implicitly presupposed that the Fall of Man never occurred and thus denied the sinfulness of man.

Herberg was less critical of some novelists, especially of George Orwell and Franz Kafka. Although Orwell only vaguely understood the significance of the Christian faith and although he frequently bordered on an irrational anti-Catholicism, he nevertheless acutely perceived that when people stopped worshipping God they made a god out of man. Because of this insight, Herberg wrote of Orwell that he was "surely not far from the seat of under-standing and grace." Kafka, on the other hand, was "the poet of the everyday-fantastic." According to Herberg, his works could be viewed on three levels: (1) on the personal-psychological level as a manifestation of the father complex, (2) on the sociopolitical level, and (3) on the metaphysical-religious level. Herberg stressed that to interpret Kafka's works on the first two levels at the expense of the third constituted a serious mistake: "Kafka was at bottom a passionate God-seeker, a searcher into the mysteries of human life and destiny." For example, Herberg pointed out, any interpretation of *The Castle* without a consideration of its metaphysical overtones would be like regarding *Pilgrim's Progress* as a commentary on the perils of traveling. *The Trial,* according to Herberg, was the most profound of Kafka's works from a theological point of view. Indeed, Herberg considered it a modern equivalent to the Job story. As he remarked concerning the execution scene in this novel, "The moment of divine punishment, of execution, is also the moment of final hope." What Kafka described was the dehumanization of modern man, and, according to Herberg, "the Church is the only institution that can challenge the dehumanization of the world."

PSYCHOLOGY
AND THEOLOGY

Herberg's interpretation of the theory of Jules H. Masserman was significant for its delineation of the relationship between theology and psychology. Masserman had published an article in the *American Journal of
Psychiatry* entitled "Faith and Delusion in Psychotherapy: The Ur-Defenses of
Man." In it Masserman sought to reverse the Freudian view that religious
"delusions" should be eliminated. Instead, he recommended that such psychological needs as the desire for immortality, for an "omnipotent servant," and
for human charitableness were essential elements of human psychology. Thus,
far from condemning these so-called delusions, as Freud had suggested, Masserman wanted to embrace them, and he thereby sought to vindicate religion.
These "ur-defenses," in Masserman's view, were as essential to man's psychology as respiration and nutrition were to the body. Thus, Herberg concluded, "Masserman's analysis constitutes a vindication of religion against the
psychoanalytic rationalists." However, Masserman's vindication of religion
was not a vindication of biblical religion. The beliefs that Masserman attempted to vindicate were, in Herberg's opinion, precisely the beliefs that
biblical religion rejected. For example, in Herberg's view the Bible categori-
cally rejected the notion of immortality in favor of a belief in the resurrection
of the body. The Bible also rejected the notion of an "omnipotent servant" who
cared for an individual. Actually, the Bible maintained that man was servant or
slave to the commands of God. And in contrast to the desire for human
charitableness, the Bible spoke of the sinfulness of man and cautioned against
placing too much reliance on human goodwill. In fact, so far was he from
agreeing with Masserman's understanding of religion that Herberg maintained
that the Bible taught antireligion.

Herberg insisted that all that Masserman had done was to provide a justification for "natural religion," not biblical religion. In short, Masserman had
substantiated that man was *Homo religiosus*. Man has always searched for a
god, Herberg pointed out, but this god has invariably been, from a biblical
point of view, an idol, for the simple reason that this god has been self-
centered and man-centered. But biblical faith was God-centered to Herberg,
and a God-centered faith called into question the very kind of security that
natural religion sought to secure. In this measure, biblical religion was anti-
religious. Biblical faith, Herberg wrote, "is indeed a faith whose very purpose
it is to 'end' all religion and bring man directly under the command, judgment,
and redeeming grace of God." The "peace that passeth understanding" could

arrive only after all human pretensions to security had been either destroyed or abandoned. As a consequence, Herberg concluded that Freud, with his rejection of religion, was closer to a biblical position than Masserman who sought to justify religion. The only difficulty with Freud's antireligion was his faith in science, which biblical faith opposed, not to mention the fact that it represented simply another form of idolatry. As Herberg explained, even Marx, with his notion of religion as the "opium of the people," a phrase he unwittingly borrowed from Charles Kingsley, was proclaiming an aspect of the biblical faith.

RELIGION IN AMERICA

Herberg thus believed that the biblical faith was the "religion to end all religions." And he was especially pleased that, in America, interest and involvement in religion were on the rise.[7] In his opinion, Chad Walsh's *Campus Gods on Trial* was "a work of apologetics in the better sense of the term" because it attacked the campus idols of progress, despair, humanitarianism, Americanism, and communism. Herberg's major disappointment with Walsh's book focused on its failure to deal adequately with the situation of religion in America, specifically with the rising tide of religious involvement and the concomitant decline of secularism. Herberg held that concern with religion was widespread on college campuses, even if the interest was expressed in nonbiblical terms. All people had their religion, for, as Herberg cited Dostoevsky, "Man must worship something; if he does not worship God, he will worship an idol made of wood or of gold or of ideas." Likewise, the college student of Herberg's day sought religion. But he was no longer secure with the utopianism of a Woodrow Wilson or a Karl Marx. Unlike the students of the 1920s, Herberg maintained, the student of the early 1950s did not smugly assume that he could solve the riddles of the universe. As a consequence, he was, as Ludwig Lewisohn said, "accessible to good." These students were accordingly more open to the prophetic faith of both Judaism and Christianity.

Herberg believed that a religious revival could be witnessed not only on college campuses but throughout the entire country as well. Between 1940 and 1954, church attendance increased at the rate of 2 percent a year, which growth, according to Herberg, was "the most rapid in all our history." And even most of those who had not been counted in the church-attendance statis-

tics considered themselves to be religious. Yet religious tensions between
Protestants and Catholics and between Catholics and Jews also increased.
These tensions included that fringe of American Protestantism that supported
segregation of the Negro, anti-Semitism, and anti-Catholicism. At the same
time, many Protestants had also exhibited a dangerous bias toward communism, demonstrated by their attitude of liberal toleration of that ideology. As
Herberg explained, Protestants were taught that communism was a Christian
heresy, and, because they did not take heresy very seriously, they were inclined to tolerate this one. Even Karl Barth, in Herberg's estimation, was
"abysmally wrong on the kind of menace Communism represents." Herberg
thus believed that Protestant ministers were particularly vulnerable to the lure
of communism.

Herberg discussed this topic before the seminarians of Andover-Newton
Theological School in December 1953, in a lecture entitled "Christian Faith
and Worldly Wisdom: A Word in Season to Some Protestant Seminarians." In
his talk, he maintained that Protestant ministers, as well as Jewish rabbis, were
often conspicuous "dupes" of Communist-front organizations. One of the
major reasons for this kind of development, according to Herberg, was that
Protestant clergymen and Jewish rabbis represented the quintessence of the
educated middle class. Thus, they reflected the sympathies of that class,
including a high-minded idealism. As Herberg noted: "It is no accident that, as
all public opinion polls agree, the educated middle class has been most consistently and abysmally wrong in its views and expectations about public affairs
in our time." This class, Herberg pointed out, greatly appreciated the efforts of
Hitler and Mussolini. The result was a religious "liberalism" that degraded the
content of the biblical faith—the biblical view of man and of the world was
overlooked. These ministers and rabbis had in effect become as secularistic in
their outlook as the rest of the population. Stripped of their theological content, the sermons of ministers and rabbis had become little more than innocent
meanderings on "ideals" and "values." Hence, Herberg felt strongly that an
irresponsible naïveté resulted.

This same secularist attitude had led to conflicts between Christians and
Jews. For example, Paul Blanshard's "vulgar anti-Catholic bias" was a consequence of his secular-statist philosophy. According to Herberg, Blanshard
implied that Romanism was equated with communism and thus anti-Ameri-
canism. The tensions reflected in this kind of error resulted whenever the issue
of church-state relations was raised, and in America it had been focused on the
problem of education. Herberg showed that, from the first, the American
educational system was the creation of American Protestantism. Originally the

word "nonsectarian," when applied to schools, did not mean "nonreligious" but rather non-Baptist, non-Methodist, and so on. In other words, nonsectarian meant "Christian and Protestant." When Catholic and Jewish immigrants first entered the public school system, the Protestant character of the system was affected. Education became associated with a "secularist" perspective, free of religious tutelage. The interpretation of the idea expressed in the word religion became a private affair. And by the 1920s the phrase "separation of Church and State" had become the byword of the secularists. Many Protestants adopted this attitude as a bulwark against what they feared of Roman Catholicism. Many Jews also adopted this secularist principle, which sadly could become idolatrous and could lead to the kind of tragedy that Jews later experienced in Nazi Germany. Herberg saw signs, however, of positive change. Even secularists were beginning to recognize the importance of religion. Protestants were reassessing their relationship to Catholicism. Catholics were attempting to adapt to a pluralistic society. And Jews were once again embracing their heritage. In passing through all the changes, Herberg held that following the biblical tradition would instill the proper confidence.

THE MEANING OF "JEWISHNESS"

To understand Herberg's position on biblical faith requires an understanding of his position on what it meant to be a Jew.[8] Here again, he insisted that "Jewishness" could be understood not in terms of a culture, a denomination, or a nation but only in relation to the Covenant. Because the Jew lived in both eternity and time, the Jew in time could only be seen as a concrete expression of a historical form that consequently was transient, relative, and localized. But, without the Covenant, the Jews had no common bond, a bond that could not be identified merely with the state of Israel. As Herberg wrote: "What makes Israeli Jews the norm? This criterion of the 'authenticity' of Jewish faith seems to me quite false." In Israel, Herberg claimed, the culture was essentially secularistic, a result of British hegemony in the 1940s. With regard to religion in Israel, he added, Orthodoxy exercised a monopoly that led many of the young people to consider religion as a vestige of the European ghettos. More importantly for Herberg, religion was viewed from the point of view of rigid legalistic ritualism and not as an existential encounter between God and man. As he pointed out, Martin Buber was without influence in the land where he lived and wrote. Consequently, Herberg held, Jewishness could only be understood from a theological point of view.

To attempt to deal with Jewish existence on any other than theological grounds resulted necessarily, according to Herberg, "in dangerous distortion and falsification." He agreed with the sociologist Carl Mayer that Jewish people were indeed unique, but he went on to elaborate that their uniqueness derived from a transcendent reality that underlay all of their varied manifestations as a culture, a race, a people, or a religion. Jews did not even constitute a "nation": "[Judaism] is a supernatural community, called into being by God to serve his eternal purposes in history. It is a community created by God's special act of covenant, first with Abraham whom he 'called' out of the heathen world and then, supremely, with Israel collectively at Sinai." Without the Covenant, Israel was nothing; the Covenant was at the very heart of the Jews' self-understanding. Any individual Jew was under the Covenant whether he liked it or not or whether he knew it or not. Just as a son could never alter the objective fact that he was a son, so the Jew was always a Jew under the Covenant. This was "an objective supernatural fact." To live an authentic life, the Jew must affirm and accept with responsibility his own Jewishness. And Jewish destiny centered on no particular nation but on both Zion and Galut, which should not be confused with the present state of Israel. To interpret the state of Israel as the final dissolution of the Galut was, Herberg held, "a new version of false messianism." Whatever happened to the state of Israel, the Covenant was eternal, and this Covenant was the foundation of Israel, which was also eternal. For this reason, to establish a lasting Jewish community on a secular basis was impossible.

The major difficulty with most American forms of Judaism in the modern world was that they had for the most part remained unaffected by neoorthodox theology. As Herberg more poignantly expressed it: "With little exception, present-day American Jewish religious thinking—Orthodox, Conservative, and Reform—remains 'liberal' in the worst sense of the word: man-centered rather than God-centered, immanentist rather than transcendental, idealistic rather than biblical, psychological rather than theological, speculative and 'philosophical' rather than existential." Secularism had affected all three forms of American Jewry. The Orthodox and Conservative tended toward routinism, and the Reform tended toward ethical monotheism. The former lacked spontaneity, and the latter lacked more traditional approaches. What was needed, in Herberg's opinion, was a dialectical interaction between tradition and spontaneity: "It is just as one-sided to hold that, in principle, religious tradition has no independent efficacy, but is merely a 'superstructural ideology,' as it is to hold that religious institutions are essentially nothing more than the embodiment of religious 'philosophies' or attitudes." The tradition, and the institutions founded on that tradition, had to leave room for the spontaneity of attitudes that were molded and profoundly shaped by the institutions and the traditions. But Herberg always worried most that self-centeredness would substitute for God-centeredness.

Herberg, however, did not entirely denigrate American Judaism. The most forceful sign of hope, he felt, came from the youth and from some Jewish scholars.[9] Martin Buber, although not an American, was "one of the greatest minds of our time" and ought to be read despite his gnostic and mystical overtones. Milton Steinberg was a man of most notable gifts and a person whom Herberg considered a friend, despite their differences. Steinberg had, in Herberg's opinion, adhered too closely to a Reconstructionist approach and was thus suffering from a "hidden secularism" that did not allow him to get to the heart of Jewish faith. Steinberg was, however, gradually discarding his "Hellenic" approach to theology just before his premature death at age forty-six. Herberg also considered some of the writings of Abraham Joshua Heschel significant—not entirely for their content, which contained some flaws, but because they would appeal to the "post-modern" person who searched for the substance of life even more than to the secular-minded person of the first half of the century. Because Herberg opposed the secularist movement of the early part of the century, he placed his hope for American Judiasm in the Jewish youth. In the 1920s, assimilation of Jews into American society was the desire of many, to the point that some predicted the dissolution of American Jewry. However, by the 1950s younger Jews were returning to Judaism as a means of self-identification. Although they had not as yet returned to the authentic Jewish tradition, there was nevertheless a new Jew emerging, free of the secularism of some of the synagogues and keenly interested in the genuine faith of the Jewish tradition, which was now being threatened not only by anti-Semitism, a perennial problem, but also by communism.

THE THREAT OF
ANTI-SEMITISM AND
COMMUNISM

Herberg considered anti-Semitism on the wane in America, where it was considered to be undemocratic and un-American.[10] Nevertheless, anti-Semitism still constantly menaced the Jew. Theologically the Jew always lived in a given society but was not of it. Consequently, the Jew remained "marginal" in every society and could never become completely acclimated to any particular one. His very being was transnational, transsocial, and transcultural, and as such he was always an outsider, an alien, a stranger, a sojourner, who called into question the world's idolatries. At the same time, the Jew lived in constant danger of becoming a "scapegoat," especially in monolithic societies such as Communist Russia. According to Herberg, communism, which should not be equated with Marxism, stressed hatred and held the notion of human rights completely irrelevant to itself. In Russia, Zionism was an "intolerable challenge" to the Communist system. As a result, anti-Semitism became an integral part of the Russian Communist culture, in which the Jew was regarded as a possible danger to the self-deifying state. In a pluralistic society such as America, the Jew could live with greater security because Protestants, Catholics, and Jews were all generally tolerated: "For better or for worse, the future of the Jew in America is bound up with America's future." For this reason, the Communist threat to America was also a threat to the American Jew.

Protestants and Catholics were of course not immune to anti-Semitism.[11] In essential agreement with Barth, Tillich, Maritain, and Berdyaev, Herberg declared that anti-Semitism was at heart anti-Christian. What had originally occurred, he believed, was that the Jew with his belief in God confronted the pagan with his paganism, and the pagan, as a result, became a Christian. Christianity therefore maintained itself by retaining its essential identification with Judaism. Anti-Semitism thus occurred when the Christian relapsed into paganism, Herberg explained; anti-Semitism was equally anti-Christian. It resulted when Protestants and Catholics emphasized the differences and overlooked the essential unity of Judaism and Christianity. According to Herberg, one of the consequences of the Nazi holocaust was to bring this point to the forefront of mass consciousness: "For the believing Christian, as for the believing Jew, there comes a point where, in order to understand his own faith, he must understand and come to terms with the faith of the other. This would appear to be obvious from the very nature of the two faiths." The unity of and the differences between Judaism and Christianity must be viewed in their proper perspectives.

JUDAISM AND
CHRISTIANITY

The unity of Christianity and Judaism had as its basis the double-covenant theory, whereby God had one covenant with the Hebrews and another with some of the Gentiles. From this perspective Judaism and Christianity were for Herberg "virtually identical in their structure of faith." In an argument reminiscent of his 1943 essay "The Christian Mythology of Socialism," Herberg listed ten points of structural identity: (1) they both believed in the God of Abraham, Isaac, and Jacob; (2) they both viewed Abraham's Covenant with God as crucial to the break from the pagan world; (3) they both agreed that God revealed himself in an encounter with man and through Scripture; (4) they both viewed man as a unitary creature and rejected a mystical or naturalistic dualism; (5) they both held that man's sin spoiled primal Creation, which was therefore in need of redemption; (6) they both viewed the world as God's creation and therefore subordinate to God; (7) they both had an ethic based on obedience to God; (8) they both were eschatological; (9) they both agreed that faith was expressed through a community and that Israel was the elect community of God; and (10) they both were historical religions in which history was viewed from the perspective of *Heilsgeschichte*, looking to a single event as the instrument of redemption.

But for all these similarities, Christianity and Judaism also differed on some important points. Herberg, citing Hans-Werner Bartsch, disagreed with the notion that Judaism was a religion of law while Christianity was a religion of grace: "The fact of the matter is that the demand of law and the gospel of grace are to be found in both religions; indeed, as Luther once exclaimed, where is the man who can properly distinguish between law and gospel?" The distinction between the two religions, for Herberg, lay in their respective relationships to the Covenant, which was "the central category of biblical thinking." Through the Covenant, Israel, as God's people, would be the vehicle whereby all of mankind would be brought under that Covenant. This path to redemption, however, did not require that all people must join with the Jewish people. Rather, through Christianity, Gentiles could become part of the Covenant community: "God's covenant with Israel is opened to all mankind through Christ." By becoming a member of the church, of the "Body of Christ," the Gentile, in effect, became an Israelite by participating in a new covenant. But the new covenant did not supplant the old one. Instead, Judaism had the task of "facing inward" toward the Jews, whereas Christianity "faces outward" toward the Gentiles. Nevertheless, Judaism and Christianity thus "represent one religious reality."

In this view, the major differences between Judaism and Christianity lay in differences of mediation, vocation, and orientation. In terms of the first, one's relationship to God was mediated through the People of Israel, but, in Christianity, it was through Christ. The Jew was consequently oriented toward Israel and the Christian toward Christ, with the former focusing on the Sinai-event and the latter on the Christ-event. In terms of vocation, the Jew witnessed for God by virtue of his very being whereas the Christian was commanded to go out and conquer the world for Christ. As such, the Jew as Jew was a constant reminder of God, but the Christian was constantly in danger of lapsing back into paganism. So one was either a Jew, a Christian, or a pagan, depending on one's status vis-à-vis the Covenant. Neither Judaism nor Christianity was better than the other, but both were better than paganism.

SECULARISM
IN EDUCATION

Herberg believed pagan tendencies in the Western world revealed themselves in secularism, in the belief in a self-sufficiency without God. One ongoing source of concern was what he perceived as a creeping secularism, especially in the American educational system.[12] Herberg felt that, in setting educational policy, the secularist sought to promote morality in the system while trying to separate morality from religion. From a Jewish point of view, such an approach was quite simply unacceptable, for religion "is quite literally the pre-supposition of all education, as it is of all thinking and living." One therefore could not ask the school systems to teach morality without religion. To attempt to do so was to advocate a separation of religion from life, and this was impossible; for, as Herberg believed, "a set of ultimate beliefs and convictions about man and the universe underlies every important part of the educational program and the educational enterprise as a whole." The beliefs and convictions were essentially religious, and teaching without beliefs and convictions simply could not be done. An academic discipline that strove to carry on the educational enterprise without religious presuppositions in Herberg's view became autonomous and subsequently would develop a philosophy that would apply to all of reality. In short, it would develop a theology, or at least "theological pretensions." Where traditional religion was ignored, as in the sciences, a "counter-religion," such as naturalism or positivism, acted as a substitute. From the point of view of biblical theology, such views were both religious and idolatrous. As Herberg exclaimed, "It is my contention that Goethe . . . is to be judged by Isaiah, Shelley and Browning by Paul, rather than the reverse."

Unlike some fundamentalists and religious liberals, Herberg insisted that secular approaches to education and the approach of biblical faith were not "irretrievably divorced." He did not recommend the retrieval of a "Medieval synthesis" as the ideal for education inasmuch as medieval culture, despite its popular image, was a heteronomous, not theonomous, culture. Herberg pointed out that modern culture was basically autonomous, characterized by emphasis on the scientific method. To this culture, biblical faith offered a dialectical yes and no. With regard to empiricism, for example, biblical faith agreed that the empirical world was the real world, but it also added that the world was created by God and was therefore neither ultimate nor self-sufficient. With regard to determinism, the biblical faith agreed that man was a natural organism but added that man was also characterized by self-transcendence. With regard to relativism, the biblical faith agreed with the "conditionedness of all human life" but added that the absolutization of the relative was sheer idolatry. With regard to progressivism, the biblical faith opposed the cyclical view of history and accepted the linear view of an ultimate consummation of history—but condemned the view that history brought its own redemption and fulfillment, which could only come from God. Finally, the scientific claim to total autonomy was rejected outright: "It is simply not true that science is a self-enclosed, self-validated, self-sufficient whole." It too depended on assumptions and postulates that were "essentially extra-scientific" and that had not been validated, such as the notion of an orderly universe, already criticized by Hume and Whitehead. On the other hand, biblical faith could not challenge science's competence in gathering factual evidence, but it could provide a standpoint by which scientists could be prevented from falling prey to the absolutization of science. Given such criticisms of modern culture, Herberg recommended a "biblical theology of education."

By a "biblical theology of education" Herberg meant the "attempt to define the nature and meaning of education in terms congenial to the categories of biblical faith" in order to bring education under the command, judgment, and redeeming grace of God. To describe this approach to education, Herberg contrasted it with the classical Greek educational ideal. For the latter, the goal of education was to exercise one's reason in order to discover the eternal verities and values. Education thus had the function of *paideia*, "self-cultivation," culminating in the unity of the soul under the rule of reason for the purpose of creating good citizens within the polis. The result of this approach to education was, in Herberg's view, a "civic totalitarianism," in which the individual was totally absorbed into society. Through education the individual freed himself from the enslavement of ignorance and illusion. In so doing, he realized his own *humanum*, "humanness," within the context of the polis.

In contrast, the biblical-realist view of education stressed not a contemplative, but an active life of decision, one of willing, of acting, and of being. The emphasis was on the heart rather than on the mind. Man's worth was transcendent not only to nature but also to society. Accordingly, humanness was achieved through a right relationship to God and with one's neighbors. Man's enslavement was due not to ignorance but to sin. Consequently, Herberg maintained, "the Bible itself knows nothing, or virtually nothing, of liberal education in our [Greek] meaning of the term." Since the Renaissance, this Greek understanding of education had come to dominate the curriculum. The result was that the Jew and the Christian came to hold to a biblical view with regard to religion and a Greek view with regard to education and culture. To counteract this trend, Herberg wrote, "I would suggest that the purpose of liberal education is to give us a more profound insight into the human situation, into man's creaturely existence in the world (in his alienation and need for God), and in this way enhance our understanding of, and sensitivity to, the condition and needs of our neighbors as well as our own." History, philosophy, literature, and art could contribute to this process; and even the study of science could allow us to understand God's creation.

From Herberg's perspective, a genuinely liberal education should concentrate on *Torah*, not on *paideia*. It should offer "a way of God-centered orientation in the world" and not seek man-centered means of enhancing one's own soul or mind about timeless truths or naturalistic facts. The emphasis should be on the personal and the historical, in which knowledge was considered the "existential insight that emerges in personal 'meeting' or encounter." The biblical view of education was thus God-centered and not man-centered, for, as Herberg recalled, "The beginning of wisdom is the fear of the Lord." Only such a theonomous approach could provide adequate conditions for achieving *humanum*. However, Herberg did warn against an overestimation of this biblical approach to education. The biblical Weltanschauung also provided merely another human perspective with its own presuppositions. As such, it too, like the idealistic or naturalistic approach to education, was subject to limitation and could also be idolatrized. But it did show a third way between what was and what ought to be inasmuch as it did not deny the sinfulness of man, as did idealism, nor did it agree with a naturalistic positivism that asserted that values have no meaning. Nevertheless, the institutions of an educational system based on a biblical perspective should be constantly called into question—as should all institutions of society.

WHIGGISM AND
PROPHETIC FAITH

Herberg's perspective produced constant criticism of all social institutions. His principal criticisms of society were directed toward both socialism and Americanism.[13] What Herberg came to affirm by 1953 was that the Whiggism of a Lord Acton, with its emphasis on the supremacy of the divine will over the will of man and human institutions, was "virtually identical with prophetic faith as applied to politics." Believing that America's founding fathers were Burkean realists, Herberg maintained that Acton and Niebuhr were both ideologically close to the founding fathers. Agreeing with Dorothy Fosdick's assessment that Niebuhr was among the "Neo-Machiavellians," Herberg wrote, "We need . . . some of Lord Acton's realism as to human nature in history and politics." Herberg also appreciated Russell Kirk's then new book *A Program for Conservatives* because it hailed Niebuhr as a representative of a novel kind of conservatism. And in reviewing Richard W. Leopold's book *Elihu Root and the Conservative Tradition*, Herberg praised Root as one of the country's very great secretaries of war. Yet he also charged that Secretary Root did not understand progressivism and the Russian Revolution. Root thus represented a general weakness in American conservatism. On the other hand, liberalism and totalitarianism were both the result of a Jewish-Christian messianism that had lost its original transcendental element.

Although Herberg inclined toward conservatism, he was nevertheless critical of both liberalism and conservatism. For example, he was more critical of Louis Hartz's *Liberal Tradition in American History* than of Clinton Rossiter's *Conservatism in America*. In maintaining that America followed an "irrational Lockeanism," Hartz was guilty of "dramatic oversimplification" by failing to provide a description of American conservatism; and, Herberg continued, "a writer [Hartz] who thinks of Edmund Burke as simply an ideologist of 'feudalism' . . . is hardly the man to do conservatism justice." On the other hand, Rossiter's book was "perhaps the single most important contribution so far made to the liberal-conservative debate." According to Herberg, liberalism developed out of eighteenth-century rationalism, was ahistorical in perspective, embraced the idea of progress, and proposed remaking society according to moral principles. Conservatism arose in reaction to the French Revolution, respected history and tradition, and possessed "a strong sense of the ambiguity of all human achievement and the perennial predicament of man in society." Unlike liberalism, conservatism viewed politics as an expediency rather than as a means by which to establish a society based on unalterable moral principles. Given these two definitions, Herberg believed that America was liberal in ideology but conservative in political practice, or, as he wrote, "Liberalism has, in a way, become a conservative tradition."

Herberg's major criticism of Rossiter's work centered on his understanding of "neo-conservatives." Herberg opposed Rossiter's recommendation that the American business class should be converted into a new "aristocracy," by which means a conservatism could reemerge. But the business community, according to Herberg, was essentially too liberal in the sense that it too was ahistorical and rationalistic in outlook. Herberg thus raised the following questions: "Is not the temper of dynamic American business too essentially liberal, too essentially radical . . . ? Who is more of a rationalistic innovator in his own field, who is less given to tradition, than the American business man, for whom 'revolutionary' is a term of the highest praise in matters of industrial engineering or marketing technique?" As a result, a "new conservatism" grounded in the American business class would actually have a weak footing. More importantly, even an authentic conservatism could not meet the crisis of the age, a crisis that could only be resolved, not in terms of conservatism or liberalism, but in terms of religion. In this respect, not even the conservative emphasis on natural law was sufficient.

From the point of view of biblical theology, the idea of natural right was "essentially a 'natural' philosophy of normative human life," which Herberg held too "natural" to be acceptable. The reason was quite simple: the concept of natural right assumed that man, unaided, could achieve a limited but universally valid knowledge of the world. In contrast, the biblical approach assumed that divine revelation was required. Furthermore, from the biblical perspective, a moral obligation was not a rational proposition but an act of obedience to a divinely revealed God. Any moral sensitivity that a person possessed was understood as derived from man's "original rightness" before the Fall. "Conscience" was therefore not of the order of reason but of faith. Moreover, natural right assumed the autonomy of man, and biblical faith condemned this position as idolatrous. According to Herberg, the natural-right doctrine was Greek in origin, not biblical. Where Christians had adapted this doctrine to theology, it produced effects detrimental to both Christianity and the doctrine. Greek philosophy assumed that human reason could discover the natural order of the world. Herberg pointed out that the Bible maintained that faith was the basis of reason and that the world, including human reason, had been perverted by sin and was redeemable only by grace.[14] However, even though natural law supplied a debatable topic, the real menace of the day, Herberg believed, was communism.[15]

One of the obvious dangers of communism was its practice of corrupting the language, of distorting and falsifying words for political effect. For example, in Communist circles the word "democracy" had come to stand for both totalitarianism and the police state, the very antitheses of the meaning of the word outside the Communist orbit. And "freedom of the press" in Communist language came to mean "control of the press by the government." This kind of "degradation of the word," as Herberg called it, began after World War I when a kind of "new dark ages" of hopelessness, cynicism, and confusion somehow introduced itself. As Herberg pointed out, Thucydides had noted the same disintegration after the Peloponnesian War, which was followed by a period in which "words lost their usual relation to things and began to be manipulated by a kind of hysterical logic." Totalitarian communism, also one of the results of the postwar decay, became the chief culprit in "semantic corruption." In democratic societies, the Communists had succeeded in introducing these semantic alterations through the liberals, "who have been converted into volunteer apologists for totalitarian Russia and the totalitarian idea." For example, the liberals would condemn an act by the United States as outright aggression whereas the same act in Russia would be viewed as merely a matter of security. Herberg warned, "Totalitarian liberalism is the chief agency in the systematic degradation of the word that is so effective a technique for undermining the ideological foundations of democracy." These liberals, including, Herberg held, some of the clergy, were unwitting agents or dupes of Russian communism, naively unaware that the East-West conflict was not merely an economic or ideological conflict, but a struggle for the soul of man. He credited Whittaker Chambers with recognizing this significant characteristic of the era.

WHITTAKER CHAMBERS AND JOSEPH MCCARTHY

Herberg proclaimed Chambers's "great virtue" to be that he recognized that the fundamental issue of human existence was the problem of faith and that communism had become the ersatz faith of modern times. He also recognized that the logic of secularism brought one to communism, both of which subsisted on a faith in man and not in God. Collectivized man, society, and state together were the objects of worship for the Communist. Herberg agreed with Chambers that the decision of the day rested on a choice between "God or Stalin." Liberals and secularists objected to this either/or decision with which Chambers confronted them. And insofar as liberals were secularists, just that far did they hold open the door for the Communist totalitarian faith. The church too must recognize that it could not be neutral in the struggle against communism, which, as Herberg reiterated, was a struggle for the control of human souls.

As Herberg went on to explain, "It is a fact that for all their sincere devotion to democratic and religious ideals, many representative spokesmen of American religion, particularly of Protestantism and Judaism, have exhibited a strange ambivalence in opposing Communism." The reason for this behavior was difficult to discern. Perhaps one of the reasons was that these ministers and rabbis felt some sympathy for the downtrodden, the oppressed, the proletariat at the same time as they seemed able to ignore some of the worst atrocities for which the Communists were responsible. Perhaps these people were also affected by a residual anti-Catholicism and thus sided with Communists against the Catholic church, particularly in Spain and Latin America. All of these reasons, coupled with the fact that "communism is a direct if illegitimate offspring of the Judeo-Christian Messianic tradition," led many not to oppose communism as vehemently as they should have. According to Herberg, the Jewish-Christian faith supported democracy, but it did not equate its faith with democracy. That would be idolatrous. Consequently, biblical faith must oppose demagoguery of every kind, whether found in the form of Russian communism or in the rantings of an American senator like Joseph McCarthy.

McCarthy, Herberg asserted, was not a conservative but a radical demagogue on a national scale.[16] "McCarthyism," a word, according to Herberg, coined by Communists, meant the attempt to run the government by rabble-rousing. This approach to American democracy was contrary to the intentions of the founding fathers, who equally opposed despotism and direct democracy. Herberg pointed out that in recent decades, through the use of mass communication systems, politicians had been able to appeal directly to the people and to overlook the constitutional process of government. The first person to take advantage of this form of rabble-rousing was, in Herberg's opinion, Franklin D. Roosevelt with his "fire-side chats." Herberg asked the rhetorical question, "What were [these fireside chats] but the re-establishment of the relation between demagogue and mob on a national scale through the miracle of modern mass communication?" A logical outcome of this method was McCarthyism, but with a slight difference: "In 'McCarthyism,' the rabble-rouser is not a cultured and aristocratic gentleman, but a crude and rather primitive plebeian, not a Pericles but a Cleon." Instead of seeking a change in policy through established means, McCarthy used the media to arouse the people and get them to deluge the White House with letters of demand.

The liberal reaction to McCarthy was not much more intelligible than was the support of the so-called nationalists. Herberg maintained that the liberals could only resort to the "delusive parallel" between McCarthy and Hitler, accusing McCarthy of leading America down the road to nazism. Herberg believed that this view had almost become "official liberal doctrine." But McCarthy possessed no private army as Hitler had, nor did he indicate any apparent religious or racial bigotry, and the established legal procedures of this country had not broken down. According to Herberg, McCarthy was a demagogue and a rabble-rouser, but, unlike Hitler or Lenin or Huey Long, he had no positive ideal, no program, and no cause other than simply opposing communism. Herberg called him "just a political swashbuckler from Wisconsin" whose public image was blown all out of proportion by those who opposed him. McCarthyism was thus "the very apotheosis of negativity; it is a conglomeration of oppositions and sentiments clinging around a vacuum." The cure for such ills was a "new conservatism," a "responsible neo-Burkean conservatism," which was "unalterably opposed to government by rabble-rousing from whatever direction it may come" and which was "dedicated to the conservation of the American constitutional tradition of freedom and order." This kind of conservatism would oppose not only communism but also rabble-rousers of any sort.

THE TASK OF
CONSERVATIVE
GOVERNMENT

Herberg outlined government's fivefold purpose: (1) to preserve peace and order, (2) to adjudicate conflicting social interests, (3) to maintain a balance in freedom and justice, (4) to strengthen the basis of stability, and (5) to promote the national interest.[17] In regard to the relationship between religion and the state, he recommended that "governmental agencies . . . teach the democratic ideal as religion." Here, religion was understood not as an ideological fetishism but as prophetic protest: "The principle of anti-idolatry seems to me quite basic in resisting absolutistic or totalistic thinking in politics. It is quite fundamental in all democratic thinking." This view included the moral convictions that there was a transcendent God above both state and society and that no one person or group possessed the necessary wisdom to rule without restraint. Opposing both autonomous and heteronomous societies, Herberg thus believed that democracy was best described "as the institutionalization of theonomy on the political level." As such, democracy emphasized the value of the individual personality and of the limitation of political power. These values were derived from the American religious tradition, which had to be affirmed in order to understand these values. Even the principle of prophetic protest had been institutionalized in America's Constitution, which provided for self-criticism, self-reform, and self-limitation.

Herberg maintained that there was no biblical basis for any particular economic system. Emphasis on economic production and labor could be found in the opening chapters of Genesis. But all property belonged, in effect, to God and we were merely stewards of the land. Because no particular system had divine sanction, Herberg offered six criteria for judging the adequacy of an economic system from a biblical point of view. First, the economic system should allow an individual to view his position in the economic process as a vocation, a calling from God. Second, it should allow for adequate incentives that have been morally evaluated. Third, within the limits of the human condition, it should allow for the greatest degree of freedom. Fourth, it should permit sufficient means for achieving economic justice and the proper distribution of goods. Fifth, it should provide economic security. And sixth, it should be efficient, in the sense that the system should continually produce the proportionate amount of goods required. Given these criteria, Herberg found both laissez-faire capitalism and socialism deficient.

Herberg asserted that free-enterprise capitalism had never really existed.

The closest anyone ever came to it was during the nineteenth century in England and America when government regulation was at a minimum. Then, a worker's major incentive was to prevent his own starvation, and he was thereby reduced to wage slavery and absolute insecurity in his job. It was a period of a "fantastic division of labor" in which many were reduced to poverty and wealth was confined to a few. Those who profited most adopted the delusive notion that this division was part of the natural order of creation. Yet capitalism of this kind had its positive side: it was efficient. As Herberg noted: "It [capitalism] was easily the most productive system the world had ever seen, and everything about it made for ever increasing productivity. Even the disorder of the recurring 'crises' apparently inherent in the system meant little on total balance." Nevertheless, out of this older capitalism grew a newer capitalism, brought about through government intervention and the rise of labor unions, which mitigated many of the evils of the earlier system. In its wake, of course, came newer problems, like statism and bureaucracy. Socialism arose in reaction to the earlier capitalism and its indictments of early capitalism were justified. But socialism with its emphasis on collectivism quickly degenerated into totalitarianism. Some thinkers, however, hoped to bring together the positive aspects of both socialism and regulated capitalism.

Herberg referred to one such thinker, Norman Thomas, as America's "Mr. Socialism" because of his social idealism. For this reason Thomas has been remembered, but the Socialist party has not.[18] Herberg explained that in the 1930s the Socialist movement lost part of its program to the New Deal. As a consequence, the Socialist movement failed, but it was a "successful failure" in that its programs were partially adopted. As Herberg put it more succinctly: "Paradoxically as the Socialist Party lies dying, its 'idea' goes marching on." Echoing the Lovestonite position of 1938, Herberg maintained that one of the reasons the movement was dying was that it had assumed the validity of a European model rather than analyze the uniqueness of the American situation. Unlike his European counterpart, the American worker was not disenfranchised—he could vote and had "rights." American Socialists thus erroneously looked upon the American worker as "backward," when in actuality he was more advanced than the European worker. In addition, the Socialists overlooked two of America's basic features: the vast resources of American capitalism and the ability of the nation to reform itself. American capitalism was quite simply not the kind of capitalism envisioned in Socialist theory: "The actual development of capitalism in this country has sensationally belied the Marxist prognosis." Moreover, Herberg insisted that Socialist goals could be achieved through the two-party system.

Herberg noted two trends in contemporary socialistic thinking: one concerned the neoliberalism of such people as Lewis Corey, Sidney Hook, and Thomas, and the second concerned what Herberg described as a "theologically grounded socialism," citing Niebuhr as a proponent. Both views were personalistic and pluralistic in outlook, and both accommodated an awareness of the danger of totalitarianism inherent in collectivism. The second, however, viewed socialism from a theological perspective and recognized that socialism was a secularized version of the Hebrew-Christian tradition and an attempt at a messianic transformation of the world. In phrases reminiscent of those in his 1943 article on Christian mythology and socialism, Herberg pointed out that the Socialist was trapped between "the earthly city of exploitation and oppression" and "the heavenly city of brotherly harmony." As such, the Socialist was in the world but not of the world. The proletariat, as "the agent of history," functioned in effect as "both the Saving Remnant and the beginnings of the Kingdom of God." Paradoxically, in the midst of Herberg's inclinations toward conservatism, he nevertheless continued to hope, as he had in 1940, for a resurgence of some kind of socialism. He wrote, "The recovery of the social idealism we admire in Norman Thomas, perhaps even the reconstitution of a social movement that will serve for our time as Socialism hoped to serve in its day, may well be waiting for a renewed appropriation of the religious heritage that makes social concern a primary responsibility of man before God." The same hope is found in Herberg's attitude toward the whole labor movement.

THE AMERICAN LABOR MOVEMENT

Herberg realized that organized labor was turning into one of the fastest growing nongovernmental organizations in the country.[19] This new position of power and prestige for labor organizations also reflected changes that had taken place since the 1930s. Then social scientists had not recognized the unions' high level of influence, largely because they had viewed unions as economic, and not political, units. As a result, no serious sociological study of American labor had been undertaken to that date. Herberg, always sensitive to shifts in the labor movement, noted a change in the ethnic constituency of some labor union locals, specifically Local No. 22 of the ILGWU and Local No. 89 of the Dressmakers Union. In 1933, Local 22 was 70 percent Jewish whereas Local 89 was a "language local" composed largely of Italians. But this Jewish and Italian dominance began to wane in 1946 mainly because

Italians and Jews had sent their children, not into the union, but to college, where they were educated to become professionals and white-collar workers. For example, Local 22 in 1946 was 63.4 percent Jewish; the membership was 51 percent Jewish by 1953. Soon, tensions in the union arose between the "oldtimers" (mainly Italians and Jews) and the "newcomers" (mainly Negroes and Latin Americans). Racial prejudice thus was not infrequently expressed, and those labels once applied to the oldtimers were now applied to the newcomers: "lazy," "irresponsible," "selfish," and the like. But, as Herberg predicted, these problems would decline as the old leadership faded from the scene.

Herberg's particular interest lay in the history of the Jewish labor movement in the United States. Dividing the history of the movement into two periods, Herberg considered the 1930s the turning point between them. By then, Jewish immigration had slowed, the Communist movement had lost its momentum, the New Deal had made a large impact on labor, the unions were increasing their power base, and the threat of nazism and anti-Semitism in Europe all played important parts in bringing about a new era in the Jewish labor movement. Before the 1930s, Jewish labor had been affected by the large influx of Jews starting in 1870 and increasing in the decades thereafter. There had been Jewish immigrants before 1870, but the Eastern European Jewish immigrants after 1870 made the largest impact on labor. Most of them were artisans and skilled laborers; very few were factory workers. Most went into the so-called Jewish trades, such as slaughtering, printing, sewing, and building. Because of their spirit of individualism and "unorganizability," as some termed it, Jewish workers were not at first susceptible to unionization. Consequently, the Jewish labor movement began not as a trade movement but as a political and ideological movement.

Jewish trade unionism thus developed from the top down, from ideological radicals who sought to organize the Jewish workers. These radicals had been indoctrinated by Eastern European revolutionary movements, and, although they constituted only a minority of the Jewish workers, they nevertheless became their leaders. According to Herberg, the "spiritual confusion, insecurity, and normlessness" of the new American situation gave the young radicals the opportunity to organize the Jewish workers. The first organizations were educational in nature and propagandistic in orientation, with the Jewish Workers Union of 1885 becoming the most prominent. It was followed by the United Hebrew Trades, which was organized by Bernard Weinstein, Jacob Magidoff, Morris Hillquit, and Henry Miller, with the assistance of Samuel Gompers. Although this union developed branches in other major cities, New York City remained the heart of the rising movement. From this organization arose the Amalgamated Clothing Workers. By 1900 the women's garment workers had organized the ILGWU, which was affiliated with the American Federation of Labor (AFL). The "moral cement" of these organizations was socialism, producing a solidarity that was also given further cohesiveness by various labor journals and newspapers. Events in Europe, like the Kishinev massacre of 1903 in Russia, led to a new wave of immigration that strengthened the now existing unions.

Through the trade unions and the public education system, the Jews gradually became acclimated to American society and institutions. The intrusion of secularist ideas, such as communism, into the unions provided the one constant threat. Indeed, were it not for the AFL, the Great Depression, and the New Deal, Herberg reiterated, the Jewish labor movement could have been ruined by Communist incursions. Many Jewish workers either broke with the American Communist party or were expelled (as we saw earlier). Some went with the Lovestonites and became the most effective leaders of their unions while effectively opposing communism within those unions. Many of these predominantly Jewish unions were among the first to support the establishment of the Committee for Industrial Organization (CIO) and ultimately sought its unification with the AFL. After World War II, the composition of the Jewish unions began to alter, eventually reaching the point where, in effect, a Jewish labor movement no longer existed, except among those Jews who were union executives. In other words, the Jewish union had become less "Jewish" and its membership had entered into the mainstream of American society. As Herberg put it: "Through the Jewish labor movement, they [the Jewish workers] became part of the United States." And the Americanization of the Jew was in part the theme of Herberg's major work, *Protestant-Catholic-Jew*.

8
PROTESTANT-
CATHOLIC-
JEW

Protestant-Catholic-Jew is Herberg's most famous work, and yet he took less time preparing it than he did either *Judaism and Modern Man* or his 1943 article "The Christian Mythology of Socialism."[1] The actual writing of the manuscript, all eleven chapters, took only eight or nine months. In part, the swiftness with which he wrote can be explained by the fact that previous articles on the topic were incorporated into the manuscript. But more revealing is the explanation that acknowledges the intensity of his concern with the topic, as witness his lectures on religion in America at various academic institutions. In any case, within the three weeks following the book's publication, over forty reviews were published and Herberg could write, "It is obvious that the book is making something of a sensation."

The title of the work is rather imposing. Besides invoking the names of the three major Western religions, it is formidably subtitled *An Essay in American Religious Sociology*.[2] Nevertheless, its goal was decidedly limited: it was intended to be "an interpretation of the religious situation . . . in mid-twentieth century America" (p. vii). In it Herberg explores the thesis that America is at once the most religious and the most secular of countries, contending that, however seemingly paradoxical the idea might be, the increasing religiosity and the increasing secularism of American society are both historically derived from the same source. That source was the successive waves of immigrants who began pouring into the country in the latter part of the nineteenth century.

The country was, of course, founded largely by English-speaking Protestants. But by the time of World War I almost every European linguistic and ethnic group was represented within its borders, not to mention many others from Asia and Africa as well. The British-American element was reduced to less than half of the population, and, according to Herberg, "Americans had become linguistically and ethnically the most diverse people on earth" (p. 7). Most of these immigrants were of peasant stock and went into, not the professions, but the trades and small-scale businesses. But there upward social mobility was possible, and each new wave of immigrants pushed the previous immigrants from beneath. Friction was inevitable. By means of the American educational system the sons of unskilled laborers could compete with the sons of professionals who had already achieved a higher position on the occupational ladder. Thus, as Herberg points out, "In America the sons of families which in Europe had remained fixed in village tradition from generation to generation found themselves caught up in a pattern of social mobility that beckoned them ever upward" (p. 9).

This upward mobility notwithstanding, Herberg describes how the immigrants wanted to preserve their old culture, especially their churches. But doing so created difficulties. The immigrants had been accustomed to their old-world village churches, but in the new world the churches located near them would often have parishioners of different linguistic and national backgrounds. For example, many of the already established Catholic churches were attended largely by Irish and German immigrants, and the Italian and Hungarian Catholics felt uncomfortable in their midst. As a consequence, they suffered both a loss of identity and dislocation. In other words, it was a question of "belonging," so important in any individual's life. People began to identify themselves, not with a village, but with a language. The "ethnic" group became important in American economic, social, and political life. Each linguistic or ethnic group began to develop its own social organizations, its own newspapers, and its own churches. Thus, the immigrants accommodated their old-world ways to the new world, and a new unity based on language, and not on the village, began to emerge.

With the second generation, however, the problems became much more perplexing. Herberg describes this generation as "doubly alienated, marginal men"—those who spoke English as their first language but also spoke the old language in their homes and who, for the most part, born in America, were Americans at the same time that they were Italian or Polish or Irish. Their "foreignness" alienated them from other Americans while their Americanness alienated them from their parents. To deal with this situation, some individuals mediated between American culture and their foreign heritage and became leaders of ethnic societies, organizations, and political blocs. For the most part, however, much of this generation sought to dissociate itself from its alien cultural background and attempted to identify completely with American culture. This attempt meant the denial of one's family background, which included one's religious background. Some even sought to become religionless. Thus, whereas the former talked of America in terms of "cultural pluralism," the latter spoke of "the melting pot." Neither view, according to Herberg, was "in touch with the unfolding American reality."

Herberg expresses his belief in *Protestant-Catholic-Jew* that those who hold to the "melting pot" theory are only partially correct. America has become known, for example, as a land of different cuisines, but certainly one cannot infer from this fact that a blending of ethnic characteristics has occurred. The heart of the matter, for Herberg, is that this country's image of itself remains "the Anglo-American ideal it was at the beginning of our independent existence." The true images of America are reflected in the *Mayflower*, Davy Crockett, George Washington, and Abe Lincoln, and not in Columbus, Pulaski, or Steuben. Consequently, this country cannot, at least for Herberg, be described as a "melting pot," but rather it is a "transmuting pot" in which assimilation of ethnic elements is seen against the background of an " 'Anglo-Saxon' model." Or as Herberg writes: "Our cultural assimilation has proceeded in essentially the same way as has our linguistic development—a few foreign words here and there, a few modifications of form, but still thoroughly and unquestionably English" (p. 21). Herberg therefore insists that the persistence of this model disproves both the "melting pot" and the "cultural pluralist" theories.

Herberg maintains that this Anglo-Saxon model was the reality that the second generation faced, however inadequately. The third generation, in contrast, realized the pervasiveness of this model. Yet the third generation also realized that, although an immigrant has to become assimilated to the language, nationality, and culture of America, the one area in which he could keep his own unique identity was that of religion. No immigrant to America was seriously expected to change his religion. And so, as Herberg asserts, "it is religion that with the third generation has become the differentiating element and the context of self-identification and social location" (p. 23).

Following Marcus Hansen's "principle of third-generation interest," Herberg agrees that "what the son wishes to forget, the grandson wishes to remember." The members of the third generation were thoroughly American. Having been born in this country, they spoke English, believed themselves to be American, and rid themselves of their "immigrant foreignness." As such, they did not feel the alienation of their fathers, yet they yearned for that sense of "belonging" that all people seek. The old ethnic group was no longer sufficient because the members of the third generation were first and foremost Americans. However, the old ethnic religion retained its appeal as a source of self-identification. The religion of the grandfathers became the means whereby the third generation could feel at home in America while confirming the roots of its ethnic heritage. One now became identified as either a Protestant, a Catholic, or a Jew, which identification, according to Herberg, was not understood as a theological distinction but rather as a social distinction. In this manner, a "new and unique social structure was emerging in America, the 'religious community' " (p. 31).

Citing the works of Ruby Jo Kennedy and August Hollingshead, Herberg agrees in *Protestant-Catholic-Jew* that statistical studies of marriages have showed a growing trend in which intermarriage was increasing between people of differing religious denominations, not along ethnic lines. This trend did not mean that ethnicity was becoming less important, but only that religious preference had become the primary means of self-identification, not nationality. As Herberg explains: "The religious community is fast becoming, if it has not already become, the over-all medium in terms of which remaining ethnic concerns are preserved, redefined, and given appropriate expression" (p. 34). Even in politics, the political parties were beginning to subsume people under the broader tripartite categories of Protestant, Catholic, Jew. Nor did this mean that old forms of discrimination and racist attitudes toward Negroes, Jews, or Catholics had ceased, but they were, in Herberg's opinion, in gradual decline. Herberg thus believed that this "triple melting pot," as Kennedy called it, was exceedingly complex with important implications not only religiously but also sociologically.

What emerges when the immigrant passes through the process of acculturation is a "new man" who identifies himself within one large religious community that is divided into three subcommunities of Protestant, Catholic, and Jew. This larger community is also religious and is known as "The American Way of Life." For this reason, Herberg maintains that "it is general conformity to this ideal [Anglo-Saxon] type that makes us all Americans, just as it is diversity of religious community that gives us our distinctive place in American society" (p. 37). Hence, American society is a unity in multiplicity. This tripartite view of American society is largely, according to Herberg, the peculiar product of the third generation. Judaism, Protestantism, and Catholicism have become the fundamental subdivisions of the "American religion." Not only do these three religions share a common underlying similarity in a theological sense, but they also share the same spiritual values with respect to American democracy. In Herberg's opinion, the validity of this view can be proved by the upsurge in religious activity throughout the country at the time of his writing.

Herberg considers the fact of the new surge of religious activity to be beyond question. Reciting the conclusions of contemporary polls, he points out that 95 percent of the American people considered themselves to be either Protestants, Catholics, or Jews, with only 5 percent claiming no affiliation. As Herberg maintains, "Religious identification is more or less a matter of course" (p. 47). Between 1926 and 1950, membership in religious institutions increased by 59.8 percent whereas the population increased by only 28.6

percent. At the turn of the century, church membership had accounted for 36 percent of the total population; by 1958, it was 63 percent. In one survey Herberg used, more people considered themselves active churchgoers than were on the official church rolls. In addition, Sunday-school attendance was on the rise, church construction had increased markedly in the suburbs, and religion was also enjoying a revival in academic communities. All of these facts in Herberg's estimation lead to the obvious conclusion that religion contributes to a sense of "belonging" as well as to the pervasiveness of religious self-identification.

Herberg explains this increase in religious awareness and observance not only in terms of religion as a means of self-identification but also in terms of the changing character structure in American society. Using the language of the sociologist David Riesman, Herberg explains that the American character has shifted from inner-directedness to other-directedness, that is, from rugged individualism to social conformism. The other-directed person is dreadfully afraid of being "different," of getting out of synchronization with his peer group. According to Herberg, this type of personality is becoming the dominant one in suburban communities, especially among professionals, junior executives, and the like. This trend in part explains the upsurge of religion; attending church is becoming a means of demonstrating that one is well adjusted socially, a means of social location. But in addition to this trend, religious activity has also increased in response to the crisis in Western civilization, which is menaced by totalitarianism and threatened by nuclear warfare. Such conditions have inevitably led to insecurity and the need for a hope that transcends the practical exigencies of everyday life. Confronted with the ever-increasing depersonalization within mass culture, the individual seeks reassurance in those very institutions that for centuries have remained the mainstay of practically every civilization—the family and religion. According to Herberg, all of these trends are represented in the rise of religion in America.

For all of their belief in formal religious ideas, Herberg notes, most Americans feel that religion is irrelevant to politics and business. He maintains that this apparent disjunction in American society points to a moral commitment to something other than beliefs normally associated with religious tenets. This common religion of all Americans, Herberg asserts, is the religion of the American Way of Life. As he explains: "It is the American Way of Life that supplies American society with an 'overarching sense of unity' amid conflict. It is the American Way of Life about which Americans are admittedly and unashamedly 'intolerant.' It is the American Way of Life that provides the framework in terms of which the crucial values of American existence are couched. By every realistic criterion the American Way of Life is the operative faith of the American people" (p. 75). And one's "way of life" is one's religion. American religion is expressed in a belief in democracy, the free-enterprise system, the Constitution, and equalitarianism. It affirms the value of the individual person, who is also graced with a basic humanitarianism. The American is optimistic and aggressive and emphasizes deeds rather than creeds—pragmatism is his philosophy. In other words, the values of this shared American religion are the values of the middle class, and the middle class "way" is the American Way.

Herberg claims that this "common faith" in American society and in the historic faiths of Protestantism, Catholicism, and Judaism reciprocally influenced each other. Indeed, the American Way of Life is "a kind of secularized Puritanism," "although it lacks the emphasis on transcendence and the doctrine of original sin so characteristic of earlier Puritanism" (p. 81). The Puritan notion of the "promised land" persisted and became part of American religion, along with the Puritan sense of vocation and dedication to duty and to work. The pietistic revivals of the nineteenth century, which downplayed the importance of theological dogma, also helped to inform the current slogan of "deeds, not creeds," which, according to Herberg, is "the hallmark both of American religion and of the American Way of Life." Furthermore, Christianity and Judaism have both been "Americanized." Not only do they promote the same American ideals held in common by all Americans but they also serve to sanction faith in the American Way of Life by advocating optimism, activism, moralism, and idealism. They support the notion, so peculiarly affirmed by American people, that religion is something good not only for the individual but for the entire community as well.

The emphasis in American religion is not so much on a particular religion as on any religion, "religion-in-general" (p. 84). Here Herberg quotes President Eisenhower: "Our government makes no sense, unless it is founded in a deeply felt religious faith—and I don't care what it is." This faith, however, is a faith in faith, a faith not in God but in religion. By extension, Herberg holds that America, unlike the European states, is a country of denominations, a country of religious pluralism, one not confined to an established church. But these denominations do fall into one of three categories of religious community, Protestant, Catholic, and Jewish, all three of which are "diverse, but equally legitimate, equally American, expressions of an over-all American religion, standing for essentially the same 'moral ideals' and 'spiritual values' " (p. 87). The focus of this religion is democracy, the "religion of religions," "a superfaith above and embracing the three recognized religions" (p. 88). Herberg insists that, despite a tendency toward idolatry, this American religion is not merely a civil religion but a "faith in faith" that is more personal than just looking at the American people as a "corporate entity" would indicate.

The American religion is an "inner, personal religion" based on a faith in faith. The very act of believing itself supplies the essential element of this religion, often expressed in such terms as the "power of positive thinking." As Herberg describes it, the mere having of faith supposedly results not only in a cure of mental disorders but also in peace of mind, normality, and self-acceptance. In other words, one does not have to have faith in a particular "thing," such as a dogma or a theological position or even God. All that is required is the mere having of faith, "the psychological attitude of having faith, so to speak" (p. 90). Herberg calls this "the cult of faith," whereby "what is important is faith, faith in faith. Even where the classical symbols and formulas are still retained, that is very often what is meant and what is understood" (p. 90). This particular characteristic of American religion also reveals itself in the three great historic faiths in America—Protestantism, Catholicism, and Judaism.

Herberg agrees that Protestantism has played a formative role in American history. Using the words of Arnold J. Toynbee, Herberg speaks in *Protestant-Catholic-Jew* of Protestantism as the response to the challenge of the American frontier. However, with increased industrialization and urbanization, Protestantism was faced with a new situation, indeed, with a new America. Whereas Protestantism had apparently faced the challenge of the frontier bravely, it seemed unprepared to face the challenge of the industrialized and urbanized society that began to develop after the Civil War. The country's economic transformation from rural to urban changed many of the Protestant denominations into established, middle-class churches. As Herberg maintains, these churches "grew increasingly remote from the outlook and hopes of the urban industrial masses" (p. 116). The Protestantism that had been the religious force behind the earlier immigrants encountered only difficulties with the newer immigrants of the late nineteenth and early twentieth centuries. The major reason for this confrontation was that the new immigrants were not primarily Protestant in origin. They also had not passed through the frontier experience. American Protestantism thus had to adapt to new, not to mention to foreign, conditions.

Herberg expresses the belief that the individualism fostered by religion and encouraged by the frontier no longer sufficed as the social basis for a changing America. This inadequacy demonstrated itself especially in the callousness much of Protestantism exhibited toward labor unions and the plight of the industrial worker. Nevertheless, some Protestants sought to meet this challenge with the establishment of such cultural and recreational centers as the YMCA and the YWCA, which provided religious education for urban young people. The Social Gospel movement made the most significant effort in this direction. Washington Gladden, for example, preached against the weaknesses of capitalism in an industrialized society, as did George D. Herron, Shailer Matthews, and F. G. Peabody. For Herberg, Walter Rauschenbush was the most impressive thinker in this movement because he preached about the need for the redemption not only of individuals but also of institutions, and he identified Christianity with a gospel of social reform. Nevertheless, although the social agencies fostered by the Social Gospel movement made impressive efforts, they were never so effective as American Protestantism had been on the frontier. Consequently, Herberg holds that the Protestant movement as it was on the frontier ended when it failed to meet the challenge of an urban-industrialized society.

Herberg nevertheless asserts that, even though the Protestant movement on the frontier may have wound down, the movement was still making some progress in the cities and Protestant thought was far from declining. Denominational growth continued, especially in the suburbs and in urban areas affected by the influx of southern Negroes and whites into industrial centers. Intellectually, Protestantism made most impressive advances with such theologians as Reinhold Niebuhr and Paul Tillich. Moreover, there was a sense, according to Herberg, in which Protestantism was still the national religion. It still constituted the largest body of Christians in America, embracing about 56 percent of the total population. Yet, Protestants increasingly viewed themselves as part of America's tripartite religious structure.

Herberg believed that Catholicism, unlike Protestantism, was never a religious movement in America. Rather, it experienced assimilation into American society as a "foreign church" (p. 136). America was at one time a "Protestant country" but never a "Catholic country," although some Catholic settlements did exist in the seventeenth century. Catholicism did not become well established until the immigrations of the nineteenth century—largely through the immigration of Irish Catholics, who would set the tone of Catholicism in America. Indeed, an attempt to permit the Irish Catholics to set up a church independent of hierarchical control was averted. Nevertheless, the Irish clergy came into greater prominence in the country, where the churches were more open to the clergy's and laymen's cooperation in running the local parishes. At the same time, the Irish character of the church was solidified by persistent anti-Catholic attacks by Protestants. Accordingly, Herberg concludes that "the

Catholic Church in the United States as we know it today is largely the achievement of the Irish Catholic immigrant, and it bears his mark" (p. 143).

Herberg points out that, because the Irish spoke English, they could act as the mediators between the larger American culture and the church. However, with the arrival of German, Slavic, and Italian immigrants, a conflict arose between the old Catholics, that is, the Irish, and the new. Parishes were established along ethnic lines, each group having its own ethnic priest. With the progress through the second and third generations, however, these ethnic lines began to blur, and Catholicism became a genuinely American institution. The church hierarchy was still composed largely of Irish clergymen, so generally the church remained Irish in tone. The Irish were, as Herberg affirms, "puritanical," democratic, and activistic, almost committing what Pius XII called the "heresy of action." In time, the Irish fused nationalism with their Catholicism to the point that for them to be American was to be Irish and Catholic. This process became so distinctive that foreign observers noted the uniqueness of American Catholicism in comparison with European Catholicism.

As one example of this distinctiveness, Herberg describes the Catholic views on the relationship of church and state. The normative Catholic view has always been, he says, to seek a union of church and state, as had been the model in Europe in the seventeenth and eighteenth centuries. In America, this position could not prevail. Most American Catholics were firmly committed to upholding the Constitution and had little, if any, desire to seek a union of church and state. Indeed, American Catholic intellectuals were reorienting their thinking on the relationship of church and state, as did the Jesuit, John Courtney Murray. What happened is that American Catholics began to see themselves as part of the American tripartite religious system. This commitment, however, did not diminish the Catholic belief that it was the one true church. Rather, as Herberg writes, "what it did involve was a deep-lying, though often unarticulated, conception of American social reality" (p. 151). In other words, the average Catholic looked on American society as pluralistic and the Catholic church as merely one religious community within the "triple melting pot," "under the benevolent aegis of American democracy."

Herberg believed that the Catholic church had been fairly successful in accommodating itself to American culture. With most of its population centered in the cities, the Catholic church constituted one of the largest Christian denominations in the country and had become the most powerful and wealthy division of the worldwide Catholic church. It had established a vast network of educational systems, and, because many of its members were from the working class, it was one of the leaders in prolabor organization and social welfare development. Indeed, according to Herberg, a "new type of American Catholic" was developing, based of course on the Irish-American model, in which diversity of opinion existed in one institution while the main guidelines of dogma remained intact. Apart from the Catholic Negroes, Puerto Ricans, and Mexicans, most Catholics had become acclimated to the church and American society. These others were still discriminated against, but Herberg expresses his belief that in time this problem would diminish. Thus, as he concludes, "American Catholicism has successfully negotiated the transition from a foreign church to an American religious community. It is now part of the American Way of Life" (p. 160).

Like the Catholic community, the American Jewish community also had its roots in the waves of immigration of the last decades of the nineteenth and the first decades of the twentieth centuries. Sephardic Jews immigrated to this country as early as 1654, Herberg reports, and the pressures of acculturation began early as well. By the 1820s some younger Jews had formed the Reformed Society of Israelites, and, although their organization was short-lived, the future of Judaism in America rested with them. By the middle of the nineteenth century most of the Jewish immigrants entering the country came from Germany. These newcomers, in Herberg's estimation, were considered by Americans to be Germans rather than Jews, and many of them joined German societies that were independent of any particular or specific religious identification. These Jews distinguished themselves not only by means of their organization of Jewish societies and institutions but also by means of their success as prosperous businessmen. Under the influence of German idealism and Protestant liberalism, the Reformed movement became a permanent part of the American Jewish community. Others, however, feeling that Reformed theology had strayed too far, developed a Conservative philosophy. Thus, by the 1880s, the Jewish community had divided itself among the Orthodox, the Conservative, and the Reform movements, without any over-arching organization under which it could be united.

Herberg explains that the greatest wave of Jewish immigration came after 1870, with the majority of immigrants arriving from Eastern Europe. According to his statistics, two and a half million Eastern European Jews came to America in the five decades after 1870. These people had a tremendous impact on the nature of Judaism in America. Mostly of peasant stock, these Jews constituted a large Jewish proletariat. Many of them were artisans, small shopkeepers, and workers in the garment industries. Consequently, they were different from the Sephardic and German Jews who had preceded them, not only in occupational skills but also in the fact that most of them settled in ghettos where Yiddish was widely spoken. Of the immigrants who arrived after 1870, two groups emerged—one that retained its traditional religious ties and a second that became more secularistic in outlook and indeed became associated with labor radicalism. Each attempted to impose its own organizations and institutions on the conditions already existing in America.

The Orthodox Jews attempted to retain the ways of the old country, but without, according to Herberg, much success. However, they were successful in establishing charitable agencies and organizations to help newly arriving Jews, in which efforts they were also aided by a Yiddish press. But those who went into the Jewish labor movement also established similar organizations, such as the Workmen's Circle. As a consequence, American Judaism at the turn of the century had divided itself into four main groups: the Sephardics, the Germans, the East European Orthodox, and the East European Jewish labor organizers. According to Herberg, although dissension, conflict, and disorder were inevitable, it was also a time of creativity. Unity among the Jews began to increase because they faced common conditions in the new country and also because of the rise of European anti-Semitism. By 1924 the National Conference of Jewish Charities, the American Jewish Committee, the Jewish Education Committee, and other unified organizations were established, and the Jewish community was becoming a well-defined ethnic group. By that time, a new structure was developing in American society, and the Jewish community became a permanent part of it.

The experience of the Jews at this point was similar to that of the Catholics. The Jews, Herberg observes, began to identify themselves as Americans and as Jews, not as some particular ethnic group. Yet, as he points out, the Eastern European Jews were slower to adapt to this newer perception—they still spoke Yiddish as a means of linguistic identity, a language that was neither German nor Russian but was instead a peculiar possession of Jews. They did not consider their doing so a rejection of America, but merely the expression of real Jewishness. Nevertheless, the second generation reacted against this identification, seeking to become Americans completely. Despite the efforts of Solomon Schechter, Mordecai M. Kaplan, and others to appeal to this second generation, they remained largely unimpressed. The members of the second generation wanted to be associated with one culture, not two, so they became either secularists or, in reaction, Zionists. Yet, as Herberg asks rhetorically, "both were also somehow strangely 'Jewish,' for was not internationalist socialism a secularized version of the 'universalist' aspect of Jewish messianism and Zionist nationalism a secularized version of the 'particularist' aspect?" (p. 185). Both arose in the 1920s and 1930s and both would wane with the third generation.

As Herberg maintains, "The emergence of the third generation changed the entire picture of American Jewry and Judaism in America" (p. 186). Appearing in the 1930s and 1940s, this generation not only returned to the religion of the grandfathers but also to the "Jewishness" of the grandfathers. Unlike, for example, the third generation of Italians and Poles who returned to the religion of the grandfathers but not to their "Italian-ness" or "Polish-ness," the third-generation Jew regained his Jewishness. But it was a Jewishness stripped of its foreign-immigrant characteristics. The third-generation Jew was not proletariat but middle class, with a college education, a white-collar profession, and a home in the suburbs in a "Jewish neighborhood." In other words, the third-generation Jew felt at home in America with his Jewishness, and thus he began to reshape American Judaism. What occurred was that Orthodox, Reform, and Conservative began to converge: "All were becoming American and therefore more and more like each other" (p. 193).

Herberg believed that the Judaism that emerged was in keeping with the Conservative Jewish tradition. Through the pressures of Americanization both the Orthodox and the Reform movements moved toward the moderate approach of Conservatism. Actually, according to Herberg, the Conservative movement had taken over a program of moderate Reformism, but it was never recognized as such. Or, as he writes: "Not Reform but Conservatism thus became the prime beneficiary of the Americanization of Judaism in this country. But this was only a matter of degree; by the mid-century all three of the 'denominations' were substantially similar expressions of the new American Jewish religious pattern, differing only in background, stage of development, and institutional affiliation" (pp. 194–95). Tensions and conflicts still existed among the three branches of Judaism, but these were gradually decreasing especially through united charitable organizations such as The Council of Jewish Federations and Welfare Funds and the United Jewish Appeal. Also, in the armed services Jewish chaplains were assigned to appeal to Jews in general, not to specifically Orthodox, Conservative, or Reform Jews. Thus, their differences notwithstanding, American Jews maintained their Jewishness by virtue of their Americanness, and Judaism became an integral part of the American Way of Life and an expression of one of the "religions of democracy."

Although Protestantism, Catholicism, and Judaism represent the three religions of American democracy, in Herberg's view they nevertheless share different positions in American society. America may have been founded on

Protestantism, but that religion too had to adapt to the influence of the two other religious communities by the middle of the twentieth century. But, Herberg points out, Catholics and Jews are the social extremes to the current "Protestant norm," and he predicts that they doubtless will conform more and more to a Protestant social pattern. In this process, tension will inevitably arise, despite the agreement these three religions now enjoy about the American Way of Life. The focus of tensions, in Herberg's estimate, will center on the relationship of church and state and the First Amendment to the Constitution. With the arrival of large numbers of Catholics, Protestants feared that they would seek a unification of church and state. Consequently, Catholics and Catholic churches were the objects of many violent attacks by Protestants. These wounds have not yet healed. But, Herberg does observe, anti-Catholic sentiment among Protestants is declining.

Herberg maintains that American Protestantism has been in the anomalous position of being a majority community while manifesting "a growing minority consciousness" (p. 234). Specifically, it fears, however baseless that fear may be, the possibility of Catholic hegemony when, in fact, the ratio of Protestants to Catholics has remained fairly constant since the 1920s. Herberg believes that this unwarranted fear had its origins in the Protestant's awareness of the fact that America was no longer, strictly speaking, a Protestant country but was instead a three-religion country. Nevertheless, this fear does explain why many Protestants have become the champions of separation of church and state, not only with regard to religion but also with regard to education. Consequently, this fear is based, not on a theological attitude, but on a secular one in which Protestants really fear for their country and their government. For Herberg, this Protestant fear arises from a failure to understand American pluralism, which embraces all, regardless of individual religious affiliation. Some Protestant theologians, such as Reinhold Niebuhr and John C. Bennett, have thus sought to give Protestant thought a new orientation that conforms to the reality of the American situation.

This same minority consciousness is particularly strong within the Jewish community, according to Herberg. The Jews are constantly on the alert against defamation, and they also fear the intrusion of the church into state affairs, whether that church be Protestant or Catholic. As Herberg expresses his belief, "Perhaps it would be more accurate to say that they have themselves taken over the entire secularist ideology on church-state relations to serve as a defensive strategy" (p. 239). Understandably, the Jew wants to preserve the secular society that gave the Jews emancipation. Like the Protestants, they too fear the Catholics most. This feeling is enhanced by the fact that the Jew lives in a

largely Christian society. For this reason, Jewish organizations are very conscious of public relations activities and of their image within society. This
concern with public image is probably the justification for the fact that rabbis
generally receive higher salaries than their Protestant counterparts, Herberg
suggests, by which means the community achieves an elevation for its rabbis
in social status and prestige. Such acts then become a means of minority-group
validation.

Any tensions that arise among the three religious groups necessarily occur,
in Herberg's view, as the country as a whole moves from Protestantism to
three-religionism. However, he does not find this situation very disturbing
because all three are united in the American Way of Life and all will gradually
adapt to the pluralistic situation. As Herberg writes, "The unity of American
life is a unity in multiplicity; it is a unity that is grounded in a 'common faith'
and is therefore capable of being re-established, despite tension and conflict,
on the level of 'interfaith'" (p. 242). Indeed, an interfaith movement was
established in the 1920s to counter rising bigotry. Later it was called the
National Conference of Christians and Jews, and it involved Catholics, Protestants, and Jews. Its stated purpose was to promote brotherhood among the
three religious communities. Further, many college campuses and cities have
interfaith days and religious-emphasis weeks. These interfaith movements
indubitably point to the common faith of Protestants, Catholics, and Jews,
which is the American Way of Life.

In the concluding chapter of the work, Herberg switches from a sociological
to a theological analysis. Originally entitled "Religion in America in the
Perspective of Jewish-Christian Faith," the tone of the chapter is one of
prophetic protest against all idolatry: "We are always prone to idolize ourselves and our works, to attribute quite uncritically final significance to our
interests, ideas, and institutions, to make of our achievements an instrument of
pride, power, and self-aggrandizement" (p. 254). This proscription also includes religion itself, for religion is for the most part the source of many
idolatries, including the religion of the American Way of Life. The widespread
upsurge in religious interest in the postwar years resulted, for Herberg at least,
in a contentless religion, a religion of self-identification and social location: "It
is thus frequently a religiousness without serious commitment, without real
inner conviction, without genuine existential decision" (p. 260). The man of
faith, as the words are understood in the biblical sense, is the man who stands
"over against" the world, not one who conforms to the world. But Americanism has become the civic religion of the American people, sanctifying and
justifying their society, their culture, and their deeds. As such, the American

civic religion is "incurably idolatrous"; as such, it lacks transcendence and prophetic judgment. Instead, religion in America is for cultural enrichment, for happiness, peace of mind, and success in business. In other words, American religion is man-centered, not God-centered, and is far removed from the biblical perspective of faith.

Seen from this particular perspective, Americans are simultaneously the most religious and the most secular of people. They participate actively in the affairs of church and synagogue, 95 percent believe in God, and most affirm the values of the Scriptures. Yet religion is compartmentalized to the extent that it plays a very small role in education, government, science, and other fields. This compartmentalization, according to Herberg, is precisely what secularism is, that which excludes God from the affairs of life. The result in America is a manifold secularism among religious people. Herberg nevertheless sees signs of a resurgence of authentic faith in American society, especially among the young people on college campuses who seek to go beyond the limits of "belonging." Moreover, Herberg maintains that some elements of the American religion point to authentic faith, and he notes that, however idolatrous American religion may be, God could still use it to fulfill his divine will: "Nothing is too unpromising or refractory to serve the divine will" (p. 272). Thus Herberg concludes his work with a prophetic judgment on the American Way of Life.

The judgment of reviewers was overwhelmingly favorable to *Protestant-Catholic-Jew*.[3] D. W. Brogan, in the *Manchester Guardian*, called it an "admirable book." The notice in the *Library Journal* referred to it as a "most significant and interesting book" that was recommended to all libraries. Reinhold Niebuhr considered it the "most fascinating essay" on American religion in recent decades, maintaining that the book contained some surprising and compelling theses. Niebuhr further believed that *Protestant-Catholic-Jew* would remain a subject of discussion for a long while, a view also held by J. Milton Yinger in the *American Sociological Review*. Nathan Glazer, who referred to Herberg's writing style as one of "architectonic grandeur," believed that Herberg's analysis of the "religion of religion," the "religion without faith," was brilliant. However, he also felt that Herberg had exaggerated the extent of the influence of this "religion of religion" on all branches of American religion, maintaining that the "religion of religion" would have little impact on Roman Catholicism in America.

Like Glazer, others thought quite highly of the work but also had some critical reservations. H. L. Short, in the *New Statesman and Nation*, criticized Herberg for not considering the possibility that a new movement was emerging in America, namely, that of pragmatic idealism, which, according to Short, "may be the genuine twentieth century American mould of the ancient Jewish-Christian tradition." Alban Baer, who at the time was a monk in Portsmouth Priory in Rhode Island, was fascinated by the work but considered Herberg's writing style too rigid, too much in tone an "academic sociological dissertation." Lee Braude, a sociologist, was critical of Herberg's ability as a sociologist. Maintaining that Herberg's work consisted mainly of speculations on secondary works, Braude asserted that "speculation, however couched in the language of sociology, is not sociology"; as a systematic sociological study, the book was therefore far from acceptable, although its value lay in fostering further research on the subject. One unnamed reviewer in the *U.S. Quarterly Book Review* criticized Herberg's concluding chapter for its having lapsed into theology rather than offering a genuine sociological conclusion with a "pragmatic value for social adjustment." And another unnamed reviewer held that the work was not so original as *Judaism and Modern Man*. Nevertheless, aside from the immediate fame that accrued to Herberg because of the work, the National Conference of Christians and Jews presented him in 1957 with a Certificate of Recognition for *Protestant-Catholic-Jew*.

9
THE
SHIFT TO
CONSERVATISM
1956–1964

In the eight years from 1956 to 1964 Herberg's reputation as a theologian and scholar expanded steadily. During this period, he published three anthologies, and he also received what he had always eagerly sought—the legitimate right to be called "Doctor." Park College, Franklin and Marshall College, and Ohio Wesleyan University all conferred on him their doctorate of letters degrees in 1956, 1960, and 1963 respectively. By far the most significant consequence of Herberg's widening reputation was the invitation he received to become a professor in the graduate school at Drew University. It was an exciting place to be for Herberg, so much so that he remained there until his retirement. His writings from 1956 to 1964 reflect the fervor with which he embraced and exercised his new academic authority.

THE CHARACTER
OF AMERICAN
RELIGION

Herberg's enthusiasm for analyzing American religion, as he had done in *Protestant-Catholic-Jew*, also continued unabated.[1] The presumed paradox of American religiosity vis-à-vis American secularity received further consideration. Utilizing Harold W. Pfautz's religious organizational forms, Herberg described the historical process whereby a cult first became a sect and finally became a church and denomination. With this development, he also saw a concomitant and increasing secularization within the organization, whereby a particular cult that developed into a denomination grew increasingly middle class in its orientation. In effect, it became "established." Yet, in America there were no established churches in the European sense. Rather what existed was a plurality of denominations. Thus, according to Herberg, "Denominational pluralism, on the American plan, means thorough-going secularization," which he defined as the widening of the gap between institutional religion and operational religion. In America, as already described in

Protestant-Catholic-Jew, this operational religion was defined by the "common religion" of the American Way of Life. Thus, the movement from cult to sect to denomination ended with the general religion of the American socioreligious community, the trifaith system.

Insofar as America has had an "established" religion, it was Protestantism in the early days of the Republic. But, according to Herberg, with increased immigration in the late nineteenth and early twentieth centuries and with the emergence of Catholicism and Judaism as important religious factors in American society, Protestantism became only one of three major religions. The effect, Herberg believed, was "Protestant paranoia," that is, fear of the growth of American Catholicism. Once the home of Protestantism, America now included "two interloper groups." Little wonder, therefore, as Herberg put it, that the Protestants began to feel dispossessed and threatened. On the other hand, the Catholics, with their social status rising in the second generation, began to feel that they were being unjustly treated by and unduly segregated from the mainstream of American society. For them, the result was "Catholic claustrophobia." However, such tensions were, in Herberg's opinion, gradually being alleviated; and Catholics, Protestants, and Jews were all developing along the lines of the syncretized religion of the American Way of Life. Even those Protestants, Catholics, and Jews who found the American Way of Life theologically to be the idolatrous result of secularization were developing an interfaith communion to oppose such idolatrous consequences.

Just as Protestants suffered from paranoia and Catholics from claustrophobia, American Jews suffered from schizophrenia, the relegation of both the religious to private life and the secular to public life. According to Herberg, such a position would be increasingly difficult to maintain. Moreover, the Jews would constantly live with the possibility of anti-Semitism, which was not just a sociological phenomenon but had a theological reality as well. To avoid this always imminent possibility, all three American religions must recognize that American society has always been pluralistic, or as Herberg termed it, a "pluriunity"—"a unity in plurality as well as a plurality in unity." Moreover, they must recognize and acknowledge their common bond: "The real and significant bond between our faiths is not that they are all American, but that they are all Biblical: we recognize Abraham as our father and the God of Israel as our God." From this premise, Herberg derived some optimism about the American interfaith movement. Nevertheless, he perceived difficulties and tensions that remained in all three branches of the American civil or national religion.

THE
UNIQUENESS OF
BIBLICAL RELIGION

*H*erberg viewed these internal tensions and conflicts, as he viewed most things, from a theological perspective.[2] His major assumption concerning the nature of American religion was that Judaism and Christianity constituted a unique religious phenomenon in history. The Jews were the people of God, and Christians shared in this uniqueness. Christianity, he asserted, "stands or falls on its conviction that it is not simply a kind of religious knowledge or view of reality, but a *unique* truth about ultimate things with a unique and all-important message about man's life and salvation." It could cooperate with other religions, such as Buddhism or Hinduism, on a secular, political, and cultural level. But it could never cooperate on a theological level. Nor did Herberg agree with the theologian Dietrich Bonhoeffer that a religionless society was in fact a Christian society. According to Herberg, and in contrast to Bonhoeffer's belief, modern man was not free of religious and metaphysical assumptions. The question therefore was which religion offered the proper perspective on the world, and that, for Herberg, was clearly the biblical perspective.

In other words, Herberg believed the choice was between a God-centered faith and an idolatrous faith. As he poignantly asserted, atheism itself was an expression of a theological interest, but usually only on the speculative plane. Existentially, no atheists existed—only, in Herberg's opinion, idolators. The "will-to-power," the "will-to-pleasure," were at bottom only manifestations of the "will-for-meaning." For example, Marx found meaning by deifying the dialectic of history. Accordingly, on the existential level of existence the question was not, Is there a God or not? or, Should one have a religion or not? but rather, In what god does one believe and in what religion does one define his existence? Here, Herberg specifically agreed with Bonhoeffer that we might unfortunately have been living in a post-Christian era, but he would not accept that we were in a postreligious era. "Every man, by virtue of being human, is Homo religiosus; every man has his religion and his god." That this was the case could be seen, according to Herberg, in the very presuppositions of the social sciences.

Herberg, as he had expressed the idea before, held that there were two major approaches to understanding ultimate reality—one either treated it as nature or treated it as history. The difference between the two affected not only one's personal philosophical perspective but cultures on a much broader scale as well. Nature, furthermore, could be interpreted either from the point of view of dynamic vitalism, in which case it resulted in paganism or romanticism—or as a rational structure, in which case it resulted in a scientific approach, which was characteristic of the mainstream of the modern intellectual tradition. In short, these two views of nature represented the Dionysian and the Apollonian understandings of reality. In Herberg's estimation, however, neither view could form the basis of social philosophy. Social philosophy required a grounding in history, an emphasis on the personality and the community, which were both historical in perspective. Moreover, because the Dionysian view of nature swallowed man up into a pantheistic scheme and the rationalistic approach led to the contemplative life, independent of the activity required of social existence, Herberg concluded, "Only when reality is understood in some sense as *history* does community receive a secure grounding in reality and social philosophy acquire the significance that alone can entitle it to that name." The conflict that arose between those who emphasized nature and those who emphasized history was essentially the conflict, metaphorically speaking, between Athens and Jerusalem.

To require that an adequate social philosophy must accept the historicity of man was to take a decidedly biblical position. Herberg then insisted that a social philosophy must be eschatological in perspective, that it required an "end" toward which history was moving: "Without an *eschaton*, history—and that, remember, means human existence—collapses into ultimate meaninglessness, into nothingness." Science, as such, was incapable of fulfilling such a transcendental need. Augustine, for Herberg, was a model of the social philosopher who was concerned not only with theology but also with the state, with marriage, with the family, and with other important elements in society. And, of course, his *City of God* was a paradigm of eschatological concern. Herberg believed that a social philosophy that focused on eschatology must be dialectical, taking into constant consideration the relationship of the "already" and the "not-yet." The tension between these categories of time could not be prematurely resolved. Thus, for Herberg, the social philosopher offered no final statements—rightness could only be achieved in the future. Social philosophy was therefore implicit theology.

Herberg considered psychology to be useful to the social philosopher but inadequate alone for the task at hand. He noted such positive contributions of Freudian psychology to the social sciences as permitting an investigation of the dynamics of man in society, providing information on the mechanisms of human behavior, and introducing motivational factors in the study of society. Yet in recent years, Herberg felt, revisionist views of Freudian psychology had challenged some of Freud's presuppositions about culture and society. One such presupposition was his rationalism—in fact, according to Herberg, Freud had made a god out of reason and scientific truth, which had led him to simplify the relationship of the tension between the ego, the id, and the superego. Herberg held that the conflict was not only among these three elements of the psyche but also within them. Conflict permeated the self, and consequently the ego was not so rational as Freud had assumed. This error led him to postulate that religion was illusory because it was not rational. What Freud lacked, as did Erich Fromm, was a recognition of the insights of the biblical tradition and the insights of existentialism. From these, he would have seen that a person was defined, not autonomously, but within a community and that despite man's sinfulness there was also a grandeur to man. Nonetheless, Freud almost unwittingly reasserted the Jewish-Christian conviction about the ambiguity of human nature.

History itself displayed this ambiguity in human nature, Herberg believed, and biblical faith operated from the perspective of history. Indeed, in the biblical view, metaphysics was acted out in history. Divine revelation was both *real* and *historical*, although it was mediated through human language and imagination. The account of this revelation was not therefore to be taken literally. The revelation is manifested at certain places and times, that is, in historical events. Revelation for Herberg was thus a divine-human encounter on the historical level of existence. This meant that the writing of history, even the most objectively written history, was nevertheless written from a theological point of view. Accordingly, he disagreed with the philosophy of history described by Arnold J. Toynbee.

TOYNBEE'S RELIGIOUS SYNCRETISM

Herberg opposed Toynbee's anti-Jewish and anti-Christian religious syncretism, the notion that all the major religions were striving toward an ultimate ecumenicity based on their common essences. In other words, for Toynbee, no religion was unique. Here, in Herberg's estimation, Toynbee began to lose his "tone of cultivated urbanity," especially when he referred to the Jewish understanding of God as "narrow," "primitive," and "immoral." And Toynbee's understanding of Christianity was a Christianity stripped of everything that was Christian in it. The result, according to Herberg, was that

Toynbee fell prey to a Greek cyclical eternalism, which believed that historical events were illusory. In contrast to this view, Herberg asserted that "in the Christian faith, as every word of the Bible is enough to prove, it is the historical and the particular that are real." Jewish-Christian religion was not composed of a set of timeless truths but rather emphasized the mighty and particular acts of God in the history of Israel and in Christ. In short, Toynbee was offended by the "scandal of particularity."

Herberg agreed with Toynbee, however, that the future of the Western world would depend on how the Western middle class responded to the challenge of nationalism and democracy. But Herberg believed that Toynbee had over-looked the ambiguities of nationalism and democracy. Smaller countries of the world, Herberg explained, were asserting their own nationalistic spirit whereas the larger ones were denouncing it as one of the evils of the age. Likewise, democracy could be either benign or sinister. For example, the emergence of mass society could lead to a destruction of human freedom through the devel-opment of a "totalitarian democracy," like communism. As Herberg noted, "Every established order strives to be totalitarian, to claim the individual [both in] body and soul." This trend did not devolve from aristocratic societies of the past but was quite simply, as Herberg had said in the late 1930s, a new phenomenon. Herberg insisted that the positive aspects of democracy could overcome these negative possibilities by the adoption of the biblically grounded faith of the Jewish-Christian religion.[3]

HISTORY AND
BIBLICAL REALISM

History, for Herberg, was the basis for theology. Indeed, he maintained that historicism was "the modern version of prophetism." In this context, human events were much more important than natural events, even though nature was part of God's creation. The biblical view stressed that to affirm history as the focal point of reality was also to affirm the significance of the individual personality: "History is the very stuff out of which human being is made: human existence is implicit history; history is explicit existence." Or as Herberg quoted Buber, "In Israel, all religion is history." Herberg confessed that when he was a Marxist he saw religion as illusory and otherworldly, but he came to realize that Marxism was really a secularized version of the Jewish-Christian theological position "in which God is replaced by the Dialectic, the 'chosen people' by the proletariat, the 'faithful remnant' and even the Messiah by the Party." In other words, Marxism was an idolatrized version of Jewish-Christian redemptive history, which Herberg finally realized was "the larger framework" he had been seeking. The appreciation Marx showed for history led Herberg to affirm the biblical view of history.

The essence of biblical religion was expressed, for Herberg, in the word "faith," the demand for an absolute commitment to God. He pointed out that for Martin Luther even those who hated God were closer to God than those who were indifferent. Indifference, in Herberg's view, was the ultimate sin whereas atheism was a kind of "inverted faith" in which the denial of God was an affirmation of God's reality. The atheist at least took God seriously. According to Herberg, what Luther actually despised was mediocre and conventional piety. In attacking this piety, an atheist (such as Nietzsche) served a divine calling—the avowed unbeliever challenged such complacency. As Herberg so succinctly wrote, "The God-obsessed God-affirmer and God-obsessed God-denier have something in common. . . . Both insist on ruthlessly tearing away the false securities we build up in the name of religion . . . the prophet out of the passion of faith, the unbeliever out of the passion of doubt, but both out of the passion of infinite concern." Thus, the unbeliever was, however negatively, closer to God than those who were indifferent and complacent.

Complacency was one of the dangers of the religion of the American Way of Life, of the idolatrous "faith in faith." As he told the Drew seminarians in a communion sermon entitled "The Incarnate Word," "You undertake the responsibility never to rest so long as there is evil in the world—which there always is!" This task was implied in the Holy Communion itself, which Herberg defined as "the supreme miracle of Christian life." The Incarnate Word, he maintained, was expressed not only through preaching and proclamation but also in the bread and wine of the sacrament. Holy Communion was therefore "the Incarnate Word, fully, really, and truly, that you are receiving—the same Incarnate Word that died on the cross, was raised the third day, and was exalted to the right hand of the Father." As proclamation, the Incarnate Word is not confined to the visible church but encompassed the whole world, the entire cosmos, because all of God's creation was part of the church. By centering on the Incarnate Word, Protestant theology, Herberg believed, would be able to avoid idolatrous faith.

Herberg acknowledged that some developments in the American three-religion society gave grounds for optimism. Protestant theology, for example, was enjoying "an intellectual renascence more impressive than anything since the eighteenth century of Jonathan Edwards." However, Protestantism had the task of closing the gap between this new development in theology on the one hand and popular religion on the other. He recognized this attempt in the work of several Protestant theologians, not the least of which was Reinhold Niebuhr.

NIEBUHR VERSUS TILLICH AND BARTH

Maintaining that *Judaism and Modern Man* was "avowedly Niebuhrian in temper and thought," Herberg began to view Niebuhr as a conservative, holding that Niebuhr's affinities were with Edmund Burke and James Madison and that he was opposed to the excesses of the French Revolution and of the Enlightenment, not to mention of utopianism as described by both Marxists and liberal idealists.[4] From Herberg's point of view, Niebuhr had arrived at the position of "a sober social and political conservatism." Maintaining that his relationship with Niebuhr was prompted by Herberg's 1943 article on Christian mythology and socialism in the *Antioch Review*, Herberg agreed with Niebuhr's personal assessment of himself that he was not a theologian in the Continental sense of a system builder. Rather, Niebuhr was a practical social philosopher with a theological bent. Like Herberg himself, Niebuhr rejected both Marxism and liberalism on the ground that they had overlooked the sinful nature of man, were utopian in perspective, and believed in the unbiblical view that history was its own redeemer. Yet, for Niebuhr, man could not be viewed as only sinful, for this perception would overlook the grandeur in man, the human capacity for self-transcendence. Neither naturalism nor idealism would suffice. Man was not simply a part of nature, nor was he a free spirit or some disembodied reason. Rather, for Niebuhr, man was a part of nature while he simultaneously transcended nature. This condition permitted the "encounter with faith" that was mediated through history. Because of Niebuhr's emphasis on history, his theological position was distinguished in Herberg's mind from the "ontologizing" theology of Paul Tillich.

The difference between Niebuhr and Tillich, according to Herberg, was that Niebuhr was biblically and historically oriented whereas Tillich was ontologically and philosophically oriented. Consequently, there were "global differences of fundamental outlook and orientation" between the two. In his three-volume *Systematic Theology*, Tillich distinguished between the power of being, the *logos* of being, and the synthesis of these two, the life of being. These ontological distinctions were translated into the language of theology by means of Tillich's crucial formula: Being-Itself = God. Although Tillich had much to say about history, it was quite simply, in Herberg's opinion, not an important category in his ontological theology. Here, Niebuhr disagreed with Tillich because he emphasized the historicity of man, which was a biblical view. The contrast between the ontological and the historical was the same as the contrast between Greek philosophy and biblical theology, and this distinction was at the heart of the difference between Tillich and Niebuhr. Furthermore, although Herberg was impressed with Tillich's massive philosophical-theological position, he sided with Niebuhr.

This distinction could lead to other contrasts between Tillich and Niebuhr. Herberg pointed out that whereas Tillich stressed that "Self-hood" was characteristic of all things, of all *Gestalten*, Niebuhr placed his emphasis on the uniqueness of man's personhood. For Niebuhr, the individual person was defined by his history. Second, whereas Tillich held that some periods of history could be described as *kairos*, as "fulfilled time," and were theonomous in orientation, Niebuhr emphasized the ambiguity of all periods of history. Third, and as a consequence of the latter, Tillich's theology was open to the possibility of a utopia whereas Niebuhr's was not. Finally, Herberg pointed out that they differed in the very conceptions of God. Tillich's Being-Itself was a "God above God" and he therefore minimized the significance of a divine-human encounter, whereas for Niebuhr such an encounter was the very core of the Christian faith.

Herberg's acceptance of Niebuhr's theological perspective also led to his appreciation of the theology of Karl Barth, to whom Herberg referred as "the master theologian of our age," "truly the Carlylean Hero as Theologian." The influence of Barth's theology was so great that Herberg maintained that those who might be anti-Barthian in their theology were nevertheless influenced by him. Herberg most admired Barth because he had restored a God-centered and Christocentric theology after the failure of liberal theology at the outbreak of World War I. Emphasizing the "wholly otherness" and transcendence of God, "Barth's word of divine transcendence, relativizing everything, absolutely everything, that was not God, seemed to provide a standpoint beyond all standpoints, a stance from which it was possible to live life courageously and resolutely, in a faith that tolerated no illusions." To everything that was not God, Barth offered a divine "No!" At first, according to Herberg, Barth's view clearly discouraged any active political participation and scorned political ideologies as child's play. Politics was "fundamentally uninteresting" when viewed against the background of the ultimate seriousness of a faith in Christ. In Herberg's estimation, this position led Barth to certain difficulties.

Although Barth believed that theology should not get involved in politics, the rise to power of Adolph Hitler and German national socialism in 1933 forced him to alter his position. According to Herberg, Barth recognized a threat to the church, a threat coming from what Barth called a "basically anti-Christian counter-church." National socialism, with its self-deification and anti-Semitism, was the "beast from out of the abyss," a phrase taken from Revelation 13. In the tradition of the sixteenth-century Swiss theologian Ulrich Zwingli, Barth called upon Christians in France, Britain, America, and Czechoslovakia to overthrow those rulers who were not following the Christocentric line. Moreover, Herberg saw a contradiction in Barth's silence about Russia, a totalitarian Communist state. According to Herberg, everything Barth "once said in denunciation of National-Socialism could be matched with easily available facts about Soviet totalitarianism, yet he [Barth] keeps silent." Barth had, in Herberg's opinion, returned to his old position of remaining indifferent to politics. In this regard, Herberg believed that Niebuhr's political views were much more realistic than Barth's inasmuch as Niebuhr denounced sinfulness wherever it might appear and not just in the instance of national socialism.

THE "FRIENDLY OUTSIDER" OF CATHOLICISM

This attachment to what he called Niebuhrian realism also appears in Herberg's attitude toward Roman Catholicism. He consistently thought of himself as a "friendly outsider" of the Catholic church.[5] Indeed, he called himself a "volunteer apologist" of that church *in partibus infidelium*. On one occasion, John Cogley introduced Herberg at a symposium at the World Affairs Center in New York as "Reinhold Niebuhr, S.J." However, for all Herberg's high regard for the church, he was not totally uncritical of it. As a loyal outsider, he believed that Catholics too hastily dismissed such people as John Dewey and Sidney Hook as secularist and irreligious, without realizing that they too could serve God's purpose. More importantly, he held that, despite Roman Catholic asceticism, the church did not take sin seriously enough and thus often overlooked the ambiguous nature of life. As in Judaism, the priestly element and not the prophetic element in great part dominated the church, and this domination frequently led Catholics not to question "the falsehood in our own truth."

Herberg also maintained that the Catholic church still struggled unsuccessfully with the problem of authority versus reason. Thus, the papal encyclical *Mater et Magistra* issued by Pope John XXIII in 1961 particularly shocked Herberg, who felt that the encyclical suffered from a confusion of perspectives. On the one hand, it properly took into account the rise of the working class and the increasing number of women in public life. On the other, it mistakenly described each nation as gradually gaining its own independence in a world of politically equal nations. At the same time that he described a world no longer divided between ruling and ruled nations, John XXIII overlooked the upsurge of totalitarian states that demand a person's body and soul, states that in effect "usurp the place of God." The document did not mention the growing power of this "demonic anti-state," the totalitarian state. As a consequence of this omission, the encyclical called for a world political community and praised the United Nations for its efforts to create one. Unfortunately, Herberg felt, the encyclical failed to notice that the world was locked in an "implacable struggle" that prevented the United Nations from becoming a supranational peace-keeping force. Furthermore, according to Herberg, the pope made the same basic error in regard to nuclear disarmament. John XXIII called for the cessation of nuclear weapon stockpiling, referring to these weapons as a "monstrous evil"—an assessment with which Herberg agreed. But Herberg pointed out that we had been at war for the previous fifteen years and that one could not disarm during a time of war. In other words, Herberg claimed that the pope talked only about ultimates whereas we always live in a world of both ultimates and *immediates.*

Herberg's great appreciation of the Catholic church involved him in the issue of aid to parochial schools and the concomitant issue of the relationship of church and state.[6] Here his approach was again historical. Religion and education have been intimately related throughout American history, he said, although not without tension and ambiguity. Herberg defined the relationship of religion and education according to three historical periods. In the first period, the Puritan era, education served the purpose of religion. In the second, which began in the later part of the nineteenth century and ran through the early part of the twentieth, education was considered a parallel enterprise to religion. In the third period, the one after World War II, religion was valued for its contribution to education. Thus, "the original relation has been reversed." In the earlier stages of this development, education was considered "non-sectarian," a term that did not mean "non-religious." Rather "it meant non-denominational religion, and in the America of that day, non-denominational religion meant a kind of generalized Protestantism."

This view changed, however, in the later part of the nineteenth century.

Then, with the influx of the new immigrants, many of whom were not Protestant, the educational scene altered. It became the business of the school system to be educational, to be divorced from religious concerns, which were in turn relegated to the home and the church. To meet the religious needs of the children, many churches, particularly the Roman Catholic, established their own, parochial, schools. At this point, the expression "separation of church and state" popularly summed up the relationship between religion and education, and the school became "the primary engine of Americanization of the millions of immigrants." The Jews, having suffered under intolerable conditions in other countries, sought to preserve the sanctity of the idea of separation of religion and education. Protestants, in the meantime, still fearing Catholic encroachments on American society, exaggerated the claim of the importance of separation of church and state. According to Herberg, then, the notion that the government itself should be "non-sectarian," which now meant "non-religious," was gradually developing. And in educational circles, especially in higher educational circles, education itself was becoming explicitly nonreligious.

Herberg maintained that the twentieth-century educational scene witnessed the arrival of a new type of educator, one who was avowedly nonreligious—the secularist, who held to "the theory and practice of human life conceived as self-sufficient and unrelated to God." But with them the secularist brought a whole host of substitute religions, such as naturalism, scientism, and positivism. In the lower grades, the substitute religion was the American Way of Life, the democratic way of life, which replaced "Christianity as the spiritual foundation of public education." For this reason, Herberg explained, to equate separation of church and state with separation of religion and state was a mistake. On the contrary, the country was established and maintained on a religious foundation, and the American Way of Life became "the operative creed of the public school"; the public school was not and had never been neutral in religious matters, only neutral toward any specific established ecclesiastical institution. Nevertheless, the counterreligion of secularism permeated the schools. Therefore, those who wanted their children to have specific religious instruction established private religious schools, a development that created a problem. Many of those who sent their children to parochial schools began to feel that their schools should be supported by public funds.

With this question of public support for parochial schools two distinct but often confused issues arose: one concerned the role of the religious school in American education in general, and the second concerned the role of the religious school in respect to "separation of church and state." According to

Herberg, the former issue was derived from the Enlightenment conception of education that stated that all citizens were in effect "wards of the state" and that the state had a monopoly on the educational system. Herberg considered this contrary to the Anglo-American tradition in which state-supported education provided educational opportunities for all. In other words, the state assisted when and where the sources of nongovernmental agencies were insufficient, a position that had the advantage of seeming to be congenial to a pluralistic vision of society in which parents have the primary responsibility for their children's education. As Herberg pointed out, this pluralistic approach to education received affirmation in 1925 when the Supreme Court rescinded an Oregon law requiring that all children receive their education in a public school. With this judicial judgment, Herberg held, the Oregon decision "became part of the American Way."

Parents could now have their children educated in an institution of their own choosing, provided that the institution met certain specified public standards. However, as Herberg pointed out, parents who sent their children to Catholic parochial schools now had the double burden of subsidizing both public and parochial schools, one subsidy in the form of taxation and the other in the form of tuition for their children's private-school education. Needless to say, these parents began to ask for public support of parochial schools. However, Protestants and Jews opposed such support on the basis of "separation of church and state," a position presumably substantiated by the First Amendment of the U.S. Constitution. This interpretation of the First Amendment was, according to Herberg, entirely erroneous: "Neither in the minds of the Founding Fathers nor in the thinking of the American people through the nineteenth and into the twentieth century did the doctrine of the First Amendment ever imply an ironclad ban forbidding the government to take account of religion or to support its various activities. Nor did the practice of the government ever recognize such a ban." Thus, the First Amendment did not ban government sponsorship of religious practices or institutions but did ban privileged religion and the establishment of a particular (state) religion.

CHURCH VERSUS STATE IN PUBLIC SCHOOLS

Religion in the public schools provided a parallel issue. In an era in which the American people were generally proreligious, Justice Douglas was able to announce in 1952 that "we are a people whose institutions presuppose a Supreme Being." Without specifying what those "institutions" were, according to Herberg his view nevertheless reflected the feeling of the majority of the American people. The third generation, with its tripartite religion of Protestant-Catholic-Jew, was emerging. This new sentiment, as Herberg had predicted, would have serious implications for the future. Because both the public school and the parochial school had much to offer in terms of American values, Herberg believed that they should cooperate without sacrificing these values. Next, he found it clear that the public school should not and could not remain religionless and that some means should be found to teach religion without offending or diminishing the significance of any particular creed. And, finally, Herberg recommended that the religion taught in the schools should not be reduced to the religion of the American Way but should have a solid biblical basis.

Herberg admitted in 1958 that his position on the relationship between religion and state reflected a perspective of "historical conservatism." He supported public aid to parochial schools for the simple reason that these schools provide a public service and are, in fact, public institutions. Moreover, his support of religion in public schools was based on the idea of divine transcendence. If a child prayed in school and acknowledged that this country was "under God," then the child was aware that there was something higher than the state that in turn judged the actions of the state. Otherwise, the danger existed that the state would equate itself with divine majesty and thus become totalitarian. Consequently, religion in public life was a public concern; and religious symbols, according to Herberg, should remain in public life. For this reason, in 1962 Herberg was greatly opposed to the decision handed down in the state of New York outlawing the Regents Prayer. In his opinion, the American people opposed this decision as a decision against the American Way and they would eventually, he predicted, "nullify it, one way or another." Or, as he more emphatically stated, "The traditional symbols of the divine presence in our public life ought not to be tampered with."

Although there were many, such as the Jesuit Virgil C. Blum, who appreciated Herberg's position on public aid to parochial schools, others were not so sympathetic. The sharpest criticism came from the Jewish community, with one person maintaining in an editorial in *Church and State* that Herberg did not represent the Jewish people of America. Another more brashly asserted that Herberg was "certainly the most stupid Jew I've ever heard of." The editor of the *American Rationalist*, Arthur B. Hewson, requested that Herberg rethink his position about " 'giving aid and comfort' to our country's enemies."

Another believed that Herberg was about to become a " 'famous name' Catholic convert." Charles W. Kegley of Wagner College wrote, "I should expect you [Herberg] to stand for education for all citizens, not indoctrination of any, and emphatically not indoctrination by those whose determination of their destiny has infallibly decreed condemnation of democracy." Nevertheless, Herberg saw no contradiction in his position which he considered to be based on a biblically sound Jewish theology as applied to a pluralistic society.

JEWISH THEOLOGY AND MARTIN BUBER

One of the dangers awaiting the Jew upon his assimilation into American society was, according to Herberg, the danger of his losing his biblical roots, of his losing the feeling of his own uniqueness and "chosenness."[7] By the third generation, the Jew no longer felt any conflict between his Jewishness and his Americanness. Indeed, as Herberg repeatedly maintained, his Jewishness was a means of fitting into the American Way of Life, into the American three-religion culture. This development was itself unique for the Jew, or, as Herberg put it, "This is something new in the whole history of the diaspora." Again, "American Jews, by and large, simply do not understand what is meant when they are told that they are in Galut; they feel at home in America, and cannot envisage the possibility of any other home." Such Jews needed to be reminded of their "chosenness," of the fact that they lived in the world but were not of the world. The reassertion of this view required the reassertion of the biblical perspective.

Although Herberg appreciated the work of such Jewish theologians as Abraham Joshua Heschel and Shalom Ben-Chorin, he always had the greatest respect for that of Martin Buber, some of whose collected writings Herberg published in 1956 under the title *The Writings of Martin Buber*. In the introduction, Herberg stated his considered opinion that Buber was "one of the most creative forces in contemporary religious thought," having influenced not only theologians but educators, poets, psychologists, and other intellectuals as well. Herberg particularly lauded Buber's emphasis on the "dialogic life," a life that required the personal encounter of "I-Thou," of the individual and God and others. Such a life was not necessarily a peaceful, serene life but was one of "holy insecurity." Rejecting both atomistic individualism and totalitarian collectivism, Buber believed that a true community could arise only out of this "I-Thou" relationship. However, unlike Herberg's attachment to Niebuhr, that

for Buber was not totally uncritical. He disagreed with Buber that no political theory could legitimately use the idea of human sinfulness, a view that
Herberg said was "surely open to doubt." The whole vindication of democracy,
according to Herberg, paraphrasing Niebuhr, rested on the sinfulness of man
—"on the conviction that no one, no matter how good or wise he may be, is
good enough or wise enough to be entrusted with unrestrained or irresponsible
power over others." Thus, Buber ran the danger of taking human sinfulness out
of the activities that make up political and social existence. His idea of
community was therefore not realizable in history but could only serve as an
eschatological possibility or a transcendent norm. Herberg, in contrast, was
interested more in concrete communities, of which the American labor movement was one.

LABOR, CONSERVATISM, AND SOCIALISM

*H*erberg's constant concern throughout his life was that a sense of community be preserved in the American labor movement. Consequently, he
consistently warned against two dangers—an encroaching bureaucratization
within the unions and the ever-present threat of communism.[8] Robert Mi-
chels's "iron law of oligarchy" applied to unions as a danger to be avoided. In
this context, two simultaneous trends operated: the tendency of a union to be a
businesslike service organization at the same time that it was "an expression
and vehicle of the historical movement of the submerged laboring masses for
social recognition and democratic self-determination." Herberg saw these two
trends in terms of their ongoing constant conflict. As an organization, a union
required a bureaucracy, but a union also was a "crusading reform movement."
However, the bureaucrat became impatient with the latter and tended toward a
totalistic view of a union as a means by which the entire life of the union
member was encompassed. As a consequence the spirit of reform was ignored.
The result, as Herberg wrote, was that "bureaucratic efficiency may be bought
at too heavy a cost." Something of the same fear existed with regard to the
constant threat of communism.

Herberg maintained that Marxist socialism could best be described as both a
triumph and a failure. It was a triumph because it brought the plight of the
working class to the attention of the world. It was a failure because it assumed
that working conditions would get worse, and it assumed that socialization of

the mode of production would bring freedom. As an ideology or Weltan-schauung it had therefore been a miserable failure. Instead of freedom, social-ism had resulted in the erection of some of the worse tyrannies in history. The conflict no longer took place between classes, between the bourgeoisie and the proletariat, but between totalitarianism and democracy. As Herberg wrote: "We are, in effect, living in a post-modern, post-Socialist world. Neither the successes nor the failures of the socialist movement are particularly relevant today. Socialism belongs to the irrevocable past, a tradition upon which we may draw, but no longer a reality by which we may live." Herberg again insisted that Marxism must be distinguished from communism even though communism was based on the political and social philosophy of Karl Marx. As such, Marxism could therefore only be understood as a perverted and secular-ized version of Jewish-Christian redemptive history. It has its roots in Jewish messianism.

According to Herberg, socialism derived its appeal from its "messianic passion for universal redemption," a view specifically originating in the bibli-cal Hebraic tradition. As noted above, it was a secularized and perverted biblical scheme of history. (By secularization Herberg meant "the denial of the transcendent and the reduction of reality to the two dimensions of nature and society.") Whereas messianism affirmed God, the "Chosen People," and the Kingdom of God, Marxism exalted history, the proletariat, and the classless society. The major difference with Marxism, however, lay in its construction that history itself became the source of redemption. Thus, in a sense, in Herberg's view, Marx was a prophet—but a false prophet, who idolatrized history itself. Significantly, Herberg pointed out, both socialism and Zionism, so similar and yet so different, emerged in America with the second-genera-tion immigrants. With the third generation and the "return" to religion, how-ever, both Zionism and socialism in the old sense began to wane. But they were not totally lost; they were only lying dormant: both, in time, would "be taken up, reassessed, and made part of the new manifestation of the messianic idea" when a new *kairos* would appear.

In the meantime, what Herberg called for to confound the Communist menace was not only a return to the biblical perspective but also a healthy American conservatism. This conservatism could not be based on the "religion of democracy" "because it is undemocratic to make democracy a religion."[9] He preferred a "biblical-realist" view of the state and democracy. Opposing both the classical view of the state as a natural extension of human nature because it identified the state and society and the positivist view of the state as a self-justified coercive power, Herberg agreed with the biblical view that man, as a personality, exceeded both the state and society in terms of relative importance. He envisioned the state as the "fruit of sin," a "protection against sin," and an "occasion of sin." In other words, the state was not of the "order of creation" but a necessity erected by man in order to minimize sinfulness. Because the state itself engaged in sinful acts, it could under no circumstance be divinized. It was therefore "clearly and properly a provisional historical institution in the order of preservation." These same characteristics also applied to society, for society also suffered from the ambiguity inherent in the sinful situation. Thus, neither the state nor society was part of the order of Creation. Rather they were both expressions of the human need for community.

Herberg noted that two perspectives on democracy derive from this same biblical perspective: totalistic democracy and constitutional democracy. The former was enhanced by the thought of Rousseau and was manifested in Communist societies in which the state was equated with society and the state presupposed the innate goodness of man. In effect, totalitarianism made a religion of state and society. Constitutional democracy, on the other hand, acknowledged the sinfulness of man as well as his grandeur. Reflecting the influence of Reinhold Niebuhr, Herberg wrote, "If it is man's capacity for justice and cooperation that makes society and the state possible, it is man's proneness to conflict and injustice that makes democracy necessary." Constitutional democracy, with its safeguards, its checks and balances, and its emphasis on the primacy of the individual thus combined the best elements of the biblical-realist view of the state and society. For these reasons, Herberg asserted that constitutional democracy had an "immense superiority" over totalitarianism—not because of its perfection but because of its recognition of human imperfection and of the ambiguity of the human condition.

The "touchstone" of Herberg's conservatism was historicism, understood not in the sense of historical relativism but in the sense of the unity, continuity, and flow of history. Here, he quoted Niebuhr to the effect that "man's being and human society are by nature historical, and the full truth about human existence can be mediated only historically." Herberg's conservatism also reflected a doctrine of natural law as it was understood by Edmund Burke, who combined natural law with a feeling for tradition and history. Ultimately, for Herberg, natural law must be grounded in God and not in the presumed rational structure of human nature. As he noted, the situational ethics of Protestants like Karl Barth came to terms with Hitler's state only belatedly whereas Catholics, with their view of natural law, did "with striking effect condemn the Nazi state as contrary to natural law and therefore no legitimate state at all and not entitled to respect or obedience in conscience." This view, in Herberg's estimation, differed radically from liberalism.

Herberg described liberalism as Jacobinism *sans guillotine*: liberalism "hopes to accomplish Jacobin ends without Jacobin means." The liberals agreed with the Jacobins in their hostility to religion and in their desire to establish a completely secularized, laic state. Religion for them was a "private affair," and the state was supposed to be blind to religion. However, as Herberg remarked, both the liberals and the Jacobins made secularism a religion. Conservatism, in contrast, viewed traditional religion as the basis of culture and society: "Religion sanctions society, but cannot become simply its handmaiden; it sustains the social order, but at the same time subjects it to a radical and what must sometimes seem a shattering criticism. Its standpoint cannot be simply that of society itself; it cannot let itself be robbed of its transcendence without letting itself be converted into an idolatrous cult sanctifying every social order simply because it is the social order that happens to prevail." The constant danger of conservatism for Herberg, however, was its tendency to transform genuine religion into a national cult. The true conservative should, he felt, not only protest against such a trend but also take up the task of leading the liberals back to the "vital center of the moral consensus of our civilization." Herberg believed that one such conservative leader was Reinhold Niebuhr.

In a letter to William F. Buckley, Jr., with whom Herberg developed a close relationship that began in 1958, Herberg wrote, "I know Reinhold Niebuhr is no favorite with you, but I honestly think that you and most 'conservatives' misunderstand him." As a consequence of this discussion, Herberg wrote an article in the *National Review* entitled "Reinhold Niebuhr: Burkean Conservative."[10] Referring to Burke as the "fountainhead of genuine conservatism," Herberg maintained that Niebuhr, like Burke, supported a "political historicism," opposed a mechanical view of society, and affirmed the need for morality with an eye to the ambiguity of the human and historical situation. Like Burke, Niebuhr also opposed the French Revolution and the French Enlightenment, with the latter's emphasis on establishing a rational society instead of a community. Thus, both Burke and Niebuhr saw the grandeur as well as the degradation of man from a perspective rooted in the Christian understanding of man.

In applying his type of conservatism to American politics, Herberg once again saw communism as a major threat.[11] American democracy today did not stand in opposition to aristocracy or monarchy but to totalitarianism: "The Neronic state was a free state in comparison with a modern Nazi or Communist totalitarianism." Unlike the Marxists, Herberg agreed with James Madison that every society was necessarily a class society and could not be otherwise. Yet Herberg saw no reason to attempt to export American democracy by force. For example, he considered it foolish to maintain that we were fighting in Vietnam to promote democracy. Rather we were fighting there, in his opinion, to stop the spread of communism. As he wrote, "What we understand by free society is *not*—repeat, *not*—a commodity for export." Consequently, in the 1964 presidential election Herberg supported Barry Goldwater instead of Lyndon B. Johnson even though he had been a strong supporter of John F. Kennedy in 1960. Goldwater, like Herberg, considered Communist totalitarianism a curse and a menace. Just as the Americans should have supported the French monarchy against the revolutionaries in 1789, the Americans should have supported, double- or triplefold, czarist Russia.

Herberg's conservatism allowed him not only to support the House Un-American Activities Committee (H U A C) but also to oppose the political maneuverings of Martin Luther King, Jr. Herberg agreed with Buckley that H U A C's name was an unfortunate one, but what bothered him most was that the liberals attacked H U A C as a right-wing organization when they should have been opposing communism. Soon, however, Herberg predicted the liberals would become known as the "stupid party," an appellation usually applied to the Republicans by the liberals. As far as King was concerned, Herberg raised the question, "Does one have the religious 'right' to violate the law?" Despite firm opposition to racial discrimination, he answered with an emphatic "No!" Referring to King as one who engaged in "rabble-rousing demagoguery" and to another civil rights leader, Ralph Abernathy, as a "fire-eating verbal revolutionary," Herberg maintained that "civil disobedience" was contrary not only to civil society but to the Christian tradition as well. Civil society demanded law and order, and the Christian tradition never justified appealing to one's own or another's conscience to engage in violence. After all, one's conscience, Herberg pointed out, could be wrong. The end result of such actions by King and Abernathy was that young Negroes felt it acceptable to break the law. Those who would end up suffering, therefore, would be the Negroes and not the hated, bigoted whites. In Herberg's view, the Negro question could only be seen as "the latest case of ethnic-migrant acculturation." It could only be resolved slowly and not by "liberal integrationism," which Herberg considered merely counterproductive.

In such a manner did Herberg combine the "biblical realism" of Niebuhr with the "political historicism" of Burke. What he affirmed therefore were the major institutions of Anglo-American history: "Without doubt, ours is the most stable society in the world." It was this society that he sought to conserve, and American labor was one key to its preservation. According to Herberg, American laborers were overwhelmingly conservative: "There are no leftists, not even leftist liberals, among the masses of American workers." Admittedly, American communism remained a constant threat, but only as a fifth column serving Soviet totalitarianism. For American democracy to survive, according to Herberg, it must constantly guard against the incursions of this Communist threat. As he believed, "We are today in a pre-war rather than a post-war situation, or rather we are in a war situation of an unprecedented kind." Herberg maintained this conservative perspective for the rest of his life.

Throughout the late 1960s Herberg continued to lecture frequently at various universities, colleges, and religious institutions across the country. In May 1967, he also presented a lecture in Germany on American religion and the biblical tradition. In addition to continuing his professorship at Drew University, he taught part-time at St. Peter's College in Jersey City, New Jersey, and at the General Theological Seminary in New York City, plus a 1969 summer-session course at the University of Southern California School of Religion. Throughout this period, one can say that Herberg's theological position remained unchanged.[1]

HISTORICISM AND MODERN THOUGHT

Herberg's basic position remained focused on the historicity of man, on man as a historical being.[2] In contrast to a phenomenological approach to man, which according to Herberg could only end in an abstraction such as "generic man," his approach emphasized that actual man was historical man. Phenomenological analysis could only reveal generic potentialities, not concrete actualities. Admitting that historicism invariably led to religiocultural relativism, he nevertheless maintained that it was not a "capricious relativism." Rather it was a religiocultural relativism that went beyond radical relativism through a leap of faith, which then could judge and evaluate all reality. For example, he said, any historian must presuppose an ethical standpoint, such as believing that human beings have value. Or the historian might even attempt to take a scientific approach to history, which would unwittingly lead to an ethical position. The so-called scientific historian could agree with such value-laden terms as "Julius Caesar was assassinated," when to be scientifically correct he should instead say that Brutus and Julius Caesar were present together and "knives became bloody." Yet the scientific historian would prefer the ethical judgment concerning Caesar's assassination. The writing of history invariably contained ethical content. And, according to Herberg, any history that attempted to provide some ethical meaning was inevitably engaging in redemptive history, that is, *Heilsgeschichte*.

Even the discipline of philosophy, through the process of secularization, ended with a kind of *Heilsgeschichte*. Secularization, Herberg maintained, involved the reduction of supernatural and transcendental reality, which was replaced by human power, which in turn converted the transcendental beginning and end of history into periods of history. This could especially be seen in Marxism. The philosopher, whether Marxist or otherwise, engaged in the quest for being either through nature or through human existence. As such, philosophy had become, in Herberg's opinion, "a 'demythologized' 'mystery' (salvation) cult." Philosophy thus was another species of religion, however generally misleading it might be. It could never free man from the ambiguity of the human condition, a condition in which, as Herberg cited Walt Whitman, men "lie awake at night and weep for their sins," in which men were constantly seeking genuine selfhood and community but were doomed to estrangement and alienation from themselves and their neighbors.

Indeed, Herberg asserted, modern man was living in a "metaphysical wasteland," afflicted not so much by atheism as by a complexity of superstitions and idolatries that threatened to undermine the theological and metaphysical tradition of the Western world. Herberg believed that Western culture had been brought to this "intellectual and spiritual blind-alley" by relativism, positivism, and secularism. All three represented a "creeping conviction" that reflected the attitudes pervading the culture. All three were logically unacceptable, Herberg held, but they had nevertheless taken hold of the minds of many. Of these three threats, the greatest was secularism, which combined both relativism and positivism to conclude that "human life is to be lived and understood as if there is nothing beyond, [which] means, in effect, to exalt to divine status, that is, to absolutize, some this-worldly (hence, merely relative) reality, value, or truth." The result was the erosion of a faith vital to the existence of the Western world. But, Herberg held out the hope, "there are signs of retrieval."

One sign of retrieval was the development in England of the philosophy of linguistic analysis, which, although derived from logical positivism, was now overturning it. Utilizing the principle of verification, logical positivism assumed that only statements that were empirically verifiable were valid, including, of course, tautological mathematical statements. According to this view, Herberg maintained, about 90 percent of our language would be dispensed with. Such a principle, however, involved logical positivism in the inherent contradiction that its own verification principle was neither mathematical nor empirically verifiable. In short, its own principle was literally nonsense. Out of these ruins came the philosophy of Ludwig Wittgenstein, who maintained that every kind of language game constituted a linguistic orbit of its own and that the language of science was not the only language game. Consequently, the way was once more open to the language games of theology and metaphysics. This was a British means of retrieval; on the Continent, the means of retrieval was existentialism.

Existentialism, Herberg explained, presupposed the value of the existing human individual. A person's life was conceived of in terms of anxiety, decision, and freedom, and one must choose to be truly oneself in order to be authentic. Otherwise, a person might choose to be a sham copy of something that one had no desire to be; that is, one could choose to live inauthentically. However bizarre and sinister such a view could become in terms of the kind of life one lived, Herberg nevertheless saw existentialism as a mode of retrieval from the sterility of positivism and scientism. Unfortunately, he observed, little communication ever took place between the existentialists and the linguistic analysts, with neither recognizing any value in the other. Nonetheless, Herberg believed they did represent both signs of retrieval and signs "of the new *post-modern* age, which, hopefully, we see dawning." What was dawning, for Herberg at least, was a more adequate religious vision of the world.

MODERN THREATS
TO RELIGION

But there were additional factors that served to make modern man religion-blind and religion-deaf. The presumed disparity between the biblical world view and the modern world view, as described by Rudolph Bultmann, was not that important, Herberg felt. Nor had the Marxist view that the association of religion with the aristocracy alienated the masses from religion. Nor was Dietrich Bonhoeffer's view—that man had "come of age," could live on his own, and had therefore no need of religion—vital. According to Herberg, almost every era had considered itself to be the ultimate in reaching maturity. Rather, Herberg asserted, the mass defection from religion could be traced to three causes: the exaltation of the technological spirit, the realization of the omnicompetent welfare state, and the triumph of mass society. In other words, he believed that modern man had been kept from religion, not by the "maturity" of the age, but by means of the dehumanization of a mass, technological society.

At issue, for Herberg, was not technology per se, which provided immense benefit to humankind. Rather the issue was the effect of the power of technology on the human spirit. The swiftness of technological advance produced in Western man an intense pressure resembling the "bends," "a monstrous sense of technological arrogance," with the result that man now considered himself his own maker, master, and even destroyer. This pervasive tendency led man to exaggerate his ability to solve technological problems, which, in principle, were always solvable, while he overlooked human problems, which required not factual and technical knowledge but wisdom. According to Herberg, it was this "technological spirit" that was hostile to religion and that tended "to dry up the very sources of religion in modern life." As an example of this technological spirit, Herberg noted President Richard Nixon's response to the astronauts' first landing on the moon: Nixon spontaneously called it the greatest event since Creation—apparently, though a Christian, overlooking the significance of the Christ-event. Nevertheless, Herberg did not oppose technology in itself, maintaining that, to cite one instance, the radio and television media could provide vehicles of communicating the genuine religious problems of the age by offering dramas and entertainments in the classical tradition of literature, in which paradigmatic problems of human life and destiny could be presented. Unfortunately, however, the nature of the message of the media was quite often determined by the "omnicompetent welfare state."

Herberg felt strongly that welfare statism minimized the significance of religion in the lives of Western man. The state acted not only as "Big Father" and "Big Brother" but also as "Big Friend" in the form of the friendly social worker. As he put it: "The modern State, in fact, becomes a divinized Welfare-Bringer." The historical process of secularization resulted in a turn from church to state, from religion to politics. People then looked, not to religion, but to the state as the source from which "all blessings flow." The functions formerly assumed by the church gradually were taken over by the state, and the church was forced to take a marginal role in society. According to Herberg, this welfare statism, combined with the technological spirit, resulted in the third cause of the defection from religion—the triumph of mass society, in which the individual person in effect became depersonalized and was "converted into a homogenized featureless unit in a vast impersonal machine." Under such conditions, the church often found itself converted into another "big business." However, Herberg insisted that the task was not to attempt to return to an age in which there was a church-centered, and not a state-centered, society, but to attempt to save not only souls but also persons by recognizing the vital significance of religion in every society.

The most persistent threat to genuine religion was, of course, totalitarianism. In Herberg's perception, "the twentieth century is the age of totalitarianism." Even the confusion among Christians about the nature of totalitarianism inadvertently contributed to its advancement. The essential characteristic of this kind of rule was the indistinguishability of the state and society, a view first conceived in ancient Greece, where the emphasis lay on the centrality of the polis. The concept of individual political freedom was thoroughly discarded in such a view. In contrast, the early Hebrews understood the distinction between the state and society and appreciated the uniqueness of the individual. Society, conceived of as a community under the Covenant, was quite natural to man. But the state served to counteract man's sinfulness and was therefore unnatural, even though ordained by God just for that purpose. Herberg explained that, according to the biblical point of view, if man were not a sinner, no need would exist for the coercive state. Given the human condition, however, the state became necessary as an "order of preservation" to minimize the possible side effects of human self-aggrandizement.

The Bible does not maintain, Herberg pointed out, that the state should receive unlimited obeisance from the people. On the contrary, a Christian was not obligated to obey a magistrate or ruler who conceived of himself as divine or who insisted that his people should worship idols. Such a government would be an illegitimate government ordained, not by God, but by Satan. This biblical understanding of the relationship of state and society and the believer's attitude toward it was, according to Herberg, adopted by the "great Augustine" and soon pervaded the thinking of the Western fathers. The first major challenge to totalitarianism, in Herberg's estimation, came from Thomas Aquinas who agreed with Aristotle that man was by nature political but added that man was also by nature a social being whose intrinsic worth was greater than that of either the state or society. Should a ruler become a tyrant, therefore, and exceed the bounds of legitimacy, Thomas allowed that rebellion and even tyrannicide might be necessary. According to Herberg, the Protestant Reformers of the sixteenth century did not improve upon this view of state and society, and most of them continued to argue the relationship of state and society along Thomistic lines.

In contrast, the totalitarian government recognized "no majesty beyond itself." It provided, in Herberg's view, an idolatrous state that demanded "worship and absolute submission." As such it asserted an absolute claim over the entire lives of its people, who were in no way considered to transcend the state in value. Nothing existed outside the state: "The State swallows up society, [and] State and society swallow up the individual." Unlike oppressive regimes of the past, in which a tyrant only demanded higher taxes or impressed citizens into the army, the modern totalitarian state sought total control over every aspect of an individual's life, including his soul. It was therefore, Herberg believed, the diabolical and illegitimate state described in Revelation 13: "the beast of the abyss." Herberg also warned that totalitarian rulers might occasionally appear to be moderate in their policies and actions, but they would revert to their traditional repressive methods when conditions were conducive. In the meantime, he saw no abatement of the totalistic claims of totalitarian states.

The Christian attitude toward totalitarianism was, for Herberg, quite clear: "With this kind of State no Christian who is serious about his Christian faith can make . . . peace." Under no circumstances should the Christian obey or even lend support to such a government. He should not even court the idea that, because such totalitarian states have held to some "liberal" principles, they have not been as bad as those of the "right" assume. On the other hand, Herberg also warned against the presumption that a democratic state was automatically a legitimate state: "The legitimate State is not identifiable with any particular system." The absolute monarchies of the eighteenth century were not democratic states, but according to Herberg they were legitimate states, entities that satisfied the requirement that they acknowledge a transcendence higher than themselves. Part of the moral crisis of the twentieth century has been that some so-called democracies of the age have not met this criterion.

Herberg believed that at the heart of the moral crisis of the age lay the fact that moral standards had in fact been repudiated. The essential problem of morality was not the disintegration of some moral code but rather an indifference to any moral code. In place of the acceptance of a moral standard, the general trend was to adopt "a self-indulgent quest for pleasure and fun." Insofar as we have morality, wrote Herberg, it was a "fun-morality" in which the sole aim was to "have a good time" and to get one's "kicks." This morality was closely related, in his view, to the growing "other-directedness" of an increasingly affluent society in which its members placed greatest emphasis on adjustment and sociability. Social adjustment became necessary, regardless of whether one was forced to wear the gray flannel suit of the businessman or the leather jacket of a beatnik. But it was also the kind of morality that stood idly by when a woman was being attacked in New York City because no one wanted to get "involved." Any kind of "serious personal involvement . . . would spoil everything."

The result of this development in moral standards could lead to our culture's reduction to a "non-moral, normless" one. Herberg thus believed that this development struck at the core of the structure of Western civilization, which was based on the idea that truth was transcendent and objective, a belief that was shared by Greek philosophers like Plato and Aristotle as well as the Hebrew prophets. The first challenge to this belief came in modern times with the introduction of relativism and with the exaltation of modern technology, which resulted in "the exaltation of power over truth as the object of man's intellectual and moral quest." Human problems quite simply became technological problems. The "higher law" gave way to no law at all. This moral crisis, as Herberg consistently maintained, was, in the final analysis, a theological and metaphysical crisis.

Neither the contextualism nor the situationalism of the "new morality," as it was called, would suffice. Herberg pointed out that situational ethics insisted that one must make moral decisions based on the concrete circumstances of a particular situation, without reference to an abstract code of law. In other words, in the language of some existentialists, situational ethics asked that a person make an "authentic" choice without reference to anything other than one's self. But, argued Herberg, this was a contentless ethic that would permit a person to treat either bravery or Hitler's worst atrocities with a presumed feeling of "authenticity" and "true inwardness." The most salutory act and the most barbaric act achieved equal status under this so-called morality. "Authenticity" used in this sense was no substitute for a fixed principle. To amend this condition, Herberg recommended affirming the "standards of tradition."

Herberg explained that Plato did not discover the three virtues of temperance, courage, and wisdom, bound together by justice. Rather, what Plato did was to analyze what was already accepted by tradition, which the Greeks referred to as the Ancestral Way. The authority of tradition was considered primal. But the Sophists called this tradition into question, which approach led to the loss of the authority of tradition, a matter of great concern to Plato and Socrates. To restore the virtues established by tradition, Plato and Socrates now sought to establish them on the basis of reason. This maneuver, according to Herberg, "was a profoundly conservative enterprise, a salvaging operation, concerned with providing the ancestral virtues with a new foundation in reason."

Likewise, the Hebrews based their ethics on tradition, but, unlike the Greeks, they considered ethics a part of religion and not separate from it. In

Hebraic thought, tradition was known as *derek abot*, "the Way of the Fathers," dating back to Moses's receiving the law on Mount Sinai. The foundation of Hebraic ethics was of course the Covenant. Even the prophets had as their task to call the strayed Israelites back to the Covenant tradition. They were, in Herberg's judgment, "thoroughly *conservative*; even conservative is too weak a word to describe their passionate backward-looking orientation." This view, as well as the Greek view, differed from the modern ethic of Sartre, who was concerned more with how one was ethical than with ethical content and principle. What was needed, according to Herberg, was an ethic that would hold the how of the existential moment and the what of ethical standards in creative tension. In other words, the moment of decision should be seen against the background of tradition. For Herberg, this tradition had to be grounded in a solid theology, especially in a biblical theology.

THE UNIQUENESS OF BIBLICAL REALISM

Herberg insisted that the biblical outlook was unique in the world. For example, he maintained that Christianity and Buddhism shared no commonality of thought whatsoever. Indeed, "they are polar opposites—with no point of contact, nothing in common, between them." Of the two, Christianity, with its historical connections to Hebraic religion, was superior to Buddhism, which had more in common with the Platonic-Greek world view. Buddhism, in Herberg's opinion, was a faith but not an authentic faith whereas Christianity was authentic religion grounded in a faith that affirmed a transcendent God. The only similarities, therefore, between the two were external and secondary historical considerations. Both began as cults that soon spread to other countries, and both subsequently became divided into two major divisions, the Greek and Latin (Christian) churches, and Hinayana and Mahayana Buddhism. Consequently, Herberg, reiterating Franz Rosenzweig, was persuaded that a person was either a Christian, a Jew, or a pagan.

Herberg also considered Jesus Christ unique in the biblical context. Continuing his adherence to Rosenzweig's view, Herberg believed that Jesus was more than just a moral teacher. He also stood in the rabbinical tradition and in line with the prophets of Israel. Yet Jesus was even more—he was the vehicle by which the Covenant of Israel was opened up to the world of the Gentiles:

"Through Christ God's covenant with Israel is—in the fulness of time—opened to all mankind." Through Christ, the Gentile, the pagan, could become part of the Covenant of Israel. Just as the Covenant was made manifest in the people of Israel, Christ, as an expression of this Covenant, was made manifest in the church, in the "body of Christ." But the church did not supersede or annul the Hebraic expression of the Covenant. Rather, Israel and Christianity were two expressions of the same covenantal faith—one for the Jews alone and one for the remainder of the world's people. In this manner, both were engaged in the struggle for the "Lord of history" against idolatry and paganism.

CONTEMPORARY DANGERS TO PROTESTANT THEOLOGY

In discussing Protestant theology in particular, Herberg noted some disturbing signs on the horizon.[3] Karl Barth had died in 1968 and Reinhold Niebuhr in 1971, leaving a serious vacuum among the ranks of Protestant theologians. Moreover, the theological views gaining prominence in America included a resurgence of a kind of Social Gospel movement. Herberg claimed that the meeting of the World Council of Churches in Sweden in 1968 sounded like a conference of the New Left political movement, with the clergy acting as "dissenters" and "ideal-mongers" seeking to express a benighted view of Christian love toward the Russians and the Chinese. Herberg believed that their attitudes were similar to the Social Gospel movement, in which ministers seemed to assume that "socialist cooperation" was closer to Christ than "capitalist competition." But of greater concern to Herberg, especially in the realm of theology, were the pernicious claims of the "Death of God" theologians.

Herberg recognized that the Death of God theologians were not atheists in the traditional sense of the word. Rather they were Christians who believed that God had once been alive but was now dead, working from the perspective of phenomenological philosophy. In this view, questions of facticity were irrelevant and things were as they appeared to be—any notion of objectivity was irrelevant. Given this perspective, it appeared that God was no longer central or relevant to the lives of Western man, and whatever meaning God might have had had been lost. Yet these theologians, such as Thomas J. J. Altizer and Harvey Cox, had retained the Jesus cult, resulting in what H. Richard Niebuhr had described as the "unitarianism of the Second Person."

But, Herberg maintained, the sense of a collapse of ultimate meaning was not new in the Western world, and the evidence provided by these theologians was "generally shallow, scrappy and journalistic."

In fact, Herberg accused them of engaging in a kind of "pseudo-sociological journalism" while deriving support, however superficially, from an impressive tradition, such as the thought of Friedrich Nietzsche, Dietrich Bonhoeffer, and Martin Heidegger. Nietzsche, for example, announced, in his *Joyful Wisdom*, the death of God. But for Nietzsche this occurrence was the source of great despair and bitterness and led to his attack on the degeneration of the world of his own age. Bonhoeffer expressed satisfaction with the world because it was a world "come of age," characterized by maturity, self-confidence, and self-sufficiency. For him man had become a religionless, autonomous individual. But Herberg felt that Bonhoeffer's thought quite simply restated the thinking of the eighteenth-century Enlightenment: "The whole business is a pitiful illusion, an aspect of utopian thinking. The world will never 'come of age' within history, just as it will never achieve perfection within history." Nor, in Herberg's opinion, was contemporary man religionless; man was *Homo religiosus* and religion a fundamental foundation of every society. As far as Heidegger's thought was concerned, Herberg believed that it had been "superficialized" by the Death of God theologians. Heidegger, like Nietzsche, expressed his unhappiness with a world in which technological mechanization had enfeebled man. An age resulted in which silence was preferred to "God-talk" and man could only wait for the "not-yet" gods of the future.

Herberg further accused the Death of God theologians of misunderstanding Christianity—they did not see that the very heart of the Christian faith was the facticity of the life, death, and resurrection of Christ. In this regard, Christianity could not be categorized with the other mystery cults of the ancient world. The early Christians vehemently insisted that Jesus the Christ was crucified "under Pontius Pilate," and this was a concrete fact of history, not the imaginary notion of some mystery cult that believed in a dying-resurrected savior. This facticity was not subject to the "bracketing-out" of the phenomenological method. The concrete historical events of Christianity could not be given the same treatment as a novel or a poem. And, according to Herberg, once this facticity was claimed, it was necessary to claim the reality of God. For Herberg, "the philosophical ground is thus taken from the 'death of God' theology; whatever else it may claim, it cannot claim to be Christian, that is, to grasp within itself the meaning of Christianity."

Not only was the philosophical basis of the Death of God theology untenable; its description of the modern world was, for Herberg, downright misleading. For these theologians the modern world could be described in a single word—secular. If, according to Herberg, this word meant what Bonhoeffer called the autonomous, self-sufficient man, then it was a mere abstraction with no concrete reality. Secular man, and even secular society, "does not exist, has never existed, and never can exist." Modern man might not be Christian, argued Herberg, but he was still religious, however idolatrous. These idolatries of the modern world, these "most lurid false faiths," should have been the object of attack by anyone who claimed to be a theologian, including these so-called Death of God theologians. But these theologians had made matters worse, in Herberg's opinion, by actually stripping Jesus of his status in the Trinity and erecting a mere "pietistic cult of Jesus." The consequence was that these theologians had erected a de-Christianized religiosity that attempted to appeal to the religiosity of all Americans. The consequence was a Christianity stripped of any real content.

For Herberg, Reinhold Niebuhr was still the Protestant theologian par excellence. In the obituary notice he wrote for Niebuhr in 1971, Herberg described him not only as "one of the finest minds of our time" but also as "the outstanding Protestant theologian in the America of our time, and one of the most significant figures in American theology since Jonathan Edwards in the eighteenth century." A few months after Niebuhr's death, Herberg offered his course "Six Types of Christian Ethics," in which, while discussing the history of Christian ethics from Augustine to Niebuhr, he spent a disproportionate amount of time on Niebuhr's ethics. Herberg explained that, although Niebuhr had begun as a Socialist of the Norman Thomas stripe, in the last ten years of his life he became a conservative in the Burkean tradition. As such, Niebuhr rejected the aims and methods of the French Revolution and preferred James Madison to Rousseau. He also rejected political pacifism, which, in Herberg's words, "is the crassest form of moral perfectionism you can find" because such pacifists perforce prefer slavery to war.

Herberg also mentioned a difference between his view of the war in Vietnam and Niebuhr's. Both had earlier held, agreeing with Hans Morgenthau, that the world's destiny would be settled in Europe. Herberg, however, changed his mind upon rereading the works of Lenin, pointing out that he "always read Lenin very frequently." In 1921 Lenin wrote that a revolution in Western Europe would come soon but that the Communists could reach Berlin by way of Asia. It was reading this remark by Lenin that changed Herberg's view whereas Niebuhr continued to hold that Europe led in importance. According to Herberg, Niebuhr did not dispute that American military presence was necessary in Southeast Asia, but he felt that Vietnam was just not so very important—his opposition to American involvement was political, not moral. Herberg agreed with this perception to a point, but he added that Vietnam was the wrong place in which to be fighting. Thailand would be the better place, he held, simply because the Thais were much better soldiers.

OMINOUS TRENDS IN THE CATHOLIC CHURCH

*H*erberg's concern for the plight of Protestant theology was equaled, if not exceeded, by his apprehension about what he considered to be ominous trends in the Catholic church.[4] For all the promise Catholic thought showed for the future, Herberg nevertheless felt misgivings about the *aggiornamento* proposed by Vatican Council II. Believing that Pope Pius IX better understood the modern world than Pope John XXIII had, Herberg opposed the very word *aggiornamento* because it meant the updating of the church, replacing what was old and worn with what was new and modern. The constant fearful possibility existed, according to Herberg, that the church would accommodate itself to the *Zeitgeist*, to "the spirit of the age," rather than oppose it and stand in prophetic opposition to it. Instead, as Herberg put it, "*Aggiornamento* invites us to look suspiciously on what is old, simply because it is old, traditional, and encourages a wholesale acceptance of what is new, just because it is new and in line with the spirit of the times." And, as he further noted, the "spirit of the age" almost always rebelled against God and the church.

Feeling himself to be an "insider" of the church, despite his Jewishness, Herberg warned that the scramble by some for modernity in the church was really a mad longing after the three great idols of secularism, nationalism, and socialism, the pursuit of which could culminate in the worst idol, totalitarianism. These three idols were making unhealthy inroads within the church, especially among secular-minded theologians and laymen who were seemingly unaware of the perils. The spirit of nationalism was clearly inappropriate in an institution that was international in scope. The church had always opposed socialism, especially that of the Communist brand. Herberg added that the church had of course to be relevant to the times, but being relevant might often mean opposing the spirit of the age. And relevance did not mean offering the liturgy in the vernacular, which despite its possible advantages could result in the development of nationalism in the church, a covert danger of far greater concern. What the church needed, therefore, was not *aggiornamento* but, as Herberg believed, "another, hopefully more adequate, more intelligent and discriminating, *Syllabus of Errors* for our time." The permanence of the church was by far more important than the current "spirit of the age."

Within five years of the council, Herberg denounced the gathering forces of subversion in the church along institutional as well as theological lines, all of which was the result of the slogan *aggiornamento*. Citing Karl Barth's reaction to Vatican II, Herberg held that the main result of *aggiornamento* was to offer to Catholics the possibility of committing all the errors of modern Protestantism and of undermining the authority of the church. The "mystique" surrounding *aggiornamento* was the result of two myths: first, that the pre–Vatican II church was in a state of disarray; and, second, that Vatican II promoted a kind of revolution in the church. Both of these myths, in Herberg's estimation, were totally ungrounded. The church was most emphatically not in a state of dilapidation, having emerged from World War II as one of the bastions of Western civilization, an opinion shared by such nonchurchmen as Sidney Hook and Paul-Henri Spaak, the Belgian Socialist leader.

Nor did the council end in a revolution within the church. This view, according to Herberg, resulted from misinterpretation and misrepresentation at the time the council concluded. On this point, he cited the French theologian, Henri de Lubac: "The day the Council ended its sessions, a deformed and deforming interpretation of it began to spread." This misinterpretation was caused largely by liberal theologians and priests, who, in the words of Jacques Maritain, "genuflect before modernity." Instead of emphasizing the "received ideas" of a culture, these liberals used *aggiornamento* as a magic word leading to incessant revision of the church "in line with what are at any moment held to be modern ideas." They did not ask if an idea was true but only if it was new. They failed to recall that Hildebrand (Gregory VII) opposed the spirit of the age, as did Pius IX, and that the church had always been at its greatest when it opposed the *Zeitgeist*. These proponents of accommodation to modernity were guilty of "reaching the point of virtual repudiation" of the authority of the Holy See.

The constant criticism of the pope by the "*aggiornamento*-liberals" was, in Herberg's opinion, the most insidious form of demoralization of the church, even though Vatican II had reasserted the prestige and position of the pope whether he was speaking *ex cathedra* or otherwise. On the other hand, Herberg stated unequivocally that "no reform movement in the Church, however desirable in itself, can have any positive value unless it is initiated, or at least strongly endorsed, by the Papacy." Instead of stressing the importance of the magisterium, its vocation and authority, the liberals introduced the vague notion of conscience. Indeed, the private conscience was put forward as infallible. But they failed to realize, Herberg noted, that conscience could also be false conscience, as in the case of a Hitler or a Stalin, each of whom also followed his conscience. The notion of following one's conscience could lead to an attitude of "anything goes" in the church as long as one was following his or her conscience. This view, in Herberg's opinion, could have dangerous consequences not only for the church but for Western civilization as well.

Herberg particularly disapproved of the liberal attitudes of Hans Kung and Garry Wills. In reviewing Kung's book *Freedom Today*, Herberg noted that, despite Kung's clarity of style, the reader remained perplexed and confused. The reason, according to Herberg, was that Kung "is rather too anxiously writing *sub specie Concilii*, which he likes to identify as both *sub specie temporis* and *sub specie aeternitatis*." In other words, Kung viewed Vatican II's position on freedom as modern and yet part of the lasting tradition of the church. For example, Kung attempted to show that the Vatican Council had succeeded in broadening the ancient church narrowness of spirit about the achievement of salvation outside the church. Vatican II now made it possible for those of even Communist persuasion to achieve salvation through their own quasi-religious faith. In doing so, however, Kung had eliminated the "scandal of particularity." According to Herberg, Kung's uncritical acceptance of *aggiornamento* had led him to confusion, and his *Freedom Today* was a "grave disappointment."

Herberg was also disappointed with *Bare Ruined Choirs: Doubt, Prophecy, and Radical Religion* by Garry Wills for its questionable, liberal interpretation of *aggiornamento*. Despite the genius of some of Wills's earlier work, the major fault in this book lay in the fact that its author was a radical and as such suffered from "a foreshortening of historical perspective." According to Wills's thesis, American institutions, both ecclesiastical and governmental, were breaking down and the Catholic church was experiencing a crisis of authority in the aftermath of Vatican II. Wills's heroic paradigm in the midst of this disorder was the dissenter Father Daniel Berrigan, whom Herberg felt to be "of no significance whatever, politically and socially, although he may constitute a minor annoyance in the Catholic Church." Herberg criticized Wills for using the example of Berrigan to argue that radicalism was on the rise when Herberg believed that both radicalism and liberalism were declining. Wills's thesis therefore represented only a "spectacular venture into the phantasmagoric world of unreality so characteristic of radical ideology."

Herberg of course agreed that the church was experiencing some disruption, but he did not blame it on Vatican II. Rather the fault lay with the progressive and propagandistic interpretation of *aggiornamento*. Further, Herberg admitted that the council had unwittingly signaled open season on the church and the pope. The pressure to "protestantize" the church had several major effects: the desire for a loosening of authority, the rejection of celibacy, the search for relevance in the modern world, and the repudiation of the authority of the magisterium and tradition. This pressure in its various forms led to the view that the church should reduce, if not eliminate, the rigidity of dogma and fixed doctrine. This desire to make the church more "Protestant" paralleled an equally harmful tendency toward what Herberg called an "idolatrized democratism," which assumed that democracy was a "law of life," whose development the church obstructed. For example, one liberal priest called for the elimination of the expression "Christ the King" from usage because it opposed democratic thought. Herberg believed that all this disruption would and should eventually strengthen the church and the pope, for "the Church, with the Pope at its head, always prevails, and Catholicism remains '*semper eadem*,' always the same, neither needing nor permitting any serious *aggiornamento*."

THE CHURCH
IN THE
MODERN WORLD

Whether Protestant or Catholic, the Christian church generally was, in Herberg's view, under constant pressure in the modern world. The centuries-old conflict within a divided Christendom had ceased, especially since Vatican II had officially ended "the cold war" between Protestants and Catholics and officially sought a rapprochement.[5] Together, the Protestants and Catholics now confronted such negative influences of the modern world as mass society and its constant depersonalization and dehumanization of the individual. Man was becoming a "featureless unit" of massive mechanization—not only of tools but of human life itself. In the midst of mass production, mass consumption, mass communications, and mass education, the church found itself in danger of becoming the representative of a mass religion by itself becoming another mass organization, big business. In America particularly, the church faced the task of dealing with a land of plenty, whose ever-increasing leisure led many to the questionable morality of "fun-ness." On the whole, many churches had almost unwittingly adapted themselves to this milieu.

The most "incredible deformation" of the church in modern times was its stratification along class lines. A church existed for the rich, the middle class, and the poor, in that order. Each stratified church carried with it its own proportion of class prejudice, class envy, class resentment, and class anxiety. Herberg acknowledged that in a fallen world, class distinctions were inevitable, but he found talk of only certain kinds of Christians as "our kind of people" shocking, especially because all Christians were presumably part of the family of God. This class stratification was made all the more heinous by the attachment to it of racial stratification, resulting in a "quasi-caste structure" that was "deeply embedded in our culture" and "entrenched in our churches." In fact, as Herberg wrote, "it is in our churches that the situation rises to its most scandalous." The church had accommodated itself to the culture in which it found itself, and as a consequence it reflected the division and divisiveness of that culture.

In other words, Herberg asserted, the church had succumbed to a secularized religion, a contentless "religion-in-general." More specifically, he held that "although almost every one in the country says he 'believes in God,' it is a religion without God; although about 90 per cent of the American people say they are Christians of one kind or another, it is a religion without Christ." The religion of America was therefore the religion of the American Way of Life, "the civic religion of Americans." To put it another way, the church had been conquered by the ways of the world. Religion had become relative whereas the culture had become absolute, expressed in a benign liberalism and an abstract unobtrusive humanitarianism. The American church was in need, in Herberg's view, of recalling that it was in the world but not of the world, of exercising its judgmentive task toward the world, and of recalling its biblical roots.

MARTIN BUBER AND
LEV SHESTOV

According to Herberg, just as the Protestants had lost their most important theologian when Niebuhr died, Judaism experienced the loss of its most important theologian with the death of Martin Buber in June 1965.[6] Considering Buber representative of the biblical-rabbinic tradition, Herberg called him the "personalist philosopher in an age of depersonalization." The uniqueness of Buber's thought, and his real contribution to modern theology, lay in his person-centered methodology. Herberg explained that Buber's method embodied the approach of neither objectivism nor subjectivism but transjectivism, in which the basic ingredient of the "I-Thou" relationship was not love but dialogue. Indeed, whereas the objective mode was best described as "I-It" and the subjective mode as "I-Me," I-Thou was the heart of the transjective mode. It required a dialogue in which the empathy of all parties was simultaneously engaged; this, for Herberg, was "truly existential thinking." Such an attitude was common to our everyday lives in which we conversed with friends and family and even those we hated. Transjective thinking, according to Herberg, overcame the barriers presented by mere objective and subjective thinking. For Buber, being itself was described in the transjective terms of dialogue, of the I-Thou relationship.

The "primary reality" was thus dialogue, the ontological ground of "person-ness," which focused on the relationship between one person and another. The functional word here was *between*. As Herberg explained Buber, "the fulness of being is in the 'between,' " which was at the heart of Buber's existential ontology. This view had epistemological consequences. Whereas the major tradition of the Western world had emphasized that man could only know "universals" while only "acquainted" with particulars, Buber maintained, as Herberg interpreted him, that we could know particulars through "encounter." Herberg noted that ordinary language philosophy supported this view. For example, it was acceptable to say "I know a great deal *about* him, but I don't *know* him." This kind of knowing of a particular was similar to the biblical view that held that knowing was always person-centered, was centered on the intercourse between two people. Not surprisingly, then, this epistemological approach also affected Buber's philosophy of religion.

One came to know God, not through a mystical experience, but through a dialogical encounter—God was "addressed," not expressed. God could not be inferred from nature or from history. Rather God was "over against us" in a meeting, an encounter, between the "person-ness" of God and one's own person. Or as Herberg expressed this idea: "The *Zwischenmenschliche*, the 'between man and man,' is the paradigm for the between man and God." Just as we knew another person not through concepts but through encounters, so we knew God. To recognize and accept another person as a person and not as a thing or a mere body was the basis for the relationship between a person and God. It was "the leap of faith" that expressed the mystery of personhood as well as the mystery of Godhood. As Herberg pointed out, this view had implications for incarnational theory, for, in speaking of the person of God, one could say that God became a person for me and out of love of me, a view that also affected Buber's understanding of ethics.

According to Herberg, Buber took the almost antinomian position of em-

phasizing the *how* of ethics to the exclusion of the what. As Herberg quoted
Buber: "Do what you do with the whole of your being." In this regard, Buber
was in the tradition of such Christian theologians as Augustine, Luther, and
Kierkegaard. Yet like these Christian theologians, Buber stopped short of a
thoroughgoing antinomianism. To do something to the fullness of your being
was to do it in the context of an I-Thou relationship with God, which meant
that the *what* of ethics necessarily followed as a consequence of this ontological condition. Nevertheless, Herberg considered Buber's ethic involved in a
crucial problem. Following existentialism and phenomenology, Buber's ethical system was self-centered: the person acted and God reacted. The biblical position was that God acted and man reacted. Although Buber was apparently aware of this dichotomy, he did not seek to reconcile the two views.
In Herberg's opinion, "phenomenology and existentialism, separately or together, require to be 'converted,' *inverted*, before they can be brought out of
their contradiction to the biblical faith, and into some kind of compatibility
with it." This disagreement with Buber notwithstanding, Herberg still believed
that Buber was one of the most important Jewish thinkers since Maimonides of
the Middle Ages.

However Herberg may have praised Buber's thought, he was not so sympathetic to the thought of the Russian Jewish intellectual Lev Shestov. Like
Berdyaev, Shestov sought to liberate "the human spirit from metaphysical
enslavement." The key to human enslavement was necessity, the necessity
imposed by fact and by logic. Socrates died in 399 B.C., an unalterable factual
necessity. The laws of identity, contradiction, and the excluded middle are
unalterable logical necessities. Some have even found a false security in these
two kinds of necessity. Shestov, on the other hand, according to Herberg,
sought liberation from necessity through the "leap of faith" to groundlessness
and ultimate freedom. Freedom was the liberating word of Jerusalem whereas
necessity was the binding word of Athens. Shestov therefore, Herberg asserted, went even beyond the paradoxes of Kierkegaard to attack directly
the view of the world based solely on reason and objective knowledge. Herberg nonetheless believed that Shestov's position was unacceptable and insufficient.

Herberg argued that Shestov was really attempting to denounce philosophy
in general in order to promote the "true" philosophy. For example, he used
reason in order to attempt to destroy reason. More importantly, Herberg
maintained, his view of the biblical faith was not genuinely biblical. Shestov
overlooked the fact that one of the principal foundations of the biblical religion
was the singular importance of history that he, however, sought to eliminate if

not annul. Moreover, the Bible had its own prescriptions and proscriptions that operated as imposingly as the goddess of Necessity. But for all these criticisms, Herberg did not totally dismiss Shestov's thought. He found considerable value in his having pointed out how much thought began with the idea of freedom but ended with slavery: "This is the shocking truth that gives real force to Shestov's radical crusade." Herberg thus considered it unfortunate that Shestov, in the school of Berdyaev as he was, was not more widely read.

AMERICAN
JUDAISM AND
NEGRO ANTI-SEMITISM

For Herberg, like Shestov, religion, and especially Judaism, was more than a metaphysical or mystical experience. It was a personal decision involving the total commitment of one's total existence. His view involved existential thinking even though, unlike Shestov, he did not denigrate the objective type of thinking found in philosophy and the sciences. In existential thinking truth was "made true" through a personal commitment. Religious faith, Herberg wrote, "is staking one's life on truth to be 'made true.'" Faith restructured one's life as a magnet rearranges metal filings. Faith thus answered the question, Who am I? For the Jew, the answer to this question was twofold—not only was he a human being but he was also a Jew, a part of the people of God. As already noted, Herberg believed that Jewishness could not be defined in terms of nationhood, culture, race, or even denomination. Being a Jew had no definition apart from the theological affirmation of God. Even atheistic Jews were nevertheless Jews: "The world will not let them not be Jews, whatever that term may mean." Jewishness involved, then, a personal decision and a commitment to the Covenant. Being a Jew was unique and was based on a unique personal decision.

Because he was unique, the Jew inevitably endured anti-Semitic slurs. In America, for example, the Jew was constantly on guard against anti-Semitism, and in this respect he suffered in much the same way the American Negro suffered, although clearly for different reasons. Here, Herberg repeated the argument made earlier that Jews had readily supported the Negroes' desire for equality in American society but had done so at little cost to themselves. They had passed resolutions in favor of Negro equality, they had supported Negro organizations with cash donations, but, as he wrote, this " 'help' has come cheap." Jewish communities had not been confronted, for the most part, with

Negroes moving into their neighborhoods. Where they had, according to Herberg, the Jews were among the first to move out. Consequently, Herberg concluded, "The fact is that American Jews . . . fully share the diffused, barely conscious dislike of blacks in the mass that seems to be endemic in white society in this country and Europe."

On the other side of the coin, the Negro was guilty of anti-Semitism, derived largely from his envy of the Jewish "minority" that had overcome the obstacles of minority status. This attitude was reflected in the Negro's use of such oversimplifications as the stereotypical Jewish landlord, employer, storekeeper, or schoolteacher, and in some cases with his association of the Jews with the Establishment. Of course, Negro anti-Semitism could not be compared with the anti-Semitism of Germany in recent times, with the "shuddering repugnance that has been the historical burden of the Jews," and in this sense Negro anti-Semitism was not really anti-Semitism at all. But for all his awareness of the need to minimize a confrontation between Negroes and Jews, Herberg did not believe that "the fatuous liberal nonsense" about integrationism was appropriate. In order to understand Herberg's reaction to this attempt to resolve the problems confronting the American Negro, one must view it, according to Herberg, in a historical perspective.

For Herberg, the most reasonable approach to the so-called Negro problem was to see it as the most recent instance of "ethnic-migrant acculturation" in America. Earlier immigrants, who had been rural peasants in the countries of their birth, became urban laborers in this country. They lived in ghettos and had their own ethnic organizations. Each ethnic group went through its own kind of family crisis, in which the younger members considered the older members' language, attitudes, and customs too reminiscent of the old world and not sufficiently American. Generally perceived by the dominant culture as constituting the lowest economic class, the new immigrants through successive generations raised their status in society, not by means of government intervention but by means of their own efforts and ingenuity. Integration into American society was thus the last stage of the process of acculturation. According to Herberg, the Negroes could be considered an analogous immigrant group, differing in one major regard—because they had been Southern slaves, they were in effect foreigners within their own country. Thus, by more than one definition, they were immigrants.

Following the work of Oscar Handlin and Irving Kristol, Herberg asserted that the Negro migrating to the North and the West began on the lowest step of the social ladder; only some were able to move gradually up the social ladder and into the suburban areas where they still found themselves segregated and discriminated against. But this segregation did not result from stigmatization based on color, which distinction, according to Herberg, has more importance in terms of sociology than in terms of biology. For example, the Japanese, Chinese, and Sicilians were being assimilated, or integrated, into the mainstream of American society even though their skin was pigmented too. They had succeeded in becoming "middle class, well educated, with solid families, with little or no delinquency or crime." They had, in other words, become "white." The drastic difference between the Negro condition and that of other immigrant groups was the economic situation. Other groups came to this country in times of great need for unskilled labor in such areas as railroad work, mining, factory work, and the like. Now the demand for unskilled labor was at a minimum, and skilled, technically trained labor was at a premium. Accordingly, the Negroes' present economic climate thus differed from that of previous immigrant groups, and these economic circumstances served to retard the Negroes' upward mobility.

This condition resulted not only in a feeling of degradation on the part of the Negro worker but also in tensions within the Negro family. The wife could often get work as a domestic helper, but the male was unable, because of his lack of skills, to enter the economic mainstream. He consequently suffered a loss of self-esteem and self-importance in the family itself. The husband might often turn to alcohol or drugs to assuage his guilt, or often would simply desert the family. According to Herberg, "this breakup of the family is encouraged by the insane 'welfare' system that prevails in most of our cities, which notoriously puts a premium on families with 'no man present.' " The government with its paternalistic attitude thus interfered, thereby making matters worse: "The Liberal mentality treats the Negro as a ward of the State." In fact, other liberal measures, such as those taken in housing and education, had produced greater segregation and intensified racial hatred.

In contrast, previous immigrant groups had been treated with "benign neglect" by the government. Herberg believed that the "only way up" for the Negro was to follow the same painfully slow, often frustrating, path of the earlier ethnic-migrant groups. The liberal approach only led to a "frustrating futility," and the radical approach of violence and confrontation could only be counterproductive and even self-destructive. Therefore, Herberg made three recommendations. First, in addressing the economic problem, he reiterated one of the recent proposals in Congress—that the government should provide subsidies to industries that trained unskilled workers in a skilled trade. This avenue was not out of line with the American tradition in which the government subsidized the building of railroads, canals, highways, and other such projects. Second, to strengthen the Negro family, Herberg recommended eliminating the welfare system in favor of "some variety of family-assistance program, possibly along the lines of the Nixon-Moynihan proposals." And finally, he recommended that self-help be encouraged, not governmental paternalism. Rather than paternalism, self-help and "benign neglect"—the same factors motivating earlier immigrants—would, in Herberg's opinion, go a long way toward bringing the Negro to the last stages of integration into American culture.

CONSERVATISM
AND THE
AMERICAN WORKER

*H*erberg's support of the working class, whether Negro or otherwise, continued unabated.[7] But his view of the working class was most emphatically not that of American liberalism. Quite the contrary, Herberg saw the labor movement in America as "the most consistently conservative element of the American people," as "the solid conservative backbone of the nation." In his opinion, the American working class was so conservative and so much a part of American culture that there existed among the workers no trace of dissension or feelings of alienation. Yet, as Herberg and others pointed out, the American worker generally voted for blatantly liberal candidates in the political arena. Voting patterns clearly did not always follow one's political philosophy, but rather one's special interests not to mention one's immigrant history and ethnic background. Moreover, many workers, such as the Irish, the Italians, and the Jews, opposed the old Yankee Protestant Republican political establishment. These reasons, plus the fact that the Democratic party had earlier courted the immigrant-ethnic communities and had succeeded in binding them to the party, led many, including the Jews, to support liberal candidates. Yet, as Herberg added, "give the worker the chance to show his political attitudes outside of, or running across, established party lines, and his essential conservatism becomes clear." Thus, Herberg felt that conservatism and liberalism did not necessarily equate with the Republican or Democratic parties per se. Rather, conservatism and liberalism had to do with differing political philosophies.

On one occasion, Herberg referred to liberalism as a "ruthless ideological dictatorship" that, along with Communist totalitarianism, was fortunately beginning to crumble in the face of a significant advance in conservatism.

Liberalism sought a secularized, laic state in the Jacobin tradition *sans guillotine*. Like the Jacobins, liberals were hostile to religion in public life, relegating it to the private sphere, which meant that liberalism, as Jacobinism, unwittingly became prey to the pseudoreligion of secularism. In this context, he noted that, after the Russian Revolution of 1917, one of the first policies of the Leninist regime declared religion a private affair. In addition, liberalism emphasized rationalism in politics, failing to appreciate any of the historical and historicist relativities of any particular situation. For example, American liberals viewed the political institutions of the British and American governments as rational, and anything that did not fit into those categories was considered not only irrational but also immoral. As it was with Thomas Paine and Thomas Jefferson, government—and society—was arranged out of and construed under abstract principles. Consequently, society could be made and remade at will.

Herberg criticized the liberals for being like Jefferson, fearing only the danger from the right and not that from the left. Accordingly, liberals were constantly searching for what was new and innovative, exercising a definite neophilia, attraction to the new. And, as a neophiliac, the liberal was unabashedly a child of the eighteenth-century Enlightenment, pursuing justice and eliminating injustice on principle alone while trying desperately to establish an ordered society. Liberalism asserted that it was for the people, but Herberg believed that this support of the people was ambiguous because liberals tried to force what was good for the people upon them when the people themselves did not know what was good. In contrast to this kind of liberalism, he observed the conservatism of the masses, who resisted the frivolity of the so-called liberal intellectuals. For Herberg, an average cab driver was better equipped to run the affairs of state, both domestically and internationally, than an intellectual. In his view, there had only been one intellectual in the White House, Woodrow Wilson, and "he [had] made a mess of things in Europe."

Using the words of an ex-liberal, John Maynard Keynes, Herberg described conservatism as "reverence, the restraints of custom, [and] respect for traditional wisdom." Conservatism, in the Burkean tradition, viewed religion, "the traditional religion of the community," as both a private and a public affair. In agreement with de Tocqueville, Herberg asserted that religion was a preservative force within society and the "main vehicle of the historical continuity upon which every society must ultimately depend." Conservatism was therefore traditionalist and historicist, and, as such, fundamentally distinct from liberalism. Unlike liberalism, conservatism did not view the American government as a model for all governments but as a government suitable only to the type of people Americans were. Whereas the liberal looked for the new, the conservative sought stability; according to Herberg, the burden of proof for the necessity of change was on those who called for it. The conservative was interested in social order and sought to eliminate only those injustices that might foment disorder. For the conservative, history could not be forced because of the ambiguousness of every human situation. Like the liberal, the conservative looked to the masses, but, unlike the liberal, the conservative viewed the backwardness and the stolidity of the masses as their virtue, not their weakness. For these conservative reasons, Herberg thought highly of the American constitutional tradition.

THE AMERICAN CONSTITUTIONAL TRADITION

Herberg believed that the state was neither of the order of creation, such as the family, nor of the order of redemption, such as the church. Rather, the state was of the order of preservation. Because the state was not of the order of creation or redemption, Herberg opposed the very idea of the totalitarian state. In contrast to the totalitarian state, which sought to impose itself on the total life of the individual, the constitutional state was self-limiting, providing for the greatest amount of freedom for the individual within the bounds of legality and public order. Herberg therefore opposed President Lyndon Johnson's Great Society because it tended toward a totalistic state, a monolithic welfare state. In other words, Johnson was coming perilously close to making the government part of the order of redemption, an idolatrous state, handing out benefits to its helpless, humble citizens. In Herberg's words, "The federal government is not, and was never meant to be, a moral agency to give the people an inspirational lead." This view, he continued, was never intended by the founders of the American Republic. The Constitution nowhere gave the government the right to provide American citizens with "an official program for the good life." The federal government, according to Herberg, should not define life's meaning and hope.

On the other hand, Herberg believed that the presidential nominations of Richard Nixon and Hubert Humphrey in 1968 demonstrated the workability of the American party machinery. The founding fathers had opposed the notion of "direct democracy," which could only lead to anarchy or despotism. Instead, they set up the electoral college by which means indirect elections could be held for the presidency and vice-presidency. When that method did not work satisfactorily, American ingenuity, still seeking a moderate approach, developed the convention system as a means of selecting the candidates for those offices. The party machine, for all its faults and political bosses, nevertheless succeeded in keeping "the even keel of the ship of state through troubled waters." In the case of Nixon and Humphrey, the party machine nominated two slightly right-of-center candidates; regardless of who won, the policies of the American government would not perceptibly alter. As Herberg believed, "This is as it should be; it guarantees stability and continuity—essential conservatism—in our political life, and this is a blessing mighty rare in the modern world."

THE FREE-ENTERPRISE SYSTEM

Proceeding from his particular theological and political stance, Herberg went on to consider several topics of the day, not the least of which was the moral status of the American businessman.[8] According to Herberg, business, especially big business, had received a "bad press" in the past. The "Robber Barons," George F. Babbitt, ruthlessness, exploitation, selfishness, and concern for profits were all words and phrases used to describe the businessman of earlier times. Herberg believed that a different perspective was required, a perspective based on moral grounds. As he pointed out, the businessman could only operate in a free, capitalistic marketplace. The authoritarian state stifled freedom, both politically and economically, and the operations of an authoritarian state were "colossally inefficient." As Herberg explained, "Whatever may be the defects of private enterprise and the free market . . . these defects are but the inadequacies and excesses of a system fundamentally sound." Granted, the free-market economy was motivated by profit and competition; it nevertheless provided greater comfort for a larger number of people in a mass, modern society. It was motivated, in Augustinian terms, by *libido dominandi*, the "lust for domination." But even these dubious motives had the effect of providing for the social well-being for a large majority of the people. Referring to Adam Smith's notion of the "invisible hand" of the free marketplace, Herberg agreed that, in pursuing his own self-interest, the businessman had promoted society's interest.

In a manner reminiscent of his position in the late 1940s, Herberg listed six criteria by which an economic system could be judged on moral grounds: efficiency, justice, freedom, incentives, security, and vocation. Judged by these criteria, the free-enterprise system, having corrected many of the grievous errors of the past, was "far and away the most productive in history." Clearly, it had not been perfected, for no economic system was perfect. Of the six criteria listed, the one that the free-enterprise system had been least effective in meeting was vocation. For example, a person might consider being a housewife, a lawyer, a teacher, or a minister as a calling, as one's vocation in life. But how could one consider work on an assembly line in a highly mechanized industry as a vocation? Herberg believed that this problem arose in a society of abundance, not in one of scarcity. Indeed, the problem was directly related to the question of leisure. With increasing leisure, one's commitment to work declined even though work had been "the most important bond with reality" for centuries. This problem was then, in Herberg's estimation, the most important one confronting the free-enterprise system of his time.

Nevertheless, the free-enterprise system had been quite successful from a moral standpoint, despite its ambiguities. Yet, Herberg pointed out, there was a danger in the free-enterprise system. The desire for profit could become an all-consuming desire on the part of the businessman—in short, it could become an idolatrous god. But the potential for this particular immorality existed not just in business but in every field of economic life, in politics, in academe, and the like. In all of these areas, Herberg explained, life was morally perilous. In examining the life of the businessman specifically, Herberg recommended that perhaps a code of ethics for businessmen could be drawn up similar to that already in effect for doctors, the Hippocratic oath. But, as he further explained, "Such a code could emerge only out of a lasting consensus, which may not yet have come into being; it is sorely needed."

OPPOSITION TO
CIVIL DISOBEDIENCE

If Herberg could see a moral justification for engaging in free enterprise, he saw little, if any, moral reason for engaging in "civil disobedience." Neither the Greek tradition, the Augustinian-Thomistic tradition, nor the Lockean tradition, according to Herberg, provide any grounds for civil disobedience: "All our major political philosophies in the West converge on the same conclusion: civil disobedience, as a systematic policy and movement, is not compatible with the stability of society or political order." In the final analysis, civil disobedience rested on the infallibility of the individual conscience and, as such, could only lead to anarchy, for individual conscience could be used to justify the most bizarre actions, such as the assassinations of Abraham Lincoln, John F. Kennedy, and Robert Kennedy. Nor could civil disobedience based on conscience or on one's fight against poverty and frustration be used to justify what were essentially criminal actions. The reason for this view, as Herberg understood it, was that social order had priority over justice: "Eternal order is the first necessity of every society."

This principle was quite clear to Herberg, for, as he argued, if there were no social order, there could be no justice and no society. Society could immediately maintain order by means of actual or threatened physical force, using policemen and armies, and less directly by means of the force of custom and tradition. In 1965 Herberg saw the order of American society being threatened by civil rights leaders, particularly by Martin Luther King. He blamed King, and other similar civil rights leaders, for what occurred in Los Angeles in Watts, where Negroes burned down or destroyed much of their own district. According to Herberg, "King and his associates have been deliberately undermining the foundations of internal order in our country. With their rabble-rousing demagoguery, they have been cracking the 'cake of custom' that holds us together." Equally disturbing to Herberg was what these civil rights leaders had been teaching thousands of younger Negroes—that it was perfectly all right to break the law. In other words, the Negroes themselves were being victimized by their own civil rights leaders.

Similar anarchistic ideas had invaded the college campus, according to Herberg, and threatened the idea of academic freedom. Originating in the idea of intellectual dissent as compatible with national unity, dissent was now bordering on the absolute—and the revolutionary. Intellectuals who supported such ideas were really, in Herberg's opinion, children of the Enlightenment who suffered from intellectual arrogance and who threatened the principle of academic freedom, the freedom to engage in research and to teach without interference. Herberg maintained that the right to academic freedom was an acquired right, not a natural, constitutional, or divine right. It was a right given to a scholar by society in the interest of the public good. Moreover, academic freedom was limited to one's field of competence and did not extend to areas outside that realm, where an academician might be protected by the First Amendment. According to Herberg, the new threat to academic freedom did not come from the church, the state, or society in general but from enraged students who sought to force an academician to teach what they wanted to hear. He believed that this threat was more dangerous than "anything that has arisen in recent times."

These student *enrages*, however, were only part of the politicalization of the university, a movement that also greatly imperiled academic life, whether it originated in the political right or in the left. According to Herberg, the possible consequences of this threat to the freedom to teach and to learn had already been demonstrated in Nazi Germany and in the Communist world. It was a freedom too precious to relinquish so easily. For this reason, Herberg was concerned that the academic community had not made any official declarations against the students who disrupted classes or occupied university buildings. Although a large majority of the faculty might have opposed such intrusions into academic life, the vocal minority who supported the students presumed themselves to be authorities on national policy. These professors thought that by virtue of their profession they should be consulted on matters of state. In such a role, in Herberg's opinion, they were not scholars or teachers, but "*philosophes*" constituting a "New Estate." In any case, he maintained, "there is, perhaps, no section of the American people that could make such a claim with worse credentials." Rather, as mentioned above, Herberg reiterated that cab drivers were more qualified to be policymakers than professors.

Of particular concern to Herberg was the possibility of anarchy on the campus. Like the revolutionary students in Paris of the 1890s, the American student radicals were moving from a "propaganda of the word" to a "propaganda of the deed," that is, to employing the tactics of violence. In other words, Herberg explained, they followed the dubious progression from being "idealist bombers" to being "simply bomb-throwing criminals" backed by the ideology of the New Left. The Old Left had been composed of Marxists who were overcome by the recuperative powers of a bourgeois society that dealt with the alienation of labor through that most bourgeois of institutions, the labor union. In contrast, the New Left looked not to labor but to intellectuals and students as the alienated. However, according to Herberg, "the revolutionary hopes that the New Left has placed in the student youth are no less illusory—and even more naive—than the fading dreams of the Old Left." The students, for example, had no real power; they were really trapped in that ephemeral stage of prolonged infantilism that resulted from being a student. Herberg regarded student black militancy in particular as the "last word in the philistine egalitarianism" of the academic community.

Herberg scorned the "Hippies" and the "Jesus Freaks" almost as much as he did the New Left. The Hippies were mostly middle-class, partially educated students who had become "inner expatriates" who now sought bliss, ecstasy, and orgiastic love while rejecting the necessity of work, production, and achievement. When Herberg referred to them as latter-day Adamites, he implicitly compared them to the second-century heretical sect that believed that Christ had overcome the sinful conditions of the world. In other words, the members of this antinomian and anarchistic sect believed they were already in Paradise and in fact were referred to as "Paradisals." Like the Adamites, the Hippies assumed their own innocence but, according to Herberg, rather naively overlooked that unacknowledged sinfulness could be detrimental both to the individual and to society. To put it another way, the Hippies had an unrealistic vision of the obvious ambiguities of life—they kept the hope of the Christian faith while ignoring the perversions, sinfulness, and frustrations of human existence which that faith took into account.

The Jesus Freaks dressed like the Hippies, talked like the Hippies, and shared in much of the same subculture as the Hippies but differed mainly on the subject of morality and religion. They were devout, pietistic Christians. Like the pietistic revivalists of the nineteenth century, the Jesus Freaks stood against established churches, seeing them as deadly, routinized obstacles to genuine spiritual growth. Citing H. Richard Niebuhr, Herberg referred to the Jesus Freaks as unitarians of the Second Person of the Trinity because their emphasis was on Jesus, not on the Trinity, and not even on Jesus the Christ. Yet, unlike his response to the Hippies, Herberg was able to see a positive element in the Jesus Freak movement. It was, in his estimation, attempting to make the Hippie movement seem to be part of the mainstream of the American tradition. Or, as Herberg wrote, "From within the counter-culture, the Jesus freaks are moving, whether they know it or not, to dissolve the counter-culture and restore sanity and sobriety." Therefore, despite their eccentricities, the Jesus Freaks, in the long run, were healthful for American society.

AGAINST
HOMOSEXUALITY AND
ABORTION

*H*erberg also entered the fray over the issues of homosexuality, abortion, and contraception.[9] In fact, he considered the increase in perversity and pornography among the "most ominous aspects of twentieth century Western decadence." Among these perversions was homosexuality, which he opposed on three grounds. The first was the biblical condemnation of homosexuality.

The Bible told that woman was created so that man's creation could be complete. The relationship between man and woman was viewed, in the Garden of Eden story, as the paradigm of human relations not only in terms of intimacy but also in terms of community. For this reason, Herberg explained, the Hebrew word *yada* means "to know" but carried the connotation of knowing in a sexual sense, that is, sexual intercourse. Biblically speaking, therefore, homosexuality was an aberrant form of human relationship. Believing that the homosexual should more often be pitied than scorned, Herberg nevertheless believed the homosexual was "a deviant, he is 'sick,' he is pathological." Biblical sociology also showed that this was the case; the family was considered the basic unit of the community, and the homosexual was of necessity excluded because he could not establish a normal family life.

Herberg also opposed homosexuality on the basis of the Greek philosophical interpretation of natural law, which he recognized as a restatement of the biblical view. By nature, a person had certain proclivities and potentialities that sought actualization. From a strictly phenomenological point of view, heterosexual relations were the norm. From this relationship derived the family, which, as Aristotle had held, was by nature the foundation of every society. Herberg pointed out that "nature" was here used in the classical sense of "the normative structure of being." Heterosexuality was normative, but this did not mean that homosexuality did not therefore exist. Herberg said, "By genetic accident or behavioral conditioning, a dog may come to dote on spinach; that does not make dogs any the less carnivorous by nature," and the same view applied to homosexuality.

Herberg also used Freud's thought in his argument against homosexuality, despite the fact that Freud's name "has so often been invoked to justify every kind of licentiousness and permissiveness." Nonetheless, Freud, too, according to Herberg, considered homosexuality a perversion on the ground that it was inconsistent with the aims of reproduction, and he viewed the sexual relationship of man and woman as the normative relationship, much as the natural-law theory did. Thus, the Bible, natural law, and Freud all affirmed heterosexuality as normative and homosexuality as abnormal. But although Herberg agreed with this consensus, he nevertheless did not feel that homosexuality should be viewed as a criminal act unless a minor was unwillingly forced to participate in a homosexual act or a homosexual displayed his propensity in a manner offensive to public decency. Under these circumstances, and not as an act between consenting adults, homosexuality should be treated by means of legal sanctions. Alternatively, the homosexual who recognized his sickness should receive not only pity but also psychological assistance from others.[10]

As far as the question of abortion and the related issue of contraception were concerned, Herberg definitely considered the former beyond the limits of a pluralistic society to decide. Quite simply, for Herberg, to argue that abortion was acceptable in a pluralistic society was to use pluralism to justify crime. As he suggested, if intrauterine abortion was acceptable on the ground that the fetus was really a part of the mother, why not extrauterine infanticide on the ground that the baby was part of the family, a view held by the ancient Greeks. This position had to be unacceptable, however, because it offended our Western sensibilities. Therefore, Herberg considered the fetus as much a living human being before birth as it was after birth. In brief, abortion was murder. In this regard, he followed the thought of Thomas Aquinas: "I regard the Thomist natural-law teaching as, by all odds, productive of the soundest moral philosophy for our purpose and one calculated to cast the most revealing light on our problems." In dealing with the question of contraception, however, he was less certain. Contraception, from a natural-law perspective, interfered with the purpose and goal of sexual intercourse, which was reproduction. But Herberg raised the almost rhetorical question, Could the natural telos of sex be primarily the bonding of the relationship between man and wife and procreation be second? Here, he only added that there was room for latitude on the pastoral and confessional level. And given this latitude on the pastoral level, Herberg informed William F. Buckley, Jr., that he definitely agreed with the 1968 papal encyclical, *Humanae Vitae*, "because it affirmed the traditional position."

Herberg took the traditional position in all matters of the present day, a day that he saw more and more as an age of expanding barbarism. The war in Vietnam was a war that had reintroduced all of the barbarisms into warfare that, in his view, the last five centuries had attempted to minimize. Russian communism had severed its ties to the traditional values of Western society and thereby constituted a far greater threat than did the Oriental communism of China. For this reason, Herberg supported President Richard Nixon's attempts at détente with the People's Republic of China. At the same time, he agreed with Vice-President Spiro Agnew that the students who opposed the war in Vietnam were "alienated peaceniks" and charged the students at the 1968 Democratic National Convention in Chicago with initiating an attack on the police, whom he called "the sons of the proletariat." Through it all he trusted the common sense of the American people. As he said in reaction to the Supreme Court decision against prayer in the public schools: "The American people have a saving grace. When some Supreme Court decisions are deviant and run against their custom and tradition, they simply ignore it. I like that. Burke was right: Custom and tradition are more reliable in constitutional democracies than the fluctuations of reform court opinions."

II
THE
FINAL
YEARS
1973–1977

On 10 April 1975, Herberg received a letter from President Paul Hardin of Drew University confirming his forthcoming retirement on 31 August 1976. In the meantime, Herberg continued to lecture not only at Drew but at other institutions as well. One lecture at Stanford University in the spring of 1973 had already brought him into contact again with Bertram Wolfe, his former colleague in the Lovestonite movement. No longer caught up in the revolutionary fervor that motivated both Herberg and Wolfe in the 1930s, Herberg now insisted that "all of history's revolutions have failed because of their own inner logic, not because of their glamorous goals," adding, "You can't remake man nor model society."[1] At Drew, he offered, in addition to his regular courses, a new seminar on the philosophy of Ludwig Wittgenstein and tutorials on the philosophies of Nietzsche and Schopenhauer. Because his health was failing, Herberg's production of articles for publication began to fall off drastically, and none appeared after the middle of 1974. Those that were published included a sociological essay on urban problems, an article on the Watergate issue, and several articles on American religion.[2]

PROBLEMS IN AMERICAN URBAN LIFE

The crisis in the American cities, Herberg maintained, not only encompassed the obvious economic and ecological problems that journalists confronted us with in our daily newspapers but also had spiritual and psychological ramifications with which few had concerned themselves. Understanding these developments required the recognition of two major population shifts: an earlier migration to the cities in order to escape the "small town" mentality, and a later migration to the suburbs in order to fulfill a desire for community. The result of this two-way movement in population was the megalopolis, composed of a central city and its surrounding suburbs. The further result was a sharp contrast between the "urban blight" of the inner city and the pronounced superficiality of the "suburban dream." But, as Herberg pointed out, the suburbanite was really a kind of expatriate urbanite, who was bound to the city economically as well as culturally. The suburbanite was far removed from the small-town rural mentality, and his actual roots were in the city. Or, as Herberg described this situation: "The suburbanite, no matter what he may think or even say, is not a small-towner." Consequently, the relationship between the city and suburb was symbiotic, and as such the two together created the megalopolis.

The moral issues raised in the inner city involved poverty, juvenile delinquency, and crime, and, of these three, "the cultural mark of the inner city is poverty." Defining poverty as a virtual culture unto itself, Herberg repeated that liberal measures and government intervention were not the means by which poverty could be cured. Rather, as with previous immigrant groups, the "only really effective" way to help the poor was "by letting them alone to help themselves" with a minimum of federal and local assistance. Needless to say, poverty did breed delinquency and crime, but here again Herberg insisted that the central cause for crime and delinquency was the lack of family cohesiveness. And, once again, he insisted that government intervention only aggravated the situation.

Neither was suburbia free of these moral issues, although the conditions under which they arose differed from those of the city. Whereas the inner-city, poverty-stricken family might have had a father who was unable to get work, the suburban father was an "absentee father" who was constantly away from home. This factor seriously weakened the suburban family and created a condition that could also lead to delinquency and crime. Add a growing "other-directed" attitude of general permissiveness, and the result, according to Herberg, spelled danger for the entire suburban family. For example, a woman's traditional role was to be a happy housewife, homemaker, and child-raiser, but with the development and mass-marketing of labor-saving devices for the home, plus a general climate of permissiveness in society itself, the wife began to feel bored, empty, and unfulfilled. The result, in Herberg's words, was "the notorious proneness of the suburban middle-class housewife to fall in with the endless succession of frantic causes . . . that give the appearance of meaningful life where all genuine meaning is being drained away by the realities of suburban life." Or, not unlike those troubled inhabitants of the inner city, many suburban housewives turned to alcohol or drugs to escape the meaninglessness of their "suburban dream."

The relationship between the city and the suburbs generated, according to

Herberg, "cultural confrontation and shock." Each had its own image of the other, and each had its own image of itself. These images conflicted: "The denizens of the central city . . . view the suburbs and the suburbanites with envy and resentment. The suburbanites, on their part, view the inner city and its hordes with a shudder of distaste and disgust, even fear, all thinly papered over with liberal platitudes and condescending pity." Herberg insisted that phantasies, whether idealistic or nihilistic, would not serve to lessen the hostility between these two groups but that only a realistic assessment of the situation would suffice as a proper starting point for some kind of reconciliation. In the meantime, good relations between the inner city and the middle-class suburbs were not enhanced when the inhabitants of the latter were released from punishment for crimes for which inner-city dwellers received convictions.

THE WATERGATE
AFFAIR

Such was the case with the Watergate affair of 1972, which, in Herberg's view, the news media exaggerated all out of proportion to its importance. For him, "the Watergate Affair remains a political scandal of a rather minor order." It provided, quite simply, another case of political espionage, which, however illegal, was nevertheless "inherent in political affairs." Or, as Herberg wrote in a more philosophical vein: "If espionage is regarded as immoral or unethical, let it be remembered that all politics, and preeminently American politics, is, in one of its dimensions at least, a struggle for power, and the struggle for power, animated by the *libide dominandi* (the lust for ruling), is not exactly the soil out of which the purest morality grows." Furthermore, he predicted, the Watergate scandal would have little effect on the next election, just as the Teapot Dome scandal of 1923 did not keep Calvin Coolidge, the vice-president under Warren Harding, from reelection in 1924. Too often, in Herberg's opinion, people believed that the true political situation was to be found in the news media. However, as he explained, this was not the case: "The realities of American politics are not to be recognized in the editorial columns of the *New York Times* or *Washington Post*."

Herberg did not minimize the shocking side of the Watergate affair, however. Specifically, he called into question the abilities and characters of President Richard Nixon's subordinates; moreover, Herberg questioned whether Nixon, whom Herberg called a "loner," was even competent to evaluate the abilities of his subordinates. But even more sinister, Herberg felt, was Senator Sam Erwin's committee, created by the Senate to investigate wrongdoings in federal elections. This committee, with the gratuitous assistance of the liberal news media, was guilty of using the same kind of tactics Senator Joseph McCarthy had employed in his early-fifties crusade against communism. Indeed, the real significance of the Watergate affair lay in the liberals' desperate attempts to undermine Nixon's landslide victory in the 1972 election. The principal vehicle of this crusade, the liberal news media, served as "the most outrageous aspect of the Watergate Affair, and should be condemned by all Americans, whether Democrats or Republicans."

AMERICAN CIVIL RELIGION

The moral question of the Watergate affair remained less important to Herberg than the issue of America's civil religion—although they were not totally unrelated. He continued to view American religion from his early-fifties perspective and especially from the point of view expressed in *Protestant-Catholic-Jew*. As he had in the earlier period, Herberg appealed to statistics to support his view of American religion. He noted that, in 1972, 95 percent of the American people considered themselves either Protestant, Catholic, or Jewish, and that over 70 percent were listed in the records of official religious institutions. Despite the incursions of Oriental religions in America in recent times, they constituted less than a fraction of 1 percent. Thus, Herberg concluded, "today this nation is the most 'churched' country in the West—which is nothing short of a revolution." Consequently, he was optimistic about the future of religion in America. The various institutions might alter their forms and expressions, but "organized religion will never die."

Religion might endure, but Herberg maintained that Judaism and Christianity would endure only if their endurance was the will of God. Despite the "tremendous revolution" in church attendance and religious affiliation, religion in America was becoming, for Herberg, more vacuous. Still in agreement with one theme of *Protestant-Catholic-Jew*, Herberg believed that religion had become a more effective form of belonging and self-identification. But this religion was not the heart of the biblical faith. Rather, it was the American Way of Life that was becoming socially sanctified—"we have religionize[d] all kinds of things," from national values to national history to national ideals to national heroes to cleanliness and education. The danger, of course, would come from setting this civil religion up alongside the biblical faith—at this point, the civil religion would become idolatrous. Would the civil religion engulf Christianity and Judaism and supersede them to the point that they would not survive? In response to such a question, Herberg answered: "If God has no purpose for Judaism and Christianity, why should they survive? If God has a purpose for them, all the forces of the world won't be able to destroy them."

Herberg explained that the idea of "civil religion" dated back to ancient Athens and Rome, where state and religion were identical. America too had its civil religion, with its own set of values, creeds, and allegiances. Herberg referred to this civil religion as the operative religion of the country. But, he noted, there was wide disagreement about the source of the operative American civil religion, and at this stage of his life he insisted that the source of American religion was not one of the established professed faiths, such as Protestantism, Catholicism, or Judaism. For Herberg, the operative religion of America was the American Way of Life in which "religion and national life [are] so completely identified that it is impossible to distinguish the one from the other." Here, he was not talking about a syncretized religion derived from all the beliefs of the American people. Rather it was "an organic structure of ideas, values, and beliefs that constitutes a faith common to Americans." In other words, the history of the nation was viewed as *Heilsgeschichte*, as redemptive history, an idea clearly derived from the Jewish-Christian view of history.

The religion of the American Way of Life was expressed in the idealism, the pluralism, the individualism, and the egalitarianism of Americans. The most familiar aspect of American civil religion was its political and economic system, the belief in the "religion of democracy" and in the free-enterprise system. The most potent symbol of this religion for Herberg was the image of the Great Seal of the United States as found on the back of a dollar bill. There, the eye of God completed an unfinished pyramid, over and under which were the mottoes *Annuit Coeptis* and *Novus Ordo Seclorum*, which mean, according to Herberg, that God had smiled on our beginnings and that we constituted a new secular order. As he concluded, "That is America in the vision of America's civil religion: a new order, initiated under God, and flourishing under his benevolent providence." Bolstering this vision was a whole host of saints, like Lincoln and Washington, and holy days, like Memorial Day, all of which represented and presented the deeply religious nature of American society.

The American Way of Life, according to Herberg, had as its source a secularized Puritanism and a secularized Revivalism. From the former, Americans derived a moralistic idealism, but one relieved of the Puritan doctrine of original sin; from the latter, Americans derived an activistic pragmatism, but one no longer exercised in the name of Christ. Recalling Sidney Mead's thoughts on the matter, Herberg held that American civil religion had moved through various stages. The first involved a syncretistic mingling of the many early Protestant views of religion and society and was followed by a religionized American Way, which in turn finally developed in this century into the exaltation of democracy as the superreligion of the American Way. One of the major means by which this religion was conveyed was the public education system that, in effect, provided theology schools for the American Way of Life. The schools taught democracy, under which every particular religious institution was subsumed, and there they might remain only as long as they did not threaten this overarching faith.

The relationship between this American civil religion and Christianity and Judaism was generally not viewed as one of conflict, in Herberg's estimation. Indeed, most Americans felt that no quarrel existed whatsoever, with the exception, perhaps, of some newly arrived immigrants or some congregants of the "old-fashioned" confessional churches, or some theologians and theologically oriented laymen: "By and large, the great mass of Americans are not aware of any tension, or friction, or conflict between America's civil religion and their professed faiths, whatever they may be." Nevertheless, according to Herberg, crucial differences between America's civil religion and the biblical faith did exist. Although the American civil religion was a genuine, noble religion, upholding probably the best way of life possible, it was neither authentically Christian nor authentically Jewish. These religions served a jealous God and could not accept any other claim to ultimacy than that God, even if that claim should be the American Way of Life. The American Way of Life "is still human, man's own construction, and not God himself."

A REASSESSMENT OF VATICAN II

The last article Herberg published in the *National Review* reassessed the gains and losses of the Vatican Council of 1965. William F. Buckley, Jr., as editor, thought quite highly of this article and told Herberg so: "That was a truly splendid piece you did on the Vatican Council—so wise, so original, and so moving."[3] Although some of the ideas contained in this article can be found in his earlier essays on the council, this one encompasses more than just an analysis of the conclusions of the council. Holding that Vatican II was a reversal of the sixteenth-century Council of Trent, Herberg asserted that not only the Western world but also the entire globe lay under the shadow of the Vatican Council II; in fact, it "may well appear as one of the most important events of the century." The Council of Trent had formalized the over-four-hundred-year-old cold war with the Protestants and had unwittingly ushered in a "third force," one that was indifferent to religion—secularism. Vatican II, however, announced an end to that cold war.

The Vatican Decree on Ecumenicity marked the beginning of reconciliation and rapprochement. The desire for reunification, according to Herberg, arose out of the "hellfire of totalitarian Europe" in which Protestants, Catholics, and even those marginally related to either began to acknowledge their common faith. Admitting that cultural rapprochement seemed nearer than theological reunification, Herberg expressed pleasure that at least Catholics and the "separated brethren" were beginning to talk to each other instead of accusing and abusing each other. But he warned against complete optimism, for out of the Vatican Council II came that pernicious and dangerous trend known as *aggiornamento*, which "embodies the worst excesses of modernism and threatens to convert even the great historical achievement of the Council into a gross and forbidding caricature." The conclusion drawn by some theologians, such as Hans Kung, was that the church was now ridding itself of that which was "outdated" and "outworn." These *frondeurs*, as Herberg called them, began to praise the honesty of the church as if the church had been dishonest since the Council of Trent. But Vatican II did not condemn Trent, because Trent had concerned itself with another set of circumstances.

Herberg emphasized that Vatican II had not forsaken its ancient responsibility to stand against "the endlessly shifting panorama of intellectual fashion and social interest." The greatest danger to the church lay in the temptation to succumb to indifference and passivity, and Herberg admitted that there was a trend, in both Europe and America, in this direction. The evidence that this trend existed, he claimed, could be found particularly on Catholic college campuses inasmuch as "Catholic academic institutions seem to be eagerly catering to this dissolutive trend" of *aggiornamento*. Nonetheless, despite his warnings, Herberg believed that this danger was temporary, for in the long run the church would remain steadfast in its commitment to proclaim "the true ultimacy of the truly ultimate."

From the middle of 1973 until his death, Herberg published no articles. His health steadily deteriorated; as it was later discovered, he was suffering from an inoperable brain tumor. He died on 26 March 1977 at age seventy-six. A memorial service was held in the Great Hall of Drew University, where noted professors, rabbis, and former students honored the memory of that man whom William Buckley described as *hors categorie*. In August of the same year, the *National Review* honored Herberg with essays by Seymour Siegel, Nathan Glazer, Lewis Feuer, Bernhard Anderson, Fritz Rothschild, and Donald Jones, all of whom had known Herberg in one capacity or another.[4] But the most appropriate eulogy was provided by Herberg himself. On 18 January 1976 he told a reporter of the Indianapolis *Jewish Post and Opinion*: "If I expected to have an effect, I would end in despair all the time. Never do I expect to have any effect. Never! I do what I can do, and I interpret God's will for me and leave the rest in the hands of God. I find that quite fulfilling." He was buried in Morris Plains, New Jersey, next to his wife, Anna.

12
CONCLUSION

On one occasion, after Herberg had spoken to a group of Russian Orthodox Christians about Berdyaev's philosophy, someone in the audience asked Herberg if he himself was Russian Orthodox because he had delivered such a splendid, sympathetic presentation of Berdyaev's position. Herberg responded that of course he was not Russian Orthodox and furthermore his talk had not included criticism of Berdyaev's views, with which he had some significant disagreements. Herberg used a similar technique when lecturing in the classroom. He would present the thought of a particular philosopher or writer, for example, Hegel, as neutrally as possible and then would ask the related question, How do we assess Hegel's impact? He and his students would then consider the problems of Hegel's thought, its contradictions, and its implications. This teaching technique, which the medieval scholastics used, provides the basic method of this work. After having already considered the development of Herberg's ideas, we are now ready to consider the question, How do we assess Will Herberg?[1]

The two most appropriate characterizations of Herberg in terms of this study came from the two people who represent the earlier and the later Herberg, and who were important persons during Herberg's life at those respective times, namely, Jay Lovestone and William F. Buckley, Jr. Lovestone said that Herberg "was like a knife—all blade—very sharp, very keen, but you can't use him, you can't get a handle on him." Lovestone found Herberg more interested in the strength of his intellectual argument than in the truth per se. For example, one former Lovestonite, who preferred to remain anonymous, told of Herberg's reactions to the Moscow Trials of 1936 that led to the executions of Gregory Zinoviev, Lev Kamenev, and others. Prior to a meeting of the Lovestonites on the subject, Herberg told a group of younger Communists in a bar on Fourteenth Street in Manhattan that he opposed the executions. However, a few hours later, during the meeting itself, he abandoned his earlier position and argued that by the year 2000 the executions would be remembered only as "a bump on the log of history."

In the introduction to the memorial essays on Herberg in the *National Review*, Buckley referred to him as a person *hors categorie*, as "one who cannot be categorized." Earlier, Buckley had held that Herberg was "among the world's truly wise men" and "among the truly erudite men of America."[2] In this vein, Herberg was once asked why he had not appeared on Buckley's television show, to which question he responded that Buckley was quite a showman, and then added, "I too know something of showmanship, you know." The interesting point is that both Lovestone's comment and Buckley's characterization are essentially the same—one cannot get a handle on Herberg, he cannot be categorized. Perhaps the most useful characterization of Herberg was one he made himself when he commented that "the kind of praise I like" is the one that says that "I stir things up."[3] In any case, the point is that, just as Lovestone's and Buckley's views of Herberg essentially agree, so too do the earlier and the later Herberg. Contrary to the general view that Herberg's thought moved from the political left to the right, I want to emphasize that the earlier and the later Herberg were essentially the same.

The evidence that supports this view appears in a work written by Herberg himself, namely, his 1943 article "The Christian Mythology of Socialism." There, it will be recalled, Herberg maintained that Marxian socialism and biblical religion were "at bottom variant mythological transcripts of a single essential reality, saying the same thing in different languages."[4] Then the conclusion must necessarily follow that the earlier Marxist Herberg and the later biblically oriented Herberg were essentially the same. In other words, Herberg's so-called conversion was a linguistic or superficial and not a substantial or radical one. I do not mean to suggest that Herberg insincerely adopted a formal theological position. Quite the contrary, he was as avid a believer in biblical religion as he had been in Marxism and an articulate apologist for both in the different periods of his thought.

My interpretation of Herberg does not depend on the assumption that his psychology was basically the same in both periods, although one could argue that such was doubtless the case. Nor does this view suggest that many of Herberg's earlier ideas were gradually adopted by the country at large, so that what was once radical became conservative and Herberg's ideas, much like those of Norman Thomas, gradually became part of American culture. Although this view has much merit, it is not the position I take here. Rather, I wish to argue that, metaphysically speaking, Herberg made no substantial change at all, except for adopting explicit ethical precepts that were decidedly lacking in Marxism. This essential unity in Herberg's thought permits us to perceive analogues in the earlier and later Herberg—just as he himself pointed to analogues between Marxism and biblical religion.

In both stages of Herberg's life, he was critical of religion. In his earlier period, he considered religion an opiate, a means of domination by the oppressive classes. In his later period, he condemned religion as idolatrous, as the absolutizing of the relative. In the one period, he believed pure, authentic

Marxist-Leninism to be the only means of achieving social harmony. In the other, he believed the authentic religion of the Bible to be the only means of achieving salvation and the Kingdom of God. In both cases, he condemned "100 percent Americanism"; in the 1930s he called it a major source of fascism, and in the 1950s he condemned the American Way of Life as the idolatrous foundation of American society. Just as he opposed Huey Long as representative of the fascistic trends in American society, he condemned Joseph McCarthy and Martin Luther King as representing new disruptions of the social order. In the 1930s, he believed that history and the dialectic provided the source of meaning for human existence, whereas in the 1950s he held that historicism and history as *Heilsgeschichte* did the same. He described human nature in both cases as ambiguous, either in the face of class struggle or in the throes of the sinful nature of man. In his first period, Herberg characterized history as consisting of contradiction that could only be resolved in that eschatological community of the future, the classless society. In his later period, he characterized history as consisting of contradiction and ambiguity that could only be resolved in the coming eschatological Kingdom of God.

He earlier believed that the proletariat constituted a vanguard party that would bring about revolution and social order, whereas he later believed that the Jews constituted the vanguard movement of authentic religion. Just as the classless society would arrive when the members of the proletariat denied their own class status, so the Kingdom of God would arrive when, as he wrote in *Judaism and Modern Man*, "the vocation of Israel is finally and completely fulfilled . . . when Israel will lose its reason for existence and all mankind will again be one."[5] From the beginning to the end of his career, Herberg believed that before these kingdoms arrived, ethical values had to play an important role in holding society together. In 1939, such ethical values transcended the great god of power, whereas later these values were grounded in a transcendent God. The Herberg of both periods considered freedom a paramount human value. In the 1930s he defined freedom within the parameters and limitations of Marxist-Leninism and later by biblical theology and within the limitations of the American Constitution.

As he wrote in the *Revolutionary Age* in January 1941, Herberg continued to hope for the rebirth of American socialism under its new name, the Kingdom of God. He stopped thinking in terms of European models and began thinking in terms of the uniqueness of the American one. In this respect, American liberalism would not suffice because he had already noted its weaknesses in the 1930s. Then, he opposed the "ultra-left sickness" of the Stalinists and Trotskyites while opposing the "shallowness" of American liberalism. By the mid–1950s, he asserted that American liberalism was becoming conservative and was gradually acknowledging its "distortions." In both periods he was a fervent opponent of Joseph Stalin. In both periods he called the American workers conservative, although he used the adjective "backward" to describe them in the 1930s. In both periods he sided with the masses vis-à-vis their leaders, whether it was the union bureaucrats versus the rank-and-file members, the church leaders versus the masses, the liberal *New York Times* versus the conservative masses, the Supreme Court versus the masses, or the black leaders like Martin Luther King versus black Americans. In the 1930s he wrote about black Americans in particular that they were suffering from a case of arrested development between the semifeudal and the proletarian stages of history. Later, he located their suffering in their arrested development in immigrant status. Instead of writing about the plight of the proletariat, he began to write about the historical development of American immigrants in their relation, not to Marxist-Leninism, but to the religion of the American Way of Life.

Similar parallels appear in other elements of Herberg's social and political thought. The five-point program he offered in 1946 and called democratic socialism would be called conservatism by the 1970s. In both cases, he agreed with the ultimate society Marx envisioned and sought a government that governed least. For example, in the 1930s he sought independence (a "Jacobin defense") of labor from government, and in the 1960s he sought independence of both labor and capital from government. Similarly, the values of the individual person that Marx had hoped to establish in a classless society, Herberg promoted in American society. By the late 1930s he acknowledged that collectivism was not an end in itself but a means of achieving a society in which the uniqueness of the individual person could blossom. For this reason, Herberg opposed any privileged classes. His logic was quite simple: if one opposed the aristocracy and the bourgeoisie as privileged classes, why not also oppose the poor people as a privileged class—which he did. As he wrote, "The Bible warns us as much against favoring the poor as against favoring the rich."[6]

Herberg, in other words, was just as conservative in his earlier period as he was later. In 1936, in a course at the New Workers School entitled "Marxism and Modern Thought," he asserted that American conservatism was a realistic political philosophy, just as Marxism was. In contrast, American liberalism was unrealistic and romantic, but it fortunately was on the decline. In 1949, while still appreciating the philosophy of Marx at the same time that he opposed communism, he maintained that communism was not of the extreme left at all, nor was fascism of the extreme right—"the whole political geography is long out of date."[7] By 1972 Herberg still opposed the intentions of communism, but he referred to Marx as "Mr. Europe of the 19th Century." In September 1973, Herberg read Ruth Bevan's *Marx and Burke: A Revisionist View*, most of which he considered to be excellent. On page 162, Bevan says, "While the theoretical differences are evident between Marx and Burke on this issue [of the objectivity of morality], in their social analyses they come around to similar moral positions." In the margin Herberg wrote, "Both [Marx and Burke] were socially and culturally conservative."[8]

This interpretation of Herberg's thought leads to the conclusion that he —perhaps unconsciously—raised Marxism to a higher level by providing it with what it decidedly lacked, namely, an explicit ethic and theology. In so doing, Herberg noted that Marxism, however distorted it might be, was historically rooted in the biblical tradition. The Lovestonites in 1941 had sought a new Marxian socialism based, not on European models, but on strictly American ones. Herberg provided the metaphysical framework for their position by offering an introductory method utilizing analogues. One could therefore remove Marxism's theory of revolution and replace it with what Herberg termed a theory of rebellion against illegitimate rulers. According to this theory, the struggle was no longer between the proletariat and the bourgeoisie but between those who supported pluralist societies and those who supported totalitarian ones. Instead of holding the view that economics provided the substructure of society, one could now hold the more general and more accurate view that religion was the basis and foundation of every society. Instead of looking forward to a social utopia, one could adopt the intermediate view of the third generation on which "so much of the future of America depends" while maintaining the eschatological vision of the Kingdom of God. Marx's philosophy, thus understood, is not incompatible with American conservatism. Not surprisingly, therefore, in his 1946 article on democracy and human nature, Herberg referred to the "economic radicals" like Marx as fundamentally agreeing with "the Founding Fathers of the American Republic."

Herberg exchanged the religion of books by Marx and Lenin for the religion of *the* book. But if one set of beliefs constitutes a parallel to another, if they are structurally identical, why then is one considered "authentic" religion and the other considered an idolatrous distortion? Why not consider Marxism (not communism) as on a par with biblical religion? The fact that Marxism has no formal theology is only a quantitative, not a qualitative difference, and in the language of Reformation theologians, such differences are called *adiaphora*. The reason Herberg made this dubious distinction between authentic and

inauthentic religion lies in his concept of secularization. He viewed secularization as a historical process of devolution from that which was originally and
"purely" religious, a decline from the era of the Bible; but such a judgment
was quite arbitrary. One could just as easily assume that Marxism was the
authentic religion and that the earlier biblical religion was a mere childlike,
immature religious manifestation ultimately fulfilled in Marxism.[9]

There is, however, a "third way," to use Herberg's phrase—one could quite
simply condemn both Marxism and biblical religion as idolatrous. Harry
Tiebout raised this possibility in an article on Herberg's *Judaism and Modern
Man.*[10] He asked, How could Christianity, Judaism, and Islam avoid the
charge of being themselves idolatrous? Herberg responded that they often did
engage in idolatry. For example, Catholicism was frequently guilty of ecclesi-
olatry, Protestantism of bibliolatry, and Judaism of nomolatry. But, Herberg
added, the prophetic faith was a "constant challenge to such self-idolatrizing
pretensions." His response, however, only begged the question, which remained, How could these religions ever know that they were *not* idolatrous?
Moreover, the mere use of biblical language did not guarantee genuine faith
because the very language of the Bible could be absolutized. Herberg could, of
course, have responded that revelation as interpreted by tradition provided the
means of avoiding idolatry. Yet revelation has the same perilous connotations
that the word "conscience" has. Revelation can be used to justify all sorts of
atrocities. Hitler, for example, justified trying to exterminate the Jews by
claiming that it was the will of the Lord that he should do so. Revelation is no
more reliable than Marxism's cunning corridors of mysterious dialectic that
ends in an illusory utopia.

Even if we assume that revelation can somehow be substantiated by traditional standards, such as those established by the Bible, the rabbinic teachings,
or church councils, we still have to ask whether Herberg's emphasis on the
Covenant was a case of absolutizing the relative. Actually, this question
resolves into the one of authentic versus inauthentic religion discussed above,
and it arises here in the context of Herberg's assertion that biblical religion was
authentic whereas others, say, Buddhism, were not. According to Herberg,
Gautama the Buddha elected to be a bodhisattva by choosing not to enter into
Nirvana because, in the words of the seventeenth-century Jesuits, he was " 'a
soul by nature Christian'—as, indeed, are all men."[11] Or, in the words of
Augustine, he was an *anima naturaliter christiani*. Otherwise, biblical religion and Buddhism, according to Herberg, were totally and radically antithetical. Yet even more significantly, Herberg responded by asserting that, with

respect to the Covenant, "historical particularity and special significance are not absolutization." In other words, the scandal of particularity made biblical religion unique in the history of humankind.

This idea of the scandal of particularity provided the basis of Herberg's insistence that only biblical religion was authentic—all other religions were idolatrous and pagan. In essence, he believed that a transcendent God participated in history by means of a double covenant with Jews and Christians, thus making them unique in the history of humankind and making them the main vehicles of *Heilsgeschichte*. Merely formulating a definition of the scandal of particularity reveals the difficulties contained within it, difficulties that Herberg considered only superficially if at all. This idea raises problems that can be considered from the points of view of linguistic analysis and historiography, which has the paramount task of dealing with particulars.

Linguistic analysis raises crucial questions about the word "transcendence." Does this word have an empirical or ontic or extensive reference; that is, is there something to which the word "transcendence" points? Assuming that the word does have some such reference, one realizes that proving it would be insurmountably difficult. One can maintain that accepting an ontic reference for the word "transcendence" is a matter of faith. But, as with the words "revelation" and "conscience," faith can be used to justify a whole host of dubious and curious beliefs. However, this question of the ontic reference of the word aside, it is clear that the word "transcendence" is quite simply another word within the orbit of all human language. Our language, including the word "transcendence," is like a mathematical language—it has no basis in nature. Rather, it derives from the human imagination and thus functions in a manner similar to the ontological proof for the existence of God—it functions only by arbitrary fiat. This view suggests that transcendence is, in the final analysis, quite immanent. Merely to claim that something is transcendent does not automatically confer ontic status upon that which has been claimed to be transcendent.[12]

A similar difficulty arises with the notion of *Heilsgeschichte*. One can claim legitimately that any particular event is unique. For example, one could hold that the Vietnam War was unique in the sense that the United States had never before engaged a massive army on the shores of Vietnam. But when viewed generically, the Vietnam War was obviously not unique. There have been other wars in which the United States participated, and indeed the Vietnam War was like all wars in that two opposing sides were killing each other. The same applies to a group of people who had what they considered to be an unusual and unique experience. For example, the Masaday Indians of the Philippines recall an airplane flying over their isolated region as a kind of redemptive event. The Christians considered the Christ-event and the Hebrews considered the Sinai-Exodus event to be unique, not because of the evidence garnered by historiography, but because of an act of faith, which is to say, because of a tour de force. Herberg viewed the scandal of particularity positively, not because the particularity of these events revealed themselves to be unique, but because some people simply asserted that they were so. *Heilsgeschichte* therefore is quite simply another interpretation of *Weltgeschichte* and it does not alter *Weltgeschichte* one iota.

Herberg, for example, criticized the "Death of God" theologians for viewing the Christ-event phenomenologically and for overlooking the particularity, the uniqueness, of that historical event. Nonetheless, when the historian views the Christ-event, he can only appeal to "authorities" and therefore must conclude that no reliable authorities substantiate Christian claims about the Christ-event. Herberg could of course have replied that the Christian interpretation was a matter of faith and that the source of the interpretation was transhistorical, but did this not mean that the Christian invariably viewed the Christ-event phenomenologically? Or would Herberg once again make the dubious claim, as noted above, that the word "transhistorical" has an ontic reference? The linguistic difficulties inherent in this problem remain insurmountable.

Herberg did not therefore recognize the commonality of the scandal of particularity. The Hebrews claimed the uniqueness of their monotheism. The Christians claimed that God actually became flesh and dwelt among us. The Buddhists proclaimed the uniqueness of Gautama the Buddha. Da Free John asserted the uniqueness of the guru who is not at all like "ordinary people." Rousseau said that he was unlike anyone else in the world. Schopenhauer believed that to receive scorn from his contemporaries provided prima facie evidence that his philosophical position was correct. The Communist vanguard considers its role and that of the proletariat unique in history. The conflict between the German National Socialists and the Jews was in effect a conflict between two groups, each claiming uniqueness. From Zoroastrianism and the Athenian Greeks to the Mormons and the Moonies, all claim a special status in history. Herberg similarly described what he considered the uniqueness of the third generation in America. The claim to particularity is almost a genetically induced psychological trait of the human species, and the scandal of the scandal of particularity is that it is so common.

More importantly, the claim of uniqueness in no way constitutes a claim of truthfulness. Given his prophetic stance, Herberg would have had to agree that the absolutization of one's presumed uniqueness would be idolatrous. It is in his prophetic stance that Herberg was most effective. As he wrote in *Protestant-Catholic-Jew*, we are prone to idolize our beliefs and institutions, as well as our ideas. Because of his prophetic stance, Herberg was critical of every idea, and for this reason Lovestone described him as a "knife—all blade" and Buckley characterized him as an *hors categorie*. The prophetic stance is, in the final analysis, not a position at all unless it is a position that admits simultaneously of absolute faith in a transcendent God and complete skepticism with respect to everything else, including the idea of God. But as Martin Heidegger pointed out, the unitary rejection of all philosophical positions is itself an interesting philosophical position. Problems exist with the prophetic stance that Herberg did not deal with.

Like Kierkegaard, Herberg maintained that one's stand on God is not necessarily a firm footing at all. He called everything finite into question, even the finite understanding of God, for all things finite are tainted with the sinfulness of man. In the late 1930s Herberg had affirmed this view when he wrote on Marxist-Leninism, but it reached full maturity with the development of his theological position. Still later, he noted that Paul Tillich acknowledged the "prophetic element in Marxism," which condemned as inhumane much of bourgeois society.[13] But neither Tillich nor Herberg acknowledged that the prophetic stance was quite simply another human perspective, and as such it was, to use Herberg's frequent designation, idolatrous—or to use a Nietzschean category, covert nihilism. It finds itself in the contradictory position of asserting the truth that there is no Truth among mankind. Herberg has unwittingly demonstrated that covert nihilism lies at the heart of the biblical tradition. Just as he held that Marxism arose out of the biblical tradition, so, we realize, does nihilism. If biblical religion were not nihilistic to the core, the question of nihilism would not have arisen. The final logic of the prophetic stance arrives at overt nihilism, which acknowledges that humankind clings to imagined values that are finally valueless.

That this is the implication of Herberg's thought clearly appears in *Judaism and Modern Man*. Although Sisyphus occasionally reaches the top of the mountain, Herberg here expressed his belief that to do so is impossible. On the one hand, he insists that life "must find fulfillment in something beyond"—obviously in God and preferably by means of biblical realism. On the other hand, one can arrive at this point "only after a desperate inner struggle in which the victory is never final." Or the Law can be used as a standard of what is right and good but "the very best we do always falls short of it." Furthermore, "salvation, like faith, out of which it is born, can never become a secure possession of ours." Salvation is embedded within history "yet is never entirely fulfilled within it." The battle of faith is "the perennial struggle of life." Herberg also says that justice can never be attained in history because love, the source of justice, fails, which means that love cannot be attained. In other words, life itself, from birth to death, is constant struggle and persistent pain, and human history is precisely the problem and not the solution of the existential questions that confront us. Yet Herberg offers a solution that lies beyond history. The solution is the eschatological Kingdom of God, but our solution here and now is to hope for this future kingdom. Hope necessarily and inevitably must be absolutized, which is to say, idolatrized. Without the idolatry of biblical eschatology, we would not absolutize technology, "secular" man, collectivism, pluralism, and the American Way of Life, for all of these are but secularized versions of that same eschatology.

The pain of the present is therefore overcome by what Nietzsche called an "imaginary teleology," which, to use the words of Augustine, is a *fantasio fornicatio*. The Kingdom of God is no more realistic and no less idealistic and utopian than the Marxist notion of a classless society. That Herberg succumbed to this covert nihilism clearly appears in his view that there are only three solutions to the problem of human existence: "(a) we may assert that while any particular event or enterprise of history is equivocal, history itself as process is meaningful; (b) we may deny that history has any meaning and look for the meaning of human life in an escape from history, in a dimension of eternity far removed from the vicissitudes of senseless change; and finally (c) we may strongly affirm the reality and significance of history but insist that its meaning, both in part and in whole, is ultimately to be resolved not within history itself but in terms of an 'end' which is beyond history and yet is directly relevant to it as final fulfillment and judgment."[4] Herberg obviously opted for the third approach and did not consider a fourth approach, that humans escape the pain of the present by positing an illusory "end" to history. In this case, (b) and (c) above are identical. What Herberg did, both as a Marxist and as a theologian, was to absolutize eschatology. Indeed, he maintained that "the meaning of history must somehow be completed if there is to be any meaning at all." A theologian might ask, Why must one's relationship to God be based on a future kingdom, unless one is using God as a means to an end? Is this not the very heart of human egocentricity? The value of the Kingdom of God, as well as a classless society, is ultimately valueless.

To offer hope when that which is hoped for is illusive, if not illusory, is the essence of covert nihilism, and this nihilism is what Herberg's prophetic stance offers. It bases its faith on the impossibility of any human solutions; it bases its hope on the knowledge of an Absolute that it forthrightly confesses can never be known; and it refuses to acknowledge that, from the perspective of its own morality, human existence, strictly speaking, ought not be. There is no comfort in saying that all questions about the existential problems that confront everyone will be resolved in the future. To provide such an answer, as both the earlier and later Herberg did, and as did Kierkegaard, Nietzsche, Heidegger, and Sartre, is not to take the metaphysical questions confronting us all with genuine seriousness. They have all missed the point. They have all in the final analysis offered an Apollonian approach to the puzzling questions before us—they have insisted on "right thinking." Just as Heidegger insisted on "right thinking" about authentic existence, Herberg insisted on "right thinking" about authentic religion. For all his emphasis on biblical realism, Herberg was finally idealistic and utopian.

Will Herberg therefore was no Diogenes seeking an honest man. Although he himself was hardly a paragon of virtue, he did carry a lamp, however faint and indistinct. His lamp was not even necessarily one of truth, but rather a lamp for searching through the ever-prevailing and all-pervading darkness. We should not worship idols, he said. But how can idolatry be avoided? Every moment of our lives involves the absolutization of the relative, and the mere use of biblical language does not free one for "authentic" religion. All religion is inauthentic. Herberg apparently never perceived these logical implications of his own position, and herein lies his greatest weakness. All other weaknesses he may have had are trivial, trite, insignificant, and merely peripheral. All people lie, if not to others, then most assuredly to themselves. Few seek the meaning of human existence genuinely and wholeheartedly. From all available evidence, Herberg did. That he failed is no judgment on his attempt—we all, in the final analysis, fail. Death is the culmination, the recognition, the realization of that failure, and the death of one individual, in this case Herberg, is a *Weltgerichte*, a final judgment on the world, as well as its gods, including the God of Abraham, Isaac, and Jacob.

Judgment implies interpretation, and a man's life demands interpretation, if for no other reason than to satisfy some of the angst of the living. Herberg's life, from beginning to end, was quintessentially religious, whether as a Marxist demanding faithfulness to a conservative Marxist-Leninist line or as a conservative American demanding allegiance to the finest religious and political traditions. He was, at bottom, a soul searching for metaphysical certainty. Like any honest intellectual, he never found it, as much as he may have believed he had. The absolutes of Marxism satisfy no more than do those of Judaism and Christianity. Like Moses and Luther, Herberg was a soul deluded. And yet a soul he was—dynamic, effusive, contradictory, paradoxical, and even, if you will, dialectical, in the classical sense of the word. He was constantly engaged in dialogue, whether with students, with professors, with politicians, or with the readers of his articles and books. His last conscious efforts were to discuss ideas. His life was a life of the mind, formally untrained, sometimes erroneous, yet truly representative of the life of prophetic protest. However, after his life the question of *why* remains. In the words of his friend, Alice Brent Nilva, he never reached a solution. Herein lies the tragedy of his or any other life, and herein is the reason Herberg is to be admired. He tried—the rest is not our business.

NOTES

CHAPTER 1

1. In *Who's Who in America*, Herberg's educational background includes the information that he received his B.A., M.A., and Ph.D. from Columbia University. However, this is not the case. For further information on Herberg's educational credentials, see the discussion between Lewis S. Feuer and Douglas G. Webb in *Canadian Review of American Studies*, Fall 1978 (pp. 233–40) and Fall 1980 (pp. 262–68).

2. "Coal Miners," 7 November 1925, p. 3.

3. *Young Worker*, 23 May 1925, pp. 1, 2.

4. "Lenin and the Youth," February 1926, pp. 166–71.

5. "The War Danger," 15 September 1927, pp. 5, 7.

6. "Military Training at the League's Schools," 6 August 1928, p. 6.

7. "The New Orientation," 9 January 1926, p. 4.

8. " 'Employee Education,' " September 1926, pp. 505–10.

9. "The Steel Making Minerals," November 1926, pp. 594–95, 600.

10. Copy in the author's possession.

CHAPTER 2

1. Herberg stated that over five hundred were expelled from the party, whereas others show a different figure. See Herberg's "The Crisis of the Communist Party of the United States," in the *International Information of the Communist Opposition*, edited by M. N. Roy and August Thalheimer, May 1930, p. 9; the introduction by Donald Clark Hodges in vol. 1 of the *Revolutionary Age* (Greenwood Reprint Corporation); Theodore Draper, *American Communism and Soviet Russia* (New York: Viking Press, 1960), p. 430.

2. "The Tenth Plenum," 1 November 1929, p. 15; "The Tenth Plenum," 15 November 1929, p. 17; "The Tenth Plenum," 1 December 1929, p. 15; "The Tenth Plenum," 15 December 1929, p. 12; "The Tenth Plenum," 1 January 1930, p. 11.

3. "The Real Meaning," 1 March 1930, pp. 6–7.

4. Cf. M. N. Roy's article "The Problem of Centralization," 20 November 1929, in *Gegen den Strom*, the central organ of the German Communist Party-Opposition, and Herberg's article "The VI Congress," 15 January 1930, p. 7.

5. See "The Crisis and Revolution," 14 March 1931, pp. 3–4; "About the XI Plenum," 30 May 1931, p. 3; "About the XI Plenum," 6 June 1931, p. 3; "The General Line," 1 December 1932, p. 5; "Soviet Recognition and the Comintern," 15 December 1933, pp. 3, 5. In January 1932, the CPUSA-Majority became known as the CPUSA-Opposition and the name of its newspaper, *Revolutionary Age*, was changed to *Workers Age*.

6. See "Against a 'New' Party," 1 December 1933, pp. 6–7.

7. Herberg Archives, Drew University, Madison, N.J., Folder 141.1.

8. "Have Communists the Right to Think?" 1 February 1930, pp. 10–11.

9. "That Duranty Interview," 10 January 1931, p. 3.

10. See "The Decay of Trotskyism," 1 December 1929, p. 8; "Whither Trotskyism?" 21 April 1930, p. 6; " 'National Socialism'—Or Factional Tail-End?" 21 May 1930, p. 13; "The 'Genius of Error,' " 15 March 1933, pp. 4, 8; review of *The Only Road* by Leon Trotsky, 1 August 1933, p. 8; "Fascism and Democracy in Hitler's Germany," 15 September 1933, p. 3; "From 'Real Communism' to 'Real Democracy,' " 1 January 1934, p. 3; "The American Trotskyist Movement," August 1930, pp. 12–15.

11. "Rosa Luxemburg," 15 February 1930, pp. 12–13.

12. See "A Discussion with an Intellectual," 10 October 1931, p. 4; "About the Theory of 'Cultural Compulsives,' " 14 November 1931, p. 3; "About the Theory of 'Cultural Compulsives,' " 21 November 1931, p. 3; "Marxism and Cultural Evolution," 14 May 1932, p. 3; " 'The Liberation of American Literature,' " 15 October 1932, p. 4; review of *Modern Monthly* edited by V. F. Calverton, 1 July 1933, p. 8; review of *Modern Monthly* edited by V. F. Calverton, 1 December 1933, p. 8; "Upton Sinclair and the Nobel Prize," 10 January 1932, p. 7, an article signed "W. H." and probably written by Herberg.

13. See "Einstein and Marx," 13 December 1930, p. 3; "Einstein and Marx," 20 December 1930, p. 3; "Einstein and Marx," 27 December 1930, p. 3; "Einstein and Marx," 4 April 1931, pp. 3–4.

14. "Darwinism and Marxism," 7 May 1932, pp. 3–4.

15. See "Two Splendid Pamphlets," 21 April 1930, p. 4; "Problems of the Negro Masses," 7 February 1931, p. 3; review of *South Carolina during Reconstruction* by Francis B. Simkins and Robert H. Moody, 15 May 1933, p. 8; review of *The Negro's Church* by Benjamin Elijah Mays and Joseph William Nicholson, 15 June 1933, p. 8.

16. See "A False Orientation in Negro Work," 14 February 1931, p. 3; "Problems of the Negro Masses," 21 March 1931, p. 3; "Problems of the Negro Masses," 28 March 1931, p. 3; "Marxism and the 'Negro Question,' " 11 July 1931, p. 4; "Jews in Russia—Negroes in the U.S.A.," 1 August 1931, pp. 3–4; "In Reply to Dr. DuBois," 5 September 1931, p. 4; "In Reply to Dr. DuBois," 12 September 1931, p. 3; "A Defense of Slavery Shattered," 26 December 1931, p. 3; "The DePriest 'Non-Partisan' Conference," 2 January 1932, p. 3; " 'We Are the Truer Guardians,' " 13 February 1932, p. 4; " 'We Are the Truer Guardians,' " 20 February 1932, p. 3; "The 100th Anniversary of Abolitionism," 9 April 1932, p. 3; "The Civil War in New Perspective," Summer 1932, pp. 54–61; "Slavery in the 'Land of the Free,' " 23 July 1932, p. 3; "Slavery in the 'Land of the Free,' " 16 July 1932, p. 4; "The Negro and Communism," 15 May 1933, p. 5.

17. See "Problems of the Crisis," 14 March 1931, pp. 3–4; "Karl Marx or Herbert Hoover," 9 May 1931, p. 3; "The Breath of Sectarianism Is Death!" 19 December 1931, p. 3; "Unemployment and the Workers," 23 September 1932, pp. 3–4; "What's Happening to America?" 1 February 1933, p. 4; "On the Hoover 'Social Trends' Report," 15 February 1933, pp. 5, 7.

18. See "Unemployment and Labor," 21 February 1931, p. 3; "The A.F. of L.

'Turns Left,'" 15 December 1932, pp. 3–4; "The Washington A.F. of L. Convention," 1 November 1933, pp. 3, 8.

19. See "The Recovery Act and the Workers," 1 July 1933, pp. 3, 7; "Labor and the Nat'l Recovery Act," 15 August 1933, p. 8; "The NRA and American Labor," October 1933, pp. 519–24; "The Real Meaning of NRA Unionism," 1 October 1933, p. 3; "The NRA and the New Swope Plan," 1 December 1933, pp. 4–5; reviews of *Labor Relations under the Recovery Act* by Ordway Tead and H. C. Metcalf, *Business under the Recovery Act* by L. Valenstein and E. B. Weiss, and *NRA Handbook*, 15 December 1933, p. 8.

20. See review of *Fascism* by Scott Nearing, 15 March 1933, p. 8; "Is America Heading for Fascism?" 1 August 1933, pp. 1, 4–5.

21. Charles S. Zimmerman Collection, ILGWU Library, New York City, Box 7, File 7.

CHAPTER 3

1. Charles S. Zimmerman, interview with author, New York City, 27 May 1980.

2. Ibid.; Saby Nahama, interview with author, New York City, 24 March 1980.

3. Charles S. Zimmerman Collection, ILGWU Library, New York City, Box 7, File 7.

4. See three untitled reports by Herberg to ILGWU Local No. 22, Charles S. Zimmerman Collection, Box 7, File 7.

5. See advertisement in *Workers Age*, 5 January 1935, p. 3.

6. See "Dressmakers Crush Dualism," 15 April 1934, p. 4; "Where Does the I.L.G.W.U. Stand?" 1 July 1934, pp. 3, 6; "Communists and the I.L.G.W.U.," 15 July 1934, pp. 3, 7.

7. See *Workers Age*, 12 September 1936, p. 4.

8. See "'The Old Federation of Gompers Is Gone!'" 2 November 1935, pp. 1, 3; "The C.I.O. and the Problems of Unity," 29 May 1937, pp. 3, 5; "'Peace' thru Disaster," 26 June 1937, pp. 2, 6; "Opportunism in the Trade Unions," 21 December 1935, p. 2.

9. See "C.P. Opportunism in Trade Union Policy," 26 October 1935, p. 3; "Working Class Unity Is Need of the Hour!" 9 November 1935, p. 4; "The C.P. and the Question of Trade Union Unity," 4 September 1937, pp. 1, 3.

10. See "The Labor Party Muddle," 2 February 1935, p. 3; "Labor Party vs. People's Front," 25 January 1936, p. 1; "Some Problems of the Labor Party," 2 January 1937, p. 4.

11. See "The Socialist Party Convention," 17 January 1931, p. 4; "Where Do the SP Militants Stand?" 16 November 1935, pp. 1, 3; "S.P. Militants' Stand on War," 23 November 1935, pp. 2–3; "Is the Socialist Party for a Labor Party?" 3 October 1936, p. 3; "Is the Socialist Party for a Labor Party?" 10 October 1936, p. 3; "The Socialists and N.Y. Elections," 28 August 1937, pp. 2, 4; "The Socialists and the Labor Party," 30 October 1937, p. 3. See also "Socialist Confusion," 6 March 1937, p. 2; "Wanted: A Simple Answer," 15 February 1936, p. 4.

12. See "Labor and Constitutional Reform," 13 July 1935, p. 2; "What Is the New Deal Labor Policy?" 3 July 1937, pp. 3, 8; "The New Deal and Trade Unions," 17 July 1937, pp. 3, 6; "New Deal Aims toward Union," 24 July 1937, p. 5; "Labor and Public Opinion," 7 August 1937, pp. 1, 3; "The New Wages and Hours Bill," 19 June 1937, p. 3; "C.I.O. and New Deal Clash," 9 October 1937, p. 3.

13. See "Roosevelt and the Liberty League," 22 February 1936, pp. 4, 6; "Roosevelt and Big Business," 7 March 1936, pp. 4, 6; "President Roosevelt's New Deal," 14 March 1936, p. 6; "Roosevelt and Labor," 30 May 1936, pp. 3, 6; "The Workers and Roosevelt's Rule," 6 June 1936, p. 3; "The Communist Party and the 'Roosevelt Question,' " 13 June 1936, p. 3; "Roosevelt's Syracuse Address," 24 October 1936, p. 4.

14. See "Who Are the Fascists in America?" 4 January 1936, pp. 1, 3; "Herberg Answers His Critic," 26 January 1936, p. 4; "War, Fascism, and the Middle Class," 1 February 1936, p. 3; "Black Legions of Fascism," 20 June 1936, p. 2; "Fascism on the American Horizon," 27 June 1936, p. 2; " 'Left' Fascists," 26 December 1936, p. 4; "The Fight against Fascism," 30 January 1937, pp. 3, 6; "The Fight against Fascism," 6 February 1937, p. 5; "A Note on Fascism in Russia of 1917," 27 February 1937, p. 4.

15. See "The Collapse of Austro-Marxism," 15 March 1934, pp. 4–5; "Estimating Austria's Revolution," 1 June 1934, p. 3; "Estimating Austria's Revolution," 15 June 1934, p. 6; "Estimating Austria's Revolution," 1 July 1934, p. 6; "Estimating Austria's Revolution," 1 August 1934, p. 7; "Facing the Dangers of the 'Lesser Evil,' " 3 August 1935, p. 2.

16. See "In the International Labor Movement," 11 April 1936, p. 6; "In the International Labor Movement," 25 April 1936, p. 6; "Civil War in Spain," 15 August 1936, pp. 3–4; "Workers Prepare to Defend Madrid," 29 August 1936, pp. 1, 3–4; "Spain and the 'Great Democracies,' " 16 January 1937, p. 4; "Jacobin Defense," 22 September 1937, p. 4; introduction to Civil War in Spain by Bertram D. Wolfe, 1937, pp. 3–4; "Revolution and People's Front," 18 April 1936, pp. 4, 6; "On the Daily Worker's 'Redefinition,' " 17 April 1937, pp. 5–6.

17. See "Some Notes on the Ethiopian Situation," 24 August 1935, p. 3; "Ethiopia and the League of Nations," 29 September 1935, p. 3; "Sanctions and the Soviet Union," 7 December 1935, p. 1; Comrades Lovestone and Herberg, "Draft Resolution on the International Working Class," February 1936, Charles S. Zimmerman Collection, Box 7, File 6.

18. See "17 Years of Socialist Construction," 1 November 1934, pp. 1–2; "Labor and Foreign Policy," 25 July 1936, p. 4; "Ultra-Radicalism vs. Marxist Foreign Policy," 1 August 1936, p. 3.

19. See "The Communist Party and the 'Roosevelt Question,' " 13 June 1936, p. 3; "Dangers of the Neutrality Bills," 20 March 1937, p. 3; "Communist Party and the Neutrality Bills," 27 March 1937, p. 5; "A Few Pages from Comintern History," 1 September 1934, p. 5; "Danger of Dual Unionism Again," 15 June 1935, p. 3; "Once Again We Ask 'Why Be Too Late?' " 27 June 1935, pp. 2, 4; "The Rise and Fall of Dual Unionism," 21 September 1935, pp. 3–4; "The Heritage of Dual Unionism," 12 October 1935, p. 3.

20. See "What We Must Learn from Lenin," 15 January–1 February 1934, p. 4;

"Trotsky's Road to Social Democracy," 15 October 1934, pp. 4, 7; "Trotskyism—Vanguard of Opportunism," 14 September 1935, p. 3; "Revolutionary Unity or New Party," 29 February 1936, p. 3; "The Case of Leon Trotsky," 18 December 1937, p. 3.

21. See correspondence between Herberg and Sidney Hook, 15 August 1931 to 27 March 1933, Herberg Archives, Drew University, Madison, N.J.; Sidney Hook to the author, 5 October 1979, 5 November 1979; "Workers' Democracy or Dictatorship?" 15 December 1934, pp. 3, 8; "Parties under Worker's Rule," 4 May 1935, p. 5; "As to a Multi-Party Dictatorship," 11 May 1935, p. 3; "Professor Hook Loses His Temper," 6 July 1935, p. 3.

22. Review of *The Passing of the Gods* by V. F. Calverton, 15 November 1934, p. 7.

CHAPTER 4

1. See "Convention of a New Beginning," 25 June 1938, p. 6; "Our Convention," 16 July 1938, pp. 1, 6.

2. See a course outline entitled "The CIO: New Problems of American Labor," which was offered at the ILGWU Local No. 22 Central Union School, Winter Term, 1937–1938, Herberg Archives, Drew University, Madison, N.J., Folder 34.1; "Broader Aspects of the C.I.O.-A.F.L. Split," 1 January 1938, pp. 1, 4; "Labor Must Have United Action," 30 April 1938, pp. 3, 8; "'The Story of the C.I.O.,'" 29 October 1938, p. 6; "The CIO—From Atlantic City to Pittsburgh," 7 January 1939, p. 3; "The Problem of Autonomy Confronts the C.I.O.," 21 January 1938, pp. 3–4.

3. See "Lenin's Political Genius," 29 January 1938, pp. 3, 5; "Lenin's Genius as Political Leader," 5 February 1938, pp. 3, 5; "Case of Bukharin," 19 March 1938, pp. 3, 6; "Another Stalin Turn?" 26 February 1938, pp. 1–2; "Stalinism Is Not Internationalism," 5 March 1938, p. 3; "On the Political Nature of the Stalinist Party," 12 August 1939, p. 3; "What Is the New Stalinist 'Party Line' Going to Be?" 30 September 1939, pp. 1–2; "The New Stalin Imperialism," 30 December 1939, pp. 1, 3; "Behind the New Imperialism of Stalinist Russia," 6 January 1940, pp. 1, 4; "Stalin's Imperialism Destroys Gains of Russian Revolution," 13 January 1940, p. 3; "Finn Labor Must Keep Independence," 20 January 1940, p. 3; "Some Remarks on Our Policy on the Russo-Finnish War," 6 April 1940, p. 3; Herberg Archives, Drew University, Folder 53.

4. See "American CP Writes Its Own Epitaph," 28 May 1938, pp. 1, 3; "The Burocracy Triumphs," 11 June 1938, pp. 1–2; "On the Political Nature of the Stalinist Party," 29 July 1939, p. 3; "Aims and Realities of Socialist Unity," 12 August 1939, p. 3.

5. See "The A.L.P. Election Policy," 13 August 1938, pp. 3–4; "Leadership in the A.L.P.," 20 August 1938, pp. 3, 5; "The ALP and the Stalinists," 31 May 1939, pp. 1–2; "The ALP and the War Issue," 4 November 1939, pp. 1, 3.

6. See Robert J. Alexander, *The Right Opposition* (Westport, Conn.: Greenwood Press, 1981), p. 134.

7. See "Neutrality and War Danger," 16 April 1938, pp. 1–2; "The O'Connell Bill," 23 April 1938, pp. 1–2; "The Fourth New Deal," 10 December 1938, p. 3; "The

Fourth New Deal," 17 December 1938, pp. 3, 5; "The Editor Answers," 1 March 1939, p. 3; review of *Men Must Act* by Lewis Mumford, 8 March 1939, p. 3; "Behind the Screen of Diplomacy," 29 March 1939, pp. 1, 3; "Issues behind Fight over Neutrality," 12 April 1939, p. 3; "Events of 1917 Show War Brings Dictatorship," 17 May 1939, p. 4; "Driving Forces behind the Administration War Policy," 11 November 1939, p. 3; "What Is F.D.R.'s War Policy Doing to the New Deal," 18 November 1939, p. 3; "Pegler 'Protects Our Wealth,'" 31 August 1940, p. 3.

8. See "Can U.S. Imperialism Defend the U.S.S.R.?" 12 March 1938, pp. 1, 5; "A Fighting Plea for Peace," 2 December 1939, p. 4; review of *The Awakening of America* by V. F. Calverton, 9 December 1939, p. 3.

9. See "Labor and Wage-Hour Legislation," 2 July 1938, pp. 3, 5; review of *The School for Dictators* by Ignazio Silone, 3 May 1939, p. 3; "Fascism Born of Real Menace," 1 July 1939, pp. 1, 3; review of *Warfare: The Relation of War to Society* by Ludwig Renn, 27 January 1940, p. 3; "Does Fascism Menace America?" 10 February 1940, p. 3; "Does Fascism Menace America?" 17 February 1940, p. 4; "Does Fascism Menace America?" 24 February 1940, p. 3; "Does Fascism Menace America?" 2 March 1940, p. 3; "Does Fascism Menace America?" 16 March 1940, p. 3. Also, on 19 January 1940 Herberg delivered a lecture to ILGWU Local No. 155 entitled "Fascism in America." For the lecture outline, see Herberg Archives, Drew University, Folder 52. See also Folder 34.1 in the Archives.

10. See "It DOES Make a Difference Who Wins," 22 June 1940, pp. 1, 4; "The United States Can and Must Stay out of the War," 29 June 1940, pp. 3–4; "Socialist Policy on the War," 10 August 1940, p. 4; "America Faces the Crucial Question of 'Appeasement,'" 7 September 1940, p. 3; "What Are the Stakes in the Coming Election?" 28 September 1940, p. 4; "Some Remarks on the Aid-to-Britain Issue," 12 October 1940, p. 3; "Is F.D.R. a Menace to American Democracy," 9 November 1940, pp. 3–4; "Some Remarks on Aid to Britain," 1 November 1940, pp. 1–2.

11. See "Rosa Luxemburg: Twenty Years After," 28 January 1939, p. 4; "The Editor Answers," 4 February 1939, p. 3; review of *Accent on Power* by Valeriu Marcu, 11 November 1939, pp. 3–4; review of *I Confess* by Benjamin Gitlow, Winter 1939, pp. 68–73; "Are We Fanatical?" 10 February 1940, pp. 3–4; "A Clinical Specimen of Trotskyist Dogmatics," 13 April 1940, p. 3.

12. The exact nature of the relationship between Niebuhr and Herberg is difficult to determine. That they knew each other is certain. How well they knew each other is not known. Herberg said that he and Anna were close friends with both Reinhold and Ursula Niebuhr and that he and Niebuhr used to take walks together in a park on the West Side of New York City. June Bingham, in her biography of Niebuhr, *Courage to Change* (New York: Charles Scribners Sons, 1961), pp. 188–90, reported that the two couples were very close; yet all of her information came from Herberg. In the Herberg papers at Drew University, the only correspondence between Herberg and Niebuhr was a Christmas card to Herberg. Richard Fox, of Reed College, who recently published a detailed biography of Niebuhr, related that there is no justification for assuming that a close relationship existed between the Herbergs and the Niebuhrs and that Bingham's description in the above passage is incorrect. Also Ursula Niebuhr wrote a letter of 16 June 1980 to me in which she says, "I believe Mrs. Bingham's biography of my husband suggests that we were all close friends. This is not so. Our

lives were too full and busy,—and my connections with Will Herberg were (mostly) academic." Bard Thompson, now dean of the Graduate School at Drew University, related that the first time he met Herberg was in Niebuhr's apartment. Because of this confusion, I have provisionally used the phrase "close acquaintanceship" in the text instead of the phrase "close friendship." However, at least from a theological point of view, Herberg made one claim that is significant. He told numerous people that when he was moving toward a formal religious position in the early 1940s and he considered becoming a Roman Catholic, Niebuhr convinced him to remain true to his Jewish heritage.

13. See a lecture outline entitled "Central Problems of Socialism," dated 30 January 1939, and a course outline entitled "Critical Problems of Marxism," dated May–June 1940, Herberg Archives, Drew University, Folder 39; "Socialist Fundamentals Reexamined," 8 June 1940, p. 4; "Socialist Fundamentals Reexamined," 15 June 1940, p. 4; "Socialist Fundamentals Reexamined," 22 June 1940, p. 3; "Some Objections to the 'Happiness Principle,'" 9 November 1940, p. 4; a course outline entitled "Marxism: An Inventory and Balance-Sheet," Herberg Archives, Drew University, Folder 141.2.

14. Jay Lovestone, interview with author, New York City, 17 June 1980.

15. See the Charles S. Zimmerman Collection, ILGWU Library, New York City, Box 15, File 5.

CHAPTER 5

1. Charles S. Zimmerman, interview with author, New York City, 27 May 1980; Alice Brent Nilva, several interviews with author (including 27 May 1980), New York City.

2. See "From Marxism to Judaism," January 1947, pp. 25–32; and a lecture to the Fellowship of Socialist Christians entitled "Religious Conviction and Social Action," given at the Union Theological Seminary, 29 April 1948, a copy of which is in the author's possession.

3. "The Christian Mythology of Socialism," Spring 1943, pp. 125–32. See also correspondence between Herberg and Bertram Wolfe, 9 June 1941, 26 June 1941, 1 July 1941, 22 July 1941, 7 July 1943, 13 July 1943, and one undated letter that was probably written in July 1941, Bertram Wolfe Papers, the Hoover Institute, Palo Alto, Calif.

4. See Herberg Archives, Drew University, Madison, N.J., Folder 159.

5. See Herberg Archives, Drew University, Folders 74, 77, 96.1, 189. See also Herberg's marginalia to Joseph S. Roucek, "A History of the Concept of Ideology," *Journal of the History of Ideas*, October 1944, p. 483, Herberg Collection, Drew University.

6. See review of *Paths to Utopia* by Martin Buber, Summer 1950, p. 26.

7. See Herberg Archives, Drew University, Folder 201.

8. See "The Crisis of Socialism," September 1944, pp. 22–31; "The Danger of Totalitarian Collectivism," December 1944, p. 33; "Socialism and the Meaning of Life," 17 March 1945, pp. 15, 18; "Socialism and the Meaning of Life," 24 March

1945, p. 10; "There Is a Third Way," December 1946, pp. 615–17; Herberg Archives, Drew University, Folders 106, 189.

9. See "Bureaucracy and Democracy in Labor Unions," Fall 1943, pp. 405–17; "The Stillborn Labor Party," May 1944, pp. 161–64; "For 'Limited' as against 'Total' Unionism," April–May 1946, pp. 51–54; "Labor and Politics in the Coming Period," Winter 1948–49, pp. 9–16; "Some Aspects of the Labor Situation," Spring 1950, pp. 16–21; an unidentified essay entitled "Organized Labor in Post-War America," probably written in 1948, Herberg Archives, Drew University.

10. See "The Ethics of Power," March 1945, pp. 19–23; "Personalism against Totalitarianism," December 1945, pp. 369–74; "Semantic Corruption," July–August 1945, pp. 8–11; "Crucial Questions—Collectivism: Totalitarian or Democratic?" 22 February 1946, pp. 473–76; "Is Control a Threat to Freedom?" July 1946, pp. 77–83; "Democracy and the Nature of Man," Fall 1946, pp. 12–19; "A Challenge to American Statesmanship," 28 May 1948, pp. 5–6; "Towards an Open World," 15 October 1948, pp. 6–8.

11. In May 1945, Herberg sent a copy of his article "Personalism against Totalitarianism" (see n. 10) to Dwight Macdonald, who at the time was editor of *Politics*. Herberg requested that Macdonald consider the essay for publication even though he may not have "sympathy for my [Herberg's] neo-religious attitude." The article was published in December. See the Dwight Macdonald Papers, Sterling Library, Yale University, Box 21, File 560.

12. See his lecture entitled "What Judaism Means to Me," given at the Jewish Theological Seminary, New York City, 6 April 1946; see also his lectures entitled "Judaism and Communism" and "Marxism and Judaism," Herberg Archives, Drew University, Folder 189.

13. See Herberg to Harry Goldberg, formerly of the Lovestonites and known then by the alias Jim Carr, 4 December 1944, 8 December 1944, 24 May 1944. Apropos of Herberg's educational background, Herberg, in the letter of 4 December 1944, wrote, "And I've always had a sneaking fondness for ivory towers—but have never seemed able to afford them." Copies in the author's possession.

14. "Rosenzweig's 'Judaism of Personal Existence,' " December 1950, pp. 541–49.

15. See "What Is Jewish Religion?" October 1950, pp. 8–13; "Assimilation in Militant Dress," July 1947, pp. 16–22; "Has Judaism Still Power to Speak?" May 1949, pp. 447–57; "Eretz Yisrael Is a 'Holy Place,' " 14 May 1948, pp. 4–5; "The Postwar Revival of the Synagogue," April 1950, pp. 315–25; Herberg Archives, Drew University, Folders 27, 79, 83.

16. See "The Theology of Antisemitism," Spring 1949, pp. 272–79; "Anti-Semitism in the Soviet Union," 5 March 1948, pp. 7–8; a thirty-page typescript entitled "Communism and Zionism," May 1948, Tamiment Library, New York University (microfilm), Reel 1777, Take 3786.

17. See "The Postwar Revival of the Synagogue," April 1950, pp. 315–25; "Has Judaism Still Power to Speak?" May 1949, pp. 447–57; a review of *The Prophetic Faith* by Martin Buber, July 1950, pp. 269–71; a lecture entitled "Martin Buber: Philosopher of Religious Existentialism," given at the Hillel Foundation at George Washington University and Rutgers University in 1954 and 1955, Herberg Archives, Drew University, Folder 108.

18. See Herberg's marginalia to Jacob B. Agus, *Banner of Jerusalem* (New York: Bloch Publishing Company, 1946), p. 48, Herberg Collection, Drew University.

19. See his discussion of Milton Steinberg's paper "The Theological Issues of the Hour," June 1949, pp. 409–28.

20. See "Secularism in Church and Synagogue," 15 May 1950, pp. 58–61; "The Church and American Politics," August 1949, pp. 198–200; Herberg Archives, Drew University, Folder 146; "Pacifists in Prison," August 1950, pp. 194–95; "Leon Bloy—Man of the Absolute," September 1947, pp. 62–71; "Socialism with Freedom," September 1950, pp. 289–91; Herberg's marginalia to Paul E. Pfuetze, "Martin Buber and Jewish Mysticism," *Religion in Life*, Fall 1947, p. 564, Herberg Archives, Drew University, Folder 108. See also a lecture entitled "Judaism, Economics, and Social Action," 24 October 1950, Herberg Archives, Drew University, Folder 193.

21. See "Beyond Time and Eternity," 18 April 1949, pp. 41–43; review of *The Theology of the Old Testament* by Otto J. Baab, October 1949, pp. 413–15; "On Petitionary Prayer," October 1948–January 1949, pp. 46–49; "What Is Man?" Herberg Archives, Drew University, Folder 223; Herberg to Herschel Matt, 4 February 1950, Herberg Archives, Drew University, Folder 27.

22. See "Education as God: The Philosophy of Samuel Alexander," April 1946, pp. 69–76; a note by Herberg, 31 October 1945, Herberg Archives, Drew University, Folder 84; additional notes by Herberg, 17 July 1941, 18 July 1941, 12 September 1941, Herberg Archives, Drew University, Folder 172; Herberg's marginalia to Willim M. Agar, *The Dilemma of Science* (New York: Sheed and War, 1941), p. 28, which Herberg finished reading 16 December 1941, Herberg Collection, Drew University.

CHAPTER 6

1. In *Commentary*, February 1947, pp. 145–51. Herberg's article appeared in the January issue. See also Herberg Archives, Drew University, Madison, N.J.

2. See Herberg to Solomon Grayzel, 27 August 1950, 21 January 1951, and Herberg to Herschel Matt, 18 August 1950, Herberg Archives, Drew University, Folder 27.

3. See Herberg's correspondence with Solomon Grayzel and related letters, Herberg Archives, Drew University, Folder 28; Herberg to Herschel Matt, 9 September 1948, ibid., Folder 27.

4. See Herberg to Solomon Grayzel, 4 December 1950, Herberg Archives, Drew University, Folder 28.

5. Throughout this chapter, all references to *Judaism and Modern Man* are to the third printing by Meridian Books, 1961. Appropriate page numbers appear in parentheses immediately after the quotations.

6. The major reviews of Herberg's book are as follows: *Kirkus*, 15 September 1951, p. 560; Julian M. Scherr's review in *Library Journal*, 1 October 1951, p. 1564; David De Sola Pool's review in *New York Times Book Review*, 18 November 1951, p. 24; *San Francisco Chronicle Book Review*, 18 November 1951; Reinhold Niebuhr's

review in *N.Y. Herald Tribune Books*, 16 December 1951, p. 8; Milton R. Konvitz's review in *Saturday Review*, 8 March 1952, p. 57; W. E. Garrison's review in *Christian Century*, 12 March 1952, pp. 312–13; K. M. Chworowsky's review in *Churchman*, 15 May 1952, p. 14; Michael Fraenkel's review in *New Republic*, 15 December 1952, p. 21.

7. For Herberg's reaction to Konvitz's review, see Herberg to Herschel Matt, 7 April 1952, Herberg Archives, Drew University, Folder 27.

CHAPTER 7

1. Herberg to Herschel Matt, 15 December 1954, Herberg Archives, Drew University, Madison, N.J., Folder 27.

2. This latter phrase is a paraphrase of Herberg's words in a letter to Herschel Matt. See Herberg Archives, Drew University, Folder 27.

3. See "On Religion and Theology," 19 March 1948, pp. 10–13; "Prophetic Faith in an Age of Crisis," July 1952, pp. 195–202; a lecture entitled "Christian Faith and Worldly Wisdom: A Word in Season to Some Protestant Seminarians," given at the Andover-Newton Theological School, 9 December 1953, a copy of which is in the author's possession; "Faith, History, and Self-Understanding," Spring 1954, pp. 14–20; "Biblical Faith and Natural Religion," January 1955, pp. 460–67; an address entitled "Hermeneutics: The Mode of Interpretation," given at Drew University, December 1955, a copy of which is also located in *Faith Enacted as History*, pp. 102–11. See also Herberg to Herschel Matt, Herberg Archives, Drew University, Folder 27; an unpublished essay entitled "Religion and the Interpretation of Life," probably written in the early 1950s but certainly after the publication of *Judaism and Modern Man*, a copy of which is in the author's possession.

4. Herberg Archives, Drew University, Folders 27, 152.1, 152.3; Herberg to June Bingham, 29 January 1954, 13 April 1955, Library of Congress, Washington, D.C.

5. See "The Integrity of the Person," 14 July 1952, pp. 18–19; "Faith and Character Structure," 25 January 1954, pp. 187–89; "Riesman's Lonely Man," 3 September 1954, pp. 538–40; "Two Philosophies of the 'Social Self,'" 19 September 1955, p. 22; Herberg Archives, Drew University, Folder 111; Herberg to June Bingham, 6 February 1955, Library of Congress, Washington, D.C.

6. See Herberg Archives, Drew University, Folders 3, 132, 134, 136, 165, 194; "'Sense of Decency,'" 5 November 1955, pp. 159–60; "Biblical Faith and Natural Religion," January 1955, pp. 460–67; Herberg Archives, Drew University, Folder 123.1; Herberg to June Bingham, 28 June 1954, Library of Congress, Washington, D.C.

7. See "The Religious Stirring on the Campus," March 1952, pp. 242–48; "Religion in the Colleges," October 1953, pp. 382–85; "'Blanshardism,' Americanism, Communism, and Romanism," February 1952, pp. 6–13; "An Underground World of Hatred and Fear," 9 October 1953, pp. 17–19; "Religious Communities in Present-Day America," April 1954, pp. 155–74; Herberg Archives, Drew University, Folders 105, 111.

8. See "Jewish Existence and Survival," January 1952, pp. 19–26; "What Is Jew-

ishness?" May 1952, pp. 21–24; "Religion and State in Israel," 14 November 1952, pp. 135–38; Herberg's marginalia to Benjamin Halperin, "The Idea of a Spiritual Home," *Jewish Frontier*, March 1955, p. 22, Herberg Archives, Drew University, Folder 3; "Tri-Focus on Judaism," 29 June 1955, pp. 759–60; review of *Man's Quest for God* by Abraham Joshua Heschel, October 1955, pp. 404–6; Herberg Archives, Drew University, Folders 209, 213.

9. See "The Religious Thinking of Milton Steinberg," November 1951, pp. 498–501; "Space, Time, and the Sabbath," June 1952, pp. 610–12; "How Can You Say 'God'?" December 1952, pp. 615–16, 618–20; review of *Eclipse of God*, by Martin Buber, July 1953, pp. 289–90; "The Cosmic Struggle," 17 July 1953, p. 372; "Religious Trends in American Jewry," Summer 1954, pp. 229–40; "I-Thou," 28 December 1955, p. 1526.

10. See *Communism vs. Judaism*, a fourteen-page mimeographed pamphlet published by the American Jewish Committee Library of Jewish Information, January 1951, Herberg Archives, Drew University, Folder 204; "Anti-Semitism on the Left," 16 January 1953, pp. 371–74; "Anti-Semitism Today," 16 July 1954, pp. 359–63; reply to Rev. John M. Oesterreicher's objections to "Anti-Semitism Today," 20 August 1954, p. 488.

11. See "Judaism and Christianity," April 1953, pp. 67–78; "A Jew Looks at Catholics," 22 May 1953, pp. 174–77; review of *The Church and the Jewish People*, edited by Gote Hendenquist, April 1955, pp. 119–21; "The Roots of Anti-Semitism," 22 August 1955, p. 20; Herberg Archives, Drew University, Folders 3, 131.1, 131.3.

12. See "Some Comments on Miss Wiley's Paper," October 1952, pp. 365–67; "The Sectarian Conflict over Church and State," November 1952, pp. 450–62; "Faith and Secular Learning," 1953, pp. 199–216; "A Jewish Point of View," May–June 1953, pp. 135–39; "Toward a Biblical Theology of Education," December 1953, pp. 259–72.

13. See "The Dissection of Babbitt Junior," 3 April 1953, pp. 653–55; "The History of a Great Historian," 13 April 1953, pp. 23–24; "Acton's Meaning for Today," 29 June 1953, pp. 17–18; review article in "Can Man Remake the World?" 31 August 1953, pp. 16–18; "A Conservative Worthy," July 1954, pp. 86–88, 90; contribution to "Critics' Choice for Christmas," 3 December 1954, p. 268; review of *Natural Right and History* by Leo Strauss, September 1954, pp. 435–39; "A Comment on Professor Hallowell's Review," September 1954, pp. 443–44; "The Great American Debate," 9 September 1955, pp. 559–62; contribution to "Critics' Choice for Christmas," 2 December 1955, pp. 239–40; Herberg's marginalia to Dorothy Fosdick, "Ethical Standards and Political Strategies," *Political Science Quarterly*, June 1952, pp. 214–28, Herberg Archives, Drew University, Folder 1, and to Lord Acton, *Essays on Church and State*, Herberg Collection, Drew University.

14. Interestingly enough, Herberg published his essay criticizing the natural-right doctrine, as presented by Leo Strauss, in September 1954. By December 1955, in the "Critics' Choice for Christmas" article in *Commonweal*, Herberg was already beginning to alter his criticism of the idea of natural right. For example, concerning Walter Lippmann's *The Public Philosophy*, he wrote, "This book is the most persuasive case for natural law in its relevance to present-day political life that I have seen."

15. See "Faith and Politics," 29 September 1952, pp. 122–25; "Spiritual Vagrants

Seeking a Night's Lodging," 26 December 1952, pp. 310–11; "The Power of Communist Ideology," March 1953, pp. 318–21; letter to the editor in support of F. Ernest Johnson's editorial article "Communists in the Pulpit," 8 June 1953, p. 80; "Communism, Democracy, and the Churches," April 1955, pp. 386–93; Herberg's marginalia to William H. Poteat, "Notes toward the Definition of Freedom," *Motive*, January 1953, p. 9, and to John C. Bennett, "The Protestant Clergy and Communism," *Christianity and Crisis*, 3 August 1953, pp. 107–10, Herberg Archives, Drew University, Folder 3.

16. See "Ten Who Would Have Changed America," 14 January 1955, pp. 410–11; "Government by Rabble-Rousing," 18 January 1954, pp. 13–16; "McCarthy and Hitler," 23 August 1954, pp. 13–15; "A Close Examination of Wisconsin's Junior Senator," 24 September 1954, pp. 610–12.

17. See "Election Gave No Mandate," 28 May 1949, p. 11; "Towards an Open World," 15 October 1948, pp. 6–8; "A Study in Fundamentals," September 1953, pp. 14–16, 33–37; "The Biblical Basis of American Democracy," Spring 1955, pp. 37–50; "The Presuppositions of Democracy," 3 June 1955, pp. 234–36; "The Spiritual Resources of Democracy," 5 August 1955, p. 451; Herberg Archives, Drew University, Folders 102, 129, 155, 181, 187.

18. See "American Marxist Political Theory," 1952, pp. 487–522; "Socialism in American Life," 11 July 1952, pp. 345–46; "What Happened to American Socialism?" October 1951, pp. 336–44; "Norman Thomas and American Socialism," December 1954, pp. 8–12.

19. See review of *American Labor Leaders* by Charles A. Madison, April 1951, pp. 189–90; "When Social Scientists View Labor," December 1951, pp. 590–96; "The Jewish Labor Movement in the United States," *American Jewish Yearbook*, 1952, pp. 1–74; "Freedom and Loyalty in Economic Life," Autumn 1952, pp. 8–12; "The Old-Timers and the Newcomers," 1953, pp. 12–19.

CHAPTER 8

1. See Herberg Archives, Drew University, Madison, N.J., Folder 27.

2. Throughout this chapter, all references to *Protestant-Catholic-Jew* are to the 1961 edition by Anchor Books, Doubleday and Co. Appropriate page numbers appear in parentheses immediately after the quotations.

3. See the following reviews of *Protestant-Catholic-Jew*: *Library Journal*, 1 September 1955, p. 1828; Reinhold Niebuhr, "America's Three Melting Pots," *New York Times Book Review*, 25 September 1955, p. 6; *Booklist*, November 1955, p. 90; *Chicago Sunday Tribune*, 13 November 1955, p. 9; Nathan Glazer, "Religion without Faith," *New Republic*, 14 November 1955, p. 18; *Catholic World*, December 1955, p. 234; *Nation*, 31 December 1955, p. 581; *Bookmark*, January 1956, p. 81; D. W. Brogan, "Religion in America," *Manchester Guardian*, 6 January 1956, p. 4; Alban Baer's review in *Commonweal*, 13 January 1956, p. 383; *U.S. Quarterly Book Review*, March 1956, p. 51; *Saturday Review*, 3 March 1956, p. 39; J. Milton Yinger's review in *American Sociological Review*, April 1956, p. 237; Lee Braude's review in

American Journal of Sociology, May 1956, p. 646; H. L. Short, "Boom on Religion," *New Statesman and Nation*, 3 May 1956, p. 189.

CHAPTER 9

1. See "That All May Be One," 21 January 1956, p. 454; "The Making of a Pluralistic Society," 1958, pp. 27–41; "Some Perils of Interfaith Life," February 1957, pp. 3–5; "Religion and Culture in Present-Day America," 1960, pp. 4–19; "Religious Revival and Moral Crisis," March 1960, pp. 209–19; foreword to *An American Dialogue*, 1960, pp. 9–13; "Protestant-Catholic Tensions in Pluralistic America," November 1960, pp. 3–11; "Protestantism in a Post-Protestant America," 5 February 1962, pp. 3–7; "Religion in a Secularized Society," Spring 1962, pp. 145–58; "Religion in a Secularized Society," Fall 1962, pp. 33–45; "Religious Group Conflict in America," 1964, pp. 143–58.

2. See "The Revolution We Are Living Through," February 1955, pp. 8–11; "Biblical Faith as *Heilsgeschichte*," March 1956, pp. 25–31; "Freud, Religion, and Social Reality," March 1957, pp. 277–84; "Imprisoned in Brotherhood," 19 April 1957, pp. 62–64; "Arnold Toynbee—Historian or Religious Prophet?" Autumn 1957, pp. 421–33; "Athens and Jerusalem," Spring 1958, pp. 178–200; review of *Psychoanalysis and Ethics* by Lewis S. Feuer, January 1959, pp. 565–69; review of *Sigmund Freud and the Jewish Mystical Tradition* by David Baedar, Autumn 1959, pp. 625–26; "Theological Presuppositions of Social Philosophy," Winter 1959, pp. 94–113; "The Strangeness of Faith," June 1960, pp. 4–7; "The Incarnate Word," a communion sermon at the Theological School of Drew University, 5 June 1961, in the author's possession; "Science and Faith," 29 October 1961, pp. 18, 20; "'Pure' Religion and the Secularized Society," 10 September 1963, pp. 188–89; "God and the Theologians," November 1963, pp. 56–58; Herberg Archives, Drew University, Madison, N.J., Folders 3, 78, 127, 128, 131.3, 228.

3. See also Herberg's marginalia to Trevor-Roper, "Arnold Toynbee's Millennium," *Encounter*, June 1957, p. 28, Herberg Archives, Drew University, Folder 170.

4. See "The Three Dialogues of Man," 16 May 1955, pp. 28–31; "Can Faith and Reason Be Reconciled?" 24 October 1955, p. 19; "The Thought of Reinhold Niebuhr," 2 April 1956, pp. 21–23; "Christian Apologist to the Secular World," May 1956, pp. 11–16; *Four Existentialist Theologians*, 1958; "Reinhold Niebuhr and Paul Tillich," October 1959, pp. 3–9, 36; "Niebuhr's Three Phases," 10 August 1960, pp. 926–27; Herberg to June Bingham, 5 June 1956, Library of Congress, Washington, D.C.; "The Social Philosophy of Karl Barth," in *Community, State and Church*, 1960, pp. 11–67; Herberg Archives, Drew University, Folder 152.3.

5. See "A Jew Looks at Catholics," 22 May 1953, pp. 174–77; "Controversy over an Encyclical," 4 November 1961, pp. 230, 232; "The New Encyclical," 7 May 1963, pp. 364–65; "The Limits of Papal Authority," 25 August 1964, pp. 730–32, 734; Martin E. Marty to author, 15 January 1980.

6. See "A Religion or Religion?" May 1956, unpaginated; "Justice for Religious Schools," 16 November 1957, pp. 190–93; foreword to *Freedom of Choice in Educa-*

tion, 1958; "Religion, Democracy, and Public Education," 1958, pp. 118–47; editorial, *Church and State*, January 1958, p. 2; reply to Nathan A. Perilman's critique of "Justice for Religious Schools," 11 January 1958, pp. 427–28; "Should the Government Help Our Parochial Schools?" January 1959, pp. 6–11; "Comment II," June 1959, pp. 102–3; "Religion and Education in America," 1961, pp. 11–51; "Religious Symbols in Public Life," 28 August 1962, pp. 145, 162; "The 'Separation' of Church and State," 3 October 1962, pp. 315, 330; "Religion and Public Life," 30 July 1963, p. 61; "Religion and Public Life," 13 August 1963, pp. 104–5; Herberg Archives, Drew University, Folder 23.

7. See "The Integration of the Jew in Contemporary America," Spring 1961, pp. 1–9; "Introduction—Martin Buber," in *The Writings of Martin Buber*, 1956, pp. 11–39. See also review of *God in Search of Man: A Philosophy of Judaism* by Abraham Joshua Heschel, Spring 1956, pp. 206–8; "Converging Trails," 18 April 1956, p. 486; review of *Die Antwort des Jona* by Shalom Ben-Chorin, Fall 1956, pp. 365–70; "At the Heart of the Mystery," 28 October 1956, p. 10; review of *A Social and Religious History of the Jews* by Salo Wittmayer Baron, Spring 1958, pp. 206–8; "Jewish Theology in the Post-Modern World," Summer 1963, pp. 364–70; Herberg Archives, Drew University, Folders 131.1, 131.3.

8. See "Marxism's Changing Face," 4 February 1955, pp. 482–84; "Jewish Labor in the U.S.," October 1955, pp. 20–21, 30–31; "Socialism, Zionism, and the Messianic Passion," Summer 1956, pp. 65–74; "Voting Habits of American Jews," 29 September 1956, pp. 617–19; "Triumph and Failure," 12 October 1956, pp. 42–44; "A 'Jewish Vote'?" 29 October 1956, pp. 28–29; "Labor's 'Hired Brains,' " 11 March 1957, pp. 17–19; "The Sociology of the Printers' Union," 3 June 1957, pp. 15–17; "A Yankee Looks at Marxism," 19 November 1960, pp. 314–15; "Communism, Christianity, and the Judgment of God," 16 January 1962, pp. 22, 37.

9. See " 'Ambiguist' Statesmanship," September 1960, pp. 7–8; "Natural Law and History in Burke's Thought," Summer 1959, pp. 325–28; "Historicism as Touchstone," 16 March 1960, pp. 311–13; "Society, Democracy, and the State," Autumn 1960, pp. 3–16; "Conservatives and Religion," 7 October 1961, pp. 230, 232; "Reinhold Niebuhr: Burkean Conservative," 2 December 1961, pp. 379, 394; "Conservatives, Liberals, and the Natural Law, I," 5 June 1962, pp. 407, 422; "Conservatives, Liberals, and the Natural Law, II," 19 June 1962, pp. 438, 458; "Five Meanings of the Word 'Historical,' " Winter 1964, pp. 327–30.

10. See also the letters between Herberg and William F. Buckley, Jr., 29 October 1961, 3 November 1961, 4 November 1961, 28 November 1962, 23 March 1962, William F. Buckley, Jr., Papers, Sterling Library, Yale University, Boxes 14, 20.

11. See "Loyalty and Security in Historical Perspective," 11 April 1955, pp. 20–22; "HUAC: Record and Appraisal," 10 April 1962, pp. 249–51; "A Religious 'Right' to Violate the Law?" 14 July 1964, pp. 579–80; "Dr. Herberg Replies," 8 September 1964, p. 784; Herberg Archives, Drew University, Folders 61, 103.1, 105, 110.2.

CHAPTER 10

1. During this interval, two events occurred that were of concern to Herberg. One involved a crisis at Herberg's institution, Drew University, which resulted in the resignations of several faculty members. The second concerned the death of Benjamin Gitlow, a former Lovestonite comrade. See "Crisis at Drew," 20 February 1967, pp. 25–27; "Benjamin Gitlow, RIP," 10 August 1965, p. 682.

2. See "A Jew Looks at Jesus," 1966, pp. 91–101; "Christian Faith and Totalitarian Rule," Winter 1966–67, pp. 63–71; "Free to Choose Our Chains," 3 January 1967, pp. 4, 8; "What Is the Moral Crisis of Our Time?" January–March 1968, pp. 63–69; "Modern Man in a Metaphysical Wasteland," Winter 1968–69, pp. 79–83; "What Keeps Modern Man from Religion?" Winter 1969–70, pp. 5–11; "Men without Gods," 27 July 1971, pp. 813–14; "The 'What' and the 'How' in Ethics," Fall 1971, pp. 350–57; Herberg Archives, Drew University, Madison, N.J., Folders 14.1, 49, 51, 65, 98, 100; Herberg's marginalia to Ellis Landoz, "Eric Voegelin and the Nature of Philosophy," *Modern Age*, Spring 1969, p. 158, Herberg Archives, Drew University, Folder 4.

3. See "Again, the Social Gospel," 13 February 1962, pp. 96, 109; "The 'Death of God' Theology—I," 9 August 1966, pp. 771, 799; "The 'Death of God' Theology—II," 23 August 1966, pp. 839–40; "The 'Death of God' Theology—III," 6 September 1966, pp. 884–85; "The Plight of American Protestantism," 5 November 1968, pp. 1109, 1126–27; "Karl Barth, RIP," 31 December 1968, p. 1310; "Reinhold Niebuhr, RIP," 29 June 1971, pp. 690–91; Herberg's marginalia to Robert North, "Pannenberg's Historicizing Exegesis," *Heythrop Journal*, October 1971, p. 394, Herberg Archives, Drew University, Folder 4.

4. See "Aggiornamento," 4 May 1965, pp. 363–64; "Post-Vatican II Theology," 3 May 1966, pp. 421–24; "What Is Religious Freedom?" 29 November 1966, pp. 1228–30; "The Church under Pressure of the World," Autumn–Winter 1967–68, pp. 13–25; "Aggiornamento," 27 August 1968, pp. 852–53; "Humanae Vitae," 10 September 1968, pp. 908–9; "Men without God," 27 July 1971, pp. 813–14; "A Crisis of Authority," 22 October 1971, pp. 1182–83; "Brilliant Overreaching," 24 November 1972, pp. 1305–6; an address entitled "The Council, the Ecumenical Movement, and the Problem of Aggiornamento," given at the Golden Jubilee National Newman Congress, Washington, D.C., 3 September 1965, Herberg Archives, Drew University, Folder 206; see also Folders 37.1, 156, and a lecture entitled "The Catholic Church: Five Years after the Council" in the author's possession.

5. Herberg's attitude toward the Protestant Reformation and Renaissance humanism was less than positive by 1970. For a clue to his perspective, see the marginalia to Judith Hook, "Italy and the Counter-Reformation," source unidentified, Herberg Archives, Drew University, Folder 37.1.

6. See "Martin Buber, RIP," 29 June 1965, pp. 530–40; "The Sweep of Jewish History," 7 November 1965, pp. 50, 52; "Man of Faith," 24 April 1966, pp. 34–35; "The Tyrant Necessity," 4 February 1967, pp. 50–51; "Judaism as Personal Decision," Summer 1968, pp. 9–20; "Scrutiny of an Enigma," 2 December 1969, pp. 1222–23; "The Jew and the Negro," 25 August 1970, pp. 900–901; "America's 'Ne-

gro Problem' in Historical Perspective," Summer 1971, pp. 207–14; *Martin Buber: Personalist Philosopher in an Age of Depersonalization*, 1972.

7. See "Conservatives, Liberalism, and Religion," 30 November 1965, pp. 1087–88; "The Great Society and the American Constitution Tradition," Summer 1967, pp. 231–35; "An American Success," October 1968, pp. 2, 5; "Conservatism, the Working Class, and the Jew," Winter–Spring 1970, pp. 25–29; notes for a lecture entitled "The Crumbling of Liberal Orthodoxies," 21 April 1970, pp. 428–29; "Words that Slay, Wisdom that Mends," 14 July 1970, pp. 738–39; "The Limits of Pluralism," 23 February 1971, pp. 198–99; lecture entitled "Conservatism, Liberalism, and the Western Tradition," 2 May 1970, in the author's possession; Herberg Archives, Drew University, Folders 4, 45, 48, 50.

8. See "The New Estate," 13 July 1965, p. 590; " 'Civil Rights' and Violence," 7 September 1965, pp. 769–70; "Who Are the Hippies?" 8 August 1967, pp. 844–46, 872; "Business Enterprise in Moral Perspective," 1968, pp. 19–30; "Inside the Outsiders," 30 July 1968, pp. 738–39; "The Student Left," 29 July 1969, pp. 754–56; "Dicta on Civil Disobedience," 18 December 1969, p. 1; "Anarchy on Campus," Winter 1969–70, pp. 2–10; "On the Meaning of Academic Freedom," 1971, pp. 1–4; "Conservatives and Jesus Freaks," November 1971, pp. 15–16; Herberg Archives, Drew University, Folder 13; William F. Buckley, Jr., Papers, Sterling Library, Yale University, Box 35.

9. See "Humanae Vitae," 10 September 1968, pp. 908–9; "The Bounds of Public Morality," 3 June 1969, pp. 545–46; "A Death-Defying Act," 7 October 1969, pp. 1007–8, 1023; "Mr. Herberg Replies," 4 November 1969, p. 1096; "The Limits of Pluralism," 23 February 1971, pp. 198–99; unpublished lecture entitled "Problems of Life and Death in the Perspective of Moral Philosophy," Herberg Archives, Drew University, Folder 15 (see also Folders 4, 41, 173); Herberg to William F. Buckley, Jr., 11 November 1969, 11 May 1971, 20 May 1971, 17 July 1971, William F. Buckley, Jr., Papers, Sterling Library, Yale University. See also a Herberg interview by Buckley, 9 July 1970 and 13 July 1970, a copy of which is in the possession of Professor Donald Jones, Drew University.

10. Herberg's opposition to homosexuality is more personally revealed in some of his letters to William F. Buckley, Jr., 11 November 1969, 13 November 1969, 24 November 1969. See William F. Buckley, Jr., Papers, Sterling Library, Yale University, Box 61.

CHAPTER II

1. See the *Stanford University News Service*, 5 April 1974, clipping in the Herberg file, Public Relations Office, Drew University, Madison, N.J.

2. See "The State of the Churches in the U.S.A. 1973—Problems and Promises," *A Study Resource by Ecumenism Research Agency*, pp. 2–5, a copy of which is in the author's possession; "City and Suburb in Symbiosis," Spring 1973, pp. 159–69; "Religion in the U.S.," 4 June 1973, pp. 54–58, 60; "America's Civil Religion," Summer

1973, pp. 226–33; "The Crisis and Its Aftermath," 1974, pp. 44–47; "Getting Back to Vatican II," 29 March 1974, pp. 366–68; "Some Comments on the Watergate Affair," July 1973, Herberg Archives, Drew University, Folder 13.

3. See William F. Buckley, Jr., to Herberg, 27 February 1974, William F. Buckley, Jr., Papers, Sterling Library, Yale University.

4. See "Will Herberg: A Tribute," *National Review*, 5 August 1977, pp. 880–87.

CHAPTER 12

1. In his notes for the introduction to his seminar entitled "Other Voices in Christian Ethics," Herberg wrote, "Scholarly inquiry demands an approach: a) *sine ira et studio* [without anger or zeal]; b) studying the material in its own context: not background for the present; c) inquiring for knowledge to be known: not as sustaining (or challenging) present positions." See Herberg Archives, Drew University, Madison, N.J., Folder 70.

2. See *National Review*, 21 April 1970, p. 428.

3. See Herberg Archives, Drew University, Folder 27.

4. Herberg had maintained this position as early as September 1941, when he wrote, "It could be shown that the whole doctrinal system of Marxian socialism bears the closest resemblance structurally to traditional Christianity." See his marginalia to Christopher Dawson, *Progress and Religion* (New York: Sheed and Ward, 1938), p. 211, Herberg Collection, Drew University.

5. See *Judaism and Modern Man* (New York: Meridian Books, 1961), pp. 268–69.

6. See Herberg's marginalia to John C. Bennett, "The Church and Power Conflicts," *Christianity and Crisis*, 22 March 1965, p. 51, Herberg Collection, Drew University.

7. See Herberg's marginalia to Arthur Schlesinger, *The Vital Center* (Boston: Houghton Mifflin Co., 1949), p. x, Herberg Collection, Drew University.

8. See Herberg's marginalia to Ruth A. Bevan, *Marx and Burke: A Revisionist View* (LaSalle, Ill.: Open Court Publishing Co., 1973), p. 162, Herberg Collection, Drew University.

9. For further discussion of the devolutionary theory of secularization, see Harry J. Ausmus, *The Polite Escape: On the Myth of Secularization* (Athens: Ohio University Press, 1982), chapters 1–5, passim.

10. See Harry Tiebout, "'Hard' Questions for Will Herberg (Based on Judaism and Modern Man)," with Herberg's marginalia, Herberg Archives, Drew University, Folder 226.

11. See Herberg Archives, Drew University, Folder 40.

12. The intention of this paragraph should not be misunderstood. What I am suggesting is a consistent prophetic stance that considers even the idea of God to be idolatrous. In this sense, "God-talk" is not only cheap but cheapening and ought to be eliminated from human vocabulary. Theologians perhaps should voluntarily go out of business—they should become metaphysicians or, better yet, historians.

13. See Herberg Archives, Drew University, Folder 169, where Herberg comments on Tillich's *Interpretation of History*. Also, Herberg on one occasion quoted Marx to the effect: "If you have to have a religion, let it be that of the Old Testament prophets." See Herberg's article, "The Christian Witness in an Emerging 'Other-directed' Culture," November 1957, p. 6.

14. See *Judaism and Modern Man* (New York: Meridian Books, 1961), p. 198.

A BIBLIOGRAPHY
OF HERBERG'S WORKS

BOOKS

Judaism and Modern Man: An Interpretation of Jewish Religion. New York: Farrar, Straus and Young, 1951. Reprint. New York: Meridian Books, 1961.
Protestant-Catholic-Jew: An Essay in American Religious Sociology. Garden City, N.Y.: Doubleday & Company, 1951. Reprint. Anchor Books, Doubleday and Co., 1960.
Faith Enacted as History: Essays in Biblical Theology. Edited with an introduction by Bernhard W. Anderson. Philadelphia: Westminster Press, 1976.

BOOKS EDITED

The Writings of Martin Buber. New York: Meridian Books, 1956.
Four Existentialist Theologians: A Reader from the Works of Jacques Maritain, Nicolas Berdyaev, Martin Buber, and Paul Tillich. Garden City, N.Y.: Doubleday Anchor Books, 1958.
Community, State and Church: Three Essays by Karl Barth. Garden City, N.Y.: Anchor Books, Doubleday & Company, 1960.

PAMPHLETS

The Heritage of the Civil War. New York: Workers Age Publishing Association, 1932.
The NRA and American Labor. New York: Communist Party, U.S.A. (Opposition), 1933.
The Theology of Reinhold Niebuhr, Outline. New York: Frontier Fellowship, n.d. [ca. early 1950].
Athens and Jerusalem: Confrontation and Dialogue. Distinguished Lecture Series, no. 3. Durham: University of New Hampshire Press, 1965.
Martin Buber: Personalist Philosopher in an Age of Depersonalization. McAuley Lecture 15. West Hartford, Conn.: McAuley Institute, 1972.

244

Bibliography of Herberg's Works

ESSAYS, ARTICLES, REVIEWS, AND MISCELLANEOUS PIECES

"Coal Miners: Here and in Russia." *Young Worker*, 7 November 1925, p. 3.
"The New Orientation—To the Masses." *Young Worker*, 9 January 1926, p. 4.
"Lenin and the Youth." *Workers Monthly*, February 1926, pp. 166–71.
" 'Employee Education' in Economics." *Workers Monthly*, September 1926, pp. 505–10.
"The Steel Making Minerals and Imperialism." *Workers Monthly*, November 1926, pp. 594–95, 600.
"The War Danger and the Youth." *Young Worker*, 15 September 1927, pp. 5, 7.
"Military Training at the League's Schools: Oppressed Must Learn Use of Arms to Cast Off Slavery." *Daily Worker*, 6 August 1928, p. 6.
"The Tenth Plenum of the ECCI: A Political Analysis." *Revolutionary Age*, 1 November 1929, p. 15.
"The Tenth Plenum of the ECCI." *Revolutionary Age*, 15 November 1929, p. 17.
"The Decay of Trotskyism." *Revolutionary Age*, 1 December 1929, p. 8.
"The Tenth Plenum of the ECCI." *Revolutionary Age*, 1 December 1929, p. 15.
"The Tenth Plenum of the ECCI." *Revolutionary Age*, 15 December 1929, p. 12.
"The Tenth Plenum of the ECCI: The United Front and Trade Union Questions." *Revolutionary Age*, 1 January 1930, p. 11.
"The VI Congress and the World Situation." *Revolutionary Age*, 15 January 1930, p. 7.
"Have Communists the Right to Think?" *Revolutionary Age*, 1 February 1930, pp. 10–11.
"Rosa Luxemburg: 'In Spite of All Her Errors She Was and Remains an Eagle!' " *Revolutionary Age*, 15 February 1930, pp. 12–13.
"The Real Meaning of the 'New Turn.' " *Revolutionary Age*, 1 March 1930, pp. 6–7.
"The 'New Turn' and the Crisis in the C.I." *Revolutionary Age*, 15 March 1930, pp. 6–7.
"Two Splendid Pamphlets." Review of *The American Race Problem* by Bishop William Montgomery Brown and *The Pope's Crusade against the Soviet Union* by Bishop William Montgomery Brown. *Revolutionary Age*, 21 April 1930, p. 4.
"Whither Trotskyism?" *Revolutionary Age*, 21 April 1930, p. 6.
" 'National Socialism'—Or Factional Tail-End?" *Revolutionary Age*, 21 May 1930, p. 13.
"The American Trotskyist Movement." *International Information of the Communist Opposition*, August 1930, pp. 12–15.
"The International Opposition Conference." *Revolutionary Age*, 22 November 1930, p. 9.
"Einstein and Marx: How Einstein 'Made' the First Page." *Revolutionary Age*, 13 December 1930, p. 3.
"Einstein and Marx: What the Theory of Relativity Is All About." *Revolutionary Age*, 20 December 1930, p. 3.
"Einstein and Marx: Theory of Relativity and Dialectical Materialism." *Revolutionary Age*, 27 December 1930, p. 3.

"That Duranty Interview: Stalin Speaks on World Politics." *Revolutionary Age*, 10 January 1931, p. 3.

"The Socialist Party Convention: Groups in the S.P.—Perspectives of the Left Movement—The Line of the Communists." *Revolutionary Age*, 17 January 1931, p. 4.

"Problems of the Negro Masses: The Negro Worker and Labor." Review of *The Black Worker* by Sterling D. Spero and Abram L. Harris. *Revolutionary Age*, 7 February 1931, p. 3.

"A False Orientation in Negro Work." *Revolutionary Age*, 14 February 1931, p. 3.

"Unemployment and Labor: American Labor and the Crisis—The Government, A.F. of L. and Unemployment—Three Lines." *Revolutionary Age*, 21 February 1931, p. 3.

"Problems of the Crisis: The Crisis and Revolution." *Revolutionary Age*, 14 March 1931, pp. 3–4.

"Problems of the Negro Masses—Which Way: Labor or Capital?" *Revolutionary Age*, 21 March 1931, p. 3.

"Problems of the Negro Masses—Which Way: Labor or Capital?" *Revolutionary Age*, 28 March 1931, p. 3.

"Einstein and Marx: Science and Determinism." *Revolutionary Age*, 4 April 1931, pp. 3–4.

"Karl Marx or Herbert Hoover: Increasing Misery or Growing Welfare." *Revolutionary Age*, 9 May 1931, p. 3.

"About the XI Plenum of the C.I.: The Plenum of the 'New Turn.'" *Revolutionary Age*, 30 May 1931, p. 3.

"About the XI Plenum of the C.I.: The Plenum of the 'New Turn.'" *Revolutionary Age*, 6 June 1931, p. 3.

"Marxism and Human Culture: Communism and Science." *Revolutionary Age*, 13 June 1931, p. 4.

"Marxism and the 'Negro Question': Roots of Negro Subjection." *Revolutionary Age*, 11 July 1931, p. 4.

"Jews in Russia—Negroes in the U.S.A.: A Lesson from the Soviet Union." *Revolutionary Age*, 1 August 1931, pp. 3–4.

"In Reply to Dr. DuBois in 'The Crisis': Communism and the Negro." *Revolutionary Age*, 5 September 1931, p. 4.

"In Reply to Dr. DuBois in 'The Crisis': Communism and the Negro." *Revolutionary Age*, 12 September 1931, p. 3.

"A Discussion with an Intellectual: Communism and the Intellectuals." *Revolutionary Age*, 10 October 1931, p. 4.

"About the Theory of 'Cultural Compulsives': Marxism and History of Science." *Revolutionary Age*, 14 November 1931, p. 3.

"About the Theory of 'Cultural Compulsives': Marxism and History of Science." *Revolutionary Age*, 21 November 1931, p. 3.

"The Breath of Sectarianism Is Death! Lessons of the Hunger March." *Revolutionary Age*, 19 December 1931, p. 3.

"A Defense of Slavery Shattered! 'Intelligence Tests' and the Negro." *Revolutionary Age*, 26 December 1931, p. 3.

"The DePriest 'Non-Partisan' Conference: The Counsel of Abject Servility." *Revolu-*

tionary Age, 2 January 1932, p. 3.

"Upton Sinclair and the Nobel Prize." *Workers Age*, 10 January 1932, p. 3.

" 'We Are the Truer Guardians . . .': The Heritage of the Civil War." *Workers Age*, 13 February 1932, p. 4.

" 'We Are the Truer Guardians . . .': The Heritage of the Civil War." *Workers Age*, 20 February 1932, p. 3.

"The 100th Anniversary of Abolitionism: Communists and Abolitionists." *Workers Age*, 9 April 1932, p. 3.

"Fifty Years after Darwin's Death: Darwinism and Marxism." *Workers Age*, 7 May 1932, pp. 3–4.

"Marxism and Cultural Evolution: About the 'Literary Class War.' " Letter to Edmund Wilson concerning Wilson's article "The Literary Class Struggle" in *New Republic*, 4 May 1932. *Workers Age*, 14 May 1932, p. 3.

"The Civil War in New Perspective." *Modern Quarterly*, Summer 1932, pp. 54–61. Later issued in slightly altered form as a pamphlet under the title *The Heritage of the Civil War*. New York: Workers Age Publishing Association, 1932.

"Slavery in the 'Land of the Free': Economics of Southern Farming." *Workers Age*, 16 July 1932, p. 4.

"Slavery in the 'Land of the Free': Economics of Southern Farming." *Workers Age*, 23 July 1932, p. 3.

"Unemployment and the Workers: The Jobless 'Self-Help' Fraud." *Workers Age*, 23 September 1932, pp. 3–4.

" 'The Liberation of American Literature': A Review of V. F. Calverton's Book." *Workers Age*, 15 October 1932, p. 4.

"The General Line and the Five Year Plan: In the Post-Conference Discussion." *Workers Age*, 1 December 1932, p. 5.

"The A.F. of L. 'Turns Left': What Happened at the Cincinnati Convention?—The A.F. of L. Proposal for Unemployment Insurance—What Now in the Trade Unions." *Workers Age*, 15 December 1932, pp. 3–4.

"What's Happening to America? On the 'Social Trends' Report." *Workers Age*, 1 February 1933, p. 4.

"On the Hoover 'Social Trends' Report: What's Happening to the United States?" *Workers Age*, 15 February 1933, pp. 5, 7.

"The 'Genius of Error' in Swamps of Opportunism: Trotsky on the German Situation." *Workers Age*, 15 March 1933, pp. 4, 8.

Review of *Fascism* by Scott Nearing. *Workers Age*, 15 March 1933, p. 8.

"The Negro and Communism: Worker's Rule and Race Prejudice." *Workers Age*, 15 May 1933, p. 5.

Review of *South Carolina during Reconstruction* by Francis B. Simkins and Robert H. Woody. *Workers Age*, 15 May 1933, p. 8.

"The Viewpoint of the International Communist Opposition," in "The Crisis in Communism (A Symposium)." *Modern Monthly*, June 1933, pp. 283–88.

Review of *The Negro's Church* by Benjamin Elijah Mays and Joseph William Nicholson. *Workers Age*, 15 June 1933, p. 8.

"The Recovery Act and the Workers: A New Menace for the Labor Movement."

Workers Age, 1 July 1933, pp. 3, 7.

Review of *Modern Monthly* edited by V. F. Calverton, nos. 3 to 6 (April to July 1933). *Workers Age*, 1 July 1933, p. 8.

"Is America Heading for Fascism? Where Does the Recovery Act Lead?" *Workers Age*, 1 August 1933, pp. 1, 4–5.

Review of *The Only Road* by Leon Trotsky. *Workers Age*, 1 August 1933, p. 8.

"Labor and the Nat'l Recovery Act: Unionism Faces a Great Test!" *Workers Age*, 15 August 1933, p. 8.

"Fascism and Democracy in Hitler's Germany: Trotsky as Champion of Reformism." *Workers Age*, 15 September 1933, p. 3.

"The NRA and American Labor." *Modern Monthly*, October 1933, pp. 519–24. Later issued as *The NRA and American Labor*. New York: Communist Party U.S.A. (Opposition), 1933.

"The Real Meaning of NRA Unionism: Some Larger Aspects of the 'New Deal.' " *Workers Age*, 1 October 1933, p. 3.

"The Washington A.F. of L. Convention: American Labor under the N.R.A." *Workers Age*, 1 November 1933, pp. 3, 8.

"Against a 'New' Party and a 'Fourth' Int'l." *Workers Age*, 1 December 1933, pp. 6–7.

"The NRA and the New Swope Plan: Larger Aspects of the Recovery Act." *Workers Age*, 1 December 1933, pp. 4–5.

Review of *Modern Monthly* edited by V. F. Calverton, nos. 7 to 10 (August to November 1933). *Workers Age*, 1 December 1933, p. 7.

Reviews of *Labor Relations under the Recovery Act* by Ordway Tead and H. C. Metcalf, *Business under the Recovery Act* by L. Valenstein and E. B. Weiss, and *NRA Handbook*. *Workers Age*, 15 December 1933, p. 8.

"Soviet Recognition and the Comintern: The Foundation of Soviet Diplomacy." *Workers Age*, 15 December 1933, pp. 3, 5.

"From 'Real Communism' to 'Real Democracy': Leon Trotsky Completes the Circle!" *Workers Age*, 1 January 1934, p. 3.

"What We Must Learn from Lenin: On Centrism and Sectarianism Today." *Workers Age*, 15 January–1 February 1934, p. 4.

"The Collapse of Austro-Marxism: Austria and Revolution." *Workers Age*, 15 March 1934, pp. 4–5.

"Dressmakers Crush Dualism." *Workers Age*, 15 April 1934, p. 4.

"Estimating Austria's Revolution." *Workers Age*, 1 June 1934, p. 3.

"Estimating Austria's Revolution." *Workers Age*, 15 June 1934, p. 6.

"Estimating Austria's Revolution." *Workers Age*, 1 July 1934, p. 6.

"Where Does the I.L.G.W.U. Stand?" *Workers Age*, 1 July 1934, pp. 3, 6.

"Communists and the I.L.G.W.U." *Workers Age*, 15 July 1934, pp. 3, 7.

"Estimating Austria's Revolution." *Workers Age*, 1 August 1934, p. 7.

"A Few Pages from Comintern History: Some Important Questions Answered." *Workers Age*, 1 September 1934, p. 5.

"Trotsky's Road to Social Democracy: 'Left' Opposition Embraces Second International." *Workers Age*, 15 October 1934, pp. 4, 7.

"17 Years of Socialist Construction." *Workers Age*, 1 November 1934, pp. 1–2.

Review of *The Passing of the Gods* by V. F. Calverton. *Workers Age*, 15 November 1934, p. 7.

"Workers' Democracy or Dictatorship? On Hook's Revival of Kautsky's Theories." *Workers Age*, 15 December 1934, pp. 3, 8.

"What Marx Really Means!" Review of *What Marx Really Meant* by G. D. H. Cole, *Modern Monthly*, January 1935, pp. 696–99.

"The Labor Party Muddle: Facing the Future by Forgetting the Past Brings Headaches to Communist Party." *Workers Age*, 2 February 1935, p. 3.

"Parties under Worker's Rule: An Answer to Sidney Hook's Concept of Parties in a Dictatorship." *Workers Age*, 4 May 1935, p. 5.

"As to a Multi-Party Dictatorship: Hook Confuses Dictatorship with Bourgeois Democracy Says Will Herberg." *Workers Age*, 11 May 1935, p. 3.

"Danger of Dual Unionism Again." *Workers Age*, 15 June 1935, p. 3.

"Professor Hook Loses His Temper: Concluding Remarks on Hook's Misconception of Dictatorship." *Workers Age*, 6 July 1936, p. 3.

"Labor and Constitutional Reform: Supreme Court Act Raises Problem of Reforming Constitution." *Workers Age*, 13 July 1935, p. 2.

"Once Again We Ask 'Why Be Too Late?'" *Workers Age*, 27 July 1935, pp. 2, 4.

"Facing the Dangers of the 'Lesser Evil': Gestures toward Coalition Government Made by Communists in France, Czecho-Slovakia, Repeat False Theories Which Brought Germany and Austria under Fascist Heel." *Workers Age*, 3 August 1935, p. 2.

"Some Notes on the Ethiopian Situation: Successful Defense Requires Reorganization of Social Life." *Workers Age*, 24 August 1935, p. 3.

"Are the U.S. Negroes a Nation?" *Negro Voice*, September 1935, unpaginated.

"Trotskyism—Vanguard of Opportunism: Present C.I. Opportunism Was First Proposed by Trotsky." *Workers Age*, 14 September 1935, p. 3.

"The Rise and Fall of Dual Unionism: What Has Happened to the Sectarian Course of the Comintern?" *Workers Age*, 21 September 1935, pp. 3–4.

"Ethiopia and the League of Nations: Fight over Sanctions Has Its Dangers for the Proletariat." *Workers Age*, 29 September 1935, p. 3.

"The Heritage of Dual Unionism: What Is the C.P. Trade Union Line Today? I." *Workers Age*, 12 October 1935, p. 3.

"C.P. Opportunism in Trade Union Policy: What Is Trade Union Course of the Communist Party Today? II." *Workers Age*, 26 October 1935, p. 3.

"'The Old Federation of Gompers Is Gone!': Significance of the A.F. of L. Convention." *Workers Age*, 2 November 1935, pp. 1, 3.

"Working Class Unity Is Need of the Hour! A Discussion of the Basis for Effective Cooperation." *Workers Age*, 9 November 1935, p. 4.

"Where Do the SP Militants Stand? An Analysis of Their Latest Programs." *Workers Age*, 16 November 1935, pp. 2–3.

"S.P. Militants' Stand on War and Road to Power: An Analysis of Their Latest Program #II." *Workers Age*, 23 November 1935, pp. 1, 3.

"Sanctions and the Soviet Union." *Workers Age*, 7 December 1935, p. 1.

"Opportunism in the Trade Unions under Cloak of Unity." *Workers Age*, 21 December 1935, p. 2.

"Who Are the Fascists in America? Fascism, the New Deal and the Liberty League." *Workers Age*, 4 January 1936, pp. 1, 3.

"Labor Party vs. People's Front." *Workers Age*, 25 January 1936, p. 1.

"Herberg Answers His Critic." Letter to the editor in reply to Edward Peters's critique of Herberg's article "Who Are the Fascists in America? Fascism, the New Deal and the Liberty League." *Workers Age*, 26 January 1936, p. 4.

"War, Fascism, and the Middle Class." *Workers Age*, 1 February 1936, p. 3.

"Wanted: A Simple Answer—A Reply to Herbert Zam's Stand on Revolutionary Unification." *Workers Age*, 15 February 1936, p. 4.

"Roosevelt and the Liberty League: The Significance of F. D. R.'s Recent Message to Congress." *Workers Age*, 22 February 1936, pp. 4, 6.

"Revolutionary Unity or New Party." *Workers Age*, 29 February 1936, p. 3.

"Roosevelt and Big Business." *Workers Age*, 7 March 1936, pp. 4, 6.

"President Roosevelt's New Deal and Big Business." *Workers Age*, 14 March 1936, p. 6.

"In the International Labor Movement: Spain and the Liberal Regime." *Workers Age*, 11 April 1936, p. 6.

"Revolution and the People's Front." *Workers Age*, 18 April 1936, pp. 4, 6.

"In the International Labor Movement: Bankruptcy of the People's Front." *Workers Age*, 25 April 1936, p. 6.

"Roosevelt and Labor." *Workers Age*, 30 May 1936, pp. 3, 6.

"The Workers and Roosevelt's Rule." *Workers Age*, 6 June 1936, p. 3.

"The Communist Party and the 'Roosevelt Question.'" *Workers Age*, 13 June 1936, p. 3.

"Black Legions of Fascism." *Workers Age*, 20 June 1936, p. 2.

"Fascism on the American Horizon." *Workers Age*, 27 June 1936, p. 2.

"Labor and Foreign Policy." *Workers Age*, 25 July 1936, p. 4.

"Ultra-Radicalism vs. Marxist Foreign Policy." *Workers Age*, 1 August 1936, p. 3.

"Civil War in Spain." *Workers Age*, 15 August 1936, pp. 3–4.

"Workers Prepare to Defend Madrid." *Workers Age*, 29 August 1936, pp. 1, 3–4.

"Is the Socialist Party for a Labor Party?" *Workers Age*, 3 October 1936, p. 23.

"Is the Socialist Party for a Labor Party?" *Workers Age*, 10 October 1936, p. 3.

"Roosevelt's Syracuse Address." *Workers Age*, 24 October 1936, p. 4.

"'Left' Fascists and the Comintern." *Workers Age*, 26 December 1936, p. 4.

Introduction to *Civil War in Spain* by Bertram D. Wolfe. New York: Workers Age Publishers, 1937, pp. 3–4.

"Some Problems of the Labor Party." *Workers Age*, 2 January 1937, p. 4.

"Spain and the 'Great Democracies.'" *Workers Age*, 16 January 1937, p. 4.

"The Fight against Fascism's Program." *Workers Age*, 30 January 1937, pp. 3, 6.

"The Fight against Fascism's Program." *Workers Age*, 6 February 1937, p. 5.

"A Note on Fascism in Russia of 1917." *Workers Age*, 27 February 1937, p. 4.

"Socialist Confusion on the Question of Unity." *Workers Age*, 6 March 1937, p. 2.

"Dangers of the Neutrality Bills." *Workers Age*, 20 March 1937, p. 3.

"Communist Party and the Neutrality Bills." *Workers Age*, 27 March 1937, p. 5.

"On the Daily Worker's 'Redefinition' of Our Political Line: 1. Inconsistency of Principle or Revolutionary Marxism?" *Workers Age*, 10 April 1937, p. 3.

"On the Daily Worker's 'Redefinition' of Our Political Line: 2. The POUM and the Spanish Revolution." *Workers Age*, 17 April 1937, pp. 5–6.

"On the Daily Worker's 'Redefinition' of Our Political Line: 3. The 'Russian Question' and the Moscow Trials." *Workers Age*, 24 April 1937, pp. 3, 5.

"The C.I.O. and the Problems of Unity." *Workers Age*, 29 May 1937, pp. 3, 5.

"CPO Convention Reflects New Stages of American Labor." *Workers Age*, 12 June 1937, pp. 1, 7.

"The New Wages and Hours Bill." *Workers Age*, 19 June 1937, p. 3.

"'Peace' thru Disaster." *Workers Age*, 26 June 1937, pp. 2, 6.

"What Is the New Deal Labor Policy?" *Workers Age*, 3 July 1937, pp. 3, 8.

"The New Deal and Trade Unions." *Workers Age*, 17 July 1937, pp. 3, 6.

"New Deal Aims toward Union Incorporation." *Workers Age*, 24 July 1937, p. 5.

"Labor and Public Opinion." *Workers Age*, 7 August 1937, pp. 1, 3.

"The Socialists and N.Y. Elections." *Workers Age*, 28 August 1937, pp. 2, 4.

"The C.P. and the Question of Trade Union Unity." *Workers Age*, 4 September 1937, pp. 1, 3.

"Jacobin Defense in the Spanish War." *Workers Age*, 15 September 1937, p. 2.

"Jacobin Defense in the Spanish War." *Workers Age*, 22 September 1937, p. 4.

"The C.I.O. and the New Deal Clash on Basic Labor Policy." *Workers Age*, 9 October 1937, p. 3.

"The Socialists and the Labor Party." *Workers Age*, 30 October 1937, p. 3.

"The Case of Leon Trotsky—A Review." *Workers Age*, 18 December 1937, p. 3.

"Broader Aspects of the C.I.O.-A.F.L. Split." *Workers Age*, 1 January 1938, pp. 1, 4.

"Lenin's Political Genius." *Workers Age*, 29 January 1938, pp. 3, 5.

"Lenin's Genius as Political Leader." *Workers Age*, 5 February 1938, pp. 3, 5.

"Another Stalin Turn?" *Workers Age*, 26 February 1938, pp. 1–2.

"Stalinism Is Not Internationalism." *Workers Age*, 5 March 1938, p. 3.

"Can U.S. Imperialism Defend the U.S.S.R.?" *Workers Age*, 12 March 1938, pp. 1, 5.

"Case of Bukharin and the Left S.R.'s." *Workers Age*, 19 March 1938, pp. 3, 6.

"Neutrality and War Danger." *Workers Age*, 16 April 1938, pp. 1–2.

"The O'Connell Bill." *Workers Age*, 23 April 1938, pp. 1–2.

"Labor Must Have United Action." *Workers Age*, 30 April 1938, pp. 3, 8.

"American CP Writes Its Own Epitaph: Earl Browder's New Constitution." *Workers Age*, 28 May 1938, pp. 1, 3.

"The Burocracy Triumphs." *Workers Age*, 11 June 1938, pp. 1–2.

"Convention of a New Beginning: A Discussion Article." *Workers Age*, 25 June 1938, p. 6.

"Labor and Wage-Hour Legislation." *Workers Age*, 2 July 1938, pp. 3, 5.

"Our Convention: Forward with the Independent Labor League." *Workers Age*, 16 July 1938, pp. 1, 6.

"The A.L.P. Election Policy: Estimate of Labor Party Tactics towards Old Parties." *Workers Age*, 13 August 1938, pp. 3–4.

"Leadership in the A.L.P.: Discussion of a Vital Problem." *Workers Age*, 20 August 1938, pp. 3, 5.

"'The Story of the C.I.O.' . . . A Book Review." Review of *The Story of the C.I.O.* by Benjamin Stolberg. *Workers Age*, 29 October 1938, p. 6.

"The Fourth New Deal: 'Continental Defense.'" *Workers Age*, 10 December 1938, p. 3.

"The 'Fourth' New Deal: 'Continental Defense' Keynote of Roosevelt Policy." *Workers Age*, 17 December 1938, pp. 3, 5.

"The CIO—From Atlantic City to Pittsburgh: Convention Reflected Achievements and Dangers." *Workers Age*, 7 January 1939, p. 3.

"The Problem of Autonomy Confronts the C.I.O.: Dangerous Situation Is Created by Top Control." *Workers Age*, 21 January 1939, pp. 3–4.

"Rosa Luxemburg: Twenty Years After—She Is Revealed Today as the Most Gifted Marxist." *Workers Age*, 28 January 1939, p. 4.

"The Editor Answers [on problem of refugees]." *Workers Age*, 4 February 1939, p. 3.

"The Editor Answers [on unemployment and war]." *Workers Age*, 1 March 1939, p. 3.

Review of *Men Must Act* by Lewis Mumford. *Workers Age*, 8 March 1939, p. 3.

"Behind the Screen of Diplomacy." *Workers Age*, 29 March 1939, pp. 1, 3.

"Issues behind Fight over Neutrality." *Workers Age*, 12 April 1939, p. 3.

Review of *The School for Dictators* by Ignazio Silone. *Workers Age*, 3 May 1939, p. 3.

"Events of 1917 Show War Brings Dictatorship: S.D.F. Editor Ignores Lessons of Past for Future." *Workers Age*, 17 May 1939, p. 4.

"The ALP and the Stalinists: C.P. Infiltration Is Grave Danger." *Workers Age*, 31 May 1939, pp. 1–2.

"Fascism Born of Real Menace." *Workers Age*, 1 July 1939, pp. 1, 3.

"On the Political Nature of the Stalinist Party: Lust for Power Motivating Force of CP Machine." *Workers Age*, 29 July 1939, p. 3.

"Aims and Realities of Socialist Unity: First Step towards Unification Is 'Socialist Block.'" *Workers Age*, 12 August 1939, p. 3.

"On the Political Nature of the Stalinist Party: Communist Party Is Instrument of Kremlin Burocracy." *Workers Age*, 12 August 1939, p. 3.

"What Is the New Stalinist 'Party Line' Going to Be? Communist Party in Right-About-Face at Moscow's Orders." *Workers Age*, 30 September 1939, pp. 1–2.

"The ALP and the War Issue." *Workers Age*, 4 November 1939, pp. 1, 3.

"Driving Forces behind the Administration War Policy: FDR Looks to War Boom as Escape from Depression." *Workers Age*, 11 November 1939, p. 3.

Review of *Accent on Power: The Life and Time of Machiavelli* by Valeriu Marcu. *Workers Age*, 11 November 1939, pp. 3–4.

"What Is F.D.R.'s War Policy Doing to the New Deal: Reconciliation with Tories Is Now on Order of Day." *Workers Age*, 18 November 1939, p. 3.

"A Review of 'I Confess.'" Review of *I Confess: The Truth About American Commu-*

nism by Benjamin Gitlow. *Modern Quarterly*, Winter 1939, pp. 68–73.

"A Fighting Plea for Peace." Review of *Keep America out of War* by Norman Thomas and Bertram D. Wolfe. *Workers Age*, 2 December 1939, p. 4.

Review of *The Awakening of America* by V. F. Calverton. *Workers Age*, 9 December 1939, p. 3.

"The New Stalin Imperialism." *Workers Age*, 30 December 1939, pp. 1, 3.

"Behind the New Imperialism of Stalinist Russia: Military Factors and Crisis of Regime Are Main Elements." *Workers Age*, 6 January 1940, pp. 1, 4.

"Stalin's Imperialism Destroys Gains of Russian Revolution: 'Defense of Soviet Union' Is Deprived of Meaning." *Workers Age*, 13 January 1940, p. 3.

"Finn Labor Must Keep Independence in Crisis: Finland Mere Pawn for British Diplomacy." *Workers Age*, 20 January 1940, p. 3.

Review of *Warfare: The Relation of War to Society* by Ludwig Renn. *Workers Age*, 27 January 1940, p. 3.

"Does Fascism Menace America? Basic Features of Fascism." *Workers Age*, 10 February 1940, p. 3.

"The Editor Replies [to criticism of Stalinism]: Are We Fanatical?" *Workers Age*, 10 February 1940, pp. 3–4.

"Does Fascism Menace America? Face of American Fascism." *Workers Age*, 17 February 1940, p. 4.

"Does Fascism Menace America? The Ideology of Fascism." *Workers Age*, 24 February 1940, p. 3.

"Does Fascism Menace America? Fascist Groups in the U.S.A." *Workers Age*, 2 March 1940, p. 3.

"Does Fascism Menace America? Fascism 'from Above' in the U.S." *Workers Age*, 9 March 1940, p. 3.

"Does Fascism Menace America? How to Defeat Fascist Peril." *Workers Age*, 16 March 1940, p. 3.

"Some Remarks on Our Policy on the Russo-Finnish War: Critical Questions in Symonds Article Considered." *Workers Age*, 6 April 1940, p. 3.

"A Clinical Specimen of Trotskyist Dogmatics." *Workers Age*, 13 April 1940, p. 3.

"Socialist Fundamentals Reexamined: Basic Dilemma of Socialism." *Workers Age*, 8 June 1940, p. 4.

"Socialist Fundamentals Reexamined: Basic Dilemma of Socialism." *Workers Age*, 15 June 1940, p. 4.

"It DOES Make a Difference Who Wins." *Workers Age*, 22 June 1940, pp. 1, 4.

"Socialist Fundamentals Reexamined: Basic Dilemma of Socialism." *Workers Age*, 22 June 1940, p. 3.

"The United States Can and Must Stay out of the War." *Workers Age*, 29 June 1940, pp. 3–4.

"Socialist Policy on the War: The Problem of Defense." *Workers Age*, 6 July 1940, p. 4.

"Socialist Policy on the War: Draft Resolution on War." *Workers Age*, 10 August 1940, p. 4.

"Socialist Policy on the War: Draft Resolution on War." *Workers Age*, 17 August 1940, p. 4.

"Pegler 'Protects Our Wealth': Sees No Sense in Conscripting—Money." *Workers Age*, 31 August 1940, p. 3.

"America Faces the Crucial Question of 'Appeasement.'" *Workers Age*, 7 September 1940, p. 3.

"What Are the Stakes in the Coming Election?" *Workers Age*, 28 September 1940, p. 4.

"Some Remarks on the Aid-to-Britain Issue: Conflicting Factors Must Be Reconciled." *Workers Age*, 12 October 1940, p. 3.

"Administration Foreign Policy and War Crisis: FDR-Wilkie Line Runs Counter to Real Interests." *Workers Age*, 26 October 1940, pp. 3–4.

"Some Remarks on Aid to Britain," *Workers Age*, 1 November 1940, pp. 1–2.

"Is F.D.R. a Menace to American Democracy: Some Lessons of Destroyer Deal Incident." *Workers Age*, 9 November 1940, pp. 3–4.

"Some Objections to the 'Happiness Principle.'" *Workers Age*, 9 November 1940, p. 4.

"Socialist Policy on War: An Analysis That Misses . . ." *Workers Age*, 7 December 1940, p. 4.

"Socialist Policy on War: Confusion without End . . ." *Workers Age*, 21 December 1940, p. 4.

"The Christian Mythology of Socialism." *Antioch Review*, Spring 1943, pp. 125–32.

"Bureaucracy and Democracy in Labor Unions." *Antioch Review*, Fall 1943, pp. 405–17.

"The Stillborn Labor Party." *Common Sense*, May 1944, pp. 161–64.

"The Crisis of Socialism." *Jewish Frontier*, September 1944, pp. 22–31.

"The Danger of Totalitarian Collectivism." Review of *The Road to Serfdom* by Frederich A. Hayek. *New Europe*, December 1944, p. 33.

"The Ethics of Power." *Jewish Frontier*, March 1945, pp. 19–23.

"Socialism and the Meaning of Life." First part of a review of *Slavery and Freedom* by Nicolas Berdyaev. *New Leader*, 17 March 1945, pp. 15, 18.

"Socialism and the Meaning of Life." Second part of a review of *Slavery and Freedom* by Nicolas Berdyaev. *New Leader*, 24 March 1945, p. 10.

"Semantic Corruption." *New Europe*, July–August 1945, pp. 8–11. Also printed in *Catholic Mind*, February 1946, pp. 95–101.

"Personalism against Totalitarianism." *Politics*, December 1945, pp. 369–74.

"Crucial Questions—Collectivism: Totalitarian or Democratic?" *Commonweal*, 22 February 1946, pp. 473–76.

"Education as God: The Philosophy of Samuel Alexander." Review of *On the Nature of Value: The Philosophy of Samuel Alexander* by Milton Konvitz. *Jewish Frontier*, April 1946, pp. 69–76.

"For 'Limited' as against 'Total' Unionism." *Labor and Nation*, April–May 1946, pp. 51–54.

"Is Control a Threat to Freedom?" *This Month*, July 1946, pp. 77–83.

"Democracy and the Nature of Man." *Christianity and Society*, Fall 1946, pp. 12–19.

"There Is a Third Way." In "Ideas for a New Party—A Symposium." *Antioch Review*, December 1946, pp. 615–17.

"From Marxism to Judaism: Jewish Belief as a Dynamic of Social Action." *Commen-*

tary, January 1947, pp. 25–32.

"Assimilation in Militant Dress: Should the Jews Be 'Like unto the Nation'?" *Commentary*, July 1947, pp. 16–22.

"Leon Bloy—Man of the Absolute." *Jewish Frontier*, September 1947, pp. 62–71.

"Anti-Semitism in the Soviet Union." *Reconstructionists*, 5 March 1948, pp. 7–8.

"On Religion and Theology: Some Comments on Max Wiener's Article." *Reconstructionists*, 19 March 1948, pp. 10–13.

"Eretz Yisrael Is a 'Holy Place.' " *Reconstructionists*, 14 May 1948, pp. 4–5.

"A Challenge to American Statesmanship." *Reconstructionists*, 28 May 1948, pp. 5–6.

"On Petitionary Prayer." *Conservative Judaism*, October 1948–January 1949, pp. 46–49.

"Towards an Open World." *Reconstructionists*, 15 October 1948, pp. 6–8.

"Labor and Politics in the Coming Period." *Christianity and Society*, Winter 1948–49, pp. 9–16.

"The Theology of Antisemitism." Review of *Christianity and the Children of Israel* by A. Roy Eckhardt. *Menorah Journal*, Spring 1949, pp. 272–79.

"Beyond Time and Eternity: Reflections on Passover and Easter." *Christianity and Crisis*, 18 April 1949, pp. 41–43.

"Has Judaism Still Power to Speak? A Religion for an Age of Crisis." *Commentary*, May 1949, pp. 447–57.

"Election Gave No Mandate; Truman Won by Plurality." Letter to the editor, *New Leader*, 28 May 1949, p. 11.

Discussion of Milton Steinberg's paper "The Theological Issues of the Hour." *Proceedings of the Rabbinical Assembly of America*, June 1949, pp. 409–28.

"The Church and American Politics." Review of *American Freedom and Catholic Power* by Paul Blanshard. *Commentary*, August 1949, pp. 198–200.

Review of *The Theology of the Old Testament* by Otto J. Baab. *Jewish Social Studies*, October 1949, pp. 413–15.

"Some Aspects of the Labor Situation." *Christianity and Society*, Spring 1950, pp. 16–21.

"The Postwar Revival of the Synagogue: Does It Reflect a Religious Reawakening?" *Commentary*, April 1950, pp. 315–25.

"Secularism in Church and Synagogue." *Christianity and Crisis*, 15 May 1950, pp. 58–61.

Review of *Paths to Utopia* by Martin Buber. *Christianity and Society*, Summer 1950, pp. 25–26.

Review of *The Prophetic Faith* by Martin Buber. *Jewish Social Studies*, July 1950, pp. 269–71.

"Pacifists in Prison." Review of *Prison Etiquette: The Convict's Compendium of Useful Information* by the Inmates. *Commentary*, August 1950, pp. 194–95.

"Socialism with Freedom." Review of *Paths to Utopia* by Martin Buber. *Commentary*, September 1950, pp. 289–91.

"What Is Jewish Religion? Reflections on Rabbi Philip Bernstein's Article in *Life*." *Jewish Frontier*, October 1950, pp. 8–13.

"Rosenzweig's 'Judaism of Personal Existence': A Third Way between Orthodoxy and

Modernism." *Commentary*, December 1950, pp. 541–49.

Review of *American Labor Leaders* by Charles A. Madison. *Jewish Social Studies*, April 1951, pp. 189–90.

"What Happened to American Socialism? Appraising the Half-Century's Record." *Commentary*, October 1951, pp. 336–44.

"The Religious Thinking of Milton Steinberg." Review of *A Believing Jew: The Selected Writings of Milton Steinberg. Commentary*, November 1951, pp. 498–501.

"When Social Scientists View Labor: The Conflict that Passeth 'Understanding.' " *Commentary*, December 1951, pp. 590–96.

"American Marxist Political Theory." In *Socialism and American Life*, vol. 1, edited by Donald Drew Egbert and Stow Persons, pp. 487–522. Princeton, N.J.: Princeton University Press, 1952.

"The Jewish Labor Movement in the United States." *American Jewish Yearbook*, 1952, pp. 1–74.

"Jewish Existence and Survival: A Theological View." *Judaism*, January 1952, pp. 19–26.

" 'Blanshardism,' Americanism, Communism, and Romanism." *New Hampshire Churchman*, February 1952, pp. 6–13.

"The Religious Stirring on the Campus: A Student Generation 'Accessible to Good.' " *Commentary*, March 1952, pp. 242–48.

"What Is Jewishness?" In the symposium "Jewishness and Diaspora." *Jewish Frontier*, May 1952, pp. 21–24.

"Space, Time, and the Sabbath." Review of *The Sabbath: Its Meaning for Modern Man* by Abraham Joshua Heschel. *Commentary*, June 1952, pp. 610–12.

"Prophetic Faith in an Age of Crisis: God-Centered Religion Meets the Challenge of our Time." *Judaism*, July 1952, pp. 195–202.

"Socialism in American Life." Review of *Socialism in American Life* edited by Donald Drew Egbert and Stow Persons. *Commonweal*, 11 July 1952, pp. 345–46.

"The Integrity of the Person." Review of *Introduction to Kierkegaard* by Regis Jolivet and *Being and Having* by Gabriel Marcel. *New Leader*, 14 July 1952, pp. 18–19.

"Freedom and Loyalty in Economic Life: Labor." *Christianity and Society*, Autumn 1952, pp. 8–12.

"Faith and Politics: Some Reflections on Whittaker Chambers' *Witness*." *Christianity and Crisis*, 29 September 1952, pp. 122–25.

"Some Comments on Miss Wiley's Paper." *Journal of Higher Education*, October 1952, pp. 365–67.

"The Sectarian Conflict over Church and State: A Divisive Threat to Our Democracy?" *Commentary*, November 1952, pp. 450–62.

"Religion and State in Israel." *Commonweal*, 14 November 1952, pp. 135–38.

"How Can You Say 'God'?" Review of *Eclipse of God: Studies in the Relation between Religion and Philosophy* and *At the Turning: Three Addresses on Judaism* by Martin Buber. *Commentary*, December 1952, pp. 615–16, 618–20.

"Spiritual Vagrants Seeking a Night's Lodging." Review of *Report on the American Communist* by Morris L. Ernst and David Loth. *Commonweal*, 26 December 1952, pp. 310–11.

"Faith and Secular Learning." In *Christian Faith and Social Action*, edited by John A.

Hutchison, pp. 199–216. New York: Charles Scribner's Sons, 1953.

"The Old-Timers and the Newcomers: Ethnic Groups Relations in a Needle Trade Union." *Journal of Social Studies*, 1953, pp. 12–19.

"Anti-Semitism on the Left." *Commonweal*, 16 January 1953, pp. 371–74.

"The Power of Communist Ideology." Review of *Bolshevism: An Introduction to Soviet Communism* by Waldemar Gurian. *Commentary*, March 1953, pp. 318–21.

"Judaism and Christianity: Their Unity and Difference—The Double Covenant in the Divine Economy of Salvation." *Journal of Bible and Religion*, April 1953, pp. 67–78.

"The Dissection of Babbitt Junior." Review of *The Shame and Glory of the Intellectuals* by Peter Viereck. *Commonweal*, 3 April 1953, pp. 653–55.

"The History of a Great Historian." Review of *Lord Acton: A Study in Conscience and Politics* by Gertrude Himmelfarb. *New Leader*, 13 April 1953, pp. 23–24.

"A Jewish Point of View." In "Religious Education and General Education: A Symposium." *Religious Education*, May–June 1953, pp. 135–39.

"A Jew Looks at Catholics." *Commonweal*, 22 May 1953, pp. 174–77.

Letter to the editor in support of F. Ernest Johnson's editorial article "Communists in the Pulpit." *Christianity and Crisis*, 8 June 1953, p. 80.

"Acton's Meaning for Today." Review of *Essays on Church and State* by Lord Acton and *Acton's Political Philosophy* by G. E. Fasnacht. *New Leader*, 29 June 1953, pp. 17–18.

Review of *Eclipse of God: Studies in the Relation between Religion and Philosophy* by Martin Buber. *Theology Today*, July 1953, pp. 289–90.

"The Cosmic Struggle." Review of *For the Sake of Heaven* by Martin Buber. *Commonweal*, 17 July 1953, p. 372.

Review article in "Can Man Remake the World? Two Approaches to Eric Voegelin's 'The New Science of Politics.'" *New Leader*, 31 August 1953, pp. 16–18.

"A Study in Fundamentals: Judaism and Economic Life." *National Jewish Monthly*, September 1953, pp. 14–16, 33–37.

"Religion in the Colleges." Review of *Campus Gods on Trial* by Chad Walsh. *Commentary*, October 1953, pp. 382–85.

"An Underground World of Hatred and Fear." Review of *Apostles of Discord* by Ralph Lord Roy. *Commonweal*, 9 October 1953, pp. 17–19.

"Toward a Biblical Theology of Education." *Christian Scholar*, December 1953, pp. 259–72.

"Government by Rabble-Rousing." *New Leader*, 18 January 1954, pp. 13–16.

"Faith and Character Structure (Some Notes on Religion in Contemporary American Society)." *Christianity and Crisis*, 25 January 1954, pp. 187–89.

"Faith, History, and Self-Understanding." *Christianity and Society*, Spring 1954, pp. 14–20.

"Religious Communities in Present-Day America." *Review of Politics*, April 1954, pp. 155–74.

"Religious Trends in American Jewry." *Judaism*, Summer 1954, pp. 229–40.

"A Conservative Worthy." Review of *Elihu Root and the Conservative Tradition* by Richard W. Leopold. *Commentary*, July 1954, pp. 86–88, 90.

"Anti-Semitism Today." *Commonweal*, 16 July 1954, pp. 359–63.

Reply to Rev. John M. Oesterreicher's objections to "Anti-Semitism Today." *Commonweal*, 20 August 1954, p. 488.

"McCarthy and Hitler: A Delusive Parallel." *New Republic*, 23 August 1954, pp. 13–15.

"A Comment on Professor Hallowell's Review of *Natural Right and History* by Leo Strauss." *Christian Scholar*, September 1954, pp. 443–44.

Review of *Natural Right and History* by Leo Strauss. *Christian Scholar*, September 1954, pp. 435–39.

"Riesman's Lonely Man." Review of *Individualism Reconsidered and Other Essays* by David Riesman. *Commonweal*, 3 September 1954, pp. 538–40.

"A Close Examination of Wisconsin's Junior Senator." Review of *McCarthy and the Communists* by James Rorty and Moshe Decter. *Commonweal*, 24 September 1954, pp. 610–12.

"Norman Thomas and American Socialism." *Jewish Frontier*, December 1954, pp. 8–12.

Contribution to "Critics' Choice for Christmas." *Commonweal*, 3 December 1954, p. 268.

"Biblical Faith and Natural Religion." *Theology Today*, January 1955, pp. 460–67.

"Ten Who Would Have Changed America." Review of *American Demagogues: Twentieth Century* by Reinhard H. Luthin. *Commonweal*, 14 January 1955, pp. 410–11.

"The Revolution We Are Living Through." *Intercollegian*, February 1955, pp. 8–11.

"Marxism's Changing Face." Review of *Marxism: The Unity of Theory and Practice* by Alfred G. Meyer. *Commonweal*, 4 February 1955, pp. 482–84.

"The Biblical Basis of American Democracy." *Thought*, Spring 1955, pp. 37–50.

"Communism, Democracy, and the Churches: Problems of 'Mobilizing the Religious Front.'" *Commentary*, April 1955, pp. 386–93.

Review of *The Church and the Jewish People: A Symposium* edited by Gote Hendenquist. *Theology Today*, April 1955, pp. 119–21.

"Loyalty and Security in Historical Perspective." Review of *Era of the Oath: Northern Loyalty Tests during the Civil War and Reconstruction* by Harold Melvin Hyman and *Red Scare: A Study in National Hysteria, 1919–1920* by Robert K. Murray. *New Republic*, 11 April 1955, pp. 20–22.

"Our Conservative Heritage Recaptured." Review of *Conservatism in America* by Clinton Rossiter. *New Leader*, 16 May 1955, pp. 14–15.

"The Three Dialogues of Man." Review of *The Self and the Dramas of History* by Reinhold Niebuhr. *New Republic*, 16 May 1955, pp. 28–31.

"The Presuppositions of Democracy." Review of *The Moral Foundation of Democracy* by John Hallowell. *Commonweal*, 3 June 1955, pp. 234–36.

"Tri-Focus on Judaism." Review of *Guideposts in Modern Judaism: An Analysis of Current Trends in Jewish Thought* by Jacob B. Agus and *Conservative Judaism: An American Religious Movement* by Marshall Sklare. *Christian Century*, 29 June 1955, pp. 759–60.

"The Spiritual Resources of Democracy." Review of *Declaration of Freedom* by Elton Trueblood. *Commonweal*, 5 August 1955, p. 451.

"The Roots of Anti-Semitism." Review of *Christianity and Anti-Semitism* by Nicolas Berdyaev. *New Republic*, 22 August 1955, p. 20.

"America's New Religiousness: A Way of Belonging or the Way of God?" *Commentary*, September 1955, pp. 240–47.

"The Great American Debate." *Commonweal*, 9 September 1955, pp. 559–62.

"Two Philosophies of the 'Social Self.'" Review of *The Social Self* by Paul E. Pfuetze. *New Republic*, 19 September 1955, p. 22.

"Jewish Labor in the U.S.: Its History and Contributions to American Life." *American Federationists*, October 1955, pp. 20–21, 30–31.

Review of *Man's Quest for God: Studies in Prayer and Symbolism* by Abraham Joshua Heschel. *Theology Today*, October 1955, pp. 404–6.

"Can Faith and Reason Be Reconciled?" Review of *Biblical Religion and the Search for Ultimate Reality* by Paul Tillich. *New Republic*, 24 October 1955, p. 19.

"'Sense of Decency.'" Review of *George Orwell* by John Atkins. *America*, 5 November 1955, pp. 159–60.

Contribution to "Critics' Choices for Christmas." *Commonweal*, 2 December 1955, pp. 239–40.

"I-Thou." Review of *Martin Buber: The Life of Dialogue* by Maurice S. Friedman. *Christian Century*, 28 December 1955, p. 1526.

"That All May Be One." Review of *The Conflict of Religions* by Philip H. Ashby. *America*, 21 January 1956, p. 454.

Review of *God in Search of Man: A Philosophy of Judaism* by Abraham Joshua Heschel. *Drew Gateway*, Spring 1956, pp. 206–8.

"Biblical Faith as *Heilsgeschichte*: The Meaning of Redemptive History in Human Existence." *Christian Scholar*, March 1956, pp. 25–31.

"The Thought of Reinhold Niebuhr." Review of *Reinhold Niebuhr: His Religious, Social and Political Thought* edited by Charles W. Kegley and Robert W. Bretall. *New Leader*, 2 April 1956, pp. 21–23.

"Converging Trails." Review of *God in Search of Man: A Philosophy of Judaism* by Abraham Joshua Heschel. *Christian Century*, 18 April 1956, p. 486. Also found in *America*, 14 April 1956, pp. 67–68.

"Christian Apologist to the Secular World." *Union Seminary Quarterly Review*, May 1956, pp. 11–16.

"A Religion or Religion? Some Comments on the Program of 'Moral and Religious Values' in the Schools." *Religion in the Schools*, May 1956, unpaginated.

"Socialism, Zionism, and the Messianic Passion." *Midstream*, Summer 1956, pp. 65–74.

Review of *Die Antwort des Jona* by Shalom Ben-Chorin. *Judaism*, Fall 1956, pp. 365–70.

"Voting Habits of American Jews." *America*, 29 September 1956, pp. 617–19.

"Triumph and Failure: Appraisal of Socialism." *Commonweal*, 12 October 1956, pp. 42–44.

"At the Heart of the Mystery." Review of *Great Age and Ideas of the Jewish People* by Salo W. Baron, Gerson D. Cohen, Abraham S. Halkin, Yehezkel Kaufmann, Ralph Marcus, and Cecil Roth, edited with an introduction by Leo W. Schwarz. *New York Times Book Review*, 28 October 1956, p. 10.

"A 'Jewish Vote'?" Review of *The Political Behavior of American Jews* by Lawrence H. Fuchs. *New Leader*, 29 October 1956, pp. 28–29.

"Some Perils of Interfaith Life: 'Americanization' Presents Subtle Dangers to Religious Cooperation." *World Alliance Newsletter*, February 1957, pp. 3–5.
"Freud, Religion, and Social Reality: 'The Incomprehensible Monster, Man.'" *Commentary*, March 1957, pp. 277–84. Also published as "Freud, the Revisionists, and Social Reality" in *Freud and the 20th Century*, edited by Benjamin Nelson, pp. 143–63. New York: Meridian Books, 1957.
"Labor's 'Hired Brains.'" Review of *Intellectuals in Labor Unions* by Harold L. Wilensky. *New Republic*, 11 March 1957, pp. 17–19.
"Imprisoned in Brotherhood: The Organization Man." Review of *The Organization Man* by William H. Whyte, Jr. *Commonweal*, 19 April 1957, pp. 62–64.
"The Sociology of the Printers' Union." Review of *Union Democracy: The Internal Politics of the International Typographical Union* by Seymour Martin Lipset, Martin A. Trow, and James S. Coleman. *New Leader*, 3 June 1957, pp. 15–17.
"Arnold Toynbee—Historian or Religious Prophet?" Review of *An Historian's Approach to Religion* by Arnold Toynbee. *Queens Quarterly*, Autumn 1957, pp. 421–33.
"The Christian Witness in an Emerging 'Other-directed' Culture: A Report on an Address by Will Herberg." *Intercollegian*, November 1957, pp. 4–11.
"Justice for Religious Schools." *America*, 16 November 1957, pp. 190–93.
Foreword to *Freedom of Choice in Education* by Virgil C. Blum. New York: Macmillan Company, 1958.
"The Making of a Pluralistic Society—A Jewish View." In *Religion and the State University*, edited by Erich A. Walter, pp. 27–41. Ann Arbor: University of Michigan Press, 1958.
"Religion, Democracy, and Public Education." In *Religion in America: Original Essays on Religion in a Free Society*, edited by John Cogley, pp. 118–47. New York: Meridian Books, 1958.
Editorial, *Church and State: A Monthly Review*, January 1958, p. 2.
Reply to Nathan A. Perilman's critiques of "Justice for Religious Schools." In "State of the Question: Two Points of View on the School Question." *America*, 11 January 1958, pp. 427–28.
Review of *A Social and Religious History of the Jews* by Salo W. Baron, in *Drew Gateway*, Spring 1958, pp. 206–8.
"Athens and Jerusalem: Confrontation and Dialogue." *Drew Gateway*, Spring 1958, pp. 178–200. Later published as *Athens and Jerusalem: Confrontation and Dialogue*. Distinguished Lecture Series, no. 3. Durham: University of New Hampshire Press, 1965.
Review of *Psychoanalysis and Ethics* by Lewis S. Feuer. *Theology Today*, January 1959, pp. 565–69.
"Should the Government Help Our Parochial Schools?" *Seminarian*, January 1959, pp. 6–11.
"Natural Law and History in Burke's Thought." Review of *Edmund Burke and the Natural Law* by Peter J. Stanlis. *Modern Age*, Summer 1959, pp. 325–28.
"Comment II" on Ordway Tead's article *Value Emphasis in College Teaching*. *Christian Scholar*, June 1959, pp. 102–3.
Review of *Sigmund Freud and the Jewish Mystical Tradition* by David Baeda. *Reli-*

gion in Life, Autumn 1959, pp. 625–26.

"Reinhold Niebuhr and Paul Tillich: Two Ways in American Protestant Theology." *Chaplain*, October 1959, pp. 3–9, 36.

"Theological Presuppositions of Social Philosophy." *Drew Gateway*, Winter 1959, pp. 94–113.

Foreword to *An American Dialogue: A Protestant Looks at Catholicism and a Catholic Looks at Protestantism*, by Robert McAfee Brown and Gustave Weigel, pp. 9–13. Garden City, N.Y.: Doubleday & Company, 1960.

"Religion and Culture in Present-Day America." In *Roman Catholicism and the American Way of Life*, edited by Thomas T. McAvry, pp. 4–19. Notre Dame, Ind.: University of Notre Dame Press, 1960.

"Religious Revival and Moral Crisis." *Union Seminary Quarterly Review*, March 1960, pp. 209–19.

"Historicism as Touchstone." *Christian Century*, 16 March 1960, pp. 311–13.

"The Strangeness of Faith." *Pulpit*, June 1960, pp. 4–7.

"Niebuhr's Three Phases." Review of *The Thought of Reinhold Niebuhr* by Gordon Harland and *Reinhold Niebuhr on Politics* edited by Harry R. Davis and Robert C. Good. *Christian Century*, 10 August 1960, pp. 926–27.

"Society, Democracy, and the State: A Biblical-Realist View." *Drew Gateway*, Autumn 1960, pp. 3–16.

" 'Ambiguist' Statesmanship." *Worldview*, September 1960, pp. 7–8.

"Protestant-Catholic Tensions in Pluralistic America." *Yale Divinity News*, November 1960, pp. 3–11.

"A Yankee Looks at Marxism." Review of *Marxism: The View from America* by Clinton Rossiter. *National Review*, 19 November 1960, pp. 314–15.

"Religion and Education in America." In *Religious Perspectives in American Culture*, edited by James Ward Smith and A. Leland Jamison, pp. 11–51. Princeton, N.J.: Princeton University Press, 1961.

"The Integration of the Jew in Contemporary America." *Conservative Judaism*, Spring 1961, pp. 1–9. Also published as "Integration of the Jew into America's Three-Religion Society." *A Journal of Church and State*, May 1963, pp. 27–40.

"Conservatives and Religion: A Dilemma." *National Review*, 7 October 1961, pp. 230, 232.

"Science and Faith." Review of *Man's Best Hope* by Roland G. Gittelsohn. *New York Times Book Review*, 29 October 1961, pp. 18, 20.

"Controversy over an Encyclical." *National Review*, 4 November 1961, pp. 230, 232.

"Some Comments on the Theological Scene at Drew." *Drew Gateway*, Winter 1961, pp. 81–87.

"Reinhold Niebuhr: Burkean Conservative." *National Review*, 2 December 1961, pp. 379, 394.

"Communism, Christianity, and the Judgment of God." *National Review*, 16 January 1962, pp. 22, 37.

"Protestantism in a Post-Protestant America." *Christianity and Crisis*, 5 February 1962, pp. 3–7.

"Again, the Social Gospel." *National Review*, 13 February 1962, pp. 96, 109.

"Religion in a Secularized Society: The New Shape of Religion in America (Lecture

1)." *Review of Religious Research*, Spring 1962, pp. 145–48.

"HUAC: Record and Appraisal." Review of *The Committee and Its Critics: A Calm Review of the House Committee on Un-American Activities* by William F. Buckley, Jr., and the editors of *National Review*. *National Review*, 10 April 1962, pp. 249–51.

"Conservatives, Liberals, and the Natural Law, I." *National Review*, 5 June 1962, pp. 407, 422.

"Conservatives, Liberals, and the Natural Law, II." *National Review*, 19 June 1962, pp. 438, 458.

"Religious Symbols in Public Life." *National Review*, 28 August 1962, pp. 145, 162.

"Religion in a Secularized Society: Some Aspects of America's Three-Religion Pluralism (Lecture 2)." *Review of Religious Studies*, Fall 1962, pp. 33–45.

"The 'Separation' of Church and State." *National Review*, 3 October 1962, pp. 315, 330.

"The New Encyclical: A Question of Perspective." *National Review*, 7 May 1963, pp. 364–65.

"Jewish Theology in the Post-Modern World." Review of *The Natural and the Supernatural Jew: A Historical and Theological Introduction* by Arthur A. Cohen. *Judaism*, Summer 1963, pp. 364–70.

"Religion and Public Life." *National Review*, 30 July 1963, p. 61.

"Religion and Public Life." *National Review*, 13 August 1963, pp. 104–5.

" 'Pure' Religion and the Secularized Society." *National Review*, 10 September 1963, pp. 188–89.

"God and the Theologians." *Encounter* (London), November 1963, pp. 56–58.

Foreword to *Politics and Catholic Freedom*, by Garry Wills. Chicago: Henry Regnery Company, 1964. Reprinted as "The Limits of Papal Authority." Review of *Politics and Catholic Freedom* by Garry Wills. *National Review*, 25 August 1964, pp. 730, 732, 734.

"Religious Group Conflict in America." In *Religion and Social Conflict*, edited by Robert Lee and Martin E. Marty, pp. 143–58. New York: Oxford University Press, 1964.

"A Religious 'Right' to Violate the Law?" *National Review*, 14 July 1964, pp. 579–80.

"Dr. Herberg Replies [to criticism of his article "A Religious 'Right' to Violate the Law?"]." *National Review*, 8 September 1964, p. 784.

"Five Meanings of the Word 'Historical.' " *Christian Scholar*, Winter 1964, pp. 327–30.

"Aggiornamento: Open Season on the Church?" *National Review*, 4 May 1965, pp. 363–64.

"Martin Buber, RIP." *National Review*, 29 June 1965, pp. 539–40.

"The New Estate: The Professors and the 'Teach-Ins.' " *National Review*, 13 July 1965, p. 590.

"Benjamin Gitlow, RIP." *National Review*, 10 August 1965, p. 682.

" 'Civil Rights' and Violence: Who Are the Guilty Ones?" *National Review*, 7 September 1965, pp. 769–70.

"The Sweep of Jewish History." Review of *The History of the Jews* by Paul

Borchsenius. *New York Times Book Review* (Part I), 7 November 1965, pp. 50, 52.

"Conservatives, Liberalism, and Religion." *National Review*, 30 November 1965, pp. 1087–88.

"A Jew Looks at Jesus." In *The Finality of Christ*, edited by Dow Kirkpatrick, pp. 91–101. Oxford Institute on Methodist Theological Studies, no. 3. Nashville, Tenn.: Abingdon Press, 1966.

"Man of Faith." Review of *The Insecurity of Freedom* by Abraham Joshua Heschel. *New York Times Book Review*, 24 April 1966, pp. 34–35.

"Post-Vatican II Theology." Review of *Freedom Today* by Hans Kung and *Dialogue with Myself* by Martin C. D'Arcy. *National Review*, 3 May 1966, pp. 421–24.

"The 'Death of God' Theology—I: The Philosophy behind It." *National Review*, 9 August 1966, pp. 771, 779.

"The 'Death of God' Theology—II: Secularization and the Collapse of Meaning." *National Review*, 23 August 1966, pp. 839–40.

"The 'Death of God' Theology—III: What Is Wrong with It?" *National Review*, 6 September 1966, pp. 884–85.

"What Is Religious Freedom?" Review of *Religious Liberty: An End and a Beginning* edited by John Courtney Murray. *National Review*, 29 November 1966, pp. 1228–30.

"Christian Faith and Totalitarian Rule." *Modern Age*, Winter 1966–67, pp. 63–71.

"Free to Choose Our Chains." Review of *Three Essays: Leonardo, Descartes and Max Weber* by Karl Jaspers. *Sunday Herald Tribune*, 3 January 1967, pp. 4, 8.

"The Tyrant Necessity." Review of *Athens and Jerusalem* by Lev Shestov. *Saturday Review*, 4 February 1967, pp. 50–51.

"Crisis at Drew." *Christianity and Crisis*, 20 February 1967, pp. 25–27.

"The Great Society and the American Constitution Tradition." *Modern Age*, Summer 1967, pp. 231–35.

"Who Are the Hippies?" *National Review*, 8 August 1967, pp. 844–46, 872.

"The Church under Pressure of the World." *Drew Gateway*, Autumn–Winter 1967–68, pp. 13–25.

"Business Enterprise in Moral Perspective," in *Moral Man and Economic Enterprise* edited by Lawrence Lavengood. Evanston, Ill.: Northwestern University Press, 1968, pp. 19–30.

"What Is the Moral Crisis of Our Time?" *Intercollegiate Review*, January–March 1968, pp. 63–69.

"Judaism as Personal Decision." *Conservative Judaism*, Summer 1968, pp. 9–20.

"Inside the Outsiders: Alienation, 'Dissent,' and the Intellectual." *National Review*, 30 July 1968, pp. 738–39.

"Aggiornamento: The Plight of American Catholicism." *National Review*, 27 August 1968, pp. 852–53.

"Humanae Vitae: Reflections on the New Encyclical." *National Review*, 10 September 1968, pp. 908–9.

"An American Success." *Encounter*, October 1968, pp. 2, 5.

"The Plight of American Protestantism." *National Review*, 5 November 1968, pp. 1109, 1126–27.

"Modern Man in a Metaphysical Wasteland." *Intercollegiate Review*, Winter 1968–69, pp. 79–83.

"Karl Barth, RIP." *National Review*, 31 December 1968, p. 1310. Reprinted with corrections under the title "Erratum." *National Review*, 28 January 1969, p. 64.

"The Bounds of Public Morality." Review of *The Vanishing Right to Life* by Charles E. Rice. *National Review*, 3 June 1969, pp. 545–46.

"The Student Left: Cause and Consequence." Review of *Seeds of Anarchy: A Study of Campus Revolution* edited by Frederick Wilhelmsen. *National Review*, 29 July 1969, pp. 754–56.

"A Death-Defying Act: The Case for Heterosexuality." *National Review*, 7 October 1969, pp. 1007–8, 1023.

"Mr. Herberg Replies [to a critique of "A Death-Defying Act: The Case for Heterosexuality"]." *National Review*, 4 November 1969, p. 1096.

"Modern Man in a Metaphysical Wasteland." *Social Education*, December 1969, pp. 931–34, 948.

"Scrutiny of an Enigma." Review of *The Jewish Mystique* by Ernest van den Haag. *National Review*, 2 December 1969, pp. 1222–23.

"Dicta on Civil Disobedience." *Virginia Law Weekly*, 18 December 1969, p. 1.

"Anarchy on Campus." *Modern Age*, Winter 1969–70, pp. 2–10.

"What Keeps Modern Man from Religion?" *Intercollegiate Review*, Winter 1969–70, pp. 5–11.

"Conservatism, the Working Class, and the Jew." *Ideas*, Winter–Spring 1970, pp. 25–29.

Notes for a lecture "The Crumbling of Liberal Orthodoxies." Quoted and assessed by William F. Buckley, Jr., "The Optimism of Dr. Will Herberg." *National Review*, 21 April 1970, pp. 428–29.

"Words that Slay, Wisdom that Mends." Review of *The Governor Listeth: A Book of Inspired Political Reflections* by William F. Buckley, Jr. *National Review*, 14 July 1970, pp. 738–39.

"The Jew and the Negro." Review of *The Confrontations: Black Power, Anti-Semitism, and the Myth of Integration* by Max Geltman. *National Review*, 25 August 1970, pp. 900–901.

"On the Meaning of Academic Freedom." In *On Academic Freedom*, edited by Valerie Earle, pp. 1–4. Washington, D.C.: American Enterprise Institute for Public Policy Research, 1971.

"The Limits of Pluralism." *National Review*, 23 February 1971, pp. 198–99.

"America's 'Negro Problem' in Historical Perspective." *Intercollegiate Review*, Summer 1971, pp. 207–14.

"Reinhold Niebuhr, RIP." *National Review*, 29 June 1971, pp. 690–91.

"Men without Gods." Review of *The Gods of Atheism* by Vincent P. Miceli. *National Review*, 27 July 1971, pp. 813–14.

"The 'What' and the 'How' in Ethics." *Modern Age*, Fall 1971, pp. 350–57.

"A Crisis of Authority." Review of *Authority and Rebellion: The Case for Orthodoxy in the Catholic Church* by Charles E. Rice. *National Review*, 22 October 1971, pp. 1182–83.

"Conservatives and Jesus Freaks." *New Guard*, November 1971, pp. 15–16.

"Brilliant Overreaching." Review of *Bare Ruined Choirs: Doubt, Prophecy, and Radical Religion* by Garry Wills. *National Review*, 24 November 1972, pp. 1305–6.

"City and Suburb in Symbiosis: The Urban Problem in New Perspective." *Intercollegiate Review*, Spring 1973, pp. 159–69.

"America's Civil Religion: What It Is and Whence It Comes." *Modern Age*, Summer 1973, pp. 226–33.

"Religion in the U.S.—Where It's Headed: Interview with Dr. Will Herberg, Philosopher, Social Historian." *U.S. News & World Report*, 4 June 1973, pp. 54–58, 60.

"The Crisis and Its Aftermath." *Ideas*, 1974, pp. 44–47.

"Getting Back to Vatican II." *National Review*, 29 March 1974, pp. 366–68.

INDEX

Kennedy, Ruby Jo, 139
Kerensky, Alexander, 15, 44, 45
Keynes, John Maynard, 195
Khaki-Shirt Army, 29
Kierkegaard, Søren, 84, 88, 190, 220, 222
King, Martin Luther, Jr., 171, 199, 214, 215
Kingdom of God, 71, 72, 96, 99, 100, 101, 102, 104, 105, 133, 168, 214, 216, 221
Kingsley, Charles, 116
Kirk, Russell, 126
Koestler, Arthur, 78
Konvitz, Milton, 91, 106
Kornilov Putsch, 44, 45
Kristol, Irving, 192
Ku Klux Klan, 23, 29, 42, 62
Kung, Hans, 186, 210

Labor, 15, 16, 27, 28, 29, 33, 35, 37, 40, 46, 47, 54, 55, 61, 63, 68, 75, 131, 132, 133, 134, 167, 172, 200, 215
Language, 72, 128, 146, 156, 159, 175, 217, 218
Laplace, Pierre, 21
Law, 80, 82, 84, 98, 179, 220
League of Nations, 45, 46
Legalism, 98, 106
Lenin, V. I., 5, 11, 12, 14, 15, 17, 21, 36, 39, 45, 48, 50, 51, 56, 58, 65, 71, 83, 130, 183, 216; Leninism, 9, 10, 11, 17, 65, 214, 220
Leopold, Richard W., 126
Lewis, John L., 3
Lewisohn, Ludwig, 116
Liberalism, 38, 39, 40, 52, 67, 76, 117, 126, 127, 128, 145, 159, 170, 186, 188, 194, 195, 214, 215
Lincoln, Abraham, 26, 45, 199, 208
Lindbergh, Charles A., 64
Linguistic analysis, 174
Linz revolt, the, 43
Literature, 18–19
Litvinov, Maxim, 46

Lloyd George, David, 40
Logic, 95
Lominadze, Besso, 10
Long, Huey, 29, 41, 130, 214
Love, 81, 97, 98, 99, 100, 113, 189, 221
Lovestone, Jay, 7, 8, 10, 15, 16, 32, 33, 46, 48, 54, 68, 212, 213, 220; Lovestonites, 7, 8, 10, 11, 13, 16, 32, 54, 68, 70, 132, 135, 204, 216
Lovett, Robert Morss, 26
Lozovsky, A. L., 10
Lubac, Henri de, 185
Luther, Martin, 122, 158, 190, 222
Luxemburg, Rosa, 15, 17, 47, 65
Lyell, Sir Charles, 21

McCarthy, Joseph, 1, 129, 207, 214; McCarthyism, 129, 130
Macdonald, Dwight, 232 (n. 11)
Machiavellianism, 77
McReynolds, Sam D., 47
Madison, James, 159, 170, 183
Magdeburg Congress (1910), 44
Magidoff, Jacob, 134
Maimonides, Moses, 190
Man, 81, 84, 89, 91, 92, 93, 96–97, 103, 105, 110, 111, 118, 122, 127, 129, 155, 169, 173
Manchurian Crisis, 16
Maritain, Jacques, 78, 84, 86, 88, 121, 185
Marx, Karl, 1, 14, 15, 18, 29, 36, 39, 47, 50, 51, 52, 53, 58, 69, 71, 73, 74, 78, 84, 89, 94, 100, 102, 116, 154, 168, 215, 216; Marxism, 1, 14, 17, 19, 20, 32, 43, 47, 50, 51, 53, 55, 56, 65, 66, 67, 69, 70, 71, 72, 73, 77, 78, 79, 94, 113, 121, 157, 158, 159, 168, 174, 213, 215, 216, 217, 220, 222
Masaday Indians, 218
Masserman, Jules H., 115
Masses, the, 9, 12, 25, 35, 41, 45, 54, 59, 61, 62, 66, 167, 172, 175, 215
Materialism, 20, 73, 79
Matt, Herschel, 91